JEANNE HIMICH FREELAND-GRAVES
THE UNIVERSITY OF TEXAS AT AUSTIN

Principles of Food Preparation
A Laboratory Manual
2ND EDITION

A Pearson Education Company
Upper Saddle River, New Jersey 07458

Printed in the United States of America
20 19 18 17 16 15 14 13 12

ISBN 0-02-339350-5

Prentice-Hall International (UK) Limited,London
Prentice-Hall of Australia Pty. Limited, Sydney
Prentice-Hall Canada Inc., Toronto
Prentice-Hall Hispanoamericana, S.A., Mexico
Prentice-Hall of India Private Limited, New Delhi
Prentice-Hall of Japan, Inc., Tokyo
Pearson Education Asia Pte. Ltd., Singapore
Editora Prentice-Hall do Brasil, Ltda., Rio de Janeiro

Preface

Principles of Food Preparation is a laboratory manual designed for use in an introductory foods laboratory at the college freshman level. It has been developed for use as an accompaniment to the fifth edition of the textbook, *Foundations of Food Preparation*. However, the incorporation of scientific as well as basic illustrations of food principles allows it to be easily used with any introductory foods or food science textbook. A knowledge of chemistry is not required, although many chemical principles are applied throughout the book.

The second edition of the manual has been revised to reflect current knowledge in food science and nutrition. Most of the food science principles throughout the chapters have been rewritten to reflect recent changes and to summarize the major points discussed in the accompanying textbook. The student should refer to a textbook for more thorough explanations about specific principles.

New experiments have been incorporated throughout the book in order to reinforce the revised food science principles. Where appropriate, new and better recipes have been substituted for some of the less successful recipes used in the first edition. Numerous recipes have also been added to applications since the application of food science principles to the final product is a primary goal of this text.

All experiments and recipes are designed for use in a 2-hour laboratory, except where noted. There are, however, more experiments than can be adequately performed in a 2-hour laboratory by a class of 16 students. Instructors should select those exercises and experiments that are most suitable for their classroom lectures.

Quantities of food products in the experiments were deliberately kept small in order to reduce the cost of each laboratory. The philosophy was to provide portion sizes suitable for tasting rather than eating. The small portions are also found in the recipes following each chapter. These recipes are designed as applications of the laboratory unit, *not* home use. Consequently, students desiring to prepare the recipes at home should double or triple the quantity of ingredients.

In many instances, proportions and ingredients have been modified from the original recipe to reduce the cost of the product. An example is the substitution of margarine for the more expensive fat, butter. Students planning on preparing the recipes at a later date should take note of this and make appropriate substitutions.

Many of the experiments and principles incorporated into this laboratory manual have been tested throughout the years by students of the Division of Nutrition and Foods of the University of Texas at Austin. The author wishes to recognize the former faculty and teaching assistants who have developed the content of these basic food science laboratories. The author is grateful to Dr. Margaret Briley for her development of the present structure of the food science laboratory. Frieda Neff, Rebecca Pobocik, Melanie Rutter, and Virginia Dougherty deserve special recognition for their helpful suggestions in preparing the second edition of this manual. Acknowledgments are also made to Dr. John Longenecker,

Head of the Division of Nutrition and Foods, and Dr. Mary Ellen Durrett, Chairman of the Department of Home Economics, for their encouragement and strong support of this venture.

Most of all, the author would like to thank her family, Dr. Glenn Graves, Candy Freeland, J. J. Freeland, and Michael Graves for their patience and willingness to at least taste all these recipes.

J. H. F.-G.

Contents

1
Sanitation

PERSONAL HYGIENE

1. It is essential to protect clothing from spills, splattering, and fire. Sleeves must be rolled up and dangling ties removed. A clean uniform, apron with a bib, or laboratory coat must be worn.
2. Loose hair must be restrained in some fashion to avoid hairs contaminating the food products. *Do not* comb hair in the laboratory.
3. Do not bring personal items, such as books and handbags to the kitchen unit. Place them in the area designated by the instructor.
4. Hands and nails must be thoroughly washed with hot, soapy water at the beginning of each laboratory period. Dry hands on *paper*, not cloth towels. Hand washing should be repeated if the hands touch any part of the body (nose, face, hair) or a commonly touched area (doorknob, telephone). Hands must also be rewashed after cleaning up spills or using the toilet.

FOOD PREPARATION AND HANDLING

1. Fruits, vegetables, soiled eggs, meats, poultry, and whole fish should be washed before use in food preparation.
2. All perishable foods, leftovers, and protein-containing foods should be refrigerated as soon as possible. Foods should be stored covered, or in a sealed container.
3. Chopping boards are used to avoid knife marks on the counter. These must be cleaned with soap and water and rinsed after each use. A sanitizer such as a chlorine bleach cleanser is necessary if meats, fish, or poultry have been cut.
4. Handle hot foods with pot holders, *not* paper towels.
5. Do not taste foods with a spoon and place the spoon back in the food. A *clean* spoon must be used for each tasting. *Never lick your fingers.*
6. Grease pans with the fat held in a piece of waxed paper. Remove the last traces of fat from a container with a rubber spatula, not the fingers.

DISHWASHING

1. Scrape all food residue from plates into the designated garbage pail. Do not scrape food into the sink unless there is a garbage disposal.
2. Rinse all dishes and utensils and stack neatly next to the sink. Remove grease remaining in pans with a paper towel.

3. Fill the sink 1/3 full with hot, 120°F (49°C), soapy water. Place all utensils in the bottom of the sink to one side. Add glassware.
4. Wash glasses with a soapy dishrag or sponge. A scouring pad will facilitate removal of stubborn spots. Rinse thoroughly in hot water, 150°F (66°C).
5. Place glasses upside down in a dish drain.
6. Wash dishes first, followed by pans and utensils.
7. Dry dishes with a cloth towel. *Do not* use the same cloth to dry the counter.
8. Hang the towel to dry. Replace with a clean one.
9. Clean the sink after each use with a dishrag and cleanser to restore its shine and remove scratches. Rinse thoroughly and dry faucet area.
10. Clean out dish drain.
11. Return dishes to cupboard.
12. Wipe off the counter and dry with paper towels.

FOOD TESTING

1. Food is not to be sampled until the instructor designates.
2. Samples of food should be removed from the product with a serving spoon. Do not touch the serving spoon to your plate. Never place your personal spoon in a food product that is not on your plate.
3. Be considerate of others when sampling food. Take small portions, leaving enough for others to taste.

CLEANING

1. Keep the counter clean and uncluttered during cooking. Close all cupboard doors and drawers. Do not allow garbage to pile up in the sink.
2. Wipe up spills as soon as they occur. Baked-on foods are difficult to remove.
3. Do not put wet items such as peelings, leftovers or scrapings in the paper wastebasket. This encourages insect and rodent infestation as well as irritable janitors. Use garbage cans with disposable, plastic liners.
4. Soak pans and dishes with high protein and starch residues in cold water as soon as possible. Soak pans and dishes with other foods in hot water.
5. The counters, range, and oven must be left free of grease, clean, and sparkling. Dirt may be removed from crevices with a brush. Use water, soap, detergents, cleanser, and scouring pads to remove dirt.
6. Turn off all electricity and gas before leaving unit.

(Courtesy of Oscar Mayer Foods Corp.)

2

Food Evaluation

OBJECTIVES

The student should be able to:

1. Identify how foods are evaluated.
2. Describe the effects of sight and smell in sensory evaluation.
3. Determine threshold concentrations of sucrose.
4. Evaluate the appearance, odor, and flavor of herbs and spices.

FOOD SCIENCE PRINCIPLES

1. Foods are evaluated according to their appearance (size, shape, color), texture (kinesthetics), and flavor (smell, taste). Overlapping attributes of food quality are mouthfeel (a composite of smell, taste, and texture), terms such as consistency and viscosity (a composite of size, shape, and texture), and presence or absence of defects (related to appearance, texture, and flavor). Words that are often used to describe these qualities include:

   a. *Appearance:* asymmetrical, bright, burnt, clear, creamy, curdled, dull, dry, fine, frothy, glossy, grainy, level, luminescent, moist, pale, pebbled, opaque, rounded, size, shape, sparkling, sticky, symmetrical, translucent, volume, and all the colors of the rainbow.

   b. *Texture:* adhesive, astringent, body, brittle, cellular, chewy, coarse, cohesive, compact, consistent, creamy, crisp, crusty, crystalline, elastic, fibrous, firm, flaky, grainy, gritty, gummy, hard, limp, lumpy, mealy, moist, mushy, pasty, porous, rubbery, silky, smooth, soggy, syrupy, sticky, stiff, stringy, structure, tender, tough, velvety, viscous, wet.

   c. *Flavor:* acid, bitter, bland, burnt, concentrated, dull, eggy, fishy, flat, foul, fragrant, fresh, off-flavor, insipid, mild, nutty, putrid, rancid, salty, sharp, soapy, sour, stale, strong, sweet, yeasty, watery, weak.

2. It is difficult to adequately evaluate food if one or more of the senses is lacking. Sight is the most important of the senses and influences the feedback received from other sensory receptors. The flavor of food is determined by its taste, mouthfeel, and most important, its odor. The ability of taste and odor detection decreases measurably with age.

3. Substances in extremely low concentrations can be detected even though they cannot be recognized. In testing it is important to taste concentrations from low to high, rather than high to low, because of adaptation of the taste receptors. The point at which a person can distinguish the presence of a substance is his or her detection threshold.

3

Experiment I: Effect of Sight in Sensory Evaluation

See the Appendix for advance preparation by the laboratory aide. This experiment is to be conducted by the instructor on 4 students. If possible, select the 4 oldest students in the class.

1. Blindfold the 4 students.
2. Uncover 1 of the 3 puréed foods.
3. Let the first student smell the food *once*.
4. Give the student a taste of the food with a *clean* spoon. Discard spoon.
5. Repeat until all the students have tasted the food.
6. Ask each student to write down on a folded piece of paper the name of the food. Record.
7. Repeat with the other 2 foods.
8. Record results in Table 2–1.

QUESTIONS

1. Why were the 4 oldest students chosen as subjects? _____
   _____

2. Why were the foods puréed for this test? _____
   _____

3. Which appears to be more important in sensory evaluation, sight or smell? _____
   _____ Why? _____
   _____
   _____

4. How important is sight in sensory evaluation? _____
   _____
   _____

TABLE 2–1 Effect of Sight in Sensory Evaluation

Food	Student's Guess				Correct Answers	
	1	*2*	*3*	*4*	*No.*	*%*
					Average % Correct	

Experiment II: Effect of Smell in Sensory Evaluation

See the Appendix for advance preparation by the laboratory aide. This experiment is to be conducted by a laboratory instructor on 4 students.

For the Student

Please come to this laboratory neither hungry nor well-fed, and free of body odors and strong-smelling cosmetics. Abstain from smoking, eating, and chewing for at least 30 minutes prior to class. Bring a pair of dark sunglasses to class.

1. Students should wear sunglasses or be in a room lighted by a red light.
2. Give each student 2 glasses, one marked **R** for rinse and filled with tap water.
3. Uncover 1 of the 3 puréed foods.
4. Give the student a taste of the food with a *clean* spoon. Discard spoon.
5. Have the student expectorate into the spittoon and rinse mouth.
6. Repeat until each student has tasted food.
7. Ask each student to write down on a piece of paper the name of the food. Record.
8. Repeat with the other 2 foods.
9. Record results in Table 2-2.

QUESTIONS

1. Why was the light dimmed in this experiment? _____
   _____

2. Why were the foods puréed? _____
   _____

3. What appears to be more important in sensory evaluation, taste or smell? _____
   _____ Why? _____
   _____

TABLE 2-2   **Effect of Smell in Sensory Evaluation**

Food	Student's Guess				Correct Answers	
	1	2	3	4	No.	%
					Average % Correct	

Experiment III: Determination of Threshold Concentration of Sucrose

See the Appendix for advance preparation by the laboratory aide.

Advance Arrangement by the Instructor

1. Arrange the plastic disposable glasses numbered 1, 2, and 3 next to the bottles containing the different sucrose solutions as shown in Table 2–3.
2. Pour 10 ml of one concentration into 1 of the 3 glasses in the same row. Make sure that the concentration corresponds with the order presented in Table 2–3. Mark the glass that contains the sugar on this chart. Reveal the code to the student at the end of the experiment.
3. Place the bottle back in position so that the student may see the concentration of the row *or* label the concentration of the row.
4. Fill the other 2 glasses in the same row with deionized water. Make sure that both the sample and blanks (deionized water) are at the same room temperature.
5. Repeat steps 2, 3, and 4 for all the concentrations.

For the Student

Please come to this laboratory neither hungry nor well-fed, and free of body odors and strong-smelling cosmetics. Abstain from smoking, eating, and chewing for at least 30 minutes prior to class.

1. Mark 2 large glasses **R** and **S**. Fill the glass marked **R** for rinse with tap water. Use the other glass marked **S** for a spittoon.
2. Rinse the mouth thoroughly with tap water and discard water into spittoon.
3. Take a sip of the liquid in the #1 glass containing the lowest concentration. The liquid should not be swallowed, but swirled around the mouth, and then expectorated into the spittoon. Do *not* take a second sip.
4. Rinse mouth. Repeat with glass #2.
5. Rinse mouth. Repeat with glass #3.
6. Circle the glass that you think has something different in Table 2–3. *Make a guess even if you do not know.* Do not taste again.
7. Repeat steps 2–6 with each concentration. Always using the *lowest* concentration not yet tasted.
8. Obtain the code from the instructor. Mark the glasses that do have the solutions in them with an X in Table 2–3.

TABLE 2–3   Code for Sucrose Solutions

mM Sucrose	Glass		
	#1	#2	#3
3	O	O	O
6	O	O	O
12	O	O	O
24	O	O	O
36	O	O	O
48	O	O	O

9. Mark which concentrations were detected by you.
10. Determine the threshold concentration of sucrose as follows:

    a. Find the lowest concentration that was correct.
    b. If the next two higher concentrations were also correct, the concentration in (a) is the threshold.
    c. If one of the next two higher concentrations was not correct, start with the next highest concentration that was correct.
    d. Repeat (a) and (b) until the threshold is determined.

11. Plot the threshold concentrations of yourself and the other students in the class in Figure 2-1.

QUESTIONS

1. Why are the solutions tasted in order from the lowest concentrations to the higher concentrations? _____

_____

2. Why is guessing allowed? _____

_____

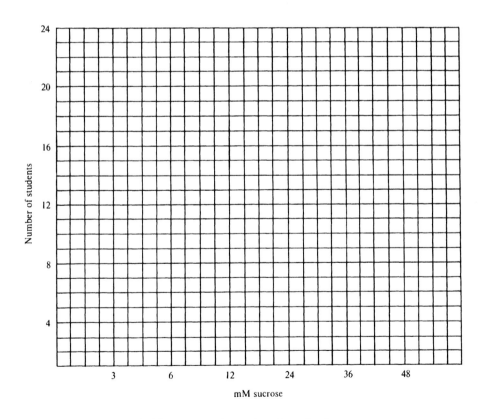

FIGURE 2-1   *Threshold concentrations of students in class.*

3. Is there a random distribution of threshold concentrations in this class? _____

_____ Why or why not? _____

_____

4. What effect would a range in ages have on the above curve? _____

_____

_____

Experiment IV: Organoleptic Evaluation of Spices and Herbs

Advance Preparation by the Laboratory Aide

1. Place a 10 ft (3.4 m) long sheet of brown paper, aluminum foil, waxed paper, or freezer paper on a counter that is infrequently used.
2. Label stations 1–20 every 6 in. (15 cm) apart.
3. Place one of the following spices or herbs and a laboratory spatula at each station. Record the station number for each spice or herb below. Reveal the code to the students at the end of the class.

Spice	Station Number	Herb	Station Number
Allspice	_____	Basil	_____
Cardamom	_____	Marjoram	_____
Cayenne	_____	Oregano	_____
Chili powder	_____	Sage	_____
Cinnamon	_____	Tarragon	_____
Cloves, ground	_____	Thyme	_____
Coriander, ground	_____		
Cumin, ground	_____		
Dill seed	_____		
Ginger, ground	_____		
Mustard	_____		
Nutmeg	_____		
Paprika	_____		
Turmeric	_____		

For the Student

1. Obtain 20 weighing papers. Label them Nos. 1–20.
2. Mark 2 glasses **R** and **S**. Fill the glass marked **R** for rinse with tap water. Use the other glass as a spittoon.
3. Place 4 weighing papers on a flat dish or in a baking pan. Bring the baking pan to the stations.

4. Place a small amount, *less* than 1/16 tsp (0.025 ml), of each of the unknowns on the corresponding marked weighing paper. It is not necessary to go in order.
5. Return to the unit with the unknowns.
6. Observe the appearance of the spice or herb. Record.
7. Pick up the piece of weighing paper to the nose. *Carefully* smell the unknown by gentle sniffing. Do not blow or breathe out. Record smell.
8. Rinse out the mouth with tap water. Discard into the spittoon.
9. Taste a small amount of the spice or herb. Do *not* swallow. Expectorate into the spittoon. Rinse the mouth with water. Record taste.
10. Repeat steps 3–9 until all the unknowns have been tested.
11. Try to guess the name of the herb or spice.
12. Determine the % correct answers by the following:

$$\frac{\text{No. correct answers}}{20} = \underline{\hspace{1cm}} \times 100 = \underline{\hspace{2cm}} \%$$

13. Record results in Table 2–4.

QUESTIONS

1. How did your number of % correct answers correspond to the class average? _____

_____

_____

2. What is the difference between a spice and an herb? _____

_____

_____

3. Why should spices and herbs be used in minute concentrations? _____

_____

_____

4. What is the average lifetime of an opened container of spices or herbs? _____

_____

Why? _____

_____

5. What factors could increase the lifetime of an herb or spice? _____

_____

Decrease it? _____

TABLE 2–4   Organoleptic Evaluation of Spices and Herbs

Station Number	Appearance	Odor	Flavor	Name	
				Your Guess	Actual
1					
2					
3					
4					
5					
6					
7					
8					
9					
10					
11					
12					
13					
14					
15					
16					
17					
18					
19					
20					
			% Correct		
				Your Average	Class Average

(Courtesy of Rice Council for Market Development.)

3
Measuring

OBJECTIVES

The student should be able to:

1. Convert measurements in English units to metric units.
2. Learn the techniques of accurate measuring.
3. Determine the accuracy of measuring equipment.
4. Recognize the importance of accurate measuring of ingredients in a recipe.

FOOD SCIENCE PRINCIPLES

1. Recipes are reproduced successfully only if the amount of each added ingredient is standardized. Standardization of amounts of solid foods are difficult due to differences in weight because of settling, aeration, structure of the molecule, packing, and films of syrup.
2. Solid and melted hydrogenated shortening, lard, and oil differ in weight. Substitution of these fats for each other is possible only if adjustments are made in measuring.
3. The degree of accuracy of measuring decreases with the number of measurements made. The least amount of error will occur when the measuring device* that is closest to the desired measurement is used.
4. Measuring devices do not always hold a standard volume. Newly purchased utensils should be checked for accuracy to determine the percent deviation from the standard. If measuring devices have deviations greater than 5%, they should not be used since the differences may adversely affect the recipe.

Exercise I: Calculating Conversions

1 Tbsp	= 3 tsp	2 c	= 1 pt
2 Tbsp	= 1 fluid oz	4 c	= 1 qt
4 Tbsp	= 1/4 c	4 qt	= 1 gal
16 Tbsp	= 1 c	16 oz	= 1 lb

*A measuring device is a utensil used to make precise measurements of a substance. Liquids are measured in a cup with a handle and pouring spout. The graduated markings on the side of the cup are used to determine the level to which the cup is filled. Solids are measured in individual fractional cups. When completely filled, each cup holds the volume designated on the cup.

6 Tbsp = ___ c   1/3 c   = ___ tsp
3/4 c   = ___ oz   1/4 lb = ___ oz
1/2 pt = ___ c   1/2 gal = ___ qt

Experiment I: Measurement of Flour

Measure the following flours by the methods listed below. Preweigh the 1-cup fractional measure. Be sure to subtract the weight of the empty cup. Record results in Table 3–1.

White Flour

   A. Dipped

       1. Dip the preweighed 1 c (250 ml) fractional measure into the flour bin until overflowing.
       2. Level with edge of spatula and weigh.
       3. Repeat.

   B. Dipped—2 Tbsp

       1. Repeat above; but remove 2 Tbsp (30 ml) flour from the cup before weighing.

   C. Sifted directly

       1. Dip the cup into the flour bin until overflowing and pour into sifter.
       2. Sift flour directly into cup.
       3. Level with edge of spatula and weigh.
       4. Repeat.

   D. Sifted, spooned

       1. Dip the cup into the flour bin until overflowing and pour into sifter.
       2. Sift onto wax paper.
       3. Spoon gently into cup. Level with edge of a spatula and weigh.
       4. Repeat.

   E. Stirred, spooned

       1. Stir flour in bin with a spoon.
       2. Repeat Part D, steps 3 and 4.

Cake Flour

       1. Repeat Part A using cake flour instead of white flour.
       2. Repeat Part D using cake flour instead of white flour.

Instant Flour

       1. Repeat Part A using instant flour instead of white flour.

Whole Wheat Flour

       1. Repeat Part E using whole wheat flour instead of white flour.

TABLE 3-1 Measurement of Flour

Variation	Empty Cup (g)	Test 1 (g)	Test 2 (g)	Average (g)	Standard[a] Weight (g)	Deviation from[b] Standard Weight (%)
White flour, *worst* dipped	29	139	141	140	143	2.1%
White flour, dipped—2 Tbsp (30 ml)					—	
sifted directly					—	
sifted, spooned *· true weight*	56.5	117.5	116.5	117	116	18%
stirred, spooned	25.1	109.9	188.9	175.4	126	−18.6 %
Cake flour, *—sifting is best* dipped	25.7	107.8	126.2	127.65	119	8.65 %
sifted, spooned					99	
Instant flour, dipped					—	
Whole wheat flour, stirred, spooned *best for whole wheat*	26g	155.2g			120	

[a] U.S. Agricultural Research Service. Average Weight of a Measured Cup of Various Foods, U.S. Department of Agriculture, *Home Economics Research Report No. 41.* 1977.

[b] % deviation from standard weight $= \dfrac{\text{Standard weight} - \text{average weight}}{\text{Standard weight}} \times 100$.

QUESTIONS

1. What is the *least* accurate method of measuring white flour? _____
   _____ Why? _____

   _____

   Which is the *most* accurate method? _____

   Which method would you recommend if you were in a hurry? _____

   _____

2. What adjustment must be made if white flour is substituted for either cake or instant flour in a
   recipe? _____
   Why? _____

Experiment II: Measurement of Sugar

Measure the following types of sugar by the methods listed below. Preweigh the 1 c (250 ml) fractional measure. Record results in Table 3–2.

Granulated

    A. Unsifted

        1. Spoon into 1 c (250 ml) fractional measure.
        2. Level with edge of spatula and weigh.
        3. Repeat.

Confectioner's (Powdered)

    A. Unsifted

        1. Repeat above using confectioner's sugar.

    B. Sifted

        1. Spoon sugar into cup until overflowing.
        2. Sift onto wax paper.
        3. Spoon gently into measuring cup.
        4. Level with edge of spatula and weigh.
        5. Repeat.

Brown

    A. Not packed

        1. Spoon brown sugar gently into cup. Do not pack.
        2. Level with edge of spatula and weigh.
        3. Repeat.

    B. Packed

        1. Spoon brown sugar into cup.
        2. Press down with rubber spatula.
        3. Repeat until cup is filled.

TABLE 3–2   Measuring of Sugar

Variation	Empty Cup (g)	Test 1 (g)	Test 2 (g)	Average (g)	Standard Weight (g)
Granulated, *just dip* unsifted	26g	227.5			196
Confectioner's, unsifted *needs to be sifted*	70	140	160	150	113
sifted					95
Brown, unpacked	25.1	147.2	152.7	149.95	—
packed *—Brown sugar should be packed*	25.9	259.2	233.3	246.25	211
free flowing					152

4. Level with edge of spatula and weigh.
5. Repeat.

C. Free-flowing (brownulated)

1. Pour into measuring cup.
2. Level with spatula and weigh.
3. Repeat.

QUESTIONS

1. How would substitution of confectioner's sugar for granulated sugar affect a recipe? _____

   _____

   Why? _____

   _____

2. Why is it necessary to pack brown sugar when measuring? _____

   _____ What adjustment must be

   made if free-flowing brown sugar is used instead? _____

   _____

Experiment III: Fats and Oils

Measure the following fats as indicated. Preweigh a 1 c (250 ml) fractional measure. Record results in Table 3–3.

Hydrogenated Shortening

    A. Solid, fractional measure

        1. Spoon fat into a 1 c (250 ml) fractional measure.
        2. Pack into cup to eliminate air.
        3. Level with edge of spatula and weigh.
        4. Empty cup using rubber spatula and paper towel.
        5. Wipe clean with paper towel.
        6. Repeat.

    B. Solid, water displacement

        1. Pour 8 oz cold tap water into 2 c (500 ml) liquid measure.
        2. Weigh.
        3. Spoon fat into cup until the water level reaches 2 c (500 ml).
        4. Weigh.
        5. Place wax paper on scale and weigh.
        6. Place fat, after shaking off excess water, onto wax paper and weigh.
        7. Repeat.

    C. Melted

        1. Measure 1 c (250 ml) fractional cup of hydrogenated shortening.
        2. Remove fat and melt hydrogenated shortening in a saucepan.
        3. Pour into 1 c (250 ml) liquid measure (preweighed).
        4. Weigh and repeat.

Lard

        1. Weigh lard as in Part A, hydrogenated shortening.

Oil

        1. Pour 8 oz (240 g) oil into 1 c (250 ml) liquid measure.
        2. Weigh and repeat.

TABLE 3–3 Measurement of Oil

Variation	Empty Cup (g)	Test 1 (g)	Test 2 (g)	Average Weight (g)	Standard Weight (g)
Hydrogenated shortening Solid, fractional	29	177	175	176	187
Solid, water displacement undrained					—
drained					—
Melted	26.63	187.6	187.6	187.6	—
Lard	36.3	214.8	213.5	214	—
Oil	280	153	160		209

QUESTIONS

1. Which is the easiest method for measuring hydrogenated fat? _____
_____ What are the disadvantages of this method?
_____

2. How does melted fat differ in weight from solid fat? _____
_____
_____
_____
_____

3. What causes the difference in volume of the melted solid fat and hydrogenated fat? _____
_____
_____

4. Would substituting oil for melted shortening affect a food product? _____
_____

Experiment IV: Measuring Liquids

Water and other liquids are measured in a graduated liquid measure. In order to be accurate, the meniscus* of the liquid should line up to the desired measurement line and be read at eye level.

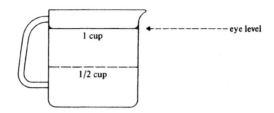

Water

A. 1 cup

 1. Fill a 1 c (250 ml) graduated liquid measure with tap water to the 1 c (250 ml) measurement line.
 2. Pour into graduated cylinder and measure.

B. 1/2 c × 2 (125 ml × 2)

 1. Fill the same cup with tap water to the 1/2 c (125 ml) measurement line.
 2. Pour into 250 ml graduated cylinder and save.
 3. Repeat steps 1 and 2.
 4. Measure number of ml.

C. 1/4 cup × 4 (50 ml × 5)

 1. Fill the same cup with tap water to 1/4 c (50 ml) measurement line.
 2. Pour into 250 ml graduated cylinder and save.
 3. Repeat steps 1 and 2 three times.
 4. Measure number of ml.

D. 1 Tablespoon × 16 (15 ml × 16)

 1. Fill 1 tablespoon with tap water.
 2. Carefully pour into 250 ml graduated cylinder and save.
 3. Repeat steps 1 and 2 fifteen additional times.
 4. Measure number of ml.

TABLE 3–4   Measurement of Liquids

Water	*Measurement (ml)*	*Standard Measure (ml)*	*Percent Deviation from Standard[a]*
1 c (250 ml)	232 mL	236.6 (250)	
1/2 c × 2 (125 ml × 2)	220 mL	236.6 (250)	
1/4 c × 4 (50 ml × 5)	199 mL	236.6 (250)	
1 Tbsp × 16 (15 ml × 16)	223 mL	236.6 (240)	

[a] % deviation from standard $= \dfrac{\text{Standard measure} - \text{measurement}}{\text{Standard measure}} \times 100.$

*A meniscus is the concave, upper surface of a liquid.

QUESTIONS

1. How is the degree of accuracy affected by the number of measurements? _____

   _____

   _____

2. How would 10 tablespoons be measured in order to achieve the most accurate measurement possible? _____

   _____

Exercise II: Calculating Metric Conversions

Liquid	*Avoirdupois (gravimetric)*
1 tsp = 4.9 ml	1 lb = 453.6 gm
1 Tbsp = 14.7 ml	1 kg = 2.2 lbs
1 c = 236.6 ml	
1 oz = 29.6 ml	28.4 gm
1 l = 1.06 qt	
1/3 c = ____ ml	2 tsp = ____ ml
3 kg = ____ lb	59 ml = ____ c
2 lb = ____ kg	4 fluid oz = ____ gm
1/2 qt = ____ ml	250 ml = ____ l

Experiment V: Determining Accuracy of Measuring Utensils

In order to be accurate, measuring utensils must be within 5% of the standard measures listed in Exercise I. Determine the volumes of the following measuring utensils by the appropriate method. Record results in Table 3–5.

Utensils

Fractionated	*Liquid*
1 c (250 ml)	1 c (250 ml)
1/2 c (125 ml)	
1/3 c (80 ml)	
1 Tbsp (15 ml)	
1 tsp (5 ml)	

A. Fractionated cups and spoons

   1. Fill to brim with tap water.
   2. Carefully pour into graduated cylinder and measure.
   3. Compare to standard volume and calculate percent deviation.

B. Liquid
    1. Fill to measurement line with tap water.
    2. Pour into graduated cylinder and measure.
    3. Compare to standard volume and calculate percent deviation.

TABLE 3–5 Measurement of Fractionated Cups

Measuring Utensil	Measurement (ml)	Standard Volume (ml)	Percent Deviation
Fractionated 1 c (250 ml)		236.6 (250)	
1/2 c (125 ml)		118.3 (125)	
1/3 c (80 ml)		78.8 (80)	
1 Tbsp (15 ml)		14.7 (15)	
1 tsp (5 ml)		4.9 (5)	
Liquid 1 c (250 ml)		236.6 (250 ml)	

QUESTIONS

1. Are the measuring utensils that you are using accurate? _____

2. Which is the more precise way to measure: using one large volume or several repeated measurements? _____ Why? _____

   _____

3. How will the deviation from the standard measurement affect recipes? _____

   _____

(Courtesy of Tea Council.)

4
Beverages

OBJECTIVES

The student will be able to:

1. Prepare and compare the different methods of brewing coffee.
2. Differentiate between the quality of brewed and instant coffee and tea.
3. Prepare and compare different varieties of tea.
4. Determine the effect of steeping time and pH on the quality of tea.
5. Prepare and compare hot cocoa and hot chocolate.
6. Assess the effect of different forms of milk on the quality of hot cocoa.

FOOD SCIENCE PRINCIPLES

1. Good quality coffee is amber brown, clear of sediment, and has a mild, brisk flavor. The goal in brewing coffee is to extract the maximum amount of caffeine and flavoring substances while minimizing the amount of polyphenols (tannins). This can be achieved if water contact with the grinds is limited and the temperature does not rise to boiling.
2. Instant coffee and tea lack the rich flavor of brewed coffee and tea. Their popularity stems from their convenience and lower cost. Freeze drying coffee improves the flavor but also increases the cost.
3. The processing of tea leaves greatly affects the flavor of the beverage. Green tea is highly astringent and light in color. A full-bodied flavor and darker color are developed when the leaves are fermented as in black tea. Oolong tea, a partially fermented tea, has flavor characteristics of both green and black tea.
4. Overextracting tea leaves results in a bitter, unpalatable beverage. Adding lemon juice changes the pH of the beverage, which results in a lighter color.
5. The flavor and color of cocoa and chocolate beverages are dependent on the processing of the cocoa bean. The high fat content of chocolate makes it more difficult to blend than powdered cocoa.
6. Decreasing the fat content of milk used in the preparation of cocoa beverages will decrease the full-bodied flavor.

Experiment I: Preparation and Comparison of Coffee Brews

1. Prepare coffee by the methods listed in Experiment I using the general principles of coffee brewing. Save a sample of the brew for comparison in Experiment II.

2. Note the amount of time that:

   a. it takes for the total preparation.
   b. the coffee grinds are in actual contact with the water.

3. Compare and evaluate the coffees for aroma, color, clarity, and flavor. Rate them according to your personal preference. Record results in Table 4–1.

General Principles of Coffee Brewing

1. The coffee pot must be absolutely clean. Residual oils that cling to the inside of the pot can taint freshly brewed coffee with a bitter flavor.
2. The correct size grind must be used for each of the different methods of coffee brewing. Too fine a grind will result in too strong a brew; too large will make it too weak.
3. Use the following guidelines to determine strength of coffee (*Note:* a cup of coffee is 6 oz (175 ml) rather than 8 oz (250 ml)):

   a. weak — 2 tsp/6 oz   (10 ml/175 ml)
   b. medium — 1 Tbsp/6 oz   (15 ml/175 ml)
   c. strong — 2 Tbsp/6 oz   (30 ml/175 ml)

4. The coffee pot should be filled to 3/4 of its capacity to prepare the best quality brew. (Several of the newer drip models are adjustable.)
5. Since coffee grinds absorb aroma from the brew, they should be removed and discarded after the brew is prepared.
6. The lid should be placed on the coffee pot as soon as the grinds are removed. See Figure 4–1.

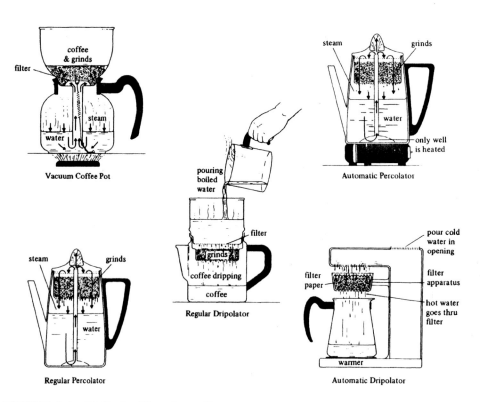

FIGURE 4–1   Methods of brewing coffee.

Percolated Coffee

A. Regular

   1. Fill coffee pot with cold water to level indicated on the side for the number of cups desired. (Or add 6 oz (175 ml) water for each cup of coffee.)
   2. Measure regular or percolator grinds into basket. Cover with perforated lid and place entire basket apparatus into coffee pot. Cover coffee pot with lid.
   3. Heat over high heat until coffee starts to percolate (hits glass top).
   4. Adjust heat so that it percolates once every 2 seconds.
   5. Percolate 7–8 minutes, depending on strength of brew desired.
   6. Measure the contact time for coffee grinds with the water prior to evaluation of the brew.
   7. Let stand 2 minutes. Remove grinds, cover, and serve.
   8. Record results in Table 4–1.

B. Automatic

   1. Follow steps 1–3 above.
   2. Let percolate until light goes off.
   3. Repeat steps 6 and 7 above.

Drip Coffee

A. Regular

   1. Assemble top reservoir.
   2. Place filter paper in top portion (if used).
   3. Measure drip coffee grinds into the upper reservoir.
   4. Bring measured amount of cold water in a separate saucepan to boil over high heat.
   5. Pour boiling water into top reservoir. Time the contact time of the water with the coffee brew.
   6. Cover and let water drip through.
   7. Remove top reservoir, cover bottom reservoir, and serve.
   8. Record results in Table 4–1.

B. Automatic

   1. Place filter paper in the filter apparatus.
   2. Measure drip coffee grinds into filter apparatus.
   3. Place glass coffee pot into position on warmer.
   4. Turn water heater on.
   5. Pour measured amount of *cold* water into designated opening on top of the assembly. Measure the contact time of the water with the coffee grinds.
   6. Let drip until all the water has run through.
   7. Turn warmer on.
   8. Remove coffee grinds and filter paper from filter apparatus.
   9. Serve immediately.
   10. Record results in Table 4–1.

Steeped Coffee

1. Pour measured amount of cold water into a coffee pot or saucepan.
2. Bring to simmer over high heat.
3. Measure regular coffee grinds. Moisten *slightly* with egg white.
4. Place coated coffee grinds on a piece of cheesecloth folded to double thickness. Tie with string to form a long, very loose pouch.
5. Add bag of coffee grinds to simmering water, 185°F (85°C) to 203°F (95°C).
6. Cover and simmer 4–5 minutes. Measure the contact time of the water with the grinds.
7. Remove bag and discard; cover and serve.
8. Record results in Table 4–1.

Vacuum Coffee

1. Pour measured amount of cold water into lower portion of vacuum coffee pot.
2. Assemble filter in position in upper portion. Set filter paper in place.
3. Firmly press upper portion of coffee pot into position on top of lower portion.
4. Measure fine coffee grinds into upper portion. Cover.
5. Heat over high heat until water leaves lower portion and is driven into upper part.
6. Adjust heat to medium to keep water in upper portion for 3–5 minutes. Stir and cover.
7. Turn heat off; water will return to lower portion of coffee pot. Measure the contact time of the water with the coffee grinds.
8. Remove upper portion. Cover lower reservoir and keep warm until served.

TABLE 4-1 Comparison of Coffee Brews

Coffee	Preparation Time (minutes)	Grind Contact Time (minutes)	Aroma	Color	Clarity	Taste	Order of Preference
Percolated, regular							
Percolated, automatic							
Drip, regular							
Drip, automatic							
Steeped							
Vacuum							

QUESTIONS

1. Which type of coffee had the best aroma? _____
   Did it also have the best flavor? _____ Why or why not? _____
   _____
   _____

2. Was the brew selected as having the best flavor prepared at the suggested temperature range of
   185°F (85°C)–203°F (95°C)? _____
   What would be the effect of using higher temperatures? _____
   _____
   _____ Lower temperatures? _____
   _____
   _____

3. Was the color the same for all brews prepared? _____
   If not, how did they differ and why? _____
   _____
   _____
   _____
   _____

4. What was the contact time between the grinds and the coffee for percolated coffee? _____
   _____ Drip coffee? _____
   Steeped coffee? _____ Vacuum coffee? _____

5. What relationship did the length of contact time have with the quality of the brew? _____
   _____

6. Why was an egg white used in making steeped coffee? _____
   _____

7. What caused the water to go into the top portion of the coffee pot when making vacuum coffee?
   _____
   Why did the water remain there? _____
   _____
   What caused the water to return to the bottom when it was removed from heat? _____
   _____
   _____

Experiment II: Comparison of Instant Coffees to Brewed Coffee

1. Prepare instant coffees by the following methods:

Instant Coffee

    a. Measure 1 rounded teaspoon of instant coffee into a cup.

    b. Measure 6 oz (175 ml) tap water, pour into a saucepan and bring to boiling point 212°F (100°C).

    or

    b. Bring water to boil in a microwave oven.

    c. Pour hot water over instant coffee; stir, and serve immediately.

2. Compare prepared instant coffee to the freshly brewed coffee (kept warm) from Experiment I.
3. Record results in Table 4–2.

TABLE 4–2   Comparison of Instant and Brewed Coffee

Coffee	Cost/ Serving	Aroma	Color	Clarity	Taste	Order of Preference
Brewed						
Instant, regular						
Instant, freeze-dried						
Instant, decaffeinated						

QUESTIONS

1. Which coffee is more expensive, instant or brewed? _____

    Regular instant or freeze-dried? _____

2. Describe the differences in flavor between instant and brewed coffee. _____

_____

    Between regular instant and decaffeinated instant coffee. _____

_____

_____

3. Why do instant coffees not taste the same as brewed coffees? _____

_____

_____

Experiment III: Preparation and Comparison of Hot Teas

1. Select a variety of teas. Suggestions are:

    a. green tea
    b. black tea
    c. mint tea
    d. oolong
    e. instant

2. Prepare the tea by the method listed below.
3. Record results in Table 4-3.

Hot Tea

1 tea bag	0.08 oz	2.2 g
or		
tea leaves	3/4–1 tsp	3–5 ml
water	1 c	250 ml

    a. Preheat teapot by filling it with boiling water.
    b. Allow the water to remain in the teapot while fresh water is boiled.
    c. Empty water from teapot. Add tea bag or tea leaves.
    d. Pour boiling water over the leaves and cover.
    e. Let the tea steep for 3–5 minutes.
    f. Remove tea bag or strain leaves.

TABLE 4-3   Comparisons of Hot Teas

Variety of Teas	Cost/Serving	Aroma	Clarity	Color	Astringency
Green					
Black					
Mint					
Oolong					
Instant					

QUESTIONS

1. Which of the teas is the most expensive? _____

    The least expensive? _____

2. Is the taste of the tea related to the cost? _____

    Why or why not? _____

    _____

3. Which tea is the most astringent? _____

    Why? _____

    _____

4. Is the color of the tea related to the degree of astringency? _____

    How? _____

Experiment IV: Preparation and Comparison of Iced Teas

Prepare the following:

1. Iced tea (brewed)
2. Instant iced tea
3. Instant iced tea, flavored with sugar and lemon

Record results of the experiment in Table 4–4.

Iced Tea

tea bag	2	
water	1 c	250 ml
ice cubes		
sugar	1 tsp	5 ml
(optional)		

1. Preheat 1 c (250 ml) Pyrex measure by filling it with boiling water.
2. Allow water to remain in the cup while fresh water is boiled.
3. Pour water out of cup. Add tea bag and fill with boiling water.
4. Let the tea steep for 8 minutes.
5. Pour equal amount of the tea into each of 2 glasses. Add cold tap water to bring each glass to 1/2 full. Fill the rest of the glass with ice cubes and stir.

Note: For purposes of comparison of flavor, do not add sugar or lemon. After comparison is made with instant tea, sugar and lemon may be added to compare brewed and instant tea with flavored tea. Record the amount of sugar and lemon added to equal the flavor of the flavored tea.

Instant Iced Tea

1. Measure amount of instant tea into a glass according to label on jar.
2. Add cold tap water and stir until dissolved.
3. Add ice cubes.

TABLE 4–4   Comparison of Iced Teas

Variety of Iced Tea	Cost/Serving	Clarity	Color	Astringency
Brewed, unflavored				
Brewed, flavored				
Instant, unflavored				
Instant, flavored				

QUESTIONS

1. Read the labels on the jars of the instant tea. What components other than tea have been added?

   _____

   Why have they been added? _____

   _____

2. How do the additives in instant tea influence the clarity? _____

   _____

   _____

   Color? _____

   Taste? _____

   _____

3. How much lemon and sugar had to be added to brewed tea to equal the flavor of the flavored

   tea? _____

   What effect does this have on cost? _____

   _____

Experiment V: Effect of Steeping Time and pH on the Quality of Tea

1. Prepare 5 cups of hot tea following the recipe in Experiment III using the following steeping times. The tea can be kept warm by covering the pot with a cloth.

   Cup a — 1.5 minutes
   Cup b — 3 minutes
   Cup c — 3 minutes
   Cup d — 6 minutes
   Cup e — 9 minutes

2. Add 1 tsp (5 ml) of lemon juice to cup c of tea steeped 3 minutes.
3. Taste and compare quality while tea is still warm.
4. Record results in Table 4–5.

TABLE 4–5   Effect of Steeping

Steeping Time (minutes)	Color	Clarity	Aroma	Astringency
1.5				
3				
With lemon juice				
6				
9				

QUESTIONS

1. Describe the effect of adding lemon juice to tea. _____

_____

Why does this occur? _____

2. What happens when tea is overextracted? _____

_____

Experiment VI: Preparation and Comparison of Cocoa and Hot Chocolate

1. Prepare the following beverages:

   a. breakfast cocoa
   b. Dutch process cocoa
   c. instant cocoa
   d. hot chocolate

2. Use the label directions in preparing the instant cocoa.
3. Prepare the other beverages by the following recipes, reserving 1 c (250 ml) of the breakfast cocoa for comparison in Experiment VII.

Breakfast Cocoa (for 2)

cocoa	1 Tbsp + 1 tsp	20 ml	water	2 Tbsp	30 ml
sugar	2 Tbsp	30 ml	milk	1 c + 2 Tbsp	280 ml
salt	dash		vanilla (optional)	drop	

    a. Mix cocoa, sugar, and salt in a small saucepan. Add water and blend.

    b. Heat over medium high heat until mixture starts to boil, stirring continuously.

    c. Lower heat and simmer 2–3 minutes. (If needed, another 1 tsp. (5 ml) of water may be added to prevent scorching.)

    d. Blend in milk and heat thoroughly to 185°C, but do *not* allow the mixture to boil.

    e. Add vanilla, if desired, and serve hot.

    f. Reserve 1 c (250 ml) for comparison in Experiment VII.

Note: A foamy cocoa can be produced by whipping with a rotary beater.

Dutch Cocoa

Follow directions above for Breakfast Cocoa but substituting Dutch Process Cocoa for Breakfast.

Hot Chocolate (for 2)

salt	dash		milk	1-1/4 c	300 ml
sugar	1 Tbsp + 1 tsp	20 ml	vanilla	drop	
water	2 Tbsp	30 ml	(optional)		
chocolate, unsweetened	1/2 oz	14 g			

1. Mix salt, sugar and water in a small saucepan.
2. Add unsweetened chocolate and stir continuously while it is melting.
3. Bring to boil; lower heat and simmer 4 minutes, continuously stirring.
4. Blend in milk and heat thoroughly to 185°F (85°C) but do *not* allow the mixture to boil.
5. Add vanilla, if desired, and serve hot.

TABLE 4-6   Comparison of Cocoas and Hot Chocolate

Beverage	Preparation Time (minutes)	Appearance (color)	Flavor	Sediment
Breakfast Cocoa				
Dutch Cocoa				
Instant Cocoa				
Hot Chocolate				

QUESTIONS

1. How does hot chocolate differ from hot cocoa? _____
   _____
   _____

2. Which beverage had the shortest preparation time? _____
   The longest preparation time? _____

3. What effect does sediment have on the flavor of the beverage? _____
   _____
   _____
   The appearance? _____

4. What causes the sediment to form on the bottom of the pan if the beverage is not continuously
   stirred? _____
   _____
   _____

Experiment VII: Effect of Milk on the Quality of Breakfast Cocoa

1. Prepare breakfast cocoa by the method in Experiment VI. Use only 1/2 of the recipe.
2. Substitute the following for the whole milk:

   a. nonfat dry milk reconstituted
   b. evaporated milk reconstituted
   c. 2% milk

3. Compare the cocoas to the reserved cup of breakfast cocoa made with whole milk. (If Experiment
   VI was omitted, prepare 1/2 recipe using whole milk.)
4. Record results in Table 4–7.

TABLE 4-7   Effect of Milk on the Quality of Cocoa

Milk Used in Cocoa	Cost/Serving	Appearance	Flavor	Sediment
Whole				
Nonfat dry				
Evaporated				
2%				

QUESTIONS

1. Does the reduced cost/serving of using nonfat dry milk compensate for the flavor difference?

   _____

   _____

2. Which cocoa had the brownest color? _____

   Why? _____

   _____

3. How does the fat content of the milk affect the quality of hot cocoa? _____

   _____

   _____

APPLICATIONS

Iced Coffee with Whipped Cream

heavy cream	1/4 c	50 ml	cold coffee	1–1/2 c	375 ml
milk	1–1/2 c	375 ml	vanilla	1/4 tsp	1 ml
sugar	1 c	250 ml			

1. Heat milk and sugar in a saucepan over medium heat, stirring constantly, until sugar dissolves. Chill.
2. Whip cream with an electric beater on medium speed until soft peaks form.
3. Pour coffee and vanilla into chilled milk.
4. Fold in 3/4 of the whipped cream.
5. Pour into chilled refrigerator trays.
6. Place in freezer until partially frozen.
7. Stir and pour into parfait glasses, 2/3 full.
8. Top with reserved whipped cream and serve.

Viennese Coffee Mix

hot cocoa mix	1/4 c	50 ml	powdered sugar	2 Tbsp	30 ml
nondairy creamer mix	1/4 c	50 ml	cinnamon	1/8 tsp	0.5 ml
instant coffee powder	3 Tbsp	45 ml	nutmeg	1/8 tsp	0.5 ml

1. Combine all ingredients.
2. Add 3 Tbsp (45 ml) to a cup. Fill with boiling water, stir, and serve.

Frozen Coffee with Chantilly Cream

strong, hot coffee	1–1/2 c	375 ml
sugar	1/3 c	80 ml
Chantilly Cream		

1. Dissolve sugar in hot coffee.
2. Pour into a refrigerator tray and freeze until ice crystals form.
3. Dip edges of 2 parfait glasses in cold water, then sugar and place in freezer to frost.
4. Spoon partially frozen coffee into frosted parfait glasses.
5. Top with Chantilly Cream.
6. Serve immediately.

Chantilly Cream

heavy cream	1/4 c	50 ml
confectioners' sugar	2 tsp	10 ml
egg white	1/4	
rum flavoring, drops	2	

1. Whip cream with an electric mixer on medium speed until stiff peaks form.
2. Gradually beat in confectioners' sugar.
3. Whip egg white with an electric mixer on medium speed until stiff peaks form.
4. Fold whipped cream and rum flavoring into egg whites.

Demitasse (for 4)

Italian or French roast coffee	6 Tbsp	90 ml
water	1-1/2 c	375 ml
lemon, slices (optional)	4	

1. Brew coffee according to the drip method on page 23.
2. Serve in demitasse or half-size cups.
3. Garnish with a slice of lemon.

Cafe au Lait (for 4)

Italian or French roast coffee	6 Tbsp	90 ml
water	1-1/2 c	375 ml
milk	1-1/2 c	375 ml
sugar (optional)		

1. Prepare demitasse using the first two ingredients.
2. Heat milk until scalding, 198°F (92°C).
3. Pour 3 oz (75 ml) demitasse and 3 oz (75 ml) hot milk simultaneously into each coffee cup.
4. Serve hot.

Note: A foamy mixture can be produced by whipping with a rotary beater.

Café Aruba

orange	1		water	1 qt	1 l
coffee	1/2 c	125 ml	heavy cream	1/2 c	125 ml
sugar (divided)	1 Tbsp	15 ml			

1. Peel orange with a vegetable peeler into thin strips. Make the strips very thin, avoiding the bitter white underneath. Set aside 1/3 of the peelings for garnish.
2. Cut the remaining 2/3s of the peelings into large pieces.
3. Combine the large pieces of orange peelings, the coffee, and 1–1/2 tsp (7 ml) sugar in the coffee basket.
4. Prepare coffee by the usual method using the indicated amount of water.
5. Meanwhile, whip cream until it is almost thickened. Add in remaining 1–1/2 tsp (7 ml) sugar. Continue beating until it has the appearance of whipped cream.
6. Finish peeling orange and cut half of the orange into thin crosswise slices. (The other half of the orange is not needed.)
7. When coffee is brewed, remove coffee basket and add orange slices. Let it mellow 10 minutes before serving.
8. Remove orange slices and pour coffee into serving cup. Cover with approximately 1/4 of the whipped cream and garnish with an orange peel.

Chocolate Soda

cocoa	1 Tbsp + 1 tsp	20 ml	club soda,	1–1/2 c	375 ml
sugar	2 Tbsp	30 ml	chilled		
water	2 Tbsp	30 ml	chocolate ice	4	
			cream, scoops		

1. Follow steps 1–4 for Breakfast Cocoa on pg. 30.
2. Pour syrup into 2 tall glasses.
3. Pour 1/4 c (50 ml) of club soda into each glass. Mix well.
4. Add remainder of club soda.
5. Add 2 scoops of ice cream to each glass.
6. Serve immediately. Garnish with whipped cream and a cherry if desired.

(Courtesy of Oregon-Washington-California Pear Bureau.)

5
Fruits

OBJECTIVES

The student should be able to:

1. Compare nutritive values of fruits.
2. Identify methods that prevent browning on the cut surface of fruits.
3. Determine the effects of sugar on the texture, tenderness, and flavor of cooked fruits.
4. Appraise baking characteristics of different varieties of apples.
5. Distinguish the effects of soaking and sugar on dried, cooked fruits.
6. Assess the effect of pH on the color of fruit juices.

FOOD SCIENCE PRINCIPLES

1. Some fruits are excellent sources of ascorbic acid and vitamin A. Raisins and prunes contain a high amount of iron. Generally, fruits are low in calories and poor sources of proteins and fats.
2. Enzymatic browning in cut fruits can be prevented by:

    a. minimizing the contact of oxygen with the cut surface by coating with sugar syrup or dry sugar.
    b. limiting the activity of the phenol oxidase enzyme by denaturing the enzyme through (i) blanching, (ii) coating with a sulfur solution, or (iii) altering the pH with acids such as ascorbic, cream of tartar, and lemon juice.

3. The firm structure of plants is due to the cellulose and hemicellulose composition of the cell wall, the solubility of pectic substances that act as cementing substances between adjacent cell walls, and the turgor (water) pressure inside the cells.

    a. Cooking softens the structure since heat converts the pectic substances between cell walls into a soluble form. (This also occurs during ripening.) Agitation during cooking softens the structure by mechanical means as the fruit is tossed around.
    b. The turgor pressure inside the cells of the fruit is dependent on the osmotic pressure of the surrounding medium (cooking liquid).

        i. When fruit is cooked in water, the water is drawn into the plant because of the higher osmotic concentration of the plant cell. The excess water swells the cell and may cause it to burst; this leads to a mushy texture in the cooked fruit.

ii. When fruit is cooked in a sugar syrup, water is drawn out of the cells near the surface of the fruit into the syrup because of its higher solute concentration. Cooking fruit in a concentrated sugar solution may cause the cells to lose so much water that they become dehydrated, tough, and shriveled. Cooking fruit in a diluted sugar solution produces a slight shrinkage and a toughening of the fruit; this enables the fruit to remain firm with its shape intact.

4. Not all varieties of apples are suitable for cooking purposes. Baking apples such as Rome and Winesap are able to hold their shape and texture when heat is applied.
5. Dried fruit reconstitutes more easily if it is soaked for a period of time before cooking. Sugar limits the rehydration of fruits and should not be added until the end of the cooking period. Tenderized fruits can be reconstituted by soaking for a short time in boiling water.   .
6. Anthocyanins are water soluble pigments in fruits that vary their color according to the pH. Acids turn the pigments red; alkaline solutions change the pigments to blue. Care must be taken when mixing fruit juices to avoid unwanted colors.

Exercise I: Comparison of the Nutritive Value of Fruits

1. Determine the nutritive value of fruits.
2. Record results in Table 5-1.

TABLE 5-1   Nutritive Values of Fruits

Fruit	Food Energy (Cal)	Protein (g)	Fat (g)	Iron (mg)	Vitamin A	Ascorbic Acid (mg)
Apple (1)						
Avocado (1)						
Banana (1)						
Cantaloupe (1/2)						
Grapefruit (1/2)						
Orange (1)						
Peach (1)						
Prunes (1 c)						
Raisins (1 c)						
Strawberries (1 c)						

QUESTIONS

1. Generally, are fruits considered good sources of proteins or fats? _____

2. What fruit is an exception to this generalization? _____

3. How does this affect its food energy (calorie) content? _____

   _____

   _____

4. Which of the above fruits are the best sources of iron? _____

   _____

   _____ Vitamin A? _____

   _____

5. Which fruits would you recommend to someone on a reducing diet who was interested in eating low-calorie but nutrient-dense foods? _____

   _____

Experiment I: Prevention of Browning on the Cut Surface of Fruit

1. Prepare the following treatments:

   a. none (leave exposed to air)
   b. dissolve 1/8 tsp (0.5 ml) ascorbic acid in 1/4 c (50 ml) water
   c. dissolve 1/4 tsp (1 ml) cream of tartar in 1/4 c (50 ml) water
   d. dissolve 2 Tbsp (30 ml) sugar in 1/4 c (50 ml) water
   e. dry sugar on a plate (for sprinkling)
   f. lemon juice in a custard cup (for dipping)
   g. pineapple juice in a custard cup (for dipping)
   h. boil 1 c (250 ml) water in a small saucepan (for blanching).

2. Peel a banana; cut off ends, and cut into 8 equal slices.
3. Do the following treatments and place the slices on a plate:

   a. none (leave exposed to air)
   b. dip in ascorbic acid solution
   c. dip in cream of tartar solution
   d. dip in sugar solution
   e. sprinkle with dry sugar
   f. dip in lemon juice
   g. dip in pineapple juice
   h. blanch in boiling water for 30 seconds.

4. Test the pH of each piece of fruit by gently touching it with pH indicator paper.
5. Let the fruit stand at room temperature exposed to air for 45 minutes.
6. Record the results in Table 5–2.

TABLE 5–2   Prevention of Browning of Fruit

Treatment	pH	Color	Texture	Flavor	Order of Preference
None					
Ascorbic Acid					
Cream of Tartar					
Sugar Syrup					
Dry Sugar					
Lemon Juice					
Pineapple Juice					
Blanching					

QUESTIONS

1. What effect does pH have on the prevention of browning in cut fruit? _____

_____

2. What is the effect of blanching? _____

_____

3. What is the disadvantage of this method? _____

_____

4. Explain why pineapple juice was effective in retarding browning. _____

_____

5. Which of the above treatments would be easiest to use when making fruit salad? _____

_____

Experiment II: Effect of Agitation and Sugar on the Texture and Flavor of Eating and Cooking Apples

Two varieties of apples should be selected, including one eating apple and one cooking apple. Recommended cooking apples include Jonathan, McIntosh, Newtown Pippin, Northern Spy, Rhode Island Greening, Stayman, Winesap, Yellow Transparent, and New York Imperial. If none of these are available, then a dual-purpose apple such as Baldwin, Gravenstein, Rome Beauty, or Wealthy can be substituted, although the results will not be as different.

1. Wash, peel, and core 2 apples of each variety. Cut each apple into 8 sections so that there are 16 pieces of each variety.
2. Reserve 1 piece of each variety for comparison.
3. Cook 3 pieces of each variety of apples by the following treatments until tender, using small saucepans.

    a. 1/2 c (125 ml) simmering water
    b. 2 c (500 ml) rapidly boiling water, stirring frequently
    c. 2 Tbsp (30 ml) sugar in 1/2 c (125 ml) simmering water
    d. 1/2 c (125 ml) sugar in 1/2 c (125 ml) simmering water
    e. 1/2 c (125 ml) simmering water until tender. Then add 1/2 c (125 ml) sugar, cook two minutes longer.

4. Evaluate pieces for texture and flavor, and the syrup for flavor. Record results in Table 5–3.

TABLE 5–3   Effect of Agitation and Sugar on Texture and Flavor of Eating and Cooking Apples

| Treatment | Eating Apple | | | Cooking Apple | | |
| | Texture | Flavor | | Texture | Flavor | |
		Fruit	Syrup		Fruit	Syrup
Water, simmering						
Water, rapidly boiling						
Thin sugar syrup						
Thick sugar syrup						
Sugar added at end						

QUESTIONS

1. Why is it important to buy the proper type of apple for cooking purposes? _____
   _____

2. What is the difference between the apples cooked in simmering vs. rapidly boiling water? ____
   _____

   Why? _____

3. What is the effect that sugar has on the flavor of the apple pieces and syrup? _____
   _____

   The texture? _____
   _____

   Explain the scientific principle for this effect on texture. _____
   _____
   _____

4. Which method would you recommend for the best all around texture and flavor? _____
   _____

Experiment III: Baking Characteristics of Different Varieties of Baking Apples

Select 3 varieties of apples. Follow the following recipe for each variety.

Baked Apples

apples	3	
brown sugar	3 Tbsp	45 ml
cinnamon	3/4 tsp	3 ml
butter	1 Tbsp	15 ml
water	3 Tbsp	45 ml

1. Wash and core apples. Remove skin from upper half to prevent splitting.
2. Place each apple in a custard cup.
3. Fill the center of the apple with 1 Tbsp (15 ml) brown sugar, 1/4 tsp (1 ml) cinnamon, and 1 tsp (5 ml) butter.
4. Add 1 Tbsp (15 ml) water to custard cup around apple.
5. Bake 30–50 minutes at 375°F (190°C) until tender. Baste occasionally.
6. Record observations in Table 5–4.

TABLE 5–4   Baking Characteristics of a Variety of Apples

Apple Variety	Shape	Texture	Flavor
No. 1 _____			
No. 2 _____			
No. 3 _____			

QUESTIONS

1. Are all apples similar in their baking characteristics? _____

   If not, what are the differences? _____

   _____

   _____

2. Which variety do you prefer? _____ Why? _____

   _____

   _____

Experiment IV: Effect of Soaking and Sugar on Cooked Dried Fruit

Select either 24 dried apricots, prunes, or plums. Soak 12 pieces in water overnight; keep the other 12 pieces dry in refrigerator and tightly covered.

1. Divide the 2 groups of dried fruits, soaked and dry, into 2 groups each.
2. All fruit should be covered with 1/2 c (125 ml) water in a small saucepan, brought to a boil, and simmered until tender.
3. The following treatments should be used:

   a. dry, cooked, water only
   b. dry, cooked, 2 tsp (10 ml) sugar added at beginning of cooking period
   c. dry, cooked, 2 tsp (10 ml) sugar added at end of cooking period
   d. soaked, cooked, water only
   e. soaked, cooked, 2 tsp (10 ml) sugar added at beginning of cooking period
   f. soaked, cooked, 2 tsp (10 ml) sugar added at end of cooking period.

4. Record results in Table 5–5.

TABLE 5–5   Effect of Soaking and the Time of Addition of Sugar on Cooked Dried Fruit

Treatment	Appearance	Texture	Flavor
Dry			
Dry, sugar at beginning			
Dry, sugar at end			
Soaked			
Soaked, sugar at beginning			
Soaked, sugar at end			

QUESTIONS

1. What effect does soaking dried fruit prior to cooking have on the quality of the final product?

   _____

   _____

2. What effect does sugar have on dried, cooked fruit if it is added at the beginning of the cooking period? _____

   _____

   The end? _____

   _____

   What is the reason for this? _____

Experiment V: Effect of pH on the Color of Fruit Juices

1. Place 2 Tbsp (30 ml) of either blackberry or raspberry juice into each of 4 small glasses.
2. Repeat above using grape and cranberry juice so that there are a total of 12 samples of 3 types of fruit juices.
3. Add 1 Tbsp (15 ml) of the liquids indicated on the chart into the glasses containing the fruit juice.
4. Measure the pH of each fruit juice tested by using pH indicator paper.
5. Record results in Table 5–6.

TABLE 5–6   Effect of pH on the Color of Fruit Juices

Treatment	Cranberry		Grape		Blackberry or Raspberry	
	pH	Color	pH	Color	pH	Color
Lemon Juice pH = _____						
Orange Juice pH = _____						
Pineapple Juice pH = _____						
1/2 tsp (2 ml) Baking Soda in 1 Tbsp (15 ml) water pH = _____						

QUESTIONS

1. What effect does pH have on the color of fruit juices? _____
_____
_____

2. Are all fruit juices affected in the same way? _____
Why or why not? _____
_____
_____

3. What practical application could this have in the preparation of a party punch? _____
_____
_____

APPLICATIONS

Fried Apple Rings

apple	1	
flour	1–2 Tbsp	15–30 ml
margarine	1-1/2 Tbsp	22 ml
cinnamon	dash	

1. Core apple but do not peel. Slice in 1/2 in. (1.3 cm) slices.
2. Roll in flour. Shake off excess.
3. Melt margarine in a skillet over medium heat.
4. Add apple slices, a few at a time.
5. Turn over when needed. Sauté approximately 10 minutes.
6. Drain on paper towels.
7. Sprinkle with cinnamon.
8. Serve hot.

Apple Brown Betty

margarine	2-1/2 Tbsp	37 ml	cinnamon	1/2 tsp	2	ml
soft bread crumbs	1-1/2 c	375 ml	nutmeg	1/8 tsp	0.5 ml	
apples, peeled,	2 c	500 ml	water	2 Tbsp	30	ml
thinly sliced			lemon juice	1 Tbsp	15	ml
brown sugar	1/2 c	125 ml	ice cream			

1. Preheat oven to 350°F (175°C).
2. Grease a small casserole with margarine.
3. Melt margarine over low heat in a saucepan. Add bread crumbs and toss until coated.
4. Combine sugar, cinnamon, and nutmeg. Sprinkle over apples. Toss until coated.
5. Place 1/2 c (125 ml) of the bread crumbs in a casserole.
6. Place half of the apple mixture on top.
7. Repeat steps 5 and 6. Repeat step 5.
8. Sprinkle with water and lemon juice.
9. Cover dish with aluminum foil.
10. Bake 25 minutes.
11. Uncover and bake for 20 minutes. If necessary, the top may be quickly browned under a broiler.
12. Serve warm with ice cream.

Triple Fruit Tart

pastry, single crust	9 in.	23 cm	strawberries, halved	3/4 c	180 ml
cream cheese	6 oz	180 g	*or*		
sugar	3 Tbsp	45 ml	bananas, sliced		
lemon juice, fresh	2 tsp	10 ml	grapes, seedless	3/4 c	180 ml
lemon peel, grated	3/4 tsp	3 ml	apple jelly	1/4 c	50 ml
peaches, peeled, fresh, *or* canned	1 c	250 ml			

1. Preheat oven to 425°F (220°C).
2. Prepare pastry for a 9-in. (23 cm) tart. Use the single crust pastry recipe on pg. 253. Place crust in a two-piece tart pan and trim edges. Be careful to pick up the tart only with the outer edge pan. Prick the crust with a fork.
3. Bake for 10–15 minutes to lightly brown the crust. Cool crust to room temperature.
4. Cream cream cheese until soft. Gradually beat in sugar.
5. Add lemon juice and peel to cream cheese mixture and stir until blended.
6. Spread cream cheese mixture in a thin layer over the bottom of the tart shell using a rubber spatula.
7. Arrange peaches in a single layer in a center line from edge to edge of the tart.
8. Arrange strawberries cut side down in a single layer on both sides of the peaches from edge to edge of the tart.
9. Arrange grapes in a single layer along side of the strawberries.
10. Melt jelly in the microwave oven or a small saucepan. Lightly brush over fruit with a pastry brush.
11. Remove outer tart pan by loosening edges with a knife and pushing center circle pan up through the middle of the outer side pan.
12. Place tart still on inner tart pan on a plate. Chill until serving.

Waldorf Salad

apples, unpeeled, diced	1 c	250 ml	raisins	1 Tbsp	15 ml
celery, diced	1/2 c	125 ml	mayonnaise	2 Tbsp	30 ml
walnuts, chopped	2 Tbsp	30 ml	lettuce leaf		

1. Combine all ingredients and toss.
2. Serve in mounds on a lettuce leaf.

Baked Banana

banana, firm	2	
margarine, melted	1 Tbsp	15 ml
brown sugar	1 Tbsp	15 ml

1. Preheat oven to 350°F (175°C).
2. Grease small baking dish with margarine.
3. Peel banana. Cut in half lengthwise. Place cut side down in baking dish.
4. Brush with melted margarine.
5. Bake 15–20 minutes until soft.
6. Sprinkle with brown sugar.

Cranberry-Orange Relish

orange, seedless	1		sugar	1 c	250 ml
cranberries	2 c	500 ml	nuts, chopped	1/4 c	50 ml

1. Wash orange. Cut into eighths.
2. Place in food blender.
3. Blend at medium speed for 5 seconds.
4. Add cranberries. Blend at medium speed for 5 seconds.
5. Stir. Blend 5 seconds.
6. Repeat step 5 until fruit is in small pieces. Do not blend to the point that it liquifies.
7. Pour into a bowl.
8. Stir in sugar and nuts.
9. Chill and let flavors blend at least 1 hour before serving.

Marshmallow Fruit Salad

mandarin orange, sections	1/2 c	125 ml	pecans, chopped	1/4 c	50 ml
			sour cream	1/2 c	125 ml
pineapple chunks	1/2 c	125 ml	marshmallows, miniature	1/2 c	125 ml
shredded coconut	1/2 c	125 ml			
banana, sliced	1				

1. Combine all ingredients in a bowl.
2. Toss lightly.
3. Chill and serve.

Orange Ambrosia

orange	1	
confectioners' sugar	1–1/2 Tbsp	22 ml
flaked coconut	1/4 c	50 ml
orange juice	2 Tbsp	30 ml

1. Peel orange. Remove outer membrane around fruit.
2. Slice oranges crosswise.
3. Sprinkle with remaining ingredients.
4. Chill 30 minutes before serving.

Broiled Grapefruit

grapefruit	1		margarine, melted	2 tsp	10 ml
brown sugar	2 tsp	10 ml	maraschino cherries (optional)	2	

1. Preheat broiler. Adjust rack so that the top of the grapefruit half will be 5 in. (12.5 cm) from the heat.
2. Cut grapefruit in half crosswise. Cut around membrane section with a knife.
3. Sprinkle each half with 1 tsp (5 ml) of sugar and drizzle with 1 tsp (5 ml) of margarine.
4. Broil 5–7 minutes until golden.
5. Top with cherry in the center of the grapefruit half.

(Courtesy of Castle & Cooke, Inc.)

6
Vegetables

OBJECTIVES

The student should be able to:

1. Compare the nutritive value of vegetables.
2. Describe the effects of method and time of cooking on the color, flavor, and texture of vegetables.
3. Determine the effect of pH on pigments found in vegetables.
4. Identify the effects of pH and salt on the flavor and texture of vegetables.
5. Discuss the discoloration of potatoes.
6. Compare the suitability of mealy and waxy potatoes for different methods of cooking.

FOOD SCIENCE PRINCIPLES

1. Deep yellow and green leafy vegetables are excellent sources of provitamin A. Ascorbic acid is found in high quantities in certain vegetables. Some green leafy vegetables have a high folic acid and calcium content. Legumes are a good source of protein and iron. In general, vegetables are low in calories.
2. Effect of cooking method and pH on color pigments in vegetables:

   a. *Carotenoids* are yellow, orange, or red pigments that are unaffected by alkali, metals, or normal cooking conditions. Cooking in an acidic medium and prolonged heating may cause a slight decrease in the intensity of color.

   b. *Anthocyanins* are pigments that are colored red in acidic media, purple at neutrality, and blue in an alkaline environment. Exposure to tin and iron will turn the pigments a greenish-blue. Their color is not changed during normal cooking, but the heat of processing will degrade some to a colorless form. Since anthocyanins are water soluble, they leach into the cooking water during cooking as heat breaks down the plant cells.

   c. *Anthoxanthins* are water soluble pigments that are colorless or white in an acidic environment, and yellow in an alkaline medium. The pigments are not greatly affected by heat but prolonged heating may turn some of them (the proanthocyanins) pink. Contact with aluminum will change the anthoxanthins to a bright yellow color, while contact with iron or copper will turn them bluish-black or reddish-brown.

   d. *Chlorophyll* is a large molecule that is either blue-green (chlorophyll a) or yellow-green (chlorophyll b). When green vegetables are cooked, plant cells rupture and release organic acids. Hydrogen ions from these acids displace the central magnesium atom in the chlorophyll to form either pheophytin a (grey-green) or pheophytin b (dull yellow-green). Formation of pheophytin can be minimized by cooking green vegetables in an uncovered pan for the first few minutes to allow volatile acids to escape.

Chlorophyll is fat soluble because of its long phytyl group. Exposure to alkali (baking soda or alkaline cooking water) can split off the phytyl group to form the sodium salt *chlorophyllin*. Chlorophyllin is a water soluble pigment with a bright green color that easily leaches into the cooking water. Exposure of chlorophyll to zinc or copper also changes its color to bright green.

3. Effect of cooking method on the taste and aroma of vegetables:

   a. Vegetables should be cooked in a small amount of water for the shortest time possible to minimize losses of sugar, organic acids, and other flavor components.
   b. Strongly flavored vegetables such as cabbage and onions should be cooked quickly in a large quantity of water in an uncovered pan. This will allow escape and dilution of sulfur components that can produce an undesirable strong flavor.

4. Effect of cooking method on the texture of vegetables:

   a. The hemicelluloses in cell walls are easily degraded by exposure to alkalis such as baking soda. The pectic substances in the intercellular cement between cells are solubilized by exposure to heat. Thus both baking soda and heat decrease the firmness of vegetables. The use of baking soda should be limited to minute amounts since it can produce a bitter flavor, mushy texture, and destroy thiamin, a B vitamin.
   b. The woody stems of asparagus and broccoli are due to the presence of lignin deposits in a secondary cell wall. Since lignin is not solubilized during cooking, woody stems cannot be tenderized and should be cut off and discarded.
   c. Cooking green vegetables in an acidic medium will help retain crispness, but it may adversely affect chlorophyll pigments, and lead to an olive-green color because of the formation of pheophytins.
   d. The cooking method and time required to produce a tender vegetable varies considerably depending on its variety, size, and maturity.
   e. Salt is added to the cooking water of vegetables because it improves flavor. Cooking vegetables in a mild salt solution will slightly retard the softening of the texture because of the increased solute concentration of the surrounding water. This may be desirable if a slight degree of crispness is desired.

5. Potatoes have a tendency to discolor both before and after cooking:

   a. Exposure of raw, peeled potatoes to air (oxygen) stimulates the formation of melanin pigments from phenolic compounds by the action of the polyphenol oxidase enzyme in the presence of copper. (Minute amounts of copper are naturally present in plant tissue.) The color changes gradually with time from a clear white to pink, to brown, and finally, to gray-black. However, the change in color will not be noticeable if the potatoes are going to be boiled; thus soaking potatoes in water before boiling is unnecessary and not recommended since it results in a loss of water-soluble nutrients.
   b. The stem-end of certain species of potatoes may darken to a bluish-gray color after cooking. This darkening is believed to be the result of a complex formed between phenolic compounds (such as chlorogenic acid) and iron when the cells are disrupted by cooking and the iron is oxidized by exposure to air. Cooking the potatoes in acidic cooking water will retard the discoloration.

6. Potatoes can be classified as mealy or waxy on the basis of their cooking properties:

   a. *Mealy* potatoes have a relatively high solids content because of their numerous, large starch grains. As starch grains gelatinize during heating, they swell and pull apart from each other;

this makes the potato light and fluffy. The fluffiness of these potatoes makes them ideal for baking. Mealy potatoes are also ideal for frying since their low sugar content prevents them from browning too quickly.

    b. *Waxy* potatoes have a low starch and high sugar content, which causes the cells to adhere to each other when cooked. The gumminess and firmness of waxy potatoes make them ideal for products in which shape is important, such as boiled potatoes, scalloped potatoes, and potato salad. The high sugar content causes waxy potatoes to brown too quickly for French frying.

Exercise I: Comparison of the Nutritive Value of Vegetables

1. Calculate the nutritive value of vegetables.
2. Record results in Table 6-1.

TABLE 6-1   **Nutritive Values of Cooked Vegetables**

Vegetable (1/2 c, 125 ml)	Food Energy (Cal)	Protein (g)	Fat (g)	Calcium (mg)	Iron (mg)	Vitamin A (I.U.)	Ascorbic Acid (mg)
Broccoli							
Cabbage							
Carrots							
Collards							
Corn							
Cowpeas							
Okra[a]							
Peas, green							
Spinach							
Squash, winter							

[a]4 pods.

QUESTIONS

1. List 3 vegetables that are the best sources of each of the following nutrients:

	Iron	*Vitamin A*	*Ascorbic Acid*
a.	_____	_____	_____
b.	_____	_____	_____
c.	_____	_____	_____

	Calcium	*Protein*	*Food Energy*
a.	_____	_____	_____
b.	_____	_____	_____
c.	_____	_____	_____

2. How do fruits in general compare to vegetables in nutritive value? _____

_____

_____

Experiment I: Effect of Cooking Method on Color, Flavor, and Texture of Vegetables

Select 1 vegetable from each of the following pigment classifications as follows:

Carotenoid: carrots, sweet potatoes, wax beans
Anthocyanin: red cabbage
Anthoxanthin: cauliflower, onion, white turnip, potato
Chlorophyll: broccoli, green beans, spinach, green cabbage

1. Prepare the selected vegetables by the appropriate method:

    a. Roots and tubers (carrots, onions, sweet potatoes, turnips, potatoes)

        1. Wash and peel.
        2. Cut into approximately 1/2-in. (1.3-cm) pieces.
        3. Divide into 7 groups.
        4. Slice 1 group thinly.

    b. Flowers (cauliflower, broccoli)

        1. Wash and cut off woody stems.
        2. Separate and cut into 7 groups of flowerets.

    c. Leafy (spinach)

        1. Wash thoroughly to remove sand.
        2. Cut off woody and bruised stems and leaves.
        3. Separate into 7 equal pieces.

   d. Leafy head (red cabbage, green cabbage)

    1. Remove core and wash.
    2. Divide into 7 equal wedges.
    3. Slice 1 wedge thinly.

   e. Beans, immature (green, wax)

    1. Wash and cut into 1–1/2-in. (3.8-cm) pieces.
    2. Divide into 7 equal portions.

2. Cook 1 portion of each vegetable by each of the following methods until tender. Record the time required. Save a small sample of each vegetable and its water for later comparison.

Steaming

   a. Pour a small amount of water into a saucepan. Add enough so that the pot will not boil dry. Bring water to a boil.
   b. Place vegetables in a steam basket and set basket in the saucepan with boiling water. Be sure water does not touch the vegetables.
   c. Cover and adjust heat to maintain the steam.
   d. Steam until tender.

Stir-Fry

   a. Add 1 tsp (5 ml) vegetable oil to wok or frying pan set on high heat.
   b. Heat until fat begins to sizzle.
   c. Sprinkle the thinly sliced vegetables with salt and monosodium glutamate.
   d. Quickly add the vegetables and stir constantly until vegetables are just tender but still crisp. **Do not** overcook!

Pressure Saucepan

   a. Place food in pressure saucepan with amount of water indicated by recipe, usually 1/4–1 c (50 ml–250 ml). Add salt.
   b. Place gasket in place on cover. Place cover on pressure pan and close tightly.
   c. Place pressure pan on stove over high heat. Allow steam to escape for 1 second to make sure pressure valve is open.
   d. Place pressure gauge over the vent tube.
   e. When the correct pressure is reached, the pressure gauge will sputter and jiggle. Adjust heat so that it jiggles 1–3 times a minute. Too many jiggles indicate excessive loss of moisture.
   f. Follow specified length of time of pressure for the particular vegetable, usually 3–5 minutes.
   g. Carefully remove pan from heat without removing the gauge. Place under cold running water until pressure completely dissipates.
   h. Push pressure gauge with a fork to test for absence of pressure. If no pressure is released, remove pressure gauge, and open pressure saucepan.

   Note: Do not force pan open. If the seal seems tight, pressure still exists. Repeat steps g and h.

Microwave

   a. Place vegetable with a small amount of water, approximately 1/4 c (50 ml), into a microwave-proof covered casserole.

    b. Set in microwave oven and microwave 3–8 minutes until *almost* tender. Stir the vegetable and rotate the dish 1/4 turn every 1–2 minutes.
    c. Remove from oven and let stand covered 5 minutes to finish cooking.
    d. Salt *after* cooking.

Boiling (large amount of water)
    a. Pour enough water into a saucepan so that it will completely cover the vegetable when added later. Add salt.
    b. Bring to a boil.
    c. Add vegetables, bring to boil again, and let simmer until tender.
    d. Drain.
    e. *Save cooking water for Experiment II.*

Boiling (small amount of water)
    a. Pour 1/2 in. (1.3 cm) of water into a saucepan. Add salt.
    b. Repeat steps b, c, and d above, except cover pan while cooking.

3. Repeat the last treatment, boiling in a small amount of water. Double the cooking time.
4. Record results in Table 6–2.

QUESTIONS

1. Which method of cookery is the fastest? _____ Why? _____
_____
_____ The second fastest? _____
Why? _____
_____

2. In general, flavor is best retained by _____
Why? _____
_____

3. Texture is least destroyed by _____
Because of _____
_____

4. Which method of cookery affects the color of chlorophyll-containing vegetables the least?
_____ The most? _____
What are the reasons for this difference? _____
_____

5. How are anthocyanin-containing vegetables affected by the different methods of cookery?
_____
Why? _____
_____
Which method would you recommend? _____

TABLE 6–2 Effect of Cooking Method and Time on the Color, Flavor, and Texture of Pigments in Vegetables

Method	Carotenoid			Anthocyanin			Anthoxanthin			Chlorophyll		
	Color	Flavor	Texture	Color	Flavor	Texture	Color	Flavor	Texture	Color	Flavor	Texture
Steam		—— min.			—— min.			—— min.			—— min.	
Stir-fry		—— min.			—— min.			—— min.			—— min.	
Pressure		—— min.			—— min.			—— min.			—— min.	
Microwave		—— min.			—— min.			—— min.			—— min.	
Boil, large amount of water, uncovered		—— min.			—— min.			—— min.			—— min.	
Boil, small amount of water, covered		—— min.			—— min.			—— min.			—— min.	
Boil, small amount of water, long time		—— min.			—— min.			—— min.			—— min.	

6. Anthoxanthin-containing vegetables are most affected by which method of cookery? _____
_____ Why? _____
_____
_____

7. Are cartenoid-containing vegetables affected in the same way as are the other pigments?
_____ Why or why not? _____
_____
_____

8. Which vegetables are best cooked by:

   steaming _____

   stir-frying _____

   pressure _____

   microwave _____

   boiling, large amount of water, uncovered _____

   boiling, small amount of water, covered _____

9. What is the effect on color of an overextended cooking time for vegetables? _____
_____

   On flavor? _____

   On texture? _____

   What else is affected by overcooking? _____
_____

Experiment II: Effect of pH on Pigments Found in the Cooking Water of Vegetables

1. Obtain the reserved cooking water from Experiment I.
2. Divide each into 3-1/3 c (80 ml) portions.
3. Test the effect of pH on color of each of the cooking waters by the following treatments:

   a. none
   b. 1/2 tsp (2 ml) baking soda
   c. 1/2 tsp (2 ml) vinegar or lemon juice

4. Observe the color changes and record results in Table 6-3.

TABLE 6-3   Effect of pH on Pigments Found in the Cooking Water of Vegetables

Pigment	Control	Alkaline (baking soda)	Acid (lemon juice)
Carotenoid			
Anthocyanin			
Anthoxanthin			
Chlorophyll			

QUESTION

Which pigment is not significantly affected by pH? _____

Experiment III: Effect of Time and Covering on the Flavor and pH of Vegetables

Select a strong-flavored vegetable and a mild-flavored vegetable from the list below:

Strong Flavor: Brassica family — cauliflower, brussel sprouts, green cabbage
　　　　　　　　Allium family — onions, leeks, garlic
Mild Flavor: carrots, celery, corn, green beans, spinach, squash

1. Prepare the vegetables as described in Experiment I, page 52, except do not slice any group. Divide into 4 portions.
2. Pour 1/2 in. (1.3 cm) water into 8 saucepans of equal size.
3. Add salt and bring to boil.
4. Add vegetables, bring to boil again, and cook the vegetables by simmering according to the following methods:

   a. 8 minutes, uncovered
   b. 16 minutes, uncovered
   c. 8 minutes, covered
   d. 16 minutes, covered

5. Test the pH of the water and record.
6. Drain.
7. Record results in Table 6–4.

TABLE 6–4   Effect of Time and Covering on the pH and Flavor of Strong and Mild-Flavored Vegetables

Cooking Method	Strong-Flavored Vegetable		Mild-Flavored Vegetable	
	pH	Flavor	pH	Flavor
Uncovered, 8 min.				
Uncovered, 16 min.				
Covered, 8 min.				
Covered, 16 min.				

QUESTIONS

1. What effect did covering the pan have on the pH of the cooking water? _____
   _____

2. Which method should be used to cook strong-flavored vegetables? _____
   _____ Why? _____
   _____

3. Which method should be used to cook mild-flavored vegetables? _____
   _____ Why? _____
   _____

Experiment IV: Effect of pH, Salt, and Cooking Time on Vegetable Color, Texture, and Flavor

1. Cut 1 large zucchini squash into 12 equal slices. Divide into groups of 3 slices.
2. Pour 1/2 c (125 ml) water into 4 saucepans of equal size and bring to a boil.
3. Add 3 pieces of zucchini to the boiling water, which has been modified by the following treatments:

   a. none
   b. 1/2 tsp (2 ml) baking soda
   c. 1/2 tsp (2 ml) white vinegar
   d. 1/2 tsp (2 ml) salt

4. Cook for 3 minutes. Remove 1 piece of squash from each saucepan and observe for color and texture.
5. Cook the other 2 pieces for 7 more minutes. Remove and observe 1 piece for color and texture; taste the other pieces for flavor.
6. Record results in Table 6–5.

TABLE 6-5   Effect of pH, Salt, and Cooking Time on Vegetable Color, Texture, and Flavor

Treatment	3 Minutes			10 Minutes		
	Color	Texture	Flavor	Color	Texture	Flavor
None						
Baking soda						
Vinegar						
Salt						

QUESTIONS

1. Which treatment produced the best product after 3 minutes? _____

   After 10 minutes? _____ Why? _____

   _____

   _____

2. Why did the baking soda produce the reaction that it did? _____

   _____

   _____

3. Why did vinegar produce a color change? _____

   _____

   _____

Experiment V: Discoloration of Potatoes

1. Peel 1 potato and cut into pieces approximately 1 in. (2.5 cm) in size. Divide into two groups. Place on two plates. Note the time.

Group I

   a. Expose pieces to air 1–1/2 hours. Observe color at 1/2, 1, and 1–1/2 hours and record results in Table 6–6.

Group II

   a. Expose pieces to air 1–1/2 hours. Observe color at 1/2, 1, and 1–1/2 hours and record results in Table 6–6.
   b. Bring 1 c (250 ml) water to boil in a small saucepan.
   c. At 1–1/2 hours, transfer the second group of potato pieces to the boiling water. Boil for 30 seconds in order to blanch them.
   d. Drain, observe color, and record in Table 6–6.

Group III

2. Meanwhile, bring 1 c (250 ml) water to boil in a saucepan.
3. Peel a second potato and cut into pieces approximately 1 in. (2.5 cm) in size.
   a. Transfer the third group of potato pieces to the boiling water and boil for 30 seconds in order to blanch them.
   b. Drain, place on a third plate, and expose to air 1–1/2 hours. Observe color at 1/2, 1, and 1–1/2 hours and record results in Table 6–6.

TABLE 6–6   Effect of Oxidation and Blanching on Discoloration of Raw Potatoes

Treatment	Time (hours)		
	1/2 Hour	*1 Hour*	*1–1/2 Hours*
Raw, exposed to air 1–1/2 hours			
Raw, exposed to air 1–1/2 hours, then blanched			
Blanched, then exposed to air 1–1/2 hours			

QUESTIONS

1. What color did the raw potatoes turn after 1/2 hour? _____
   After 1 hour? _____ After 1–1/2 hours? _____
   Why did this occur? _____
   _____

2. What happened when the potatoes that had been exposed to the air for a long time were blanched?
   _____
   _____

3. How did these potatoes compare to those that had been freshly peeled? _____
   _____

4. Is it necessary to soak potatoes in water after peeling if there is going to be a delay in cooking?
   _____ Why or why not? _____
   _____

5. What is another reason not to soak potatoes? _____
   _____

Experiment VI: Comparison of Mealy and Waxy Potatoes in Cooking

Select 4 potatoes of equal sizes from each of the following varieties:

Mealy: Russet, Idaho
Waxy: Red Pontiac, New Round White, California Long White

Prepare one potato from each of the above groups by the following methods:

Baked Potato

1. Preheat oven to 400°F (200°C).
2. Wash and scrub 1 waxy and 1 mealy potato.
3. Place potatoes in oven and bake 60 minutes or until they yield to pressure of finger.
4. Remove from oven, cut in half and fluff up.

Mashed Potato

Prepare 1 waxy and 1 mealy potato in the following manner:

potato	1		salt
milk or cream	1 Tbsp	15 ml	pepper
butter	2 tsp	10 ml	

1. Bring 2 c (500 ml) of water to boil in a saucepan.
2. Wash potato, peel and cut into large pieces.
3. Add potato pieces to boiling water, bring to boil again, cover and simmer 20–25 minutes until done.
4. Drain.
5. Mash potato pieces with the milk, butter, salt and pepper.

French Fries

Prepare 1 waxy and 1 mealy potato in the following manner:

1. Wash potato and peel.
2. Cut into lengthwise strips, 1/4–3/8 in. (6-9 mm) wide.
3. Fill a deep saucepan or deep fat fryer 1/2 full with vegetable shortening or salad oil. Heat to 375°F (190°C).
4. Place potatoes in basket until it is 1/4 full.
5. Lower basket into hot fat. (Excessive foaming can be controlled by raising basket again.) Keep the potatoes separated with a *long* handled fork.
6. Fry 5–7 minutes, until potatoes are golden.
7. Drain and salt.

Microwave Scalloped Potatoes

Prepare 1 waxy and 1 mealy potato in the following manner:

potato	1		pepper	dash	
margarine	2 tsp	10 ml	milk	1/2 c	125 ml
flour	2 tsp	10 ml	onion, minced	2 tsp	10 ml
salt	1/4 tsp	1 ml	paprika	dash	

1. Wash potato. Peel, remove eyes, and cut into thin slices.
2. Microwave butter 30 seconds.
3. Add flour, salt and pepper. Blend in thoroughly.
4. Gradually add milk; stirring constantly.
5. Microwave mixture 3 minutes or until thickened.
6. Grease a small casserole dish.
7. Place half of the potato slices in it.

8. Sprinkle with 1 tsp (5 ml) of the onions.
9. Pour half the sauce over the potatoes and onions.
10. Repeat steps 7, 8, and 9.
11. Microwave 8 minutes, stirring at 5 minutes.
12. Let stand 4 minutes; sprinkle with paprika and serve.

Observe appearance and taste and record results in Table 6–7.

QUESTIONS

1. Which potato is the best for baking? _____

   Why? _____

   _____

2. Mashed potatoes are lighter and fluffier with what type of potato? _____

   _____ Why? _____

   _____

3. Which potato creates a better French fry? _____

   Why? _____

   _____

4. Scalloped potatoes best hold their shape when which type of potato is used? _____

   _____ Why? _____

   _____

TABLE 6–7   The Suitability of Mealy and Waxy Potatoes for Baked, Mashed, French Fried, and Scalloped Potatoes

Variety	Appearance	Flavor	Texture	Doneness
MEALY, baked				
mashed				
French-fried				
scalloped				
WAXY, baked				
mashed				
French-fried				
scalloped				

Experiment VII: Factors Affecting the Quality of a Baked Potato

Select 2 potatoes of equal sizes from the following varieties:

Mealy: Russet, Idaho
Waxy: Red Pontiac, Main, New, Round White, California Long White

1. Preheat oven to 400°F (200°C).
2. Wash and scrub potatoes. Use an icepick to make hole for thermometer.
3. Wrap one potato of each variety with aluminum foil. Keep one of each unwrapped.
4. Put potatoes in oven and bake for 45 minutes until done.
5. Record temperature of potatoes at 15, 25, 35, and 45 minutes.
6. Remove from oven, cut in half, push up on skin to fluff, and observe texture of inner potato and skin.
7. Record results in Table 6-8.

QUESTIONS

1. What is the effect of foil-wrapping on the time required to bake potatoes? _____
   _____ Why? _____

   _____

   On the texture of the skin? _____

   Why? _____

2. How does the texture of a mealy potato differ from that of a waxy potato? _____

   _____

   Which do you prefer? _____ Why? _____

   _____

TABLE 6-8   Factors Affecting the Quality of a Baked Potato

| Variety of Potato | Temperature at Time (minutes) | | | | Final Texture |
	15	25	35	45	
Mealy, unwrapped					
foil-wrapped					
Waxy, unwrapped					
foil-wrapped					

APPLICATIONS

Harvard Beets

beets, canned or cooked	1 c	250 ml	salt	1/2 tsp	2 ml	
			vinegar	2 Tbsp	30 ml	
beet liquid	1/4 c	50 ml	margarine	1-1/2 tsp	8 ml	
cornstarch	2 tsp	10 ml				
sugar	1 Tbsp	15 ml				

1. Blend together the liquid, cornstarch, sugar, and salt in a saucepan.
2. Bring to a boil over direct heat with constant stirring. The liquid should boil until it is clear.
3. Remove from heat; add margarine and vinegar; stir to blend; add cooked beets.
4. Heat over low heat until the beets are heated.

Pennsylvania Dutch Red Cabbage

tart apple, pared and cubed	1/2 c	125 ml	carraway seed	1/8 tsp	0.5 ml
			vinegar	1 Tbsp	15 ml
red cabbage, shredded	1 c	250 ml	water	1 Tbsp	15 ml
oil	1 Tbsp	15 ml	salt	1/4 tsp	1 ml

1. Sauté apple and red cabbage in oil.
2. Stir in remaining ingredients.
3. Cover pan and cook until just tender, about 10 minutes.

Mexican Sour Cream Corn

margarine	1 Tbsp	15 ml	pimento, chopped (optional)	2 tsp	10 ml
onion, chopped	2 Tbsp	30 ml			
garlic clove, minced	1/4		cheese, cubed	1 oz	28 g
			salt	1/4 tsp	1 ml
green chili, canned	2		corn, 1/2 frozen pkg.	5 oz	60 g
			sour cream	3 Tbsp	45 ml

1. Preheat oven to 375°F (190°C).
2. Melt margarine in skillet.
3. Add onion and garlic. Sauté 5 minutes until soft.
4. Cut green chilies into thin strips. Add chili and pimento to skillet. Sauté 5 more minutes.
5. Add corn and salt. Mix thoroughly.
6. Pour corn mixture into small casserole. Mix in cheese cubes.
7. Cover tightly with aluminum foil and bake 20 minutes.
8. Remove corn from oven; uncover and dot sour cream on top of corn.
9. Recover casserole, return to oven to heat sour cream for 3–5 minutes.

Zucchini Stir-Fry

zucchini	1/2 lb	250 g	margarine	1 Tbsp	15 ml
mushrooms	2 oz	60 g	olive oil	1 Tbsp	15 ml
	(1/2 c)	(125 ml)	oregano	1/8 tsp	0.5 ml
green pepper	1/2		salt	1/4 tsp	1 ml
onion	1/2		pepper	1/8 tsp	0.5 ml
tomato	1				

1. Prepare vegetables:

   a. Cut zucchini and mushrooms into 3/8 in. (38 mm) slices.
   b. Cut green pepper lengthwise into strips that are 5/8 in. (63 mm) wide.
   c. Cut onion into 1/8 in. (13 mm) slices.
   d. Cut tomato in half crosswise and then cut each half into 4 wedges.

2. Heat margarine and oil in a skillet over high heat.
3. When oil sizzles, add green pepper, and cook 1 minute.
4. Push green pepper to one side. Add zucchini in a single layer in the pan and cook until bottom side just starts to brown. Turn over and cook 30 more seconds.
5. Push zucchini and green pepper to one side. Add onions in a single layer and cook 1 minute.
6. Push all vegetables to side. Add mushrooms in a single layer and cook 1 minute.
7. Add tomatoes and oregano. Stir-fry tomatoes until they just begin to cook, approximately 30 seconds. Vegetables should still be tender-crisp, not soft.
8. Season with salt and pepper and serve.

Spaghetti Squash (plain)

spaghetti squash, small,	1/2		salt	1/2 tsp	7 ml
cut in half lengthwise			white pepper	1/8 tsp	0.5 ml
margarine	1 Tbsp	15 ml			

1. Place the squash cut side down in a Dutch oven. Add 2 in. (5 cm) of water. Cover pan and bring to a boil.
2. Lower heat to medium-low and let it simmer 20 minutes.
3. Drain squash.
4. Use a large spoon to remove seeds and the gummy material directly underneath them. Discard seeds and membranes.
5. Use a fork to separate strands of squash. Discard shell.
6. Place strands of squash in a bowl. Add margarine, salt, and pepper. Toss until well coated.

Spaghetti Squash with Meat Sauce

spaghetti squash, small	1		mushrooms, canned	2 oz	60 g
ground beef, lean	1/2 lb	250 g	black olives, pitted,	2 Tbsp	30 ml
onion, chopped	1/2		sliced		
garlic clove, minced	1/2		salt	1/2 tsp	2 ml
green pepper, chopped	1/2		oregano	1/4 tsp	1 ml
carrot, grated	1/2		basil	1/4 tsp	1 ml
tomato sauce, canned	8 oz	250 g	pepper	1/8 tsp	0.5 ml
tomatoes, coarsely	1 c	250 ml	sugar	1/8 tsp	0.5 ml
chopped, drained			Parmesan cheese	2 Tbsp	30 ml
water	1/4 c	50 ml			

1. Prepare spaghetti squash by the method above.
2. Meanwhile, prepare meat sauce:

    a. Break beef into large chunks and add to a nonstick skillet over medium-high heat. Cook 1 minute.
    b. Add onion, garlic, green pepper, and carrot. Cook until meat is browned.
    c. Add tomato sauce, tomatoes, water, mushrooms, black olives, salt, oregano, basil, pepper, and sugar. Bring to a boil, cover, lower heat and simmer 30–60 minutes.

3. Mound spaghetti squash on a plate. Pour meat sauce in the middle. Serve with Parmesan cheese.

Baked Winter Squash

acorn or butternut	1	
squash, small		
salt	1/8 tsp	0.5 ml
margarine	2 Tbsp	30 ml
brown sugar	2 Tbsp	30 ml

1. Preheat oven to 375°F (190°C).
2. Cut squash in half. Scoop out seeds and fiber with a large spoon and discard.
3. Place 2 pieces of aluminum foil large enough to wrap squash halves shiny side up in a roasting pan.
4. Place squash halves cut side up in the center of each piece of foil. (If they will not stand up without falling over, cut a thin slice off the bottom to level them.)
5. Sprinkle each half with the salt and brown sugar. Dot with margarine.
6. Wrap each half tightly with foil and bake 35 minutes.
7. Unwrap, baste, and serve.

Note: Squash may also be cooked in a covered casserole in a microwave oven for 6 minutes.

Baked Tomato

tomato	1	margarine	1 tsp	5 ml
salt	dash	bread crumbs,	1 Tbsp +	20 ml
pepper	dash	Italian flavored	1 tsp	
onion slice,	1			
paper thin				

1. Preheat oven to 375°F (190°C).
2. Wash tomato. Cut 1/2 in. (1.3 cm) slice off stem and end of tomato.
3. Place tomato, stem end up, in a small casserole or custard cup.
4. Sprinkle cut surface with salt and pepper. Cover with paper thin slice of onion.
5. Melt margarine in saucepan or microwave in small bowl.
6. Add bread crumbs and mix thoroughly.
7. Press bread crumb mixture firmly over the onion slice.
8. Bake 25 minutes and serve.

7

Salads, Emulsions, and Gelatin

(Courtesy of Lawry's Foods, Inc.)

OBJECTIVES

The student should be able to:

1. Discuss the formation and three phases of emulsions.
2. Prepare and compare temporary, semi-permanent, and permanent emulsions.
3. Determine the factors that affect the crispness of salad greens.
4. Prepare and compare different types of salads.
5. Discuss the factors affecting the preparation of gelatin.

FOOD SCIENCE PRINCIPLES

1. An emulsion is a colloidal dispersion of one liquid in another when both liquids are mutually antagonistic or immiscible. Agitation or physical force is required to disperse the molecules. An emulsion has three phases: the dispersed phase (usually watery), the continuous phase (usually oily), and an emulsifier phase.
2. Emulsions are classified on the basis of their stability:

   a. *Temporary emulsions* have a thin viscosity and a slight degree of stability. Homemade French dressing is an example: the vinegar or lemon juice is the continuous phase, the oil is the dispersed phase, and the mustard or paprika is the emulsifier. Agitation of these ingredients produces a temporary emulsion that will collapse with time with the emulsifier collecting at the interface.

   b. *Semi-permanent emulsions* have a viscosity similar to thick cream and a high degree of stability. Examples are commercial salad dressings and soups that are prepared using stabilizers or starches.

   c. *Permanent emulsions* have a very thick viscosity (semi-solid) and are very stable. Mayonnaise is made from large quantities of oil and small amounts of acid that are combined with the aid of lecithin, a highly effective emulsifier found in egg yolk.

3. Cooked salad dressings are mixtures of egg, acid, starch, fat, and seasonings. Flour is used as the primary thickener; this reduces the fat and kilocalorie content compared to mayonnaise.

68

4. Salad greens are fragile and rapidly dehydrate. Washing in cold water is essential for cleaning as well as for recrisping. Vegetables are best recrisped in a covered container in the refrigerator. Salad greens should never be covered with a salty solution (such as a salad dressing) until the last moment before serving due to the effect of osmosis drawing water out of the cells. The transfer of water out of the cells to an area of higher solute concentration (the salty dressing) causes dehydration and wilting of the greens.

5. It is best to soften unflavored gelatin in water before it is dispersed in a liquid. Otherwise it will clump when boiling water is added. If the gelatin is separated by grains of sugar, however, the amount of clumping is reduced when boiling water is added.

6. Factors that affect gelation include:

   a. *Concentration of gelatin:* A minimum concentration of 1.5–2% gelatin is necessary for gelation. Too much gelatin produces a gummy product.

   b. *Sugar:* Sugar decreases the strength of a gel because it competes with water for binding sites on the gelatin molecules.

   c. *Acid:* Acids produce a more tender product because a gel is most rigid between a pH of 5 and 10.

   d. *Salts:* Salts present in foods such as milk or hard water produce a firmer gel.

   e. *Physical interference:* Solids and mechanical agitation physically interfere with bond formation. When fruits or nuts are added to gelatin salads, the amount of water is decreased in proportion to the amount of gelatin. Solids are added only after some thickening has occurred, i.e., bond formation has developed, so that the gel structure will keep them from either sinking to the bottom or rising to the top depending on their density.

   f. *Enzymes:* Proteolytic enzymes prevent gelation because they denature proteins. Some examples are bromelin in raw pineapple and actinidin in raw kiwifruit. The protein is easily destroyed by cooking or by the heat of processing (canning).

   g. *Temperature and time:* The formation of the gel network is a slow process that is increased by cool temperatures. If the liquid is cooled very quickly, a weak gel will form because of weak bonds; if the liquid is cooled slowly, a firmer gel with strong bonds will form.

7. Foams increase the lightness and volume of gelatin and decrease the intensity of its color. Egg white and milk foams are added to gelatins to produce sponges and creams.

Experiment I: Effect of Emulsifiers on Oil and Vinegar

1. Label 8 test tubes 1–8.
2. Pour into each the amounts of oil and vinegar shown in Table 7–1. Use red wine vinegar for a color contrast.
3. Add 1/4 tsp (1 ml) of the emulsifiers listed in the table to test tubes 2–4.
4. Add 1/8 tsp (0.5 ml) of each emulsifier listed in the table to test tubes 5–8.
5. Shake each test tube 50 times.
6. Observe the test tubes for 10 minutes.
7. Record results in Table 7–1 at the end of 10 minutes.

TABLE 7-1   Effect of Emulsifiers on Oil and Vinegar

Test Tube No.	Oil (ml)	Vinegar (ml)	Emulsifier	After 10 Minutes
1	20	10	None	
2	20	10	Egg yolk	
3	20	10	Mustard	
4	20	10	Paprika	
5	20	10	Mustard + paprika	
6	15	15	Mustard + paprika	
7	20	1	Mustard + paprika	
8	1	20	Mustard + paprika	

QUESTIONS

1. Why did the oil and vinegar separate when no emulsifier was added? _____
_____
_____

2. Explain why egg yolk can function as an emulsifier. _____
_____

3. Which has better emulsifying qualities, dry mustard or paprika? _____

_____

4. How does the ratio of oil to vinegar influence the stability of the emulsion? _____
_____
_____

5. Which combination of oil-vinegar ratio and emulsifier produced the most stable emulsion?
_____

Experiment II: Preparation and Comparisons of Temporary Emulsions

1. Prepare the following temporary emulsions:

French Dressing

oil	1/3 c	80 ml	salt	1/2 tsp	2 ml
vinegar	1–1/2 Tbsp	22 ml	pepper	dash	
sugar	1–1/2 Tbsp	22 ml	celery salt	dash	
paprika	2 tsp	10 ml	garlic, 1 clove		
parsley	1/4 tsp	1 ml	crushed		
tarragon, dried	1/4 tsp	1 ml			

    a. Place all ingredients except garlic in a blender.
    b. Blend for several minutes.
    c. Add crushed garlic.
    d. Let flavors blend for at least 30 minutes.
    e. Remove garlic and serve.

Italian Dressing

olive oil	1/4 c	50 ml	dry mustard	1/8 tsp	0.5 ml
wine vinegar	1/4 c	50 ml	pepper	dash	
Parmesan cheese	1 Tbsp	15 ml	garlic, clove	1/8	
salt	1/2 tsp	2 ml	green onion,	1 Tbsp	15 ml
oregano, dried	1/4 tsp	1 ml	chopped		

    a. Place all ingredients except onion in a blender.
    b. Blend for several minutes.
    c. Add onion.
    d. Let flavors blend for at least 30 minutes before serving.

Caesar Salad Dressing

olive oil	1/3 c	80 ml	pepper	1/4 tsp	1 ml
lemon juice	1/4 c	50 ml	garlic, clove	1/8	
Parmesan cheese	2 Tbsp	30 ml	egg	1	
salt	1/2 tsp	2 ml	anchovy, minced	1	

    a. Bring enough water to cover an egg to a boil in a small saucepan. Add egg. Simmer for 2 minutes and remove egg.
    b. Place oil, lemon juice, cheese, salt, pepper, and garlic in a blender.
    c. Blend for several minutes.
    d. Add coddled egg to dressing in blender. Blend 1 more minute.
    e. Remove from blender. Mix in anchovies.
    f. Allow flavors to combine for several minutes before serving.

2. Take a 5 ml sample of each dressing when it is first blended. Pour sample into a test tube. Record the time it takes for the emulsion to break.
3. Observe appearance of each dressing. Taste each dressing for flavor after it has been allowed to mellow for 30 minutes.
4. Record results in Table 7–2.

TABLE 7–2   Temporary Emulsions

Emulsion	Emulsifier	Time for Separation to Begin	Texture	Flavor
French dressing				
Italian dressing				
Caesar Salad dressing				

QUESTIONS

1. Which of the temporary emulsions was the most stable? _____
   The least stable? _____
2. Why was the texture of the Caesar dressing different from the others? _____
   _____
   _____

Experiment III: Preparation and Comparison of Semi-Permanent and Permanent Emulsions

1. Prepare the following semi-permanent emulsion:

Tomato Curry Dressing

tomato soup, condensed, undiluted	3 Tbsp	45 ml	dry mustard	1/2 tsp	2 ml
			curry powder	1/4 tsp	1 ml
oil	2 Tbsp	30 ml	salt	1/8 tsp	0.5 ml
vinegar, apple cider	1 Tbsp	15 ml	parsley, dried	1/8 tsp	0.5 ml
sugar	2-1/2 tsp	12 ml	pepper	dash	
onion, minced	1/2 tsp	2 ml			

    a. Add all ingredients in a deep bowl.
    b. Beat with a wire whisk or rotary beater until well blended.
    c. Chill until serving.

2. Prepare the following permanent emulsions:

Old-Fashioned Mayonnaise

egg yolk	1/2		cayenne pepper	dash	
dry mustard	1/4 tsp	1 ml	vinegar	1 Tbsp	15 ml
sugar	1/4 tsp	1 ml	oil	1/2 c	125 ml
salt	1/4 tsp	1 ml			

  a. Combine egg yolk with mustard, sugar, salt, and cayenne pepper in a small, *deep* bowl.
  b. Stir in vinegar. Beat 1 minute with a wire whisk or a rotary beater.
  c. Slowly dribble in 1 tsp (5 ml) of oil while beating mixture until oil has been thoroughly incorporated, creating a smooth, well-blended, and creamy mixture.
  d. Repeat step c until 1 Tbsp (15 ml) of the oil has been incorporated to make a smooth, well-blended, and creamy mixture.
  e. Take rest of oil and slowly pour it into mixture while beating, until all has been incorporated.
  f. Refrigerate until serving.

Electric Mixer Mayonnaise

Follow the preceding recipe but use an electric mixer rather than a rotary beater or wire whip.

Blender Mayonnaise

  a. Combine the ingredients in steps a and b for "Old-Fashioned Mayonnaise" in a blender. Use 1/4 of a beaten *whole* egg rather than an egg yolk.
  b. Add 1 tsp (5 ml) oil and begin blending again.
  c. Continue blending while adding 1 tsp (5 ml) of oil at a time until all of the oil has been used.

3. Prepare cooked salad dressing:

Cooked Salad Dressing

nonfat dry milk	1 Tbsp	15 ml	cayenne pepper	dash	
flour	1 Tbsp	15 ml	water	1/4 c + 2 Tbsp	80 ml
sugar	1-1/2 tsp	7 ml	egg	1	
salt	1/2 tsp	2 ml	lemon juice	1 Tbsp + 1 tsp	20 ml
dry mustard	1/2 tsp	2 ml	margarine	1 Tbsp + 1 tsp	20 ml

  a. Set up bottom pan of double boiler with water on stove. Heat over medium-high heat.
  b. Place top pan of double boiler on counter. Sift together nonfat dry milk, flour, sugar, salt, dry mustard, and cayenne pepper into top pan.
  c. Add water and stir until flour and sugar are dissolved.
  d. Beat the egg in a custard cup with a fork until well blended. Slowly dribble in lemon juice to the beaten egg.
  e. Restir flour–water mixture. Blend in egg–lemon juice mixture.

   f. Place top pan of double boiler on bottom pan. Stir constantly until thickened. Then cook additional minute, stirring constantly.

   g. Remove top pan from heat and immediately stir in margarine. Mix until well-blended.

   h. Place in a bowl. Cover and chill.

4. Open jars of commercial French dressing, mayonnaise, and mayonnaise-type salad dressing. Place 1/4 c (50 ml) of each in a small bowl.

5. Estimate the cost per 1 Tbsp (15 ml) of each dressing.

6. Observe the appearance and texture of the different types of salad dressing. Taste each for flavor.

7. Record results in Table 7–3.

QUESTIONS

1. What is the difference in viscosity and stability between the semi-permanent and permanent emulsions? _____

_____

Why? _____

_____

2. Why is it necessary to cook the starch when preparing a starch-thickened salad dressing? _____

_____

3. Account for the difference in price of commercial mayonnaise-type salad dressing and mayonnaise. _____

_____

Which is higher in kilocalories? _____ Why? _____

_____

4. Which method of preparing mayonnaise produced the thickest emulsion? _____

Why? _____

_____

5. Why must the oil be added slowly in very small quantities when preparing mayonnaise? _____

_____

6. Compare the flavor of homemade to commercial mayonnaise. _____

_____

TABLE 7–3   Comparison of Semi-Permanent and Permanent Emulsions

Type	Cost/1 Tbsp (15 ml)	Appearance	Texture	Flavor
Salad dressing, homemade, commercial, starch base				
commercial, starch base				
Mayonnaise, homemade, hand-beaten				
electric mixer				
blender				
commercial, oil base				
Cooked salad dressing, homemade				
commercial				

Experiment IV: Effect of Storage Conditions on the Crispness of Lettuce

slightly limp lettuce leaves (unwashed iceberg lettuce leaves
   left at room temperature for 2 hours)
3 plastic bags
masking tape for labeling
cookie sheet (with sides)

1. Prepare lettuce leaves by tearing them into pieces approximately 4–5 in. (10–12.5 cm) square. Divide into 6 groups making sure that the degree of wilting is evenly distributed between the groups.
2. Prepare labels for the following treatments of the limp lettuce leaves:

   a. none
   b. washed in cold water, shaken slightly
   c. washed in cold water, shaken slightly, and refrigerated uncovered
   d. washed in cold water, shaken slightly, and refrigerated covered
   e. washed in cold water, dried with paper towel, and refrigerated covered
   f. washed in salt water (1 Tbsp/1 c or 15 ml/250 ml), shaken slightly, and refrigerated covered

3. Prepare the lettuce leaves according to the treatments listed in step 2. For the covering in 2d, e, and f, place the lettuce pieces in a plastic bag.
4. Place 2c, d, e, and f on a cookie sheet and place in refrigerator for 1-1/2 hours. Let 2a and b remain at room temperature uncovered.
5. Remove pan from refrigerator. Unwrap 2d, e, and f. Observe relative crispness of all samples and record results in Table 7–4.

TABLE 7–4   Effect of Storage Conditions on the Crispness of Lettuce

Washing Procedure	Preparation Procedure	Storage Condition	Covering	Crispness
None	None	Room	No	
Cold water	Shaken slightly	Room	No	
Cold water	Shaken slightly	Refrigerated	No	
Cold water	Shaken slightly	Refrigerated	Yes	
Cold water	Dried	Refrigerated	Yes	
Salt water	Shaken slightly	Refrigerated	Yes	

QUESTIONS

1. Why is lettuce normally washed before storage? _____
   _____

2. Why should greens be refrigerated? _____
   _____

3. What effect does storage with droplets of water clinging to the leaves have on the recrisping of
   lettuce? _____
   Covering? _____
   Why? _____
   _____

4. Explain what happened to the lettuce washed in salt water. _____
   _____
   _____

5. What practical application does question 4 have concerning the adding of salad dressing to
   greens? _____
   _____

Experiment V: Preparation and Comparison of Salads

1. Prepare several of the salad recipes found in Applications.
2. Calculate the cost/serving of each salad.
3. Compare each of them for appearance, texture, and flavor.
4. Record results in Table 7–5.

TABLE 7–5   Comparison of Salads

Salad	Cost per Serving	Appearance	Texture	Flavor

Experiment VI: Dispersion of Gelatin

1. Label 6 test tubes 1–6.
2. Place 1/4 tsp (1 ml) unflavored gelatin in each test tube.
3. Do the following treatments for each tube, then immediately shake the test tubes until the gelatin is dissolved. Record time for dispersion in Table 7–6.

   Tube 1: Add 1 Tbsp + 1 tsp (20 ml) *cold* water.
   Tube 2: Add 1 tsp (5 ml) tap water. Shake gently but do not invert. Let soak 5 minutes. Then add 1 Tbsp (15 ml) *cold* water.
   Tube 3: Add 1 Tbsp + 1 tsp (20 ml) boiling water.
   Tube 4: Add 1 tsp (5 ml) tap water. Shake gently but do not invert. Let soak 5 minutes. Then add 1 Tbsp (15 ml) *boiling* water.
   Tube 5: Add 1 tsp (5 ml) sugar. Mix well. Add 1 Tbsp + 1 tsp (20 ml) *boiling* water.
   Tube 6: Add 1 tsp (5 ml) sugar. Mix well. Add 1 tsp (5 ml) tap water. Shake gently but do not invert. Let soak 5 minutes. Then add 1 Tbsp (15 ml) *boiling* water.

QUESTIONS

1. What was the effect of prior soaking on plain gelatin when boiling water was added? _____

   _____

2. Which is the best method of dispersing plain gelatin? _____

   _____

   Why? _____

3. Why is sugar added to powdered dessert gelatin mixes? _____

   _____

TABLE 7–6   Dispersion of Gelatin

Test Tube No.	Gelatin	Prior Soaking	Water Temperature	Dispersion Time (minutes)
1	Plain	No	Cold	
2	Plain	Yes	Cold	
3	Plain	No	Boiling	
4	Plain	Yes	Boiling	
5	Sugared	No	Boiling	
6	Sugared	Yes	Boiling	

Experiment VII: Factors Affecting Gelation

small metal gelatin molds or cups	8	
gelatin	2-1/4 tsp (1 pkg)	7 g
sugar	2 Tbsp + 1 tsp	35 ml
lemon juice	1 tsp	5 ml
milk	2 Tbsp + 1 tsp	35 ml
pineapple *or* kiwifruit, crushed, canned, drained	2 Tbsp + 2 tsp	40 ml
pineapple *or* kiwifruit, crushed, raw, drained	1 Tbsp + 1 tsp	20 ml

1. Label 8 small metal gelatin molds or cups.
2. Prepare gelatin. Use the basic method below for mold #1 (control) but vary the preparations of molds 2–8 according to the following treatments.

Basic Method (Mold #1)

    a. Place 1/4 tsp (1 ml) unflavored gelatin and 1 tsp (5 ml) sugar in mold. Mix well.
    b. Add 1 tsp (5 ml) cold tap water. Stir slightly and let soak 2 minutes.
    c. Add 1 Tbsp + 1 tsp (20 ml) boiling water to gelatin and water. Stir until *completely* dissolved.
    d. Add 2 Tbsp + 1 tsp (35 ml) ice water. Stir and place in coldest section of refrigerator. (If time is limited, molds may be placed in freezer initially to chill faster, but watch them carefully and do not permit ice crystals to form.)
    e. Record time required for gelation.

Variations

    Mold #2: Double amount of gelatin used.
    Mold #3: Double amount of sugar used.
    Mold #4: Reduce ice water to 1 Tbsp (30 ml) in step d. Add 1 tsp (5 ml) lemon juice.
    Mold #5: Use milk instead of ice water in step d.
    Mold #6: Reduce sugar to 1/2 tsp (2 ml) in step a. Reduce ice water to 1 Tbsp (15 ml) in step d. Add 1 Tbsp + 1 tsp (20 ml) crushed, drained, canned pineapple or kiwifruit that has been cooked 2 minutes, crushed and drained.
    Mold #7: Repeat instructions for mold #6 but do not add fruit until mixture is chilled and has the consistency of unbeaten raw egg white. Watch this carefully because this mixture will gel faster than the basic method because of the reduced amounts of water and sugar.
    Mold #8: Repeat instruction for mold #7 but instead use crushed, drained, *raw* pineapple *or* kiwifruit.

3. Chill until firm or until time indicated by laboratory instructor. Unmold gelatin onto labelled plates.
4. Measure height of gels. Evaluate them for appearance and texture. Record results in Table 7–7.

TABLE 7-7   Comparison of Treatments that Affect Gelation

Mold No. / Treatment	Time Required for Gelatin (minutes)	Appearance	Texture	Height (mm)
1 Control				
2 Double gelatin				
3 Double sugar				
4 Acid				
5 Milk				
6 Pineapple or kiwifruit, canned or cooked, added immediately				
7 added when thickened				
8 raw, added when thickened				

QUESTIONS

1. List the factors that increase the strength of a gel. Briefly explain the scientific reason for their effect. _____

_____

_____

_____

2. List the factors that decrease the strength of a gel. Briefly explain the scientific reason for their effect. _____

_____

_____

_____

_____

3. Explain why some raw fruit cannot be used in the preparation of gelatin salads. _____

_____

_____

_____

4. Explain why a gelatin salad should be slightly thickened before solids are added. _____

_____

_____

Experiment VIII: Preparation and Comparison of Gelatin Desserts

1. Prepare the following gelatin desserts. Record preparation time for each.

Orange Gelatin

gelatin	1 Tbsp	15 ml	orange juice	1/3 c	80 ml
water	1/3 c	80 ml	concentrate, frozen		
boiling water	1/2 c	125 ml	ice water	1/2 c	125 ml
sugar	1/2 c	125 ml	lemon juice,	2 Tbsp	30 ml
			fresh		

a. Soak gelatin in water 5 minutes to soften.
b. Add boiling water. Stir until gelatin is *completely* dissolved.
c. Mix in sugar. Stir until dissolved.
d. Mix orange juice concentrate and water together. Stir in lemon juice.
e. Pour into gelatin. Blend well.
f. Pour 1/2 of the mixture into individual molds. Chill.
g. Reserve the other 1/2 for the following recipe.

Orange Sponge

a. Obtain 1/2 of the above recipe.
b. Place in ice water in refrigerator to chill.
c. Beat 1 egg white until stiff, but not dry.
d. When gelatin is the consistency of unbeaten egg white, whip it until it foams.
e. Fold in egg white foam.
f. Pour into individual molds.
g. Chill.

Spanish Cream

gelatin	1 tsp	1 ml	egg yolk	1	
sugar	2 Tbsp	30 ml	vanilla	1/4 tsp	1 ml
milk	3/4 c + 1 Tbsp	195 ml	egg white	1	

a. Bring water to boil in the bottom half of a double boiler.
b. Combine gelatin and 1/2 of the sugar in the top pan. Slowly stir in milk. Place on bottom pan.
c. Heat, stirring occasionally, until sugar dissolves.
d. Beat egg yolk.
e. Pour in a small amount of the hot gelatin mixture into the egg yolk, stirring constantly.
f. Gradually add more of the hot mixture, continuing to stir.
g. Add warmed egg yolks back to gelatin mixture, stirring constantly.
h. Continue cooking for 2–4 minutes until mixture thickens.
i. Remove pan from heat. Pour mixture into a bowl.
j. Stir in vanilla.
k. Cool until mixture is slightly thickened.
l. Beat egg white with an electric mixer until foamy. Gradually add sugar in a small stream while continuing to beat. Beat until the egg white is stiff, but not dry.
m. Fold thickened custard into egg white foam.
n. Spoon into mold.
o. Chill.

Chocolate Bavarian Cream

gelatin	1 tsp	5 ml	chocolate chips	3 oz	90 g
sugar	2 Tbsp + 2 tsp	40 ml	vanilla	1/2 tsp	2 ml
			egg white	1	
milk	1/2 c	125 ml	heavy cream	1/4 c	50 ml
egg yolk	1		confectioners' sugar	2 tsp	10 ml

a. Follow steps a–g in the recipe above. Add chocolate chips in step g. Stir until melted.
b. Follow steps h–l in the recipe above.
c. Whip confectioners' sugar and cream until the peaks are soft and hold their shape.
d. Fold whipped cream into gelatin.
e. Fold egg white into gelatin mixture.
f. Spoon into individual molds.
g. Chill.

2. Observe appearance. Taste for texture and flavor.
3. Record results in Table 7–8.

TABLE 7-8   Preparation and Comparison of Gelatin Desserts

Dessert	Preparation Time (minutes)	Appearance	Texture	Flavor
Orange gelatin				
Orange sponge				
Spanish cream				
Chocolate Bavarian cream				

QUESTIONS

1. Why is the gelatin softened prior to the addition of boiling water? _____

   _____

   _____

2. What is the effect of adding egg white to a gelatin dessert? _____

   _____

   _____

3. How is the texture of a gelatin dessert changed by the addition of milk or cream as an ingredient?

   _____

   _____

   Why? _____

   _____

APPLICATIONS

Antipasto Salad

artichoke hearts, canned	2 oz	60 g	watercress bunch	1/4		
			iceberg lettuce, head	1/4		
mushrooms, fresh, sliced	2 Tbsp	30 ml	romaine, head	1/4		
pimento strips	1 Tbsp	30 ml	cherry tomatoes, halved	1/3 c	80 ml	
pitted black olives	1/4 c	50 ml				
Italian dressing	1/2 c	125 ml				

1. Combine artichoke hearts, mushrooms, pimento strips, and black olives in a large salad bowl.
2. Pour Italian dressing over the ingredients. Mix and let marinate 1 hour.
3. Wash greens and drain. Tear into bite-sized pieces. Reserve a few large leaves of romaine to act as liners for the salad bowl.
4. Add greens and tomatoes to salad bowl. Toss gently until well-mixed.
5. If desired, serve with the following: cooked, cold cauliflower; cooked, sliced asparagus; radish roses; pickled peppers; strips of pepperoni.

Salad Esmeralda

zucchini	1/2		bacon slice	1
Italian dressing	1/4 c	50 ml	red onion, thinly sliced	1/2
cream cheese	1-1/2 oz	45 g	romaine, head	1/2

1. Thinly slice zucchini.
2. Pour Italian dressing over zucchini. Marinate 30 minutes.
3. Cut cream cheese into cubes.
4. Fry bacon in skillet over high heat until crisp. Drain on paper towels. Crumble.
5. Add all ingredients to the salad bowl.
6. Toss gently until well mixed.

Parmesan Cheese Dressing

oil, olive	1/4 c	50 ml	salt	1/2 tsp	2 ml
vinegar, red wine	1/4 c	50 ml	pepper	1/8 tsp	0.5 ml
sugar	1 tsp	1 ml	oregano	1/4 tsp	1 ml
garlic salt	1/8 tsp	0.5 ml	Parmesan cheese	2 Tbsp	30 ml

Combine all ingredients thoroughly.

Vegetable Marinated Salad

vegetable of choice	1/2 lb	250 g	roasted red pepper,		
olive oil	2 Tbsp	30 ml	minced	2 tsp	10 ml
lemon juice	2 Tbsp	30 ml	green pepper	2 tsp	10 ml
salt	1/4 tsp	1 ml	capers	1 tsp	5 ml
garlic clove, minced	1/4		parsley, minced	1 tsp	5 ml
sweet pickle relish	2 tsp	10 ml	pepper	dash	
onion, minced	1 tsp	5 ml	Boston or red tip		
			lettuce leaves		

1. Select a vegetable such as asparagus spears, whole green beans, sliced carrots, sliced fresh mushrooms, or sliced tomatoes. If using asparagus, green beans, or carrots, cook in boiling water until tender, no more than 5 minutes. Do not cook fresh mushrooms or tomatoes.
2. Combine remaining ingredients except lettuce leaves.
3. Wash and dry lettuce leaves. Arrange on a serving plate.
4. Decoratively place vegetable on top of lettuce leaves.
5. Pour dressing on top of vegetable. Let vegetable marinate 15–20 minutes. Serve at room temperature.

Romaine and Mushroom Salad

scallions	2	Caesar Salad Dressing	1/4 c	50 ml
mushrooms, raw	4	Romaine lettuce	2 c	200 g
garlic clove	1			

1. Wash fresh mushrooms and romaine. Dry mushrooms with paper towel. Shake excess water off romaine.
2. Prepare Caesar Salad Dressing, pg. 71.
3. Cut garlic clove in half. Rub cut sides over the inside of the salad bowl. Discard.
4. Thinly slice white section of scallions. Add to salad bowl.
5. Slice mushrooms 1/8–1/4 in. (3–6 mm) thick with the stems left intact. Add to salad bowl.
6. Pour Caesar Salad Dressing over scallions and mushrooms. Toss. Let marinate 2–3 minutes.
7. Break romaine into 2–3 in. (5–7.5 cm) pieces.
8. Gently toss all ingredients.
9. Serve immediately.

Spinach Salad

bacon, slice	1		hard-cooked egg,	1	
spinach, fresh, 1/2 pkg.	5 oz	150 g	chopped		
			bean sprouts	1/4 c	50 ml
water chestnuts, canned	2		green onions	1	
mushrooms, fresh	2		Sweet and Sour Dressing		

1. Fry bacon in skillet over high heat until crisp. Drain on paper towels. Crumble.
2. Wash spinach free of all sand and drain. Discard any bruised leaves or stems. Cut off any tough, thick stems. Break large pieces into a manageable size.
3. Slice water chestnuts and mushrooms into 1/8 in. (3 mm) slices.
4. Add remaining ingredients and crumble bacon. Toss salad.
5. Pour Sweet and Sour Dressing (see recipe below) over salad; toss, and serve immediately.

Sweet and Sour Dressing

oil	1/4 c	50 ml	catsup	2 Tbsp	30 ml
vinegar, cider	2 Tbsp	30 ml	salt	1/2 tsp	2 ml
sugar	2-1/2 Tbsp	37 ml	pepper	dash	

Combine all ingredients thoroughly.

Creamy Cole Slaw

sugar	1-1/2 Tbsp	22 ml	celery seed	1/2 tsp	2 ml
vinegar, apple cider	1-1/2 Tbsp	22 ml	pepper	1/4 tsp	1 ml
			mayonnaise	1/2 c	125 ml
mustard	2 tsp	10 ml	carrot	1	
salt	1/4 tsp	1 ml	cabbage	1/2 small head	
paprika	dash				

1. Combine sugar, vinegar, mustard, salt, paprika, celery seed, and pepper in a small bowl. Stir until sugar is dissolved.
2. Add mayonnaise and beat well with a wire whisk until blended.
3. Grate carrot; shred cabbage. Place in a bowl.
4. Pour dressing over cabbage and carrot. Mix well and chill.

Celery Seed Dressing

sugar	2 Tbsp	30 ml	vinegar, cider	1 Tbsp +	20 ml
onion, grated	1/2 tsp	2 ml		1 tsp	
dry mustard	1/4 tsp	1 ml	oil	1/4 c	50 ml
salt	1/4 tsp	1 ml	celery seed	3/4 tsp	3 ml

1. Combine sugar, onion, dry mustard, salt, and 1 tsp (5 ml) of the vinegar.
2. Beat with a rotary beater.
3. Add 1 tsp (5 ml) oil. Beat until thick and creamy.
4. Continue beating while adding the remaining oil very gradually.
5. Gradually beat in remaining vinegar.
6. Stir in celery seed.
7. Let flavors blend for at least 30 minutes before serving.
8. Serve with fruit salad.

Molded Fruit Salad

strawberry dessert gelatin, pkg.	3 oz	90 g	crushed pineapple, canned	1/2 c	125 ml
water, boiling	1 c	250 ml	banana	1	
strawberries, frozen, thawed	3/4 c	180 ml	pecans, chopped	1/2 c	125 ml
			sour cream	1 c	250 ml

1. Dissolve strawberry jello in boiling water in a bowl.
2. Mix in strawberries and pineapple.
3. Mash banana and add to mixture. Stir well.
4. Pour 1/2 of mixture into mold.
5. Place the two mixtures in the refrigerator.
6. Combine nuts with sour cream.
7. Layer sour cream over partially thickened gelatin in mold.
8. Top with remaining gelatin.
9. Chill.

Sea Foam Salad

lime dessert gelatin, pkg.	3 oz	90 g	cream cheese	4 oz.	120 g
			heavy cream	1/2 c	125 ml
pears, can	15 oz	450 g			

1. Place jello in a bowl.
2. Drain juice from pears.
3. Bring pear juice to a boil over high heat.
4. Pour over jello. Stir until it is dissolved. Allow to cool to lukewarm.
5. Cream the cream cheese in a separate bowl. Blend 1 Tbsp (15 ml) cream until smooth.
6. Add cream cheese to jello. Beat until well blended.
7. Chill until partially thickened.
8. Mash pears.
9. Whip cream until soft peaks form.
10. Fold thickened gelatin into mashed pears.
11. Fold pear-gelatin mixture into whipped cream.
12. Pour into a mold and chill.

(Courtesy of Rice Council for Market Development.)

Cereals and Pasta

OBJECTIVES

The student should be able to:

1. Assess the cost and nutritive value of breakfast cereals.
2. Demonstrate and discuss the gelatinization of breakfast and starchy cereals.
3. Prepare and compare pasta.

FOOD SCIENCE PRINCIPLES

1. Processed breakfast cereals generally have an increased cost compared to the natural fo Breakfast cereals are generally fair sources of plant protein but good sources of iron, thiamin, a riboflavin.
2. Cereals are cooked with water in order to gelatinize the starch. Long cooking times are often necessary to allow the starch grains to swell and lose the raw, starchy taste. Cooking times can be decreased by pregelatinization or the addition of disodium phosphate. These permit rapid rehydration but increase the tendency of the cereal to congeal.
3. Grains of rice often stick together because of the presence of starch. Two methods can be used to separate grains: (a) soaking in cold water before cooking or (b) sautéing in hot fat. The soaking will wash away excess starch and the sautéing will seal the starch in the grains. The soak method is often used in the preparation of Spanish rice; however, water-soluble nutrients are lost as they leach into the soak water. Sautéing is often used in the preparation of a pilaf; however, it is easy to burn the rice if one is not careful.
4. Homemade pasta is superior in flavor and texture to commercial pasta, but the extensive preparation time limits its popularity. Pasta made from durum flour cooks quicker than that made from durum semolina but it is stickier and has less of a "bite."

Exercise I: Cost and Nutritive Value of Breakfast Cereals

1. Determine the number of servings for each breakfast cereal listed in Table 8–1 from the nutrition label. Calculate cost/serving.
2. Calculate the nutritive value/serving of each cereal without added milk.
3. Record results in Table 8–1.

TABLE 8-1   Cost and Nutritive Value of Breakfast Cereals

Cereal	Cost	Servings/ Package	Cost/ Serving	Percent U.S. RDA per Serving				
				Food Energy (kcal)	Protein (g)	Iron (mg)	Thiamin (mg)	Ribo-flavin (mg)
Cheerios								
Corn Flakes								
Cream of Wheat								
Puffed Rice								
Rice Krispies								
Shredded Wheat								
Total								
Wheat Chex								
Wheaties								

QUESTIONS

1. Which cereals are the most economical? _____

   _____

   The most expensive? _____

2. Breakfast cereals are considered good sources of which nutrients? _____

   _____

3. How would the addition of milk affect the nutritive value of cereals? _____

   _____

Experiment I: Gelatinization of Breakfast Cereals

1. Prepare the breakfast cereals found in Table 8–2 according to the basic method of cooking cereals. Use ingredients and cooking times listed in Table 8–2.
2. When the mixture first thickens, remove a small sample of the cereal and place in a custard cup. Compare initial sample to final cooked product.

Basic Method of Cooking Breakfast Cereals

    a. Place water and salt in a saucepan over medium heat. Bring to a boil.

    b. Add cereal slowly while constantly stirring.

    c. Lower heat and simmer for the time indicated in Table 8–2.

TABLE 8-2   Preparation of Breakfast Cereals[a]

Product	Cereal[b]	Water c (ml)	Simmering Time (minutes)
Cream of Wheat	2-1/2 Tbsp (37 ml)	1-1/4 (300 ml)	10
Grits	3 Tbsp (45 ml)	1 (250)	3–5
Oats, quick-cooking	1/3 c (80 ml)	3/4 (180)	1
Oats, rolled	1/3 c (80 ml)	1 (250)	5

[a] Add 1/4 tsp (1 ml) salt/1 c (250 ml) water.
[b] One serving.

3. Measure volume of cooked product and calculate % increase.
4. Observe appearance and texture. Taste cereal for flavor.
5. Record results in Table 8–3.

TABLE 8-3   Comparison of Gelatinized Breakfast Cereals

Cereal	Volume			Appearance		Texture		Flavor	
	Initial	Final	% Increase[a]	Initial	Final	Initial	Final	Initial	Final
Cream of Wheat									
Grits									
Oats, instant									
Oats, rolled									

[a] % increase = $\dfrac{\text{Final volume} - \text{initial volume}}{\text{Initial volume}} \times 100$.

QUESTIONS

1. Why are cereals cooked? _____

   _____

2. Which type of cereal had the biggest increase in volume? _____

   Why? _____

   _____

3. Why are cereals cooked beyond the point at which they first thicken? _____

   _____

4. How were the oats made instant? (Check the label.) _____

   _____

Experiment II: Gelatinization of Grains

1. Prepare 1/4 c (40 ml) of the grains found in Table 8–5, using the ingredients and methods listed in Table 8–4.

TABLE 8–4   Preparation of Grains[a]

Cereal	Amount of Water to Add to 1/4 c (60 ml) Cereal	Cooking Time (minutes)	Method
Rice, short-grain	3/4 c (180 ml)	15	1
long-grain, converted	1/2 c + 1 Tbsp (140 ml)	15	2
instant	1/4 c (60 ml)	—	3
brown	1/2 c + 1 Tbsp (140 ml)	40	2
wild	3/4 c (180 ml)	60	2
Pearl Barley	3/4 c (180 ml)	45	1[b]
Bulgur	1/2 c (125 ml)	—	4
Millet	3/4 c + 1 Tbsp (195 ml)	40	1[b]

[a] Add 1/4 tsp (1 ml) salt/1 c (250 ml) water.
[b] Cover can be removed during last 5 minutes to separate grains.

Basic Methods of Preparing Grains

Method #1

    a. Place cold water, salt, and cereal in a saucepan over medium-high heat.
    b. Bring to a boil. Stir and cover.
    c. Lower heat and simmer until end of cooking period.

Method #2

    a. Add water and salt to a saucepan over medium-high heat. $\frac{1}{2}c + 1T$
    b. Bring to a boil.
    c. Stir in cereal and cover. $\frac{1}{4}c$
    d. Lower heat and simmer until end of cooking time.

Method #3

    a. Add water and salt to a saucepan over high heat.
    b. Stir in cereal.
    c. Cover and turn off heat.
    d. Let stand 5 minutes until served.

Method #4

    a. Place cereal in a bowl.
    b. Add salt to water in a saucepan.
    c. Bring water to a rolling boil and pour over cereal in bowl.
    d. Let stand until cereal is soft and fluffy, not more than 30 minutes.
    e. Pour off excess water and use.

2. Measure volume of cooked cereal and calculate percent increase.
3. Observe appearance and texture. Taste cereal for flavor.
4. Record results in Table 8–5.

TABLE 8–5 Comparison of Gelatinized Cereals

Cereal	Volume (ml)			Appearance	Texture	Flavor
	Initial	Final	% Increase			
Rice short-grain						
long-grain						
instant						
brown						
wild						
Barley						
Bulgur						
Millet						

QUESTIONS

1. Which cereal product produced the largest increase in volume? _____

   Why? _____

2. Why is the appearance of instant rice so much different from that of long-grain or short-grain

   rice? _____

   _____

3. Why is wild rice so expensive? _____

   _____

4. How does brown rice differ from white rice? _____

   _____

Experiment III: Separation of Rice Grains

1. Cook 1/4 c (50 ml) long-grain rice with 1/2 c + 1 Tbsp (140 ml) water and 1/8 tsp (0.5 ml) salt
   according to the following methods:

   a. Cover rice with water and stir. Let stand 15 minutes. Discard water. Repeat. Rinse rice
      thoroughly and drain in a colander. Cook rice according to Basic Method #1 in Experiment II.
   b. Melt 1/4 tsp (1 ml) margarine in 1/4 tsp (1 ml) oil over medium-high heat in a saucepan. Add
      rice and sauté 2-3 minutes, stirring constantly so that it does not brown. Add water and salt.
      Bring to boil and stir. Cover, turn heat to low, and simmer 15 minutes.
   c. Basic Method #1 in Experiment II.
   d. Basic Method #1 but add 1/2 tsp (2 ml) margarine to the water before cooking.

2. Place on plates. Evaluate for appearance, texture, and flavor.
3. Record results in Table 8–6.

TABLE 8–6 Comparison of Methods for Separating Rice Grains

Method	Appearance	Texture	Flavor
Soak			
Sauté			
Standard			
Standard, plus fat			

QUESTIONS

1. Which method produces the most separate starch grains? _____

   Why? _____

   What is its disadvantage? _____

   _____

2. Which method is second best for separating starch grains? _____

   Why? _____

   What is its disadvantage? _____

   _____

Experiment IV: Preparation and Comparison of Pasta

1. Prepare homemade egg noodles by the following recipe. Keep a record of the preparation time.

Homemade Egg Noodles

egg, beaten	1/2		flour	1/2 c	125 ml
milk	1 Tbsp	15 ml	cornstarch		
salt	1/4 tsp	1 ml			

   a. Mix together the egg, milk, and salt.
   b. Gradually add the flour to form a very stiff dough.
   c. Knead for approximately 10 minutes. Let the dough rest for 10 minutes.
   d. Roll dough as thinly as possible over a floured surface.
   e. Sprinkle lightly with cornstarch.
   f. Roll dough up like a jelly roll. Slice dough crosswise in 1/4 in. (6 mm) lengths. Unroll noodle dough slices.
   g. Spread to dry for 1-1/2-2 hours. [In the laboratory, the drying time can be decreased by placing the noodles on a cookie sheet in a warm oven that is not over 212°F (100°C).]
   h. Bring 1 quart (1 l) water and 1 tsp (5 ml) salt to a boil.
   i. Drop noodles in boiling water and stir.
   j. Cook, uncovered, for 10 minutes.
   k. Drain and save a sample of the cooking water.

2. Prepare commercial egg noodles according to package directions using the minimum cooking time. Save a sample of the cooking water.
3. Prepare two types of commercial spaghetti: one regular (made from durum *flour*) and the other labeled as being made from durum *semolina*. Cook both types according to package directions using the minimum cooking time. Save a sample of the cooking water.
4. Observe the appearance of the pastas and their cooking water. Bite into the pasta and evaluate the texture and flavor.
5. Record results in Table 8–7.

TABLE 8–7   Comparison of Pasta Products

Pasta	Preparation Time (minutes)	Cooking Water	Pasta		
		Appearance	Appearance	Texture	Flavor
Egg noodles, homemade					
commercial					
Spaghetti, durum flour					
durum semolina					

QUESTIONS

1. Why are commercial egg noodles more popular with consumers than homemade noodles?
   _____

2. What is the difference between egg noodles and other forms of pasta? _____
   _____

3. Why did the cooking water change appearance? _____
   _____

4. Which spaghetti had the clearest cooking water? _____
   Why? _____
   _____

APPLICATIONS

Tabbouleh

bulgur wheat	1/2 c	125 ml	tomatoes, ripe	2	
water, boiling	1 c	250 ml	salt	1/2 tsp	2 ml
parsley, minced	1/2 c	125 ml	pepper	1/8 tsp	0.5 ml
mint, fresh, minced	2 Tbsp	30 ml	olive oil	2 Tbsp	30 ml
or			lemon juice, fresh	2 Tbsp	30 ml
dried mint	2 tsp	10 ml	lettuce leaves	4	
onion, chopped	1/2				

1. Place wheat in a medium deep bowl. Pour boiling water over top. Cover with a plate or aluminum foil and set aside for 30 minutes.
2. Combine parsley, mint, and onions.
3. Coarsely chop tomatoes. Sprinkle with salt and pepper.
4. Add tomatoes to parsley mixture.
5. Drain bulgur wheat. Add wheat to tomato–parsley mixture.
6. Combine olive oil and lemon juice. Pour over tabbouleh and toss to mix.
7. Chill until serving.
8. When ready to serve, place lettuce leaves on a plate and mound tabbouleh on lettuce.

Garlic Cheese Grits

grits	1/4 c	50 ml	garlic cheese	1-1/2 oz	45 g
water	1/2 c	125 ml	sharp cheddar	1-1/2 oz	45 g
milk	1/2 c	125 ml	cheese, grated		
margarine	2 Tbsp	30 ml	egg, beaten	1/2	

1. Preheat oven to 350°F (175°C).
2. Grease a small casserole.
3. Place grits in a saucepan.
4. Gradually stir in water and milk. Cook over medium high heat until thick, 3–5 minutes.
5. Add margarine and blend thoroughly. Remove from heat.
6. Stir in cheese and egg until mixture is smooth.
7. Pour into casserole.
8. Bake 35 minutes until it bubbles.
9. Let the grits stand for 5 minutes before serving.

Sicilian Pasta

olive oil	2 Tbsp	30 ml		pine nuts	2 Tbsp	30 ml
garlic, minced	1 clove			broccoli florets	1 c	250 ml
Italian tomatoes, chopped	14 oz	420 g		raisins	2 Tbsp	30 ml
				pasta (twists or shells)	1/4 lb	125 g
salt	1/2 tsp	2 ml				
pepper	1/8 tsp	0.5 ml				

1. Preheat oven to 400°F (200°C).
2. Heat olive oil in a skillet over medium heat.
3. Add garlic and sauté 30 seconds.
4. Add tomatoes, salt, and pepper. Bring to a boil; reduce heat to low and simmer 10 minutes.
5. Meanwhile, toast pine nuts:

    a. Place pine nuts in a single layer on a cookie sheet.
    b. Bake approximately 5 minutes until they start to turn light brown.
    c. Immediately remove from oven and let cool. Watch them carefully because they burn easily.

6. Meanwhile, prepare broccoli:

    a. Cut broccoli florets in half.
    b. Place florets stem side down in 1 in. (2.5 cm) of water in a saucepan.
    c. Cover and bring to a boil. Cook 2–3 minutes until tender-crisp.
    d. Drain and set aside.

7. Add raisins to tomato sauce. Simmer an additional 5 minutes.
8. Meanwhile, prepare pasta according to package directions.
9. Combine pasta, tomato sauce, broccoli, and pine nuts. Serve immediately.

Rice with Hot Chilies and Cheese

rice, cooked	1 c	250 ml		jalepeno or chili, canned, seeded, minced	1/2 tsp	2 ml
parsley, dried	1/2 tsp	2 ml				
oregano, dried	1/4 tsp	1 ml				
salt	1/8 tsp	0.5 ml		cheddar cheese, grated	2 oz	60 g
pepper	dash					
sour cream	1/2 c	125 ml		paprika	dash	

1. Preheat oven to 350°F (175°C).
2. Grease a 5 in. (12.5 cm) square casserole dish.
3. Toss cooked rice with parsley, oregano, salt, and pepper.
4. Place half of rice in casserole dish.
5. Combine jalepeno and sour cream. Spread 1/2 c (125 ml) over layer of rice.
6. Sprinkle half the cheese over the sour cream.
7. Repeat steps 4, 5, and 6.
8. Sprinkle with paprika.
9. Bake in oven 15 minutes or until cheese melts.
10. Serve hot.

Spanish Rice

oil	1 Tbsp	15 ml	water	1/2 c	125 ml
onion, chopped	1/3 c	80 ml	chili powder	1/4 tsp	1 ml
pepper, minced	1/3 c	80 ml	basil	1/8 tsp	0.5 ml
rice	1/3 c	80 ml	sugar	1/8 tsp	0.5 ml
tomatoes, canned,	3/4 c	180 ml	salt	3/4 tsp	3 ml
coarsely chopped			pepper	dash	

1. Heat oil in heavy skillet over medium-high heat.
2. Add onion and pepper to hot oil. Sauté 3–5 minutes until soft.
3. Add rice and stir-fry until lightly browned. Do not allow the rice to burn.
4. Add remaining ingredients.
5. Bring to a boil, stir, and cover. Lower heat and simmer 20 minutes. Do *not* stir. Check occasionally to see if more liquid is needed. One or 2 Tbsp (15–30 ml) water may be added if necessary.

Sour Cream Noodles

salt	1 tsp	5 ml	pepper	1/8 tsp	0.5 ml
noodles	4 oz	120 g	scallions or chives,	1 Tbsp	15 ml
sour cream	1/2 c	125 ml	chopped		
garlic salt	1/4 tsp	1 ml	margarine	2 Tbsp	30 ml

1. Bring 2 qts (2 l) of water to a boil with the salt.
2. Add noodles to boiling water, and stir. Boil, uncovered, 10 minutes (or according to package directions) until noodles are cooked but still firm (á la dente).
3. While noodles are cooking, combine sour cream, garlic salt, pepper, and scallions. Mix well.
4. Drain noodles in a colander.
5. Melt margarine in the saucepan in which the noodles were cooked.
6. Add noodles back to saucepan. Toss gently to coat with margarine.
7. Add sour cream mixture to noodles; toss gently.
8. Serve promptly.

Vermicelli with Butter and Cheese

salt	1/4 tsp	1 ml	pepper	dash	
vermicelli	4 oz	120 g	Romano cheese,	1 Tbsp	15 ml
butter	2 Tbsp	30 ml	grated		
parsley	1/2 tsp	2 ml			

1. Bring salt and 2 qts (2 l) of water to a boil in a saucepan.
2. Add vermicelli, stirring constantly. Boil 4–5 minutes over medium-high heat until the spaghetti is cooked but still firm (á la dente).
3. Drain.
4. Melt butter in the saucepan in which the vermicelli was cooked. Add parsley.
5. Return drained vermicelli to pan and toss gently to coat with parsley and butter.
6. Sprinkle with grated cheese. Toss again.
7. Serve immediately.

(Courtesy of American Egg Board.)

9
Starch

OBJECTIVES

The student should be able to:

1. Identify types and functions of substances that separate starch granules.
2. Describe the effect of the type of starch, overheating, sugar, and acid on the quality of cooked starch pastes.
3. Prepare and compare cornstarch-thickened puddings and starch products made from white sauces.

FOOD SCIENCE PRINCIPLES

1. When liquid is added to dry starch granules, the exterior portion of the granules becomes sticky while the interior remains dry; resulting in lumps. This can be prevented by separating the granules before liquid is added by: coating with fat, surrounding with sugar, or dispersing in a cold liquid.
2. When starch is mixed in cold water, it absorbs a small amount of water that produces a reversible swelling. When the mixture is heated, the water further penetrates the starch grains and causes them to lose their birefringence. This slow, irreversible breakdown of structure is called *gelatinization.*
3. Continued heating of starch in hot water beyond gelatinization causes the granules to swell enormously and soften to form a starch paste (pasting). This thickening is due to the increasingly larger size of the granules, starch exudate that has leaked out from the granule, and evaporation of water. As these events take place, the starch paste slowly loses its raw flavor.
4. Starch is a mixture of amylose and amylopectin polysaccharides whose relative proportion is a major factor in the way it behaves during cooking. Starches from wheat such as flour thicken at temperatures near the boiling point into a cloudy gel, and undergo retrogradation when chilled. Starches containing large amounts of amylopectin such as potato, waxy cornstarch, and tapioca, thicken at lower temperatures and become clear; but they do not gel or undergo retrogradation.

    Instant and canned puddings contain high amounts of pregelatinized and amylopectin starch, respectively, which become hydrated when heated.

    Browning flour by dry heat breaks down the starch molecules into dextrins. Dextrins are sweeter than starch but have less effective thickening properties.

5. Factors affecting thickened starch pastes:

   a. *Sugar:* Sugar delays gelatinization but does not affect pasting. In small amounts, it has a tenderizing effect on starch gels but large amounts decrease gel strength.
   b. *Acids:* The thickening ability of starch is decreased by the breakdown of starch granules. This breakdown can be minimized by cooking and thickening the starch before acid is added.
   c. *Overheating and overstirring:* Completely gelatinized starch should not be stirred unless necessary or over heated because the swollen starch grains are easily broken. This will result in a thinning of the mixture.

6. White sauces are a mixture of flour and milk, with some fat added for flavor. The consistency is dependent on the proportions of the thickening agent (flour) to the liquid (milk). White sauces are the basis for foods such as cream sauces, soufflés, gravies, and scalloped dishes.

Experiment I: Separation of Starch Granules

1. Place the following separating substances into 4 small saucepans:

   a. none.
   b. 1 Tbsp (15 ml) melted fat. Melt in saucepan.
   c. 1/4 c (50 ml) cold water.
   d. 1 Tbsp (15 ml) sugar.

2. Add 1 Tbsp (15 ml) flour to each of the saucepans. Stir to dissolve.
3. Bring 2 c (500 ml) water to a boil. Pour 1/4 c (50 ml) boiling water into each saucepan, stirring constantly.
4. Turn heat to high. Stir until mixture boils.
5. Observe consistency of sauce.
6. Record results in Table 9–1.

TABLE 9–1   Separation of Starch Granules

Separating Substances	Consistency	Practical Use
None		
Melted fat		
Cold water		
Sugar		

1. Explain why lumps occur when liquid is added to flour. _____
_____
_____

2. How may lumps be prevented in starch-thickened sauces? _____
_____
_____

3. Briefly describe how each of the following act as a separating substance when mixed with flour:

Melted fat   _____

Cold water   _____

Sugar   _____

Experiment II: Effect of Starch Variety on Hot and Cooled Starch Pastes

1. Prepare starch pastes with the ingredients in Table 9–2. (Brown flour over medium heat in heavy skillet. Do not burn.)
2. Add 2 Tbsp (30 ml) *cold* water to each of the ingredients. Stir until dissolved. Add 1/4 c + 2 Tbsp (90 ml) cold water and stir until dissolved again.
3. Heat each paste over medium heat. Stir occasionally until the sauce thickens. (Do not overstir.) Reduce heat and keep warm 2–3 minutes.
4. Pour 1/4 c (50 ml) of each of the starch pastes into separate custard cups. Place in the freezer to chill quickly. Do not allow ice crystals to form.
5. Pour 1/4 c (50 ml) of each of the hot starch pastes onto waxed paper. Observe appearance and consistency. Measure the size of the spread. (The spread is the diameter of the paste after it has stopped spreading.)
6. Remove cooled starch paste from freezer. Unmold from the custard cup onto waxed paper. Observe appearance, consistency, and spread.
7. Record results in Table 9–2.

QUESTIONS

1. Which of the cooked starch pastes were clear? _____
_____

Cloudy? _____

2. How is the appearance of the starch paste related to its amylose and amylopectin content?
_____
_____
_____

3. Which of the starch pastes had the thinnest consistency? _____
_____

Thickest? _____

TABLE 9-2   Effect of Starch Variety on Hot and Cooled Starch Pastes

Variety of Starch	Quality Tbsp (ml)	Appearance		Consistency		Size of Spread (mm)	
		Hot	Cold	Hot	Cold	Hot	Cold
Flour, all purpose	1 (15)						
browned	1 (15)						
instant	1 (15)						
whole wheat	1 (15)						
Cornstarch	1/2 (8)						
Cornstarch	1 (15)						
Potato	1 (15)						
Tapioca	1 (15)						

4. What effect did browning the flour have on its thickening ability? _____

_____

Why? _____

5. How does the thickening ability of cornstarch compare to that of flour? _____

_____

Why is there a difference? _____

_____

6. Which starches gel when cooled? _____

_____

Why? _____

Experiment III: Preparation and Comparison of Cornstarch-Thickened Puddings

1. Prepare chocolate pudding by the following recipe. When the pudding first thickens (step c), remove half and place in a custard cup. To the mixture in the custard cup, beat in the following: 1/2 egg yolk, 1 tsp (5 ml) margarine, and 1/4 tsp (1 ml) vanilla. Continue cooking the remaining pudding according to the recipe.

Chocolate Pudding

sugar	1 c	250 ml	egg yolk (divided)	1	
cornstarch	1 Tbsp	15 ml	beaten		
salt	dash		margarine (divided)	2 tsp	10 ml
milk	1 c	250 ml	vanilla (divided)	1/2 tsp	2 ml
baking chocolate	1/2 oz	15 g			

   a. Combine sugar, cornstarch, and salt in a saucepan.
   b. Gradually add milk. Add baking chocolate.
   c. Cook over medium heat until mixture thickens and boils, stirring constantly. Boil 1 minute, stirring constantly. Remove from heat.
   d. While stirring egg yolk in a custard cup, drop a small amount of the hot pudding into the egg yolk. Gradually add more pudding while continuing to stir, until at least 1/4 c (50 ml) has been added.
   e. Then stir pudding while gradually adding the egg yolk mixture back to the pudding.
   f. Return to cook over medium heat until the mixture bubbles for 1 minute, stirring constantly.
   g. Remove from heat. Stir in margarine and vanilla.
   h. Spoon into serving dish. Chill.

2. Prepare 1/4 package of commercial chocolate pudding mix according to the instructions on the label. Pour into a custard cup.
3. Prepare 1/4 package of an *instant* commercial chocolate pudding mix according to the instructions on the label. Pour into a custard cup.
4. Open a canned chocolate pudding and pour into a custard cup.
5. Calculate cost per 1/2 c (125 ml) serving for a pudding.
6. Compare the puddings for appearance, consistency, and flavor.
7. Record results in Table 9–3.

TABLE 9–3 Comparison of Cornstarch-Thickened Puddings

Variation	Cost/Serving	Appearance	Consistency	Flavor
Homemade, cooked short time				
cooked long time				
Commercial mix cooked				
instant (pregelatinized)				
Canned, (high amylopectin)				

QUESTIONS

1. Why are puddings cooked beyond the point at which they first thicken? _____
   _____
   _____

2. Compare homemade puddings to commercial pudding mixes: _____
   _____
   _____

   To canned puddings: _____
   _____
   _____

Experiment IV: Effect of Sugar, Acid, and Overheating on Thickened Starch Pastes

1. Prepare 4 cornstarch pastes by the following methods:

   a. Place 1 Tbsp (15 ml) cornstarch into each of 4 saucepans.
   b. Add one of the following separating substances to each

      Pan 1:   1/4 c (50 ml) sugar
      Pan 2:   2 Tbsp (30 ml) lemon juice
      Pan 3:   2 Tbsp (30 ml) cold water
      Pan 4:   2 Tbsp (30 ml) cold water

   c. Stir until dissolved.
   d. Add the following amounts of cold water to

      Pan 1:   1/2 c   (125 ml)
      Pan 2:   1/4 c + 2 Tbsp   (80 ml)
      Pan 3:   1/4 c + 2 Tbsp   (80 ml)
      Pan 4:   1/2 c   (125 ml)

   e. Heat over medium heat until thickened. Lower heat and keep warm 2–3 minutes.

2. Continue heating Pan 4 over high heat. Boil mixture 3 minutes, stirring constantly.
3. Add 2 Tbsp (30 ml) lemon juice to thickened cornstarch in Pan 3.
4. Pour 1/4 c (50 ml) of each hot paste onto waxed paper. Observe appearance and consistency. Measure size of spread.
5. Place the remainder of each paste into separate custard cups. Place in freezer to chill. Do not allow ice crystals to form.
6. Unmold chilled cornstarch pastes onto waxed paper. Observe appearance, consistency, and spread.
7. Record results in Table 9–4.

TABLE 9-4   Effect of Sugar, Acid, and Overheating on Thickened Starch Pastes

Treatment of Starch Paste	Appearance		Consistency		Size of Spread (mm)	
	Hot	Cold	Hot	Cold	Hot	Cold
Sugar						
Acid, initial						
thickened						
Overheating and over-stirring						

QUESTIONS

1. What is the effect of the addition of sugar on a starch paste? _____
   _____
   _____

2. When should acid be added to starch paste? _____
   _____ Why? _____
   _____

3. How does overheating or overstirring a thickened starch paste affect the viscosity? _____
   _____
   _____
   _____

Experiment V: Preparation and Comparison of Starchy Food Products

1. Prepare white sauces by one of the following methods using a wire whisk. Use the proportions of ingredients given in Table 9-5 to prepare 1 c (250 ml) of sauce.

White Sauce—Roux Method

   a. Melt fat over low heat in a saucepan.
   b. Stir in flour. Cook mixture 1 minute until it is thick and smooth, stirring constantly.
   c. Remove from heat. Add a small portion of the liquid and stir until completely blended. Gradually add the rest of the liquid while continuously stirring.
   d. Return to heat. Bring to a boil and simmer 1 minute, stirring continuously.

TABLE 9-5   Ingredients for Preparation of a White Sauce

White Sauce	Liquid 1 c (250 ml)	Flour Tbsp (ml)	Fat Tbsp (ml)	Seasoning Dash	Use
Thin	Milk or thin cream	1 (15)	1 (15)	Salt	Cream soup
Medium	Milk or thin cream	2 (30)	2 (30)	Salt	Creamed dishes, scalloped dishes, gravy
Thick	Milk or thin cream	3 (45)	3 (45)	Salt	Souffles, cooked salad, dressings
Very thick	Milk or thin cream	4–5 (60–70)	4 (60)	Salt, pepper	Croquettes, souffles

White Sauce—Starch Paste Method

    a. Mix small amount (1/4) of the cold liquid with the flour to form a smooth paste.
    b. Melt fat over medium heat in a saucepan.
    c. Add remaining liquid to the fat and bring to a boil.
    d. Slowly add starch paste to the boiling mixture, stirring constantly.

White Sauce—Starch Dispersion Method

    a. Combine flour with cold liquid in a saucepan.
    b. Heat starch dispersion over medium heat until it thickens.
    c. Add fat and stir until dissolved.
    d. Bring to a boil and simmer 1 minute, stirring constantly.

2. Use the white sauces to prepare the following:

    a. Thin white sauce: Cream of Potato soup or Creamed Spinach.
    b. Medium white sauce: Welsh Rarebit.
    c. Thick white sauce: Macaroni and Cheese, Cheese Soufflé.
    d. Very thick white sauce: Cream of Cauliflower Soup.

3. Observe appearance and texture. Taste for flavor.
4. Record results in Table 9–6.

TABLE 9-6   Comparison of Products Made from White Sauce

White Sauce	Product	Appearance	Flavor	Texture
Thin				
Medium				
Thick				
Very thick				

QUESTIONS

1. What causes a starch paste to thicken as it is cooked? _____
   _____
   _____

2. Name two ways lumps are prevented in the preparation of a white sauce. _____
   _____
   _____

3. Why are the thickened white sauces cooked 1 minute after they have thickened? _____
   _____
   _____

APPLICATIONS

Cream of Potato Soup

margarine	2 tsp	10 ml	chicken broth	1/2 c	125 ml
onion, minced	1 Tbsp	15 ml	salt	1/8 tsp	0.5 ml
celery, minced	1 Tbsp	15 ml	thin white sauce	1/2 c	125 ml
potatoes, peeled, diced	1/2 c	125 ml	green onion, minced	1 tsp	5 ml

1. Melt margarine in a saucepan over medium-high heat.
2. Add onion and celery. Sauté 5 minutes until soft.
3. Add potatoes, chicken broth, and salt.
4. Bring to a boil. Cover, lower heat, and simmer 10–15 minutes until potatoes are tender.
5. Warm white sauce over low heat. Gradually add cooked potatoes and broth, stirring constantly.
6. Pour into serving bowl.
7. Spinkle with minced onion.

Welsh Rarebit

medium white sauce	1/2 c	125 ml	egg, beaten	1/2	
dry mustard	1/4 tsp	1 ml	cheddar cheese, grated	1/2 c	125 ml
cayenne pepper	dash		toast points		

1. Add dry mustard and cayenne pepper to heated white sauce.
2. Allow to cool slightly.
3. Slowly stir in egg.
4. Heat over low heat, stirring constantly, until mixture is thickened and smooth.
5. Stir in cheese until it melts.
6. Pour over toast points and serve hot.

Macaroni and Cheese

thick white sauce	1/2 c	125 ml	sharp cheddar	3/4 c	180 ml
dry mustard	1/4 tsp	1 ml	cheese, grated		
onion, grated	3/4 tsp	3 ml	Worchestershire	1/4 tsp	1 ml
salt	dash		sauce		
pepper	dash		macaroni, cooked	3/4 c	180 ml

1. Preheat oven to 350°F (175°C).
2. Grease a small casserole.
3. Combine dry mustard, onion, salt, and pepper with white sauce in a saucepan over low heat.
4. Stir in cheese and Worchestershire sauce. Continue stirring until it is well blended.
5. Combine macaroni with cheese sauce.
6. Pour into casserole and bake 20–30 minutes until the cheese sauce bubbles.

Cheese Soufflé

margarine	2 Tbsp	30 ml	cayenne pepper	dash	
flour	2 Tbsp	30 ml	cheddar cheese, grated	4 oz	120 g
milk	3/4 c	180 ml	eggs	2	
salt	1/4 tsp	1 ml	cream of tartar	1/8 tsp	0.5 ml
Worchestershire sauce	1/4 tsp	1 ml			

1. Preheat oven to 350°F (175°C).
2. Wrap outside of soufflé dish with a greased 4 in. (10 cm) wide band of triple thickness aluminum foil. Make sure that at least 3 in. (7.5 cm) of foil is above the rim of the dish. If necessary, secure in place with a string.
3. Prepare cheese sauce:

   a. Melt margarine over low heat in a saucepan. Stir in flour and mix continuously until mixture comes to a boil. Cook 1 minute, stirring constantly.
   b. Remove from heat. Slowly add milk, continuously stirring.
   c. Return to heat. Boil and stir 1 minute.
   d. Stir in salt, Worchestershire sauce, and cayenne pepper.
   e. Add grated cheese and stir until melted.
   f. Remove from heat and allow to cool for 2 minutes.

4. Separate eggs into whites and yolks.
5. Beat together egg yolks until blended. Set aside.
6. Beat egg whites with electric beater until foamy. Add cream of tartar, and continue beating until peaks are stiff but not dry.
7. Pour blended yolks into cheese sauce, stirring continuously.
8. Gently fold cheese sauce into beaten egg whites.
9. Pour into soufflé dish and bake 30 minutes. A knife inserted halfway between center and the edge should come out clean.
10. Serve immediately.

Cream of Cauliflower Soup

very thick white sauce	1/2 c	125 ml	egg yolks	1–1/2	
cauliflower, frozen,	7 oz	210 g	heavy cream	1/4 c	50 ml
partially thawed			cayenne pepper	dash	
chicken stock	3 c	750 ml	lemon juice	1/4 tsp	1 ml
salt	1/4 tsp	1 ml	green onion, chopped	1 Tbsp	15 ml
lemon juice	1/2 tsp	2 ml			

1. Remove 1/4 of the cauliflower florets for garnish. Slice the remaining cauliflower 1/4 in. (6 mm) thick.
2. Bring the chicken stock and salt to a boil in a saucepan.
3. Add the sliced cauliflower. Lower heat and simmer until it can easily be mashed.
4. Meanwhile, cook the remaining florets in a saucepan covered with water and the lemon juice until tender. Plunge the florets into cold water to stop cooking; drain.
5. Remove cauliflower from chicken stock and purée it with a sieve or the back of a spoon. Do *not* use a blender.
6. Combine puréed cauliflower and white sauce in a saucepan by beating. Heat mixture over medium heat until it simmers. Do not allow the mixture to boil.
7. Beat together the egg yolks and heavy cream. Slowly pour a small amount of the hot soup into this mixture, stirring constantly. Gradually add a little of the hot soup to warm the egg yolks. Then slowly pour the hot egg yolk mixture into the soup, continuously stirring.
8. Add cayenne pepper, lemon juice, and florets to the soup. Heat through.
9. Serve sprinkled with green onions on top.

Chicken Croquettes

very thick white sauce	1/2 c	125 ml	lemon juice	1/2 tsp	2 ml
parsley, dried	1/2 tsp	2 ml	cooked chicken,	3/4 c	180 ml
poultry seasoning	1/8 tsp	0.5 ml	diced		
pepper	dash		egg	1/2	
egg, beaten	1/2		water	1 tsp	5 ml
soft bread crumbs	1/4 c	50 ml	dry bread crumbs	1/4 c	50 ml

1. Stir parsley, poultry seasoning, and pepper into warm white sauce.
2. Mix a small amount of the hot sauce into the egg, beating constantly. Gradually add more of the sauce.
3. Slowly pour the egg mixture into the hot sauce, stirring constantly.
4. Place pan over low heat and cook 1 minute, stirring constantly. Do not boil. Remove pan from heat.
5. Mix in the soft bread crumbs, lemon juice, and cooked chicken.
6. Cool in freezer until chilled. Do not allow ice crystals to form.
7. Beat together the egg with the water.
8. Shape croquettes into small cones or cylinders.
9. Dip in egg and roll in bread crumbs.
10. Let the croquettes dry on a rack for 30 minutes.
11. Preheat fat in a deep-fat fryer to 375°F (190°C). Follow directions for the basic method of deep-fat frying, page 243.
12. Deep-fry 2–3 minutes until golden brown.
13. Drain on paper towels.

Note: Croquettes may be kept warm in an oven at 250°F (120°C).

(Courtesy of American Egg Board.)

10
Eggs

OBJECTIVES

The student should be able to:

1. Determine the effect of storage on egg quality.
2. Describe factors affecting the quality of hard-cooked, poached, and scrambled eggs.
3. Compare the effects of different methods in preparing eggs and custards.
4. Evaluate the effects of milk, acid, and alkali on the coagulation of eggs.
5. Discuss factors affecting the quality of custards, egg foams, and meringue.

FOOD SCIENCE PRINCIPLES

1. A fresh grade AA egg should be compact when cooked, with the yolk centered in, and covered by a thick film of egg white. Eggs stored at room temperatures, rather than refrigerator temperatures, lose moisture and CO_2. The loss of CO_2 increases the alkalinity and thinning of the egg white. Support of the chalazae for the egg yolk is lost and the yolk no longer remains centered.

    When appearance is important for fried, poached or baked eggs, fresh eggs of AA grade should be used. For scrambled eggs, custards, and other products where eggs are an incorporated ingredient, older eggs and grades of lower quality can be used.
2. Coagulation of egg proteins is dependent on the following factors:

    a. *Temperature:* The temperature at which egg white and egg yolk coagulate differs because of their different proteins. Undiluted egg white coagulates at temperatures from 144°–149°F (62°–65°C) and egg yolk coagulates from 149°–158°F (65–70°C).
    b. *Concentration:* Dilution of egg proteins raises the temperature at which the proteins coagulate.
    c. *Acid:* Adding acid to egg white (which is naturally alkaline) decreases the pH to near the isolectric point of the egg proteins. At the isolectric point, proteins are least stable and most sensitive to denaturation (coagulation). Hence, small amounts of acid lower the coagulation temperature of most egg proteins.
    d. *Sugar:* Sugar elevates the temperature of coagulation and produces a more tender coagulum.
    e. *Salt:* Salt lowers the temperature of coagulation.

3. Hard-cooked eggs should be simmered under 185°F (85°C), never boiled. Boiling or overcooking produces a tougher, rubbery egg white. It may also produce a greyish-green film at the yolk-white interface from a reaction between the iron in the yolk and the sulfur in the white.

    Plunging the just-cooked egg into cold water to cool quickly will minimize this reaction. Rapid cooling reduces the pressure toward the outer part of the egg and draws hydrogen sulfide away from the yolk.

4. Microwave-cooked scrambled eggs are fluffy, moist, and a highly desirable product. Although cooking eggs in a double boiler requires a great deal of time, this method of cookery produces the creamiest scrambled eggs.

5. Egg yolks have the greatest thickening ability, followed by whole egg, with whites having the least. But two egg yolks substituted for one whole egg raise the temperature at which a gel forms. Two egg whites will lower the temperature at which a gel forms.

6. The type of milk used in a custard can significantly affect its flavor. Evaporated milk as a result of its processing, has a distinct color and flavor. The use of nonfat dry milk in the preparation of a custard produces a product lacking in richness and body.

7. Factors affecting formation and stability of egg-white foams:

    a. *Temperature:* Egg whites at room temperature reach a greater volume more quickly than refrigerated eggs because of the lowered surface tension of the warmer egg whites. However, the stability of the foam is not as great.

    b. *Concentration:* Dilution with water will increase volume but decrease the stability of an egg-white foam.

    c. *Acid:* Acids decrease the pH to near the isolectric point so that proteins are more sensitive to denaturation. Thus, acids decrease the time required to produce an egg-white foam and the foam is very stable.

    d. *Sugar:* Sugar increases the time required for development of a foam but the foam is stable.

    e. *Fat:* The addition of even a minute amount of fat interferes with the formation of an egg-white foam. Egg yolks are a common source of fat contamination.

    f. *Overbeating:* The peak of stability of egg-white foam occurs before maximum volume occurs. Thus, overbeating produces an unstable foam that has a tendency to collapse and become coarse.

8. The amount and time of addition of sugar to an egg-white foam can greatly affect the product. For optimal results, sugar is added *when the foam barely flows in the bowl.* The amount added at one time should be small, and the foam should be beaten after each addition. If sugar is added to egg white before beating has begun, extensive beating is necessary to produce a foam; this foam will be stable but reduced in volume. If a foam is beaten to the stiff stage after adding sugar, it will have a dull surface after baking.

9. The accumulation of liquid at the meringue/filling interface, called "weeping," is due to under-coagulation of the foam and is minimized by hot pudding or pie fillings. Overcoagulation of foams causes amber droplets of syrup to collect on the surface of the meringue. This beading is minimized by cool fillings. To best avoid both problems, bake meringues on hot fillings in a *hot oven 425° F (220°C) for a short time (about 4-1/2 min.).* This method also produces a more tender, less sticky meringue.

Experiment I: Effect of Storage on Egg Quality

Select 1 egg that has been stored for 1–2 weeks at room temperature and 1 egg that has been refrigerated for the same period of time.

1. Place eggs in a bowl of water. Observe whether they will float.
2. Carefully crack open egg and slip onto a *flat* dish.
3. Observe the appearance of the egg.
4. Measure the spread of the egg white at its widest point.
5. Touch the edge of the egg white pH indicator paper to determine its pH.
6. Fry both eggs by one of the following methods. Use the *same* method for each condition of storage.

Fried Egg

Standard Method

egg	1		salt	
fat	2–3 Tbsp	30–45 ml	pepper	

   a. Melt fat in a skillet over low heat until it sizzles.
   b. Carefully slip egg from the dish into the skillet.
   c. Cook until egg white is completely firm.
   d. Baste egg with fat occasionally to coagulate film of egg white over surface of yolk.
      or
   e. Gently turn egg over once without breaking yolk. Cook 1 minute more.

Low-Fat Method

egg	1	1	salt
fat	1/2 tsp	2 ml	pepper

   a. Melt fat in a skillet over low heat until it sizzles. Tilt pan and turn so that fat coats bottom of pan, or spray with a vegetable oil spray.
   b. Carefully slip egg from dish into the skillet.
   c. When egg white is firm around the edges, add 1–2 Tbsp (15–30 ml) water to the skillet surrounding the egg.
   d. Cover tightly and cook 3 minutes or until egg white is completely coagulated. Baste occasionally with the water.

7. Observe appearance of egg. Measure spread of egg white.
8. Season and serve.
9. Record results in Table 10–1.

TABLE 10-1   Effect of Storage Conditions on Egg Quality

Storage Condition	pH	Floating Ability	Position of Yolk	Appearance of White	Spread of White (cm)
Refrigerator, raw					
fried					
Room temperature, raw					
fried					

QUESTIONS

1. Why does 1 egg float? _____

_____

2. Which egg yolk is not centered? _____ Why not? _____

_____

3. What relationship does the appearance of the egg white have to do with the distance that it spreads? _____

_____

Experiment II: Factors Affecting the Coagulation Temperature of Egg Proteins

1. Separate an egg into its yolk and white. Beat each component separately with a fork.
2. Blend a whole egg until thoroughly mixed.
3. Place 1 tsp (5 ml) blended egg white into each of 5 test tubes.
4. Repeat step 3 using egg yolk or whole egg.
5. Add the following treatments to each set of eggs. Shake until well blended.

   a. none
   b. 1 tsp (5 ml) water
   c. 1/4 tsp (1 ml) lemon juice or vinegar
   d. 1/4 tsp (1 ml) sugar
   e. 1/4 tsp (1 ml) salt

6. Place a beaker filled with warm water on the burner of a stove. Arrange a thermometer to a ring stand so that the bulb of the thermometer is immersed in the water.
7. Turn heat to high. Hold the test tubes containing the nontreated whole yolk and white of the egg in the water being heated. Observe and record the temperature at which each egg component coagulates.
8. Repeat step 7 with treatment 5b; 5c; 5d; 5e.
9. Record results in Table 10-2.

TABLE 10-2   Factors Affecting the Coagulation Temperature of Egg Proteins

Treatment	Temperature of Coagulation		
	White	Yolk	Whole Egg
None			
Dilution (water)			
Acid			
Sugar			
Salt			

QUESTIONS

1. Which component of the egg coagulated at the lowest temperature? _____

   What was the effect of combining the egg yolk and egg white? _____

   Why? _____

2. How did the following affect the coagulation temperatures:

   Acid: _____

   Sugar: _____

   Salt: _____

3. What practical application would this experiment have for the preparation of poached eggs?

   _____

Experiment III: Factors That Affect the Quality of Hard-Cooked Eggs

Select 6 eggs that have been stored for 1–2 weeks at room temperature and 6 eggs that have been refrigerated for the same period of time.

1. Hard-cook 2 of the refrigerated eggs and 2 of the room temperature eggs in 2 separate saucepans according to the following recipe. Cool 1 egg from each saucepan according to the recipe; allow the other egg to cool slowly at room temperature.

Hard-Cooked Egg

   a. Bring a quantity of water that is sufficient to completely cover the egg to boiling in a saucepan over high heat.
   b. Slip egg in saucepan with a spoon; be careful not to crack egg.
   c. Cover, lower heat, and simmer 20–25 minutes.
   d. Remove egg from water with a slotted spoon.
   e. Cool under running cold water. Crack open and peel.

2. Follow step 1 above but do not lower heat. Boil vigorously for 10 minutes.
3. Repeat step 1 except boil vigorously for 20 minutes.
4. Cut cooled eggs in half. Observe and record results in Table 10–3.

TABLE 10-3   Factors That Affect the Quality of Hard-Cooked Eggs

Cooking Method	Storage Condition							
	Refrigerator				Room Temperature			
	Position of Yolk	Color Surrounding Yolk	Texture of Yolk	Tenderness of White	Position of Yolk	Color Surrounding Yolk	Texture of Yolk	Tenderness of White
Simmered, fast cool								
slow cool								
Boiled, 10 min, fast cool								
slow cool								
Boiled, 20 min, fast cool								
slow cool								

Experiment IV: Factors Affecting Quality of Poached Eggs

Select 4 Grade AA fresh eggs and 1 egg that has been allowed to deteriorate by being stored at room temperature for 1–2 weeks.

1. Cook 1 fresh egg and the deteriorated egg according to the following recipe:

Poached Eggs

    a. Bring 2 in. (5 cm) of water in a saucepan to boil.
    b. Crack open egg and slip onto a dish.
    c. Holding edge of dish close to surface of water, carefully slip egg into water.
    d. Lower heat and simmer until coagulated (3–5 minutes).
    e. Remove with a slotted spoon and drain briefly on a paper towel.

2. Follow basic recipe except add 1 Tbsp (15 ml) vinegar to step 1.
3. Follow basic recipe except add 1/2 tsp (2 ml) salt to step 1.
4. Cook 1 fresh egg according to the above recipe except create a whirlpool by stirring the water in circles with a spoon. Add the egg to the swirling water.
5. Record results in Table 10-4.

TABLE 10-4   Factors Affecting the Quality of Poached Eggs

Variation	Egg White Thickness over Yolk	Appearance of Egg White	Flavor
Simmering water, fresh egg			
+ vinegar			
+ salt			
deteriorated egg			
Swirling water			

QUESTIONS

1. What is the most striking difference between a poached fresh egg and a poached deteriorated egg?

_____

_____

2. What is the effect of the addition of vinegar? _____

_____

Why? _____

_____

3. What is the effect of the addition of salt? _____

_____

Why? _____

_____

4. Why was the water swirled and what effect did this have on the final product? _____

_____

_____

Experiment V: Factors Affecting the Quality of Scrambled Eggs

1. Prepare scrambled eggs (see Figure 10–1) by each of the following recipes. Record the preparation time for each method.

FIGURE 10-1   *Creamy scrambled eggs are produced by cooking over low heat and using minimal stirring. (Courtesy of American Egg Board.)*

Scrambled Eggs

Low Temperature

egg	1		pepper	dash	
milk	1 Tbsp	15 ml	margarine	1 tsp	5 ml
salt	dash				

    a. Place egg, milk, salt, and pepper in a small bowl or cup.

    b. Blend with a fork until mixture is a uniform color.

    c. Melt margarine in a small skillet over medium low heat.

    d. Pour egg mixture into pan.

    e. When egg begins to set at bottom, gently lift the mixture with a spatula to allow the liquid to run underneath. *Avoid overstirring.*

    f. Continue lifting and *gently* stirring until eggs are nearly coagulated, 3–5 minutes. (*Note:* Eggs will continue to coagulate for a short time after they are removed from heat.)

Double Boiler

    a. Follow basic recipe except melt margarine in a double boiler placed over *simmering* water.

    b. Stir *occasionally* until creamy.

Microwave

    a.   Melt margarine 45 seconds in a heat-resistant bowl. (Fat is not necessary but is included for comparative purposes.)

    b.   Follow steps 1 and 2 of the basic recipe.

    c.   Pour egg into dish; cover loosely with wax paper; microwave 1 minute.

    d.   Stir; if egg is not cooked; microwave another 10–15 seconds. (Do not overcook. Egg will become firmer with standing.)

2. Repeat basic recipe except eliminate milk as ingredient. Record preparation time.

3. Repeat basic recipe except use an egg substitute in place of a fresh egg. Record preparation time.

4. Repeat basic recipe for scrambled eggs except cook eggs over high heat. Record preparation time.

5. Record results in Table 10–5.

TABLE 10–5   Factors Affecting the Quality of Scrambled Eggs

Cooking Method	Preparation Time (minutes)	Appearance	Moistness	Flavor
Low temperature, milk				
no milk				
egg substitute				
High temperature				
Double boiler				
Microwave				

QUESTIONS

1. What is the effect of high temperatures in the preparation of scrambled eggs? _____

_____

_____

2. Which cooking method produced the lightest product? _____

Why? _____

_____

3. Which cooking method produced the creamiest product? _____

Why? _____

_____

4. What is the purpose of adding milk in the preparation of scrambled eggs? _____

_____

5. Does the egg substitute make a suitable replacement for fresh eggs? _____

_____ Why or why not? _____

_____

Experiment VI: Factors Affecting the Quality of Custards

1. Prepare baked and stirred custard (see Figure 10–2) according to the basic recipe.

FIGURE 10–2 *Custards are gels formed from the enmeshment of milk by the coagulated egg protein. (Courtesy of American Egg Board.)*

Egg Custard (for 2)

Basic Recipe

milk	1/2 c	125 ml	vanilla	1/2 tsp	2 ml
egg	1/2		salt	dash	
sugar	1 Tbsp	15 ml	nutmet	dash	

    a. Scald milk to 185°F (85°C) for 1 minute. Cool the milk by placing the pan in cool water.
    b. Blend egg, sugar, vanilla and salt in a bowl until thoroughly mixed.
    c. Add milk to egg mixture and blend.

Baked
    a. Preheat oven to 350°F (177°C).
    b. Follow basic recipe.
    c. Pour equal amounts of egg-milk mixture into 2 custard cups.
    d. Sprinkle with nutmeg.
    e. Place cups into a pan of *hot* water 1 in. (2.5 cm) deep.
    f. Bake for 45 minutes or until a knife inserted 1 in. (2.5 cm) from side of cup comes out clean. Test by gently shaking. Do **not** allow custard to curdle from overcooking.

Stirred
    a. Follow basic recipe except do not add vanilla or salt in step (b).
    b. Pour egg-milk mixture into the top of a double boiler. Place the top over the bottom of a double boiler filled with *simmering* water. Do not allow the water to touch the top pan.
    c. Heat over medium heat 20 minutes until the mixture coats the back of a spoon, 172–183°F (78–84°C).
    d. Remove pan from bottom of double boiler and place in cool water. Stir.
    e. Add vanilla and salt. Stir again.
    f. Serve sprinkled with nutmeg if desired.
    Note: If custard curdles from overcooking, beat mixture with a rotary beater until smooth again.

2. Repeat preparation of custards using the following teatments:

    a. baking without being immersed in water.
    b. doubling the amount of egg yolk (to 1 yolk).
    c. doubling the amount of egg white (to 1 white).
    d. doubling the amount of whole egg (to 1 egg).
    e. substituting reconstituted evaporated milk for whole milk, that is equal amounts of cold water and evaporated milk.
    f. substituting reconstituted nonfat dry milk for whole milk.
    g. doubling the amount of sugar.
    h. eliminating the sugar.
    i. adding 1 tsp (5 ml) of lemon juice to step (b) of the basic recipe.

3. Record results in Table 10–6.

TABLE 10-6   Factors Affecting the Quality of Custards

Treatment	Baked			Stirred		
	Appearance	*Texture*	*Flavor*	*Appearance*	*Texture*	*Flavor*
None						
Baking with-out water				—	—	—
2 × egg yolk						
2 × egg white						
2 × whole egg						
Evaporated milk						
Nonfat dry milk						
2 × sugar						
No sugar						
Lemon juice						

QUESTIONS

1. Why is stirred custard different in texture from baked custard? _____

   _____

   _____

2. What happens when a custard is allowed to overcook? _____

   _____

3. Why does surrounding the custard with water minimize curdling? _____

   _____

   Why must the water be *hot*? _____

   _____

4. What is the effect of adding extra egg yolks to a custard? _____
_____

Extra egg whites? _____
_____

Extra whole egg? _____
_____

5. What effect does the type of milk have on the quality of a custard? _____
_____
_____

6. What is the function of sugar in a custard? _____
_____
_____

7. How does lemon juice affect custard? _____
_____
_____

8. Why is vanilla added after the stirred custard has been cooked rather than at the beginning?
_____
_____
_____

Experiment VII: Factors Affecting the Appearance and Volume of Egg-White Foams

1. Blend 3/4 c + 2 Tbsp (210 ml) egg white.
2. Place 2 Tbsp (30 ml) of egg white into a 2 c (500 ml) measure.
3. Place one of the measuring cups with egg whites in the freezer to chill.
4. Beat egg whites until foamy using one of the following treatments:

   a. Add 1 Tbsp (15 ml) tap water
   b. Add 1/8 tsp (0.5 ml) cream of tartar
   c. Add 2 Tbsp (30 ml) sugar
   d. Add 1/2 tsp (2 ml) egg yolk
   e. Continue beating until peaks are dry and curdled
   f. Use the chilled egg whites
   g. None (room temperature egg whites)

5. Beat egg whites until the peaks are stiff, not dry, hold their shape, and the foam no longer slips when the bowl is tilted (see Figure 10–3). Do not overbeat except for step 4e above. Record beating time.
6. Observe appearance; level with rubber spatula and record volume.
7. Let samples stand 15 minutes.
8. Repeat step 6.
9. Record results in Table 10–7.

TABLE 10–7   Factors Affecting the Appearance and Volume of Egg-White Foams

Treatment	Beating Time (minutes)	Initial		After 15 Minutes	
		Appearance	Volume	Appearance	Volume
Dilution (water)					
Acid					
Sugar					
Fat (egg yolk)					
Overbeating					
Cold temperature					
Room temperature					

FIGURE 10–3   In egg whites beaten to the stiff-peak stage, only the tips of peaks fall over when the beater is pulled away. (Courtesy of American Egg Board.)

QUESTIONS

1. Which treatment produced the largest increase in volume? _____
_____ The least? _____
Why? _____
_____

2. How did water increase the volume? _____
_____
Was it stable? _____ Why or why not? _____
_____

3. Which treatment produced the most stable foam? _____
Why? _____
_____

4. Which treatment produced the least stable foam? _____
Why? _____

5. What are the practical applications of this experiment? _____
_____

Experiment VIII: Effect of Time of Addition of Sugar on the Appearance, Beating Time, and Volume of Egg-White Foam

1. Preheat oven to 375°F (190°C).
2. Place 2 Tbsp (30 ml) of egg white into a 2 c (500 ml) measure.
3. Add 2 Tbsp (30 ml) sugar to the egg whites at one of the following steps:
   a. in the beginning
   b. when the egg white is foamy
   c. when the peaks are soft, rounded, and fall over
   d. when the peaks are stiff and hold their shape
   e. when the peaks are dry and very stiff
4. Beat the egg whites until the peaks are stiff for all except 3e, in which the egg whites are beaten dry. Do not overbeat. Record beating time.
5. Observe appearance; level with rubber spatula and record volume.
6. Place even-sized mounds on a baking sheet. Bake until the meringues are evenly browned.
7. Remove from oven and observe. Record results in Table 10–8.

TABLE 10–8   Effect of Time of Addition of Sugar on Beating Time, Volume, and Appearance of Egg-White Foam

Addition of Sugar	Beating Time	Volume	Appearance		Comments
			Raw	Baked	
Beginning					
Foamy					
Soft peaks					
Stiff peaks					
Dry					

QUESTIONS

1. At what point should sugar be added in the preparation of egg white foam? _____
   _____

2. What happens when sugar is added at the beginning of the beating period? _____
   _____

3. What is the result of overbeating egg whites? _____
   _____

4. Which method produced the best volume? _____ Was the foam
   stable? Why or why not? _____
   _____
   _____

Experiment IX: Effect of Temperature on the Quality of Meringue

1. Preheat 2 ovens; one to 425°F (220°C) and one to 325°F (160°C).
2. Prepare 1/2 package of commercial pudding mix. Use 1 c (250 ml) milk unless label direction indicates otherwise.
3. Pour prepared pudding into 4 small pie pans or custard cups.
4. Place 2 of the pie pans into a larger pan. Surround the pie pans with hot water to keep the pudding hot. Cover and keep warm.
5. Place the other 2 pie pans in cold water. Cool to 50–60°F (10–15°C).
6. Beat 1 egg white until soft peaks form. Add 1–1/2 Tbsp (22 ml) sugar and beat until peaks are stiff.

7. Spread 1/4 of the meringue on top of the puddings. Make sure the meringue touches the sides of the dish.
8. Bake 1 hot and 1 cold pudding topped with meringue at 425°F (220°C).
9. Bake the other hot and cold pudding topped with meringue at 325°F (160°C).
10. Observe appearance. Cut, observe again and record results in Table 10–9.

QUESTIONS

1. Which combination of oven and pudding temperatures produced the best product in terms of appearance? _____

   In terms of minimal leakage? _____

   Why? _____

   _____

2. Why did the weeping occur? _____

   _____

TABLE 10–9   Effect of Temperature on the Appearance and Leakage of Meringue

Oven Temperature	Surface		Inner	
	Appearance	Weeping	Appearance	Leakage
Hot, hot filling				
cold filling				
Cold, hot filling				
cold filling				

APPLICATIONS

Huevos Rancheros

Salsa Ranchero	1/2 c	125 ml	tortillas (optional)	2
oil	2 Tbsp	30 ml	eggs	2

1. (Optional) Heat oil in skillet. Add tortillas and fry lightly on both sides for 30 seconds. Do not allow tortillas to become crisp. Drain tortillas on paper towel and place on serving plate.
2. Fry eggs in oil according to Standard Method in Experiment I.
3. Place eggs on tortillas; cover with Salsa Ranchero and serve.

Salsa Ranchero

tomato	1		garlic clove	1/2	
chili serrano, seeded	1/4		oil	1 Tbsp	15 ml
			onion	2 Tbsp	30 ml
or			salt	1/8 tsp	0.5 ml
jalepeno, canned, seeded	1/4				

1. Broil tomato 4–6 in. (10–15 cm) from heat for approximately 10 minutes until it is cooked and the skin is blistered and charred.
2. Slip skin off tomato.
3. Place tomato, chili, and garlic in a blender. Blend for 10 seconds.
4. Heat oil in a skillet over medium heat. Add onions and sauté 5 minutes until soft.
5. Add salt and tomato-chili mixture to skillet.
6. Cook 5 minutes until sauce is reduced.

Deviled Eggs

eggs, hard-cooked	3		lemon juice	1 tsp	5 ml
mayonnaise	2 Tbsp	30 ml	salt	1/8 tsp	0.5 ml
Worchestershire sauce	1/2 tsp	2 ml	pepper	dash	
			onion, grated	1/2 tsp	2 ml
mustard, prepared	1/2 tsp	2 ml	paprika (optional)	dash	

1. Split hard-cooked eggs in half lengthwise.
2. Scoop out yolk and mash.
3. Add remaining ingredients and mix thoroughly.
4. Spoon yolk mixture back into egg white shells.
5. Sprinkle with paprika if desired.
6. Chill and serve.

Salzburger Nockerl

Chocolate sauce			cream of tartar	1/4 tsp	1 ml
almonds, sliced	2 Tbsp	30 ml	salt	dash	
margarine			flour	1-1/2 Tbsp	22 ml
sugar (divided)	1/4 c	50 ml	vanilla	3/4 tsp	3 ml
eggs	3				

1. Preheat oven to 375°F (190°C).
2. Prepare chocolate sauce.
3. Spread almonds on aluminum foil on a cookie sheet. Toast in oven until lightly browned. Set aside. Watch carefully because these easily burn.
4. Grease a 7-in. (18 cm) ceramic casserole dish with margarine. Sprinkle with 2 tsp (10 ml) sugar. Shake out any excess sugar and set aside.
5. Separate eggs into yolks and whites. Discard one of the yolks.
6. Place the 3 egg whites into a deep bowl. Beat egg whites with an electric beater at medium speed until foamy. Add cream of tartar and salt and beat at high speed until soft peaks form.
7. *Gradually* beat in 2 Tbsp + 1 tsp (35 ml) sugar. Beat until egg whites form stiff peaks. Set aside.
8. Beat egg yolks in a separate small deep bowl until light-colored. Gradually beat in 1 Tbsp (15 ml) sugar. Continue beating until the mixture is very thick and lemon-colored. The total beating time will be at least 5 minutes.
9. Add the flour to the egg yolks and beat until smooth.
10. Add the vanilla to the egg yolk and beat until blended.
11. Pour the egg yolk mixture over the egg whites. Fold in just until color is uniform.
12. Pour foam as three mounds in the casserole dish. Use a rubber spatula to swirl each mound up to create a peak.
13. Bake 10 minutes or until golden.
14. Sprinkle with toasted almonds.
15. Serve hot with a portion of the hot chocolate sauce drizzled over the top of each serving.

Chocolate Sauce

unsweetened chocolate	1 oz	30 g	cold water	2/3 c	180 ml
sugar	1-1/2 Tbsp	22 ml	vanilla	3/4 tsp	3 ml

1. Combine chocolate, sugar, and cold water in a small, heavy saucepan.
2. Cook over medium-high heat, stirring constantly until mixture just starts to boil.
3. Immediately lower heat and let simmer approximately 30 minutes. The mixture will become thicker as the water evaporates.
4. Remove from heat and stir in vanilla.
5. Serve warm.

French Omelet

margarine	1 Tbsp	15 ml
eggs	3	
water	1 Tbsp	15 ml
salt	1/4 tsp	1 ml
pepper	dash	

1. Beat all ingredients together until well blended with a fork or rotary beater. Avoid producing a foam.
2. Melt margarine in a 10 in. (25 cm) Teflon frying pan over low heat.
3. When margarine bubbles, tilt pan to cover the bottom and sides with fat. Add eggs.
4. Turn heat to medium. Begin sliding skillet back and forth while lifting eggs with a spatula to let uncooked portion run underneath.
5. Discontinue the lifting when eggs begin to completely coagulate to avoid tearing holes in the omelet.
6. Check bottom of omelet; if not brown, let it cook a few more seconds to lightly brown the bottom.
7. Loosen around the edge with a spatula.
8. Pour or sprinkle filling on 1/2 of the omelet if desired. Keep filling 1/2 in. (1.8 cm) from edge.
9. Tilt pan; loosen omelet with spatula and fold. Serve.
   or
9. Tilt pan; loosen omelet with rubber spatula and roll onto the serving dish.

Italian Omelet

margarine	2 Tbsp	30 ml	basil	1/8 tsp	0.5 ml
zucchini, thinly	1/2 c	125 ml	salt	1/4 tsp	1 ml
sliced			pepper	1/8 tsp	0.5 ml
onion slice	2		Romano cheese	1 Tbsp	15 ml
eggs	3		tomato, fresh,	1/4	
water	3 Tbsp	45 ml	diced		
oregano	1/4 tsp	1 ml			

1. Melt 1 Tbsp (15 ml) margarine in a small skillet over medium-high heat. Add zucchini and onion. Sauté 5–8 minutes until tender.
2. Combine the eggs, water, oregano, basil, salt, and pepper in a bowl. Beat with a fork until the eggs are just blended.
3. Melt the remaining margarine in an omelet pan.
4. Stir zucchini mixture into eggs.
5. Follow steps 3–7 for preparing a French Omelet. Do not fold.
6. Sprinkle cheese and diced tomato over omelet.
7. Broil 4–6 in. (10–15 cm) from heat until cheese melts.
8. Tilt pan and slide omelet onto a dish unfolded.

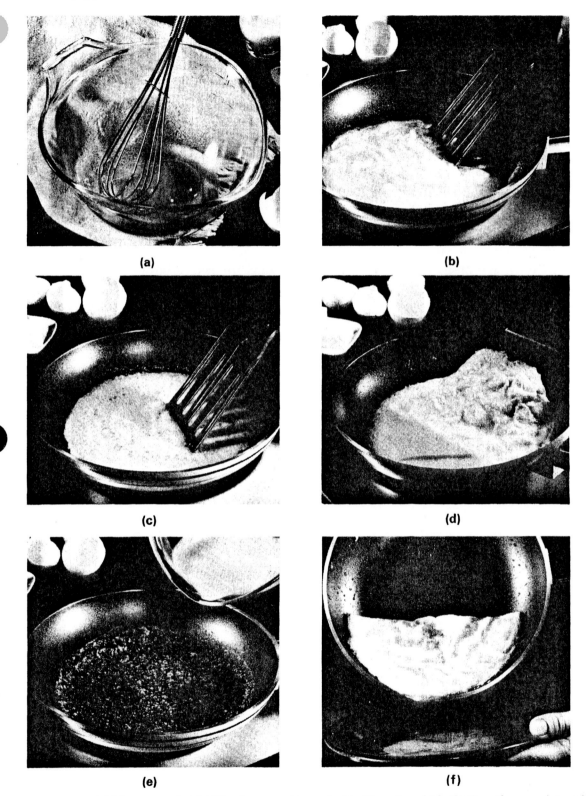

(a)

(b)

(c)

(d)

(e)

(f)

FIGURE 10-4   Making an omelet. (a) Blend eggs, water, and salt with a wire whisk. (b) Pour the egg mixture into sizzling fat. (c) Carefully draw cooked portions at edges toward the center. (d) Slide pan rapidly back and forth to keep mixture in motion while gently lifting eggs. (e) Fill the omelet with a filling when the top is still moist and creamy. (f) Turn the omelet out of the pan onto a heated plate. (Courtesy of American Egg Board.)

Puffy Omelet

eggs	2	
water	2 Tbsp	30 ml
salt	dash	
pepper	dash	
margarine	1–1/2 tsp	7 ml

1. Preheat oven to 325°F (160°C).
2. Separate eggs into whites and yolks.
3. Beat egg yolks and pepper with rotary beater until thick and lemon-colored.
4. Beat egg whites with electric beater until foamy. Add salt and water. Beat until peaks are stiff, but not dry.
5. Melt margarine in a 10 in. (25 cm) skillet over low heat.
6. Pour egg yolks down the side of the bowl of the egg white foam. Carefully fold in foam until the whites and yolks are well blended.
7. Turn heat to medium. When margarine is hot enough to sizzle a drop of water, add egg mixture. Level with spatula.
8. Cook 1 minute.
9. Place in oven for 15 minutes. A knife inserted in center should come out clean.
10. Remove from oven. Loosen underneath with a spatula. Fold in half and serve.

Quiche Lorraine

pie crust, 6 in., (15 cm)	1		egg	1	
dried beans or rice	1/3 c	80 ml	half and half	1/2 c	125 ml
bacon slices	4		salt	1/4 tsp	1 ml
swiss cheese, grated	1 oz	30 g	cayenne pepper	dash	
onion, minced	2 Tbsp	30 ml			

1. Preheat oven to 425°F (220°C).
2. Prepare pie crust:

    a. Follow recipe for pie crust on page 253.
    b. Prick bottom and sides of crust with a fork.
    c. Cover with wax paper. Fill with dried beans or rice.
    d. Bake 5 minutes until firm.
    e. Remove paper and beans. Cool.

3. Fry bacon over high heat until crisp. Drain on paper towels and crumble.
4. Mix together egg, half and half, salt, and cayenne pepper.
5. Sprinkle bacon, cheese, and onion on the pie crust.
6. Place pie pan on rack in oven. Pour egg mixture on top of bacon mixture.
7. Bake 15 minutes at 425°F (220°C). Lower heat to 350°F (175°C) and bake 10–15 minutes longer. A knife inserted halfway between the center and edge should come out clean.
8. Let stand 10 minutes before serving.

(Courtesy of American Dairy Association.)

OBJECTIVES

The student should be able to:

1. Compare the nutritive value, cost and quality of milks.
2. Identify the effects of using different forms of milk in preparing milk products.
3. Determine the effect of pH, temperature, and rennin on the coagulation of milk.
4. Distinguish factors which affect formation of milk foams.

FOOD SCIENCE PRINCIPLES

1. Homogenized milk seems richer than pasteurized milk because the milk fat particles are more evenly distributed. Reconstituted non-fat dry milks and low-fat milks and their products lack the full-bodied flavor of whole milk because of the reduction in fat content.

   An economical but palatable substitute for whole milk is to mix it half and half with reconstituted non-fat dry milk.

   Evaporated milk has a characteristic taste and brown color that results from the reaction of lactose and milk proteins during the canning process.

   Sour cream and yogurt have the same amount of calories as the cream and milk from which they are produced.

2. The proteins of milk may be coagulated by the following:

   a. *Heat:* Whey proteins are sensitive to heat and begin to coagulate at 150°F (66°C). These coagulated proteins form a precipitate along the sides and bottom of the pan and on the surface of the heated milk. The major protein in milk, casein, is relatively unaffected by heating during normal cooking temperatures and times. However, if the concentration of protein is high, such as in evaporated and sweetened condensed milks, casein will curdle more readily.

   b. *Acid:* When the pH of milk falls below 5.2, casein begins to coagulate because the negative charges that stabilize calcium phosphocaseinate micelles are neutralized by the positive charges of the hydrogen ions (from the acid). Casein salts are formed and the milk curdles.

   The curds formed by acid are soft and fragile with a high moisture content. They are relatively low in calcium because most of the calcium remains in the whey.

133

c. *Rennin:* Rennin is an enzyme that is sold commercially as an extract called rennet. When rennet is added to milk, the milk clabbers in a two-step reaction. In the first step, rennin cleaves a bond in kappa-casein to form para-kappa-casein, a protein with exposed chemical groups. In the second step, the exposed chemical groups in para-kappa-casein react with calcium to form a curd because kappa-casein no longer is present to stabilize the colloidal dispersion of casein micelles.

Rennin has optimal activity at 104°F (40°C) and a pH of 6.7. If the milk has been warmed over 149°F (65°C) and cooled, it will not clot effectively because of an interaction between kappa-casein and beta-lactoglobulin.

The curds formed by enzymes such as rennin are tough and rubbery with a low moisture content. These curds contain the majority of the calcium.

3. Combination of milk with acid foods is difficult because of curdling. The instability can be minimized by:

   a. adding the acid food to the milk (rather than the milk to the acid).
   b. heating both the acid food and milk before combination.
   c. thickening either the acid food or milk before combination.
   d. serving the combination promptly.

4. Factors that affect milk (and cream) foams:

   a. *Viscosity:* Increasing the viscosity will increase the stability of the foam. This can be achieved by the addition of excess solids (NFDM), crystals (chilled evaporated milk), or gelatin. Viscosity is also increased when proteins are coagulated from the addition of an acid during the whipping of milk or cream.
   b. *Concentration of fat:* Increasing the fat content will increase the ease of formation and stability of foams.
   c. *Temperature:* Cool temperatures cause the fat droplets to harden and clump together more easily than when they are warm and soft.
   d. *Sugar:* Sugar helps prevent overbeating by delaying curdling. But it should not be added until the end of the whipping period because prior addition increases beating time and decreases the volume of a foam.

Experiment I: Comparison of Milk Forms

Select several of the following milk forms:

Whole pasteurized milk	Reconstituted NFDM mixed half and
Whole homogenized milk	half with whole milk
2% milk	Reconstituted evaporated milk
99% fat-free milk	Buttermilk
Reconstituted nonfat dry milk	Sweetened condensed milk
(NFDM)	Goats milk

Half and half
Light cream
Heavy cream
Nondairy creamer
Sour cream
Yogurt, plain
Yogurt, fruit-flavored

1. Calculate the nutritive values of milk forms in Table 11–1.
2. Determine cost/serving from the price stamped on the container or a price list posted in the laboratory.
3. Observe each sample and taste for flavor. Do *not* sample directly out of the container. Use a clean tablespoon to remove a sample from the container and place the sample in a glass.
4. Record results in Table 11–1.

QUESTIONS

1. What is the effect of homogenization on the appearance and viscosity of milk? _____

_____

_____

2. What single factor appears to be most significant in creating a "full-bodied, rich flavor" in milk? ____

_____

Why? _____

_____

3. When a restricted budget is necessary, what would be the most acceptable milk form in terms of palatability as well as cost? _____

_____

4. How does sweetened condensed milk differ in composition from evaporated milk? _____

_____

_____

_____

_____

5. How does nondairy creamer differ in taste from fresh cream? _____

_____

_____ In cost? _____

_____

6. What is an advantage of using a nondairy creamer? _____

_____

A disadvantage? _____

7. How does the calorie content of yogurt differ from that of low-fat milk? _____

_____

_____

8. In what way does the addition of sweetened fruits to yogurt affect its calorie value? _____

_____

TABLE 11-1 Comparison of Milk Forms for Nutritive Value, Cost, Appearance, and Flavor

Milk Form	Nutritive Value/Serving[a]					Cost/ Serving[a] (¢)	Appearance	Flavor
	Energy (cal)	Protein (g)	Fat (g)	Calcium (mg)	Vitamin A (IU)			
MILK Whole, pasteurized								
Whole, homogenized								
2%								
99% fat free								
NFDM								
NFDM, whole milk								
Evaporated, undiluted								
Buttermilk								
Sweetened condensed milk								
Goat's								
CREAM Half & half								
Light								
Heavy								
Nondairy								
Sour								
YOGURT Plain								
Fruit-flavored								

[a]Serving sizes: milks and yogurt—1 c (250 ml); creams—1 Tbsp (15 ml).

Experiment II: Effect of Milk Form on the Quality of Pudding

Select 4 of the milks used in Experiment I.

1. Divide a package of *instant* pudding mix into 4 equal parts.
2. Add 1/2 c (125 ml) of milk to each part.
3. Beat with a rotary beater or the lowest speed of an electric beater 2 minutes or until thickened.
4. Chill.
5. Calculate cost/1/2 c (125 ml) serving.
6. Observe appearance and texture. Taste for flavor.
7. Record results in Table 11–2.

QUESTIONS

1. Which type of milk produced the best quality pudding? _____

   Why? _____

2. Which type of milk produced the least desirable pudding? _____

   Why? _____

3. Is the decreased cost/serving worth the difference in quality? _____

   Why or why not? _____

   _____

TABLE 11–2   Effect of Milk Form on the Cost and Quality of Pudding

Milk Form	Cost/Serving	Appearance	Flavor	Texture
1. _____				
2. _____				
3. _____				
4. _____				

Experiment III: Effect of pH and Temperature on the Coagulation of Milk

1. Add 1 Tbsp (15 ml) of lemon juice to 1 c (250 ml) of chilled whole milk. Stir.
2. Add 1 tsp (5 ml) of baking soda to 1 c (250 ml) of chilled whole milk. Stir.
3. Heat 2 c (500 ml) of milk in a saucepan until it scalds. Add 2 tsp (10 ml) lemon juice. Stir. Cover and keep warm.
4. Let stand for 30 minutes and observe.
5. Test the pH of each milk mixture with pH indicator and record.
6. If a curd forms, drain the mixture through a piece of cheese cloth folded in half. Squeeze to remove excess whey and reserve for tasting.
7. Wash curds in strainer. Chill.
8. Add a dash of salt and 2 Tbsp (30 ml) of cream to half of each of the curds to form creamed cottage cheese.
9. Record results in Table 11-3.

QUESTIONS

1. What effect does pH have on the coagulation of milk? _____
   _____
   _____

2. What is the effect of temperature on the coagulation of milk? _____
   _____
   _____

3. Which nutrients are found in the curd? _____
   _____

   The whey? _____

4. Why is cottage cheese marketed as "creamed"? _____
   _____

TABLE 11-3   Effect of pH and Temperature on the Coagulation of Milk

Condition	pH	Formation of Curd	Taste	
			Plain Curds	Creamed Curds
Acid, chilled				
heated				
Alkaline				

Experiment IV: Effect of Temperature and Rennin on the Coagulation of Milk

1. Dissolve 2 rennet tablets in 5 tsp (25 ml) cold water.
2. Add by stirring, 1 tsp (5 ml) rennet mixture to 1 c (250 ml) milk that has been treated by one of the following methods:
   a. chilled by refrigeration
   b. warmed to 160°F (71°C) for 5 minutes, chilled
   c. warmed to 105°F (41°C)
   d. warmed to 160°F (71°C) for 5 minutes, chilled, warmed to 105°F (41°C)

3. Place the cups containing the chilled milk and one of the warmed milks in a pan containing crushed ice. Pack ice around cup and refrigerate.
4. Keep the other warm milk and the boiled milk in a warm place in the room.
5. Let stand 25 minutes and observe.
6. Cut through curd to break into a few *large* pieces. Lift with slotted spoon and place on a display plate.
7. Compare curd formed by rennin to that formed by acid in Experiment III.
8. Record results in Table 11–4.

TABLE 11–4   Effect of Temperature and Rennin on the Coagulation of Milk

Temperature Conditions	Formation of Curd	Appearance of Curd	Comparison to Curd Formed by Acid
Chilled			
Warmed 160°F (71°C), chilled			
Warmed 105°F (41°C)			
Warmed 160°F (71°C), chilled, warmed 105°F (41°C)			

QUESTIONS

1. Which temperature conditions were the optimum for producing a curd? _____
   _____

2. What effect did chilling the milk have on enzyme activity? _____
   _____

3. What was the effect of warming the milk to 160°F (71°C)? _____
   _____

   Why did this happen? _____
   _____

4. How did the curds formed by the action of rennin differ from those formed by acid? _____
   _____
   _____
   _____

5. Which nutrients are found in the curd? _____
   _____

   The whey? _____
   _____

Experiment V: Combination of Milk with Acid Foods

1. Prepare the following combination in a saucepan over medium-low heat using 1/2 c (125 ml) tomato juice and 2 Tbsp (30 ml) milk. Use 1/2 tsp (2 ml) of flour to thicken where indicated. Hot refers to simmering temperatures of 185°F (85°C). Cold refers to refrigerator temperatures. If available, use a microwave oven to heat the milk.

   a. cold milk to cold tomato juice
   b. hot milk to cold tomato juice
   c. hot tomato juice to hot milk
   d. cold tomato juice to hot thickened milk
   e. hot tomato juice to hot thickened milk
   f. hot thickened tomato juice to cold milk

2. Observe appearance and record.
3. Heat and keep warm over medium-low heat for 15 minutes. Be careful not to scorch.
4. Observe appearance and record results in Table 11–5.

TABLE 11-5   Appearance of Milk Combined with Acid Foods

Combination		Appearance	
Add	*To*	*Initial*	*After 15 Minutes*
Cold milk	Cold juice		
Hot milk	Cold juice		
Hot juice	Hot milk		
Cold juice	Hot, thickened milk		
Hot juice	Hot, thickened milk		
Hot, thickened juice	Cold milk		

QUESTIONS

1. Which combination of unthickened liquids produces the best initial appearance? _____

   _____

2. What happens when this combination is kept warm for a period of time? _____

   _____

3. How does thickening of one of the liquids affect the stability of the mixture? _____

   _____

   _____

   Why? _____

4. Is there a change in stability when the thickened mixture is heated for a period of time? _____

   _____

   Why or why not? _____

   _____

5. Which of the above combinations produced the most stable mixture? _____

   _____

6. How could this information be applied in cooking? _____

   _____

   _____

Experiment VI: Factors Affecting Milk Foams

1. Prepare whipped foams in graduated 2 c (500 ml) liquid measuring cups. Use a rotary beater or an electric mixer on medium speed to produce a foam that forms mounds. Do not overbeat because a broken emulsion in a milk foam cannot be recombined. Because only a few seconds of extra beating of whipped cream can turn it into butter, stop beating as soon as it has the appearance of whipped cream.

2. Prepare whipped foams using 1/2 c (125 ml) of heavy cream by the following methods. Record preparation time for each method.

   a. *Room temperature:* Use cream that is at room temperature.
   b. *Chilled:* Use beaters, cup, and cream that have been chilled in the refrigerator or freezer.
   c. *Sugar added initially:* Follow step 2b. Dissolve 1 Tbsp (15 ml) sugar in cream prior to beating.
   d. *Sugar added at end:* Follow step 2b. Fold in 1 Tbsp (15 ml) sugar when whipping is completed.
   e. *Overwhipped:* Whip cream until emulsion breaks and butter is formed. Drain butter, squeeze out liquid, and press together into a block.

3. Prepare whipped foams using 1/2 c (125 ml) of undiluted evaporated milk by the following methods:

   a. *Room temperature:* Follow instructions for 2a.
   b. *Chilled:* Place beaters, cup and milk in freezer until crystals appear. Whip milk.
   c. *Addition of lemon juice and sugar:* Follow instructions for 3b. Fold in 1 Tbsp (15 ml) lemon juice and 2 Tbsp (30 ml) sugar when whipping is completed.
   d. *Addition of gelatin:* Dissolve 1 tsp (5 ml) gelatin in 1/4 c (50 ml) water. Add to NFDM solids and whip as in 4a.

4. Prepare whipped foams using 1/2 c (125 ml) nonfat dry milk (NFDM) solids and 1/3 c (80 ml) ice water by the following methods:

   a. *Standard:* Whip solids and water until the foam stands in mounds.
   b. *2 × water:* Double the amount of water to 150 ml and whip.
   c. *Addition of lemon juice and sugar:* Follow instructions for 4a. Fold in 1 Tbsp (15 ml) lemon juice and 2 Tbsp (30 ml) sugar when whipping is completed.
   d. *Addition of gelatin:* Dissolve 1 tsp (5 ml) gelatin in 1/3 c (80 ml) cold water. Add to NFDM solids and whip as in 4a.

5. Level each of the foams with a spatula and measure volume.
6. Observe appearance and stability.
7. *Optional:* Place a funnel fitted with filter paper in a graduated cylinder. Place foam in top of funnel. Let stand 30 minutes. Measure and record volume of drainage.
8. Calculate cost per 1/3 c (80 ml) serving.
9. Observe appearance and stability. Taste for flavor.
10. Record all results in Table 11–6.

TABLE 11-6   Factors Affecting Milk Foams

Milk Foam	Cost/ Serving	Prepara-tion Time (minutes)	Volume (ml)	Drainage (ml)	Appearance		Stability		Flavor
					Initial	30 Min.	Initial	30 Min.	
HEAVY CREAM room temperature		5 m	150		foamy	foamy	soft but stable	same	
chilled		5 m	175	0	thick, chunky	same	very stable	same	
sugar, added initial		3 m	133.5	1	white/ wet	glossy	not strong	runny	
sugar, added end		10 m	140	½ ml	white; fluffy	same	peaks	still stiff	
over-whipped		1 m	118.3	3.5	yellow/ fluffy	pry yellow	light, fluffy	light, firm	
EVAPORATED room temperature		5 ½ s	300	100 ~~225~~	fluffy, porous	liquid	solid	runny	
chilled		1.5 m	450	25	thick, foamy	foamy; good	foamy, runny	milky, good →	
+ lemon juice and sugar		1 m. y	450	25	thick	some	good	good	
+ gelatin		8	140	1	thick white	white air	thick	some	
NFDM standard		15 m	300 ml	270 ml	watery	very whipped; runny	watery	stands	
2 × water		5 m	600	60	watery foamy	foamy	watery	stands	
+ lemon juice and sugar		15	500	10	tan white	white	liquid	stable	
+ gelatin		25	250	250	yellow	off white	very runny	foamy liquid	

QUESTIONS

1. What is the effect of temperature on the formation of milk foams? _____
   _____

2. In what way does sugar affect the stability of milk foams? _____
   _____

   Acid? _____

3. Explain the effect of gelatin in producing a stable foam. _____
   _____
   _____

4. If there is no fat in nonfat dry milk solids, how can a foam be produced? _____
   _____
   _____

5. Which method produces the least expensive but acceptable product? _____
   _____

6. Which foam is the easiest to prepare? _____
   The most expensive? _____

7. Which of the foams, heavy cream, evaporated milk or nonfat dry milk solids, was the most
   stable? _____
   Why? _____
   _____

   The best appearance? _____
   The most palatable? _____

● **APPLICATIONS**

Chocolate Peanut Butter Float

cocoa	1 Tbsp + 1 tsp	20 ml	milk	1-1/2 c	375 ml
sugar	2 Tbsp	30 ml	peanut butter	2 Tbsp	30 ml
salt	dash		vanilla ice	4 scoops	
water	2 Tbsp	30 ml	cream		

1. Follow steps 1–4 for Breakfast Cocoa, pg. 30.
2. Remove pan from heat. Pour syrup into a blender.
3. Add milk and peanut butter to the blender.
4. Blend at high speed for 5 seconds.
5. Add 2 scoops of ice cream. Blend just until smooth.
6. Pour into 2 serving glasses.
7. Add a scoop of ice cream to each glass.
8. Serve immediately.

Frosted Chocolate Milkshake

cold milk	1 c	250 ml
chocolate syrup	2 Tbsp	30 ml
chocolate ice cream, scoops	4	

1. Prepare a frosted glass by dipping glass in ice water and placing it in the coldest part of the freezer.
2. Place all ingredients in a blender.
3. Blend until thick and creamy.
4. Pour into a frosted glass and serve immediately.

Baked Rice Pudding

milk	1-1/4 c	300 ml	sugar	3 Tbsp	45 ml
water	1/4 c	50 ml	egg, beaten	1	
instant rice, uncooked	1/4 c	50 ml	nutmeg	dash	
			salt	1/8 tsp	0.5 ml

1. Scald milk and let cool.
2. Bring water to a boil over high heat in a saucepan.
3. Remove pan from heat. Stir in rice. Cover and let stand 5 minutes.
4. Bring water to boil in the lower half of a double boiler.
5. Combine milk, sugar, egg, nutmeg, and salt in the top pan of the double boiler. Place top pan in position. Do not let the boiling water touch the top pan.
6. Stir in cooked rice.
7. Heat 15 minutes, stirring occasionally.
8. Preheat oven to 350°F (175°C).
9. Grease a small casserole dish with margarine.
10. Pour mixture into casserole dish.
11. Bake 20 minutes until lightly browned.

Corn Chowder

bacon slice	1		heavy cream	1/4 c	50 ml
onion, chopped	1/3 c	80 ml	milk	3/4 c	180 ml
green pepper, chopped	3 Tbsp	45 ml	salt pepper	1/4 tsp dash	1 ml
frozen corn	3/4 c	180 ml	nutmeg	dash	
pimento, chopped	2 tsp	10 ml			

1. Fry bacon in a skillet over high heat until crisp. Drain on paper towels. Crumble.
2. Add onions and green peppers. Sauté until onions turn soft.
3. Add corn and pimentos. Cover, and simmer 10–15 minutes, stirring occasionally.
4. Stir in heavy cream, milk, salt, pepper, and nutmeg.
5. Simmer 3 minutes. Do not allow to boil.
6. Pour into serving bowl. Top with crumbled bacon.

(Courtesy of Wisconsin Milk Marketing Board, Inc.)

Cheese

OBJECTIVES

The student should be able to:

1. Compare the nutritive value, cost, uses, and quality of cheeses.
2. Identify market forms of cheeses.
3. Describe the effect of heat on cheeses.
4. Distinguish the effect of cheese variety on the quality of cheese sauce.
5. Prepare and compare products made with cheeses.

FOOD SCIENCE PRINCIPLES

1. Cheese, a highly concentrated form of milk, is rich in nutrients. The protein, calcium, riboflavin, vitamin A, sodium, and food-energy values of most cheeses are high.
2. Cheese varieties are differentiated according to their flavor, body, and texture. Factors that influence these are:

    a. type of milk used
    b. quantity of salt, colors, and other seasonings
    c. bacterial species and mold used for innoculation
    d. manufacturing and processing methods
    e. environmental conditions during ripening, such as temperature, humidity, and curing time

3. In general, cheese may be classified as the following:

    a. *Unripened cheese:* Unripened cheese has a high moisture content and is eaten fresh within a few weeks. The curd is soft and fragile because it has been coagulated primarily by acid.
    b. *Ripened cheese:* Ripened cheese has a low moisture content and is ripened for 3 months to 2 years before it is eaten in order to develop its flavor and texture. The curd is tough and rubbery because it has been coagulated by the action of an enzyme such as rennin. During ripening, the action of enzymes, bacteria, molds, or yeast hydrolyze the casein curds to amino acids and ammonia, the fat to fatty acids and acetate, and the lactose to lactic acid. The breakdown of these nutrients changes the rubbery "green" cheese to a soft and sometimes crumbly solid.

4. Cheese is a high protein, high fat food that is sensitive to heat. When heated, the proteins coagulate and the fat melts. When overheated, the coagulated proteins become tough and rubbery and the fat emulsion may break. The time of heat penetration can be decreased by increasing the surface area via shredding or dicing.

5. Some types of cheeses are more suitable than others for use in cheese sauces and blended products. Green cheese is difficult to use in cooking because it does not blend well and does not have much characteristic flavor. Sharp cheese blends better and has more flavor than mild cheese because it has been ripened longer. The stringiness of cheddar cheese can be modified by combining it with a white sauce that helps keep the fat emulsified. Process cheeses blend easily and are resistant to fat separation because of the presence of emulsifiers.

Exercise I: Calculation of Cost and Nutritive Value of Cheeses

1. Calculate the nutritive value of cheeses in Table 12–1.
2. Determine the cost/lb of cheese by visiting a supermarket or from a price list posted in the laboratory.
3. Record results in Table 12–1.

TABLE 12–1 Cost and Nutritive Value of Cheeses

Cheese	Cost/lb (500 g)	Food Energy (Cal)	Protein (g)	Fat (g)	Calcium (mg)	Vitamin A (I.U.)	Ribo-flavin (mg)	Sodium (mg)
Blue								
Cheddar								
Cottage								
Cream								
Parmesan								
Process American								

QUESTIONS

1. Which cheeses are the most economical? _____

   The most expensive? _____

2. Which two cheeses have the lowest calcium content? _____

   Why? _____

3. Cheeses, in general, are considered excellent sources of which nutrients? _____

   _____

Exercise II: Comparison of Market Forms of Cheese

Select a variety of the cheeses listed in Table 12–2.

1. Divide each type of cheese into a sufficient number of cubes for everyone to taste.
2. Observe the appearance and texture of each cheese.
3. Sniff the odor and taste for flavor.
4. Record results in Table 12–2.

QUESTIONS

1. What is the effect of ripening on the texture of cheeses? _____

   _____

   _____

   Why does this occur? _____

   _____

2. How is the flavor related to the degree of ripening? _____

   _____

   _____

3. Why is the texture of processed, low-fat, low-cholesterol, and spread cheeses different from the

   texture of the cheese from which it was made? _____

   _____

   _____

4. Why is the curd of soft, unripened cheeses so different from that of the other types of cheeses?

   _____

   _____

   _____

TABLE 12–2   Comparison of Market Forms of Cheese

Variety of Cheese	Appearance	Texture	Odor	Flavor	Uses
HARD, RIPENED, GRATING Parmesan					
Romano					
HARD, RIPENED Cheddar					
Colby					
Edam					
Provolone					
SEMISOFT, RIPENED Brick					
Muenster					
SOFT, RIPENED, BACTERIA Brie					
Camembert					
SOFT, RIPENED, MOLD Blue					
Gorgonzola					
SOFT, UNRIPENED Cottage					
Cream					
PROCESS American					
SPREAD _____					
LOW-FAT, LOW-CHOLESTEROL _____					

Experiment I: Effect of Heat on Cheeses

1. Grate 4 tsp (20 g) of the following cheeses: blue, sharp Cheddar, mild Parmesan, and process American.
2. Divide each of the grated cheese into 2 parts of 2 tsp (10 g) each.
3. Cover 2 broiler pans with aluminum foil, dull side out.
4. Arrange 5 quarter slices of bread on each broiler pan.
5. Turn oven to broil.
6. Sprinkle 2 tsp (10 ml) of each of the cheeses over the bread. Each broiler pan should have 5 quarter slices of bread with 5 different types of cheese.
7. Place 1 broiler pan in the oven.
8. Broil until the cheeses begin to melt.
9. Remove pan from oven. Observe appearance.
10. Cut each piece of bread in half and note the stringiness of the cheese.
11. Taste each cheese for texture and flavor.
12. Repeat step 7, 9, 10, 11. Instead of step 8, broil until *just* before the cheeses begin to char.
13. Record results in Table 12–3.

QUESTIONS

1. What is the effect of overheating cheeses? _Dries out & hardens_

2. Which type of cheese has the best appearance when melted? _cheddars_

The least amount of stringiness? _parmesan_
Why? _hard cheese_

TABLE 12–3 Effect of Heat on Cheeses

Variety of Cheese	Melted				Overheated			
	Appearance	Stringiness	Texture	Flavor	Appearance	Stringiness	Texture	Flavor
Blue	melted, inconsistent	crumbly	creamy, stretchy	tangy	bloated	no flex	soft, dry	rotten
Cheddar, process American	waxy, rubbery	none	dry	bland	bloated	no flex	crispy	burnt
sharp	dark yellow, greasy	slight	dry	little more bite	puckered, deflated	no flex	hard	bland, burnt
mild	dry	dry	rubbery	bland	dry, crispy	minimal	hard, rubbery	bland, burnt
Parmesan	dry	not elastic	tough	sharp, strong	bloated	tough	really hard	rotten

Experiment II: Effect of Cheese Variety on the Quality of Cheese Sauce

1. Grate 1 oz (30 g) of the following cheeses: Blue, process American, sharp Cheddar, cheese spread, Mozzarella, and Parmesan.
2. Prepare 3 c (750 ml) of thin white sauce, pg. 106.
3. Divide the white sauce into six 1/2 c (125 ml) portions and place each in a small saucepan over low heat.
4. Add 1 oz (30 g) of each cheese to each saucepan, stirring constantly. Record the time it takes for the cheese sauce to become homogeneous.
5. Observe the color and consistency. Taste for flavor.
6. Record results in Table 12–4.

QUESTIONS

1. Which type of cheese produces the best cheese sauce? _____

   Why? _____

2. Should any of the above cheeses *not* be recommended for use in a cheese sauce? _____

   Why or why not? _____

   _____

3. Which type of cheese took the longest time to achieve homogeneity? _____

   _____ Why? _____

TABLE 12–4   Effect of Cheese Variety on the Quality of Cheese Sauce

Variety of Cheese	Preparation Time (minutes)	Color	Consistency	Flavor
Blue				
Cheddar, process American				
sharp				
spread				
Parmesan				

APPLICATIONS

Cheese Manicotti

Crepes (12)

milk	1 c	250 ml
eggs	2	
flour	1–1/4 c	310 ml
olive oil	2 tsp	10 ml
salt	dash	

Filling

ricotta cheese	1–1/2 c	375 ml
Parmesan cheese	3 Tbsp	45 ml
parsley, minced	3 Tbsp	45 ml
egg, beaten	1	

Topping

tomato sauce	2 c	500 ml
mozzarella cheese, grated	1/3 c	80 ml

1. Measure milk and set aside.
2. Beat eggs with a wire whisk until well blended.
3. Gradually beat in approximately 1/2 the flour until batter is smooth.
4. Add 2 Tbsp (30 ml) of the measured milk to the egg–flour mixture.
5. Beat batter until smooth. Beat in remaining flour.
6. Beat in remaining milk, olive oil, and salt.
7. Let batter rest 5 minutes.
8. Preheat electric crepemaker.
9. Pour batter into a pie plate the size of the crepemaker.
10. Prepare crepes: Follow manufacturer's instructions for the crepemaker *or* insert teflon part of crepemaker into batter for 3 seconds. Immediately turn over and let crepe cook until the batter sets and the crepe can be lifted up at the edges, approximately 2 minutes. If the batter seems too thin, 1 Tbsp (15 ml) flour can be beaten in. If the batter becomes too thick toward the end, a small amount of milk can be added.
11. Gently remove crepe and place on a plate. The crepes can be stacked on top of one another because they will not stick together. The crepes are *not* cooked on the second side.
12. Preheat oven to 350°F (175°C).
13. Prepare filling while crepes are cooking:
    a. Combine cheeses and parsley.
    b. Add egg and mix until smooth and creamy.
14. Prepare manicotti:
    a. Spoon a thin layer of spaghetti sauce on the bottom of an 8 × 8 in. (20 × 20 cm) square baking dish.
    b. Place a heaping Tbsp of filling in a horizontal position at one end of a crepe. Spread filling in a thick line to within 3/4 in. (2 cm) of edges. Roll crepe up like a jelly roll. Tuck ends under.
    c. Place crepes seam side down in baking dish.
    d. Repeat until the filling is gone.
    e. Cover crepes with a thin layer of tomato sauce.
    f. Sprinkle with mozzarella cheese.
15. Bake crepes until heated through and sauce bubbles, approximately 20 minutes.

Note: If a crepemaker is not available, crepes can be made in a non-stick frying pan. Place a small amount of olive oil in pan until it sizzles. Add 1 Tbsp (15 ml) batter and immediately turn pan back and forth to help shape and spread the batter. The crepe should be approximately 5 in. (13 cm) in diameter. Cook only 1–2 minutes until batter is set and crepe can be lifted up at edges. Remove with spatula *without cooking second side.*

New York Cheesecake

graham cracker crumbs	1/2 c	125 ml	egg, beaten	1	
			lemon juice, fresh	1 tsp	5 ml
margarine, melted	2 Tbsp	30 ml	vanilla	1/2 tsp	2 ml
cream cheese	6 oz	180 g	Strawberry topping	(see below)	
sugar	1/3 c	80 ml			

1. Preheat oven to 350°F (175°C).
2. Grease a 6-in. (15 cm) pie pan with margarine.
3. Mix together the graham cracker crumbs and the melted margarine.
4. Reserve 1 Tbsp (15 ml) of the crumbs for a topping. Press remaining crumbs into a crust for the pie pan. Chill in freezer.
5. Cream cream cheese until soft.
6. Gradually beat in sugar.
7. Beat in egg until smooth. Add lemon juice and vanilla and beat until smooth.
8. Pour mixture into crumb crust.
9. Sprinkle remaining 1 Tbsp (15 ml) graham cracker crumbs on top.
10. Bake approximately 30–35 minutes until pie is firm. (Do *not* insert a knife to check for doneness. Cheesecakes are not cooked as long as custards and overcooking produces a dry filling.)
11. Remove from oven and chill in freezer until filling is cool. Do not allow ice crystals to form. (At home, chill in the refrigerator 2 hours.)
12. Serve with Strawberry Topping.

Strawberry Topping

water	1/4 c	50 ml	red food coloring	1/8 tsp	0.5 ml
cornstarch	1-1/2 tsp	7 ml	frozen strawberries,	5 oz	150 g
sugar	2 Tbsp	30 ml	thawed	(1/2 c)	(125 ml)

1. Combine water, cornstarch and sugar in a small saucepan.
2. Bring to boil and cook 1 minute, stirring constantly.
3. Add red food coloring to syrup.
4. Combine thickened syrup and strawberries.
5. Chill until serving.

Almond Cheesecake

graham cracker	1/3 c	95 ml	vanilla	1/4 tsp	1 ml
crumbs	+ 1 Tbsp		almond extract	1/8 tsp	0.5 ml
sugar	1 Tbsp	15 ml			
cinnamon	1/4 tsp	1 ml	*Sour Cream Topping:*		
margarine, melted	2 Tbsp	30 ml	sour cream	1/4 c	50 ml
cream cheese	4 oz	120 g	sugar	1 Tbsp	15 ml
sugar	3 Tbsp	45 ml	vanilla	1/8 tsp	0.5 ml
egg, beaten	1 + 1 tsp	1 + (5 ml)	almond extract	1/8 tsp	0.5 ml

1. Preheat oven to 350°F (175°C).
2. Grease a 6-in. (15 cm) pie pan with margarine.
3. Mix together the graham cracker crumbs, sugar, cinnamon, and the melted margarine.
4. Press crumbs into a crust for the pie pan. Bake in oven 6 minutes.
5. Cream cream cheese until soft.
6. Gradually beat in sugar.
7. Beat in egg until smooth. Stir in vanilla and almond extract.
8. Pour mixture into crumb crust.
9. Bake 25 minutes.
10. Meanwhile, prepare sour cream topping: Mix together sour cream, sugar, vanilla and almond extract.
11. Remove cheesecake from oven. Spread sour cream topping on top. Return to oven and bake an additional 10 minutes.
12. Remove from oven and chill in freezer until filling is cool. Do not allow ice crystals to form. (At home, chill in the refrigerator 2 hours.)

Cheese Spoon Bread

cornmeal	1/4 c	90 ml	pepper	dash	
	+ 2 Tbsp		milk	1 c	250 ml
water	1/2 c	125 ml	cheese, grated	4 oz	120 g
shortening	1 Tbsp	30 ml	eggs, beaten	1–1/2	
sugar	1–1/2 tsp	7 ml			
salt	1/2 tsp	2 ml			

1. Preheat oven to 325°F (160°C).
2. Grease a small casserole dish or loaf pan.
3. Combine cornmeal, water, shortening, sugar, salt, and pepper in a saucepan. Add 1/2 of the milk.
4. Cook over medium heat, stirring constantly, until mixture comes to a boil.
5. Remove pan from heat.
6. Reserve 1/3 of the cheese for a topping. Add the other 2/3 of the cheese to the hot mixture. Stir until it is melted.
7. Pour in remaining milk and eggs, stirring constantly.
8. Pour mixture in dish.
9. Bake 35–40 minutes or until a knife inserted halfway between the center and edge of the dish comes out clean.
10. Serve hot from the baking dish.

Chili Con Queso

onion, minced	2 Tbsp	30 ml	tomatoes, canned,	1/2 c	125 ml
green chilies,	2 tsp	10 ml	chopped		
canned, chopped			cheese, grated	1 c	250 ml

1. Combine onion, chilies, and tomatoes in a saucepan.
2. Bring to a boil; lower heat and simmer until onion is soft.
3. Stir in cheese until it melts.
4. Serve hot with corn or totilla chips.

Cheese Sticks

flour	1 c	250 ml	sharp cheddar cheese,	3/4 c	180 ml
salt	1/4 tsp	1 ml	grated	(3 oz)	(90 g)
paprika	dash		water	2–3 Tbsp	30–45 ml
margarine	1/3 c +	80 ml			
(divided)	1 Tbsp	15 ml			

1. Preheat oven to 400°F (200°C).
2. Rub flour into a pastry cloth and the cloth sleeve of a rolling pin.
3. Sift together flour, salt, and paprika.
4. Cut in 1/3 c (80 ml) margarine with a pastry blender until it is the size of peas.
5. Mix in cheese.
6. Sprinkle water on the mixture while stirring with a fork until the mixture leaves the sides of the bowl and forms a cohesive mass. Do not add more water than needed.
7. Turn dough onto a piece of wax paper. Pick up wax paper. *Gently* squeeze and pat dough into a ball without touching it with the hands.
8. Place on floured pastry cloth. Gently press the ball down with the palm of the left hand while using the right hand as a guide. Do not allow cracks to form.
9. Quickly and lightly, use short strokes to roll a rectangle 7 in. × 8 in. (18 cm × 20 cm).
10. Dot with 1 Tbsp (15 ml) margarine.
11. Fold the corners into the center.
12. Repeat steps 9–11.
13. Wrap the folded dough in wax paper.
14. Chill for 30 minutes in the refrigerator or 10 minutes in the freezer.
15. Roll dough into a rectangle 1/4 in. (6 mm) thick.
16. Use a pastry wheel to cut strips of dough 1/2 in. × 4 in. (1.3 cm × 10 cm).
17. Place strips on a baking sheet.
18. Bake 8–10 minutes.

Cream of Cheese Soup

water	3/4 c	180 ml	chicken bouillon	1/2	
potatoes, diced	1 c	250 ml	cube		
onion, chopped	2 Tbsp	30 ml	flour	1 Tbsp	15 ml
celery, chopped	1/4 c	50 ml	milk	1 c	250 ml
parsley, dried	1/2 tsp	2 ml	extra sharp cheddar cheese,	2 oz	60 g
salt	1/4 tsp	1 ml	grated		
pepper	dash		cayenne pepper	dash	

1. Bring water to a boil over high heat.
2. Add potatoes, onion, celery, parsley, salt, pepper, and bouillon cube.
3. Cover; lower heat and simmer 12–15 minutes until potatoes are tender.
4. Blend flour with a small amount of cold milk.
5. Stir into cooked vegetable mixture. Add remaining milk.
6. Bring to a boil and simmer 1 minute.
7. Remove from heat. Stir in cheese until melted.
8. Stir in cayenne pepper and serve immediately.

(Courtesy of National Live Stock and Meat Board.)

13●

Meat

OBJECTIVES

The student should be able to:

1. Identify the predicted tenderness, primal cut, and nutritive value of retail cuts of meat.
2. Determine the effect of oven and end-point temperature on cooking losses, appearance, juiciness, flavor, and texture of meats.
3. Assess the effect of broiling distance on the quality of broiled meats.
4. Evaluate methods of home tenderization of meats.
5. Prepare and compare dry and moist methods of meat cookery.

FOOD SCIENCE PRINCIPLES

1. Tenderness of meats can be predicted by the type of cut. Muscles that are highly exercised such as the abdomen, shoulder, and rump contain large amounts of connective tissue. These muscles are less tender than the infrequently exercised muscles of the upper, central portion of the carcass such as the rib and loin primal cuts.

   Other factors affecting tenderness include the formation of actinomyosin (during rigor mortis, thaw rigor, or cold shortening), degree of aging, age of the animal, processing methods (enzymes, acid, salts and polyphosphates, mechanical manipulation, electrical stimulation, hot-boning, and temperature conditioning), and cooking methods (starting and cooking temperatures and time).

2. Meats are excellent sources of protein, iron, and zinc. The fat content of meat is dependent on the species and cut of meat. Higher grades of tender beef generally have a high saturated fat content. Organ meats contain high levels of trace minerals and cholesterol.

3. During cooking, heat affects the following:

   a. *Proteins:* The initial heating activates enzymes naturally present in the meat. These enzymes degrade muscle proteins until they are denatured by high temperatures. Thus cooking meat at low temperatures for long periods of time allows more protein degradation than that cooked quickly at high temperatures. The denatured proteins fragment and shorten, and cause the meat to shrink. Also, immobilized water is lost, which dehydrates the muscle and creates decreased juiciness and increased toughness and cooking losses. High oven and broiling temperatures accelerate these events.

Proteolytic enzymes in commercial meat tenderizers are believed to become activated with heating. Papain, for example, becomes increasingly active between 131°–167°F (55–75°C) to attack and degrade muscle proteins as well as act on collagen whose coiled structure has been disrupted by heat. After application of a commercial meat tenderizer, it is unnecessary to wait before cooking because tenderization does not begin until the meat is heated.

b. *Connective Tissue:* Collagen is the white connective tissue that forms the wall of muscle fibers and binds them into bundles. At 102°F (39°C), the coils of collagen begin to unwind. At 149°F (65°C), collagen denatures, loses its strength, and shrinks to approximately a quarter of its original length. With sufficient heat, moisture, and time, collagen is hydrolyzed (solubilized) to form gelatin. The other major connective tissue, elastin, is not softened to any great extent during cooking.

c. *Fat:* High temperatures melt fat; the melted fat may be absorbed by the meat or become part of the drippings. Surface fat may prevent moisture loss from evaporation. Melted fat increases the perception of juiciness because it stimulates the secretion of saliva in the mouth.

d. *Flavor:* Heat develops the flavor and aroma of meat through formation and interaction of volatile substances, coagulation and breakdown of proteins, melting and decomposition of fats, and caramelization and breakdown of carbohydrates.

4. The color of meat is primarily due to the concentration of the pigment myoglobin. The concentration of myoglobin varies according to species, age of the animal, amount of exercise and stress, exposure to oxygen and heat, and conditions of storage and processing. Levels increase with advancing age, frequent exercise, and high requirements for oxygen (organs).

Inside the anaerobic environment of the muscle, myoglobin is a purple-red color. When the meat is cut and exposed to air, it forms oxymyoglobin, which has a bright red color. With continued exposure to air, oxymyoglobin is slowly oxidized to metmyoglobin, which has a brownish-red color. The change in color is due to the oxidation of the iron molecule in myoglobin from the ferrous ($+2$) to the ferric ($+3$) state. If storage is continued, the metmyoglobin is changed into a variety of decomposition products that have greenish or faded colors.

When red oxymyoglobin is heated, it is denatured to the greyish-brown globin hemichrome. This change in color can be used as an index of doneness. However, it is more accurate to use a meat thermometer. The following guidelines can be used to assess doneness:

a. *Rare:* bright red interior, thin surface layer of brown; 140°F (60°C).
b. *Medium:* pink interior, deep surface layer of brown; 160°F (71°C).
c. *Well done:* uniformly brown; 170°F (77°C).

5. Methods of cooking meats can be classified as the following:

a. *Dry heat methods:* Dry heat methods of cookery are roasting, oven- and pan-broiling, and deep-fat, pan- and stir-frying. These methods are used most often for tender cuts of meat because the amount of connective tissue is small and cooking is unnecessary to hydrolyze the collagen. Cooking decreases the tenderness of tender cuts of meat because heat denatures proteins. Some dry heat methods may be appropriate for less tender cuts of meat if cooking temperatures are kept low for a prolonged period of time or a thin piece of meat is cut thinly across the grain (London broil).

b. *Moist heat methods:* Moist heat methods include pan- and oven-braising, simmering (stewing), steaming, and pressure-cooking. These heat methods are used for less tender cuts of meat because slow cooking with moist heat tenderizes the meat through collagen hydrolysis. If the temperature is kept low for long periods of time, tenderization also occurs from enzyme activity.

6. Less tender cuts of meats can tenderized at home by:

   a. Mechanical means: grinding, pounding, cubing, slicing thinly
   b. Enzymes: preparations catalyze hydrolysis of proteins
   c. Moist heat: slowly solubilizes collagen to gelatin
   d. Marinating: acids increase moisture retention
   e. Cooking at low temperature 250°F (120°C) for a long time: solubilizes collagen to gelatin.

**Exercise I: Identification of Characteristic Bone, Primal Cut, and
Predicted Tenderness of Retail Cuts of Meats**

Identify the characteristic bone, primal cut, and predicted tenderness of the following retail cuts of meat (Table 13–1). Use the beef, pork, lamb, and veal charts by the National Live Stock and Meat Board, which can be found in most textbooks.

QUESTIONS

1. What factors influence the predicted tenderness of meats? _____

   _____

2. Of what importance is the characteristic bone in determining the primal cut of a piece of meat

   _____

3. What relationship does the primal cut have to the predicted tenderness of a cut of meat?

   _____

   _____

TABLE 13-1   Identification of Characteristic Bone, Primal Cut, and Predicted Tenderness of Retail Cuts of Meats

Retail Cut	Characteristic Bone	Primal Cut	Predicted Tenderness
BEEF arm steak			
blade roast			
brisket			
flank steak			
pin-bone sirloin steak			
rib roast			
round steak			
shank cross cuts			
short ribs			
T-bone steak			
PORK arm steak			
Boston butt			
center loin roast			
rib chop			
smoked ham			
spareribs			
LAMB crown rib roast			
leg			
rib chop			
loin chop			
VEAL cutlets			
loin chop			
rib chop			
rump roast			

Exercise II: Calculation of Cost/Serving and Nutritive Value of Meats

1. Calculate the nutritive value of meats in Table 13–2.
2. Determine the cost/lb (500 g) of meats from supermarket ads or from a price list posted in the laboratory. Divide the cost/lb (500 g) by the number of servings/lb (500 g) to determine the cost/serving.
3. Record results in Table 13–2.

TABLE 13–2   Calculation of Cost/Serving and Nutritive Value of Meats

Cooked Meat 3 oz. (90 g)	Cost/lb (500 g)	Serving/lb (500 g)	Cost/Serving	Nutritive Value				
				Food Energy (Cal)	Protein (g)	Fat (g)	Iron (mg)	Zinc (mg)
Chuck roast								
Hamburger								
Sirloin steak								
Beef liver								
Pork luncheon meat[a]								
Loin pork chops								
Ham								
Bacon[b]								
Veal cutlet								

[a] 2 oz. (60 g).
[b] 2 slices.

QUESTIONS

1. Which meat is the most expensive in terms of cost/serving? _____

   The least expensive? _____

2. Which meat has the greatest amount of nutrients for the least cost/serving? _____

   The least amount? _____

3. What is the average protein content/serving of muscle meats? _____
_____

4. What nutrient is most associated with the food energy of the meat? _____
_____

5. Is the cost of meat related to its nutritive value? _____

6. Which meat cannot be considered a good source of protein? _____
Why? _____
_____

7. Meats are good sources of which two minerals? _____
1. _____
2. _____

Experiment I: Effect of Oven Temperature on Cooking Losses of Meat

1. Preheat 4 ovens to: 325°F (160°C)   425°F (220°C)
    375°F (190°C)   475°F (245°C)
2. Preweigh broiler pan and a small dish with a thermometer resting on it.
3. Divide 1–1/3 lb (625 g) of hamburger into 4 parts and shape 4 balls of meat of equal size. Weigh each meat ball and record weight.
4. Insert a meat thermometer into the center of the meat ball. Reshape the meat if necessary to firmly hold the thermometer.
5. When oven is at designated temperature, place 1 meat ball on 1 broiler pan in oven. Bake until the thermometer registers 160°F (71°C).
6. Remove broiler pan from oven and record internal temperature. Remove meat ball from broiler pan and place on dish.
7. Remove thermometer from meat. Weigh meat ball and dish.
8. Weigh broiler pan to calculate weight of drippings.
9. Record results in Table 13–3.

QUESTION

Which oven temperature produced the least amount of cooking loss? _____
_____ The best appearance? _____
The juiciest product? _____ Why? _____
_____

TABLE 13-3   Effect of Oven Temperature on Losses of Meat

Weight (g)	325°F (160°C)	375°F (190°C)	425°F (220°C)	475°F (245°C)
Broiler pan + drippings				
Broiler pan				
Drippings				
Dish + cooked meat				
Dish				
Raw meat				
Cooked meat				
Evaporation[a]				
% loss[b]				
Time required to reach 160°F (71°C).				

[a] Evaporation = Raw weight − (cooked weight + weight of drippings).

[b] $\% \text{ loss} = \dfrac{\text{Raw weight} - \text{cooked weight}}{\text{Raw weight}} \times 100.$

Experiment II: Effect of Final End-Point Temperature on Losses, Appearance, and Juiciness in Meat

1. Preheat 3 ovens to 325°F (160°C).
2. Preweigh 3 broiler pans and 3 small dishes with a thermometer resting on them.
3. Divide 1 lb (500 g) into 3 parts and shape 3 balls of meat of equal size. Weigh each meat ball and record in Table 13-4.
4. Insert a meat thermometer into the center of each meat ball. Reshape the meat if necessary to firmly hold the thermometer. Place on broiler pan.
5. When the oven is at 325°F (160°C), place 1 broiler pan in each oven. Bake until the thermometer registers the following:

   Oven A: 140°F (60°C).
   Oven B: 160°F (71°C).
   Oven C: 170°F (77°C).

6. Immediately remove broiler pan from oven and remove meat from broiler pan. Place on weighed dishes. Remove thermometer from meat and *immediately* cut open meat balls. Observe appearance and juiciness.
7. Weigh meat balls and dishes.

8. Weigh broiler pan to calculate weight of drippings.
9. Taste one-half of the cut meat balls for texture and flavor.
10. Record results in Table 13–4.

TABLE 13–4 Effect of Final End-Point Temperature on Losses, Appearance, Juiciness, Texture, and Flavor of Meat

Parameter	140°F (60°C) Rare	160°F (71°C) Medium	170°F (77°C) Well-done
Weight (g) Broiler pan + drippings			
Broiler pan			
Drippings			
Dish + cooked meat			
Dish			
Raw meat			
Cooked meat			
Evaporation[a]			
% loss[b]			
Appearance			
Juiciness			
Texture			
Flavor			

[a]Evaporation = Raw weight − (cooked weight + weight of drippings).

[b]$\% \text{ loss} = \dfrac{\text{Raw weight} - \text{cooked weight}}{\text{Raw weight}} \times 100.$

QUESTIONS

1. Describe the exterior and interior color of meat cooked to the final end-point temperatures of:

	Exterior	*Interior*
140°F (60°C)	_____	_____
160°F (71°C)	_____	_____
170°F (77°C)	_____	_____

2. Which final end-point temperature produced the greatest cooking losses? _____
   The juiciness meat ball? _____
   The most tender meat ball? _____ The most flavorful
   meat ball? _____

3. Summarize the advantages and disadvantages of cooking meat to the following stages:

Rare: _____
_____

Medium: _____
_____

Well-done: _____
_____

Experiment III: Effect of Distance from Heat in Broiling

Select one of the following meats:

pork chop, lamb chop, minute steak, hamburger patty, ham steak,
bacon, tender beef steak

1. Weigh 3 pieces of meat that are approximately the same size.
2. Preweigh the broiler pan and 3 small dishes.
3. Place 1 piece of meat on the broiler pan. Place pan on first (upper) rack of oven. Measure and record distance from top of meat to the broiler using a ruler.
4. Repeat step 3 using the second and third racks.
5. Remove pan from oven. Preheat broiler.
6. When broiler is hot, place pan on first rack. Record time. Broil until brown and halfway cooked. Turn and broil until done. Record preparation time.
7. Repeat step 6 using the second rack. Cook the second piece of meat to the same degree of doneness as the first.
8. Repeat step 6 using the third rack.
9. Remove pan from oven. Place meat on dish; immediately cut open and observe appearance.
10. Weigh dish and meat. Subtract weight of preweighed dish to determine weight of cooked meat.
11. Weigh broiler pan to determine weights of drippings.
12. Record results in Table 13–5.

TABLE 13–5   Effect of Distance from Heat in Broiling

Weight (g)	Distance from Broiler					
	Rack 1		Rack 2		Rack 3	
	Inches (cm)	Minutes	Inches (cm)	Minutes	Inches (cm)	Minutes
Raw meat						
Dish + cooked meat						
Dish						
Cooked meat						
Broiler pan + drippings						
Broiler pan						
Drippings						
Evaporation						
% loss						
Appearance						
Tenderness						
Juiciness						

QUESTIONS

1. Which distance from the broiler produced the least amount of cooking losses? _____ _____ How was this related to evaporation? _____ _____ _____

2. Which distance from the broiler cooked the meat in the shortest time? _____ _____ How did this affect the juiciness of the meat? _____ _____

3. What conclusion can be derived from this experiment? _____ _____ _____

Experiment IV: Methods of Tenderization of Meat

Purchase the following cuts of meat for this experiment (see Figure 13–1):

round steak	1–1/4 lb	625 g
round steak, cubed	1/4 lb	125 g
round steak, ground	1/4 lb	125 g

1. Cut the 1–1/4 lb (625 g) steak into 5 pieces of equal sizes. Weigh each and record.
2. Prepare each piece of meat according to the following methods of tenderization. Repeat the method of enzyme tenderizing, allowing the meat to stand for 30 minutes before cooking.

Braised Beef

margarine	1/2 tsp	2 ml	water	1/4 c	50 ml
oil	1/2 tsp	2 ml	salt	dash	
round steak	1/4 lb	125 g	pepper	dash	

a. Heat margarine and oil in small skillet over medium high heat until sizzling.
b. Add beef and sear on both sides until brown.
c. Add water. Bring to boil, lower heat and simmer 45 minutes.
d. Weigh and record.
e. Season and serve.

FIGURE 13–1   Round steak is tenderized mechanically with a meat hammer. (Courtesy National Live Stock and Meat Board.)

Marinated Beef

red wine vinegar	1/4 c	50 ml	clove	1	
bay leaf, crushed	1/2		salt	dash	
onion slice, 1/4 in. (6 mm)	1		pepper	dash	
carrot slice	3		round steak	1/4 lb	125 g
celery leaves	3				

    a. Combine all ingredients except beef in a saucepan.
    b. Heat to boiling; lower heat and simmer 1 minute.
    c. Pour hot marinade over meat.[1]
    d. Marinate 30 minutes to 1 hour; basting occasionally.
    e. Drain meat and pan-fry steak. Follow method in Experiment V.
    f. Weigh and record.

Enzyme-Tenderized Beef

meat tenderizer	1/8 tsp	0.5 ml
round steak	1/4 lb	125 g

    a. Moisten beef with water.
    b. Sprinkle tenderizer over surface of meat.
    c. Pierce meat deeply with a fork at 1/2 in. (1 cm) intervals.
    d. Cook steak *immediately*. Follow recipe for pan-frying in Experiment V.
    e. Repeat above; allow the steak to stand for 30 minutes before cooking.

3. Shape ground meat into a patty that matches the size and shape of the other pieces of meat. Weigh and record. Pan-fry according to the method in Experiment V. Weigh and record.
4. Pound both sides of 1/4 lb (125 g) of round steak with a wooden meat hammer or back of the large spoon. Pan-fry according to the method in Experiment V. Weigh and record.
5. Weigh cubed round steak. Pan-fry according to the method in Experiment V. Weigh and record.
6. Observe, taste, and compare the beef tenderized by the different methods.
7. Record all results in Table 13–6.

QUESTIONS

    1. Why does braising tenderize meat? _____

    _____

    2. What is the effect of marinating meat on tenderness? _____

    _____

    Why? _____

    _____

    3. Why should enzyme-tenderized meat be cooked immediately? _____

    _____

    Why was the meat pierced with a fork? _____

    _____

[1]Hot marinade is being used only as a time-saver in the laboratory. Normally meat should be marinated for 24 hours in a cold marinade.

4. What effect did grinding meat have on tenderness? _____

_____

Why? _____

Cubing meat? _____

Pounding meat? _____

5. Which of the tenderization methods produced the most tender product? _____

_____

The best textured product? _____

The most juicy product? _____

6. Which of the methods produced the least amount of cooking losses? _____

_____

TABLE 13–6   Effect of Tenderization Methods on Cooked Meats

Tenderization Method	Initial Weight	Final Weight	% Cooking Loss[a]	Tenderness	Texture	Flavor	Juiciness
Braised							
Marinated							
Enzyme, 0 minutes							
30 minutes							
Ground							
Pounded							
Cubed							

[a] % cooking loss $= \dfrac{\text{Initial weight} - \text{final weight}}{\text{Initial weight}} \times 100$.

Experiment V: Preparation and Comparison of Dry and Moist Methods of Meat Cookery

Select meats to be prepared by dry and moist methods of cookery. Use either the basic method in each section or prepare a recipe which illustrates an application of the basic method.

1. Wipe the meat with a dampened paper towel to remove bits of bone and foreign material.
2. Weigh the raw meat and record.
3. Prepare meats according to the basic method or selected recipe. Check with the laboratory teacher for instructions.
4. Keep a record of the preparation time.
5. Weigh the cooked meat and record. Calculate % cooking losses by the following formula:

$$\frac{\text{Raw weight} - \text{cooked weight}}{\text{Raw weight}} \times 100 = \% \text{ cooking loss}$$

6. Observe appearance and juiciness. Determine tenderness by ease of penetration with a fork and ease of chewing. Taste for flavor.
7. Record results in Table 13–11 on pg. 179.

Dry-Methods of Meat Cookery

Roasting

1. Select a tender cut of meat which is at least 2 in. (5 cm) thick.
2. Use the basic method of roasting to prepare a rare roast beef, one half of a smoked ham, a leg of lamb or a veal loin roast, or prepare Creamy Meatloaf, pg. 181.

Roasting—Basic Method

1. Preheat oven to 325°F (160°C) for small roasts; 300°F (150°C) for large meats.
2. Place meat, fat side up, on a rack in an *uncovered* pan. Do not add water.
3. Insert the bulb of a meat thermometer into the middle of the largest muscle of the meat (or the center of the meatloaf).
4. Cook the meat according to Table 13–7. Remember that the temperature of large roasts may continue to increase as much as 5–10°F (3–6°C) after the meat is removed from the oven.
5. Let the meat stand for 15–20 minutes before carving.
6. Season meat only as it is sliced.

Oven-Broiling

1. Select a tender cut of meat which is 1–3 in. (2.5–7.5 cm) thick. Thinner pieces of meat will overcook and toughen. Thicker pieces of meat will not cook all the way through.
2. Use the basic method of oven broiling to prepare beef steak, beef patties or lamb chops, or prepare Lamb Shish-Kabob, pg. 183.

Oven-Broiling—Basic Method

1. Slash fat and connective tissue to edge of the muscle so that it will not curl up during cooking. (Connective tissue is the thin, elastic membrane that surrounds the muscle.)
2. Place on *greased* broiler pan. If aluminum foil is used, use it on the bottom pan only. The top rack must have holes in it to allow melted fat to drip through. Otherwise accumulated fat may cause a dangerous grease fire.

FIGURE 13-2 *Five basic methods of cooking meat. (a) Roasting. (b) Broiling. (c) Pan-frying. (d) Braising. (e) Stewing. (Courtesy of National Live Stock and Meat Board.)*

TABLE 13-7   Timetable for Roasting Meats at 300°F (150°C) to 325°F (160°C)[a]

Retail Cut of Meat	Rare		Medium		Well-done	
	°F (°C)	Min./lb (0.5 kg)	°F (°C)	Min./lb (0.5 kg)	°F (°C)	Min./lb (0.5 kg)
BEEF rib (4–6 lbs; 1.8–2.7 kg)	140 (60)	26–32	160 (70)	34–38	170 (77)	40–42
tenderloin, whole	140 (60)	45–60 total				
PORK[b] ham, fresh leg, bone-in					170 (77)	35–40
smoked, half cook-before-eating			160 (70)	22–35		
fully cooked	140 (60)	18–24				
smoked, arm picnic					170 (77)	35
loin, center					170 (77)	30–35
LAMB leg (5–7 lbs, 2.3–3.2 kg)	140 (60)	20–25	160 (70)	25–30	170 (77)	30–35
shoulder, boneless	140 (60)	30–35	160 (70)	35–40	170 (77)	40–45
VEAL leg			165 (74)	25–30		
loin			165 (74)	25–30		

[a]Compiled from publications of the National Live Stock and Meat Board.
[b]Fresh pork (not smoked) should be roasted at 325–350°F (160–175°C).

3. Turn oven to broil.
4. Set broiler pan on rack so that the top portion of approximately 1 in. (2.5 cm) thick cut of meat is 2–3 in. (5–7.5 cm) from the coils. Place thicker cuts 3–5 in. (7.5–12.5 cm) away.
5. Use Table 13–8 as a guideline for cooking times.
6. Broil until the top surface is brown and it is a little more than half done. This is the side that will be served.
7. Season with salt and pepper. Turn the meat over with tongs. Do *not* pierce the meat with a fork.
8. The meat can be checked for doneness by cutting with a knife near the bone and observing the color.

TABLE 13-8   Timetable for Broiling Meats[a]

Retail Cut of Meat	Rare		Medium		Well Done	
	°F (°C)	Min./lb (0.5 kg)	°F (°C)	Min./lb (0.5 kg)	°F (°C)	Min./lb (0.5 kg)
BEEF patties 1″ × 3″ (2.5 × 7.5 cm)	140 (60)	15	160 (70)	25		
tender steaks 1″ (2.5 cm)	140 (60)	15–20	160 (70)	20–30		
1–1/2″ (3.8 cm)	140 (60)	28–30	160 (70)	22–35		
2″ (5 cm)	140 (60)	35–40	160 (70)	45		
PORK bacon					(4–5 min.)	
ham slice, 1 in. (2.5 cm)					170 (77)	16–20
rib or loin chops, 3/4–1″ (1.8–2.5 cm)					170 (77)	15–20
LAMB chops 1 in. (2.5 cm)			160 (70)	7–11		
1–1/2 in. (3.8 cm)			160 (70)	15–19		

[a]Compiled from publications of the National Live Stock and Meat Board

Pan-Broiling

1. Select a fatty, tender cut of meat that is less than 1 in. (2.5 cm) thick.
2. Use the basic method of pan broiling to prepare bacon, smoked ham steak, or ground beef patty. Cooking time will be approximately half that of oven broiling.

Pan-Broiling—Basic Method

1. Select a *heavy* skillet. This is essential since lightweight skillets have a tendency to warp and develop hot spots.
2. Heat skillet over medium high heat.
3. Rub fatty edge of meat over skillet to lightly grease pan. Add meat. Do not add fat or water. Do not cover.
4. Slowly cook each side until meat browns. Turn occasionally with tongs. Do not pierce the meat with a fork. Remove any excess fat that accumulates.
5. Reduce heat and finish cooking.

Pan-Frying

1. Select a tender cut of meat that is less than 1 in. (2.5 cm) thick.
2. Use the basic method of pan frying to prepare beef steak, veal chop, pork rib chop, or lamb rib chop; or, prepare Fried Liver, pg. 184, or Veal Piccata, pg. 184.

Pan-Frying—Basic Method

1. Repeat steps 1 and 2 for pan broiling.
2. Heat fat or oil over medium heat. Do not allow fat to smoke or burn.
3. Add meat to hot fat; cook until brown. Do not cover.
4. Season and turn with tongs.
5. Brown second side or cook until done. Regulate heat so that meat does not burn.
6. Excess fat on the cooked meat may be reduced by briefly draining the meat on a paper towel.

Stir-Frying

1. Select a tender cut of meat.
2. Use the basic method of stir frying, or prepare Stir-fried Beef and Broccoli, pg. 181.

Stir-Frying—Basic Method

1. Select a wok (electric, if possible) or a large or electric frying pan.
2. Prepare all ingredients by cutting them into shapes that are uniform in size and thickness. Meat should be sliced thinly across the grain.
3. Prepare sauce of cornstarch (1 tsp or 5 ml) to 1/3 c (80 ml) liquid. Set aside.
4. Add a small amount of oil, 1 Tbsp (15 ml), to the heated wok.
5. When oil sizzles, add vegetables one at a time and stir-fry 1–2 minutes between each addition. Add slower cooking vegetables (celery, broccoli, green pepper) first, followed by quick cooking vegetables (cabbage, onions, mushrooms) last.
6. Remove vegetables to plate.
7. If needed, add additional oil to the wok.
8. Add meat and stir-fry 2–3 minutes until meat is just browned. Do not overcook.
9. Add sauce to meat. Heat until thickened.
10. Return vegetables to pan and stir to mix.
11. **Optional**: Cover pan for 15 seconds–2 minutes to reheat vegetables. Remember that the vegetables will continue to cook, so do not overcook. Vegetables should be tender crisp, not limp.
12. Serve immediately.

Moist Methods of Meat Cookery

Pan-Braising

1. Select a less tender cut of meat.
2. Use the basic method of pan-braising to prepare Swiss Steak, pg. 185.

Pan-Braising—Basic Method

1. **Optional**: Pound meat with a meat hammer to tenderize.
2. **Optional**: Rub flour seasoned with salt and pepper into both sides of the meat. Shake off any excess flour. Meat may also be dipped next in an egg-milk mixture and further coated with bread crumbs.

3. Heat fat or oil in a heavy skillet over medium-high heat. Do not allow the fat to burn or smoke. Or meat may be browned in its own fat.
4. Sear both sides of meat until brown.
5. Pour off and discard excess fat.
6. Add a small quantity of liquid 1/4–1/2 cup (50–125 ml) to pan. Bring to a boil.
7. Cover with a tightly fitting lid.
8. Reduce heat and simmer until done. Use Table 13–9 as a guideline in determining cooking times.
9. Check occasionally to make sure liquid has not boiled away. If necessary, add more water if needed.
10. Remove meat from pan. Remaining liquid may be thickened for a gravy.

TABLE 13–9   Timetable for Braising Meats[a]

Retail Cut	Average Size	Hours
BEEF arm pot roast	3–5 lbs (1.3–2.3 kg)	2-1/2–3-1/2
round	3/4–1 in. (1.8–2.5 cm)	1–1-3/4
PORK chops	3/4–1-1/2 in. (1.8–3.8 cm)	3/4–1
spareribs	2–3 lbs (0.9–1.3 kg)	1–1/2
shoulder steaks	3/4 in. (1.8 cm)	3/4–1
LAMB breast, stuffed	2–3 lbs (0.9–1.3 kg)	1-1/2–2
neck slices	3/4 in. (1.8 cm)	1
shoulder chops	3/4–1 in. (1.8–2.5 cm)	3/4–1
VEAL breast, stuffed	3–4 lbs (1.3–1.8 kg)	1-1/2–2
chops	1/2–3/4 in. (1.3–1.8 cm)	3/4–1
steaks		3/4–1
cubes	1–2 in. (2.5–5 cm)	3/4–1

[a]By permission of the National Live Stock and Meat Board.

Oven-Braising

1. Select a less tender cut of meat.
2. Use the basic method of oven-braising to prepare beef pot roast or veal steaks, or prepare Oven-braised Pork Chops, pg. 185.

Oven-Braising—Basic Method

1. Preheat oven to 300–325°F (150–160°C).
2. Follow steps 1–8 for the basic method of pan-braising. Aluminum foil may be used as an alternative cover for step 7.
3. Place meat in oven and cook according to Table 13–9.

Simmering (Stewing)

1. Select less tender cuts of meat at least 1 in. (2.5 cm) thick.
2. Use the basic method to prepare beef stew.

Simmering (Stewing)—Basic Method

1. Cut meat into 1- in. (2.5 cm) cubes. If lack of time is a significant factor for the laboratory and a pressure cooker is not available, cut into 1/2 in. (1.3 cm) cubes to reduce cooking time.
2. **Optional**: Rub flour seasoned with salt and pepper into meat. Shake off excess flour.
3. Heat fat or oil in a heavy dutch oven over medium high heat. Do not allow the fat to burn or smoke.
4. Add meat and brown on all sides.
5. Pour off and discard excess fat. Return meat to pan.
6. Add enough liquid to cover pieces of meat. Cover and bring to a boil. Reduce heat to simmer.
7. Cook until tender using Table 13–10 as a guideline for cooking times.
8. Prepared vegetables may be added 45 minutes before the end of the cooking period. Vegetables should be added in this order: carrots, celery, onion, and potatoes. Add each vegetable separately and allow the water to boil for a few minutes before the next vegetable is added.
9. Seasonings, spices, wine, and herbs may be added when liquid is added to the browned meat. Since the flavor of herbs may be reduced with long cooking times, the stew may be "freshened" by the addition of more herbs or wine 15 minutes before the end of the cooking period.
10. Remove meat and vegetables. Prepare a gravy with the remaining liquid, if desired.

Pressure Cooking

1. Select a less tender cut of meat.
2. Use the method recommended by the instruction book for the pressure cooker, or prepare Viennese Goulash, pg. 182 or Veal Marengo, pg. 186.

TABLE 13–10   Timetable for Simmering (Stewing) Meats[a]

Retail Cut	Average Weight lbs (kg)	Hours	Min./lb (0.5 kg)
BEEF brisket	4–6 (1.8–2.7)		40–50
stew[b]		1-1/2–2-1/2	
PORK ham, smoked arm picnic	5–8 (2.3–3.6)	3-1/2–4	45
country-style ribs		2–2-1/2	
LAMB stew[b]		1-1/2–2	
VEAL stew[b]		1	

[a]Compiled from publications of the National Live Stock and Meat Board.
[b]1–1-1/2 in. (2.5 to 3.8 cm) cubes.

TABLE 13–11 Preparation and Comparison of Dry and Moist Methods of Meat Cookery

Method Cookery	Raw Weight (g)	Cooked Weight (g)	% Cooking Loss	Preparation Time (minutes)	Appearance	Tenderness	Flavor	Juiciness
DRY roasting								
oven-broiling								
pan-broiling								
pan-frying								
stir-frying								
MOIST pan-braising								
oven-braising								
simmering (stewing)								
pressure cooking								

QUESTIONS

1. Which dry method of cooking meat produces the least % cooking loss? _____
_____ How is this releated to the juiciness? _____
_____

2. Which dry method of cooking meat produces the leanest meat? _____
_____ Why? _____
_____

   The greasiest? _____ Why? _____
_____

3. How does moist cooking tenderize less tender cuts of meat? _____
_____
_____

4. What would happen if less tender cuts of meats were cooked by dry methods? _____
_____
_____

5. What would happen if tender cuts of meats were cooked by moist methods? _____
_____
_____

6. Which method of moist meat cookery, braising or stewing, produces a stronger meat flavor?
_____ Why? _____
_____

7. How would the addition of bones to a stew affect its flavor? _____
_____

8. What is the advantage of preparing a stew rather than braised meat when the cost of meat is
   expensive? _____
_____

APPLICATIONS

Stir-Fried Beef and Broccoli

beef round steak	1/2 lb	500 g	green onions	3	
cornstarch	1–1/2 tsp	7 ml	soy sauce	1–1/2 tsp	7 ml
egg white	1/2		catsup	1–1/2 tsp	7 ml
salt	1/4 tsp	1 ml	red wine vinegar	1/2 tsp	2 ml
pepper	1/4 tsp	1 ml	sugar	1/4 tsp	1 ml
monosodium glutamate	1/4 tsp	1 ml	oil (divided)	1 Tbsp +	20 ml
hot pepper sauce	4 drops			1 tsp	
broccoli florets	1 c	250 ml	garlic, minced	1/2 clove	
mushrooms, fresh, sliced 1/4 in. (0.6 cm)	1 c	250 ml			

1. Slice meat across the grain into thin strips approximately 1–1/2 in. (3.8 cm) long.
2. Combine cornstarch, egg white, salt, pepper, monosodium glutamate, and pepper sauce in a bowl.
3. Add meat and toss well so that meat is evenly coated. Let meat marinate 20–30 minutes.
4. Prepare vegetables:

   a. Cut broccoli florets in halves or thirds to achieve a uniform size.
   b. Slice mushrooms if not already sliced.
   c. Diagonally cut green onions in 1-in. (2.5 cm) pieces.

5. Combine soy sauce, catsup, vinegar, and sugar in a small bowl or custard cup. Set aside.
6. Preheat wok on high heat. Add 1 Tbsp (15 ml) oil.
7. When oil sizzles, add garlic and cook 30 seconds.
8. Add broccoli; stir-fry 2 minutes.
9. Add onions to broccoli; stir-fry 2 minutes.
10. Add mushrooms to broccoli and onions; stir-fry 1 minute. Remove vegetables from wok to a plate.
11. Add the remaining 1 tsp (5 ml) oil to the wok.
12. When oil sizzles, add beef. Cook 2–3 minutes, just until beef is browned on all sides. [If recipe is to be doubled, cook only 1/2 lb (500 g) meat at one time.]
13. Add soy sauce mixture to beef. Cook and stir until sauce is thickened.
14. Return vegetables to pan and toss with beef. Cover and cook 20 seconds to heat through.
15. Serve immediately.

Creamy Meat Loaf

ground beef	1/2 lb	250 g	garlic salt	1/4 tsp	1 ml
bread crumbs, soft	1/2 c	125 ml	Worchestershire sauce	1 tsp	5 ml
			oregano	1/4 tsp	1 ml
sour cream	1/2 c	125 ml	parsley	1/2 tsp	2 ml
onion soup mix	1/4 oz	7 g	pepper	1/16 tsp	0.3 ml
			egg, beaten	1/2	

1. Preheat oven to 325°F (160°C).
2. Combine all ingredients. Shape into a loaf, 4 in. × 3 in. × 1–1/2 in. (10 cm × 7.5 cm × 3.8 cm).
3. Place meatloaf in an uncovered roasting pan. Insert meat thermometer in the middle of the loaf.
4. Bake 35–45 minutes or until temperature reaches 160°F (70°C).
5. Remove meat thermometer, place on serving dish and serve.

Viennese Goulash

margarine, divided	2-1/4 tsp	11 ml	salt	1/4 tsp	1 ml
oil	2 tsp	10 ml	pepper	1/8 tsp	0.5 ml
onion, thinly sliced	1		tomato sauce,	2 Tbsp +	40 ml
beef round or	1/2 lb	250 g	canned	2 tsp	
stew meat			chicken bouillon	1/2 tsp	2 ml
paprika	1 Tbsp	15 ml	powder		
cider vinegar	1-1/2 Tbsp	22 ml	lemon peel	1/3 lemon	
water	3/4 c	180 ml	garlic, minced	1/2 clove	
caraway seed	1 tsp	5 ml	flour	2 tsp	10 ml
marjoram	1/4 tsp	1 ml			

1. Melt 2 tsp (10 ml) of the margarine and the oil in a pressure saucepan.
2. Add onions and sauté until golden.
3. Meanwhile cut meat into 3/4-in. (1.8 cm) cubes. Cut off and discard any fat.
4. Add paprika, vinegar, and remaining margarine (1/4 tsp or 1 ml) to onions.
5. Add meat to onion mixture. Toss well and brown meat, occasionally stirring. Remove to platter, using rubber spatula to scrape out pan.
6. Add water to pan. Return pan to heat and heat briefly while stirring to dissolve any sauce sticking to the bottom of the pan.
7. If the pressure cooker has a round metal disc with holes in it, place it in the pan. Add meat on top of disc. If no disc is available, just add back meat.
8. Add caraway seed, marjarom, salt, pepper, tomato sauce, and powdered chicken bouillon, lemon peel, and garlic to meat and mix well.
9. Cover and close pan. Turn heat to high.
10. Let steam escape a few seconds through the valve to make sure it is open. Place gauge set at 15 lbs over the valve. When the valve first jiggles, record time. Turn heat to medium-low or so that the gauge jiggles 1–4 times/minute. *Do not let it jiggle more often or the meat may burn. If an electric burner is used, it may be necessary to initially remove the pan from heat for a short time to control the number of jiggles.*
11. Cook meat for 25 minutes after the gauge first jiggles.
12. Remove pan from heat and allow to cool 4 minutes.
13. Reduce pressure instantly by placing the still closed pressure cooker under cold running water in the sink. When the hissing stops, nudge gauge with fork to see if steam will still spurt out. If there is no steam, remove gauge with fork, and open pressure cooker.
14. Remove metal disc with a fork, leaving the goulash in the pan. Scrape off any sauce clinging to the disc with a rubber spatula into the pan.
15. Mix flour in 1 Tbsp (15 ml) water. Add to goulash in pan.
16. Return pan to heat and cook mixture until it boils, stirring constantly for 1–2 minutes.

Note: If recipe is to be doubled, do not double flour or water in step 15.

Yogurt-Spiced Lamb Shish-Kabob

lamb, 1-in. (2.5 cm) cubes	1/2 lb	250 g	green pepper	1	
Yogurt-spiced marinade			tomato	1	
onion	1		mushrooms	4	

1. Cut any fat or tendons off lamb cubes.
2. Prepare Yogurt-Spiced Marinade (see below). Add lamb and marinate 30–60 minutes at room temperature. (At home marinate 3–4 hours.)
3. Bring enough water to cover the onion to boil in a small saucepan. Peel onion and cut into quarters. Add onion to boiling water. Boil 2 minutes and drain.
4. Seed green pepper and cut into eighths.
5. Quarter tomato.
6. Remove lamb from marinade. Thread lamb onto 2 metal skewers, alternating with vegetables.
7. Place remaining marinade in a small saucepan. Cook over medium-low heat while lamb is broiling. Do not reduce it too much or the marinade will be too dry.
8. Broil shish-kabob 5 in. (13 cm) from heat until lamb is lightly browned on outside. Turn only once for each side. Do not overcook or the lamb will be tough. Remember that the lamb cube is also cooked in the interior by the metal skewer that conducts heat.
9. Serve shish-kabob hot with cooked marinade as a sauce.

Yogurt-Spiced Meat Marinade

coriander, ground	1 Tbsp	15 ml	garlic cloves, crushed	3	
cumin, ground	1 Tbsp	15 ml			
cardamon, ground	1 Tbsp	15 ml	ginger root, grated	1 Tbsp	15 ml
chili powder	1 tsp	5 ml	or		
salt	1/2 tsp	2 ml	ginger ground	1 tsp	5 ml
pepper	1/8 tsp	0.5 ml	honey	3 Tbsp	45 ml
margarine	2 Tbsp	30 ml	yogurt	1 c	250 ml

1. Combine corinader, cumin, cardamon, chili powder, salt, and pepper.
2. Melt margarine in a skillet over medium-high heat. Add combined spices and cook 2–3 minutes.
3. Combine cooked spices with remaining ingredients in a bowl.

Sweet and Sour Chinese Ribs

spareribs or back ribs	1 lb	500 g	oil	1 Tbsp	15 ml
honey	1/4 c	50 ml	garlic, minced	1/2 tsp	2 ml
catsup	1/4 c	50 ml	ginger, ground	1/4 tsp	1 ml
onion, minced	1/4 c	50 ml	pepper	1/8 tsp	0.5 ml
vinegar, red wine	2 Tbsp	30 ml	cornstarch	1 tsp	5 ml
Worchestershire sauce	2 Tbsp	30 ml	water	2 Tbsp	30 ml
soy sauce	1-1/2 Tbsp	22 ml			

1. Cut into individual ribs. If using spareribs, cut off excess flap of meat and skin.
2. Combine remaining ingredients except cornstarch and water in a small saucepan. Bring to a boil over medium-high heat; reduce heat and simmer 10–15 minutes, stirring occasionally.
3. Combine cornstarch with water in a custard cup. Add to sauce and boil 1 minute, stirring constantly.
4. Place ribs on broiler rack. Baste with sauce.
5. Broil 5 in. (13 cm) from heat 5–8 minutes. Turn over and broil second side 5 minutes.
6. Serve hot with remaining sauce.

Fried Liver

bacon slices	2		pepper, sliced	1/2	
liver	1/2 lb	250 g	onion, sliced	1/2	
flour	1/4 c	50 ml	tomatoes, canned,	2/3 c	160 ml
salt	1 tsp	5 ml	drained		
pepper	1/4 tsp	1 ml	salt	1/2 tsp	2 ml

1. Fry bacon over high heat until crisp. Remove from fat, drain on paper towels, and crumble.
2. Cut liver into serving pieces.
3. Mix together flour, salt, and pepper.
4. Roll liver in seasoned flour. Shake off excess flour.
5. Sauté sliced pepper in fat over medium-high heat for 2 minutes. Add onion, fry 1 more minute. Remove pepper and onion to a small bowl and cover with aluminum foil to keep warm.
6. Add liver slices to pan and fry until brown on both sides.
7. Coarsely chop tomatoes. Mix with 1/2 tsp (2 ml) salt. Pour over liver.
8. Bring to a boil; reduce heat and simmer 10 minutes.
9. Return pepper and onion to pan and heat through.
10. Sprinkle bacon bits on top and serve.

Veal Piccata

veal scallopini	1/2 lb	250 g	salt	1/4 tsp	1 ml
1/4–1/16 in. thick			pepper	1/8 tsp	0.5 ml
(.6–.16 cm)			parsley, dried	1/2 tsp	2 ml
flour	2 Tbsp	30 ml	lemon	1/2	
butter	2 Tbsp	30 ml			

1. Pound veal with a meat hammer to 1/4–1/16 in. (0.6–.16 cm) thick. Cut into serving pieces.
2. Coat veal with flour. Shake off any excess flour.
3. Squeeze lemon into a small glass to obtain its juice. Remove any seeds. Add parsley and stir.
4. Melt butter in a skillet over medium-high heat. Do *not* allow the butter to brown or smoke.
5. Add veal and quickly brown on both sides.
6. Sprinkle salt and pepper on veal; lower heat and cook 3–5 minutes longer.
7. Pour lemon juice and parsley over veal. Cook 1 more minute.
8. Serve promptly.

Swiss Steak

bacon slices	2		onion, minced	1/2	
flour	1/4 c	50 ml	carrot, minced	1	
salt	1/2 tsp	2 ml	celery stalk,	1	
pepper	1/4 tsp	1 ml	minced		
round steak,	1/2 lb	250 g	tomato sauce	1/2 c	125 ml
1/4 in. thick			beef bouillon	1/2	
(0.6 cm)			cube		

1. Fry bacon in heavy skillet until crisp. Remove pan from heat. Remove slices and allow to drain on paper towels.
2. Mix flour, salt and pepper in a bag.
3. Cut steak into serving pieces. Place each piece individually into bag containing seasoned flour. Shake off excess flour while meat is still in the bag.
4. Use a meat hammer to pound both sides of the steak to 1/8 in. (3 mm) thickness.
5. Place pan containing bacon drippings over medium-high heat. Quickly brown meat on both sides. Remove browned meat from pan to a dish.
6. Add onion, carrot and celery to the remaining fat. Sauté 5 minutes until golden.
7. Dissolve bouillon cube in 1/2 c (125 ml) boiling water.
8. Add meat back to pan. Spoon vegetables on top of meat.
9. Pour tomato sauce and hot bouillon over meat.
10. Bring to boil; cover; lower heat and simmer 45 minutes. If necessary, more water may be added to prevent scorching.

Oven-Braised Pork Chops

pork chops	1/2 lb	250 g	egg, beaten	1	
flour	2 Tbsp	30 ml	milk	1 Tbsp	15 ml
salt	1/4 tsp	1 ml	bread crumbs	1/3 c	80 ml
pepper	1/8 tsp	0.5 ml	vegetable oil	2 Tbsp	30 ml

1. Preheat oven to 350°F (175°C).
2. Remove outer fat from pork chops.
3. Mix flour, salt and pepper in a bag.
4. Add pork chops individually to the bag containing flour. Shake off excess flour while still in the bag.
5. Mix egg and milk together.
6. Spread bread crumbs on a sheet of wax paper.
7. Dip floured pork chops into egg-milk mixture; then roll in bread crumbs.
8. Heat oil in a small skillet, over high heat. Do not allow the oil to burn or smoke.
9. Add the chops and quickly brown on both sides.
10. Place browned chops in casserole dish. Add 1/4 c (50 ml) water.
11. Cover and place in oven. Bake 25–30 minutes.

Veal Marengo

veal stew meat	1/2 lb	250 g	parsley, dried	1/8 tsp	0.5 ml
flour	1 Tbsp	15 ml	thyme, dried	1/8 tsp	0.5 ml
salt	1/4 tsp	1 ml	bay leaf	1/2	
pepper	dash		tomatoes, canned,	1/4 c	50 ml
oil or shortening	1 Tbsp	15 ml	drained		
onion, chopped	1/4		bouillon or	1	
garlic clove,	1/3		chicken cube		
minced			hot water	1/2 c	135 ml

1. Cut veal stew meat into 1–1-1/2 in. (2.5–3.8 cm) cubes.
2. Combine flour, salt, and pepper.
3. Roll veal cubes in flour. Reserve remaining flour for gravy.
4. Heat oil in the bottom pan of a pressure cooker over medium-high heat.
5. Add veal and brown meat on all sides. Remove meat and place on a plate.
6. Add onion and garlic. Sauté 2–3 minutes until golden.
7. Add veal and remaining ingredients to pressure cooker.
8. Cover and place on high heat. Let steam escape for a few seconds out of the valve to make sure it is open. Place control gauge set at 10 lbs over valve.
9. After control gauge first jiggles, cook for 20 minutes. Readjust heat so that gauge jiggles 1–4 times/minute.
10. Remove from heat. Allow to cool slowly for 5 minutes.
11. Place pressure pan in sink under cold running water to reduce pressure. The pressure should be reduced in 15–45 seconds or when the hissing stops. Check to see if pressure is reduced by nudging gauge with a fork. If nothing happens, remove gauge with fork, and open pressure cooker.
12. Mix remaining seasoned flour with 1/4 c (50 ml) cold tap water.
13. Place pressure cooker containing veal over high heat. Bring to a boil. Slowly add cold starch suspension, stirring continuously. Boil 1 minute.
14. Serve hot.

(Courtesy of Western Growers Association.)

14
Plant Proteins

OBJECTIVES

The student should be able to:

1. Assess the nutritive value of legumes, nuts, and seeds.
2. Know how to combine complementary plant proteins.
3. Determine the effect of pH on the rehydration of dried legumes.
4. Demonstrate the production of dairy-like products from vegetable proteins.
5. Prepare and compare meat analogs to meats.
6. Experiment with the use of vegetable proteins as a meat extender.
7. Prepare and compare foods made with high protein-containing plant foods.

FOOD SCIENCE PRINCIPLES

1. Legumes, nuts, and seeds are good sources of protein and fiber. Nuts and seeds are high in calories due to their high fat content. Some minerals are found in these plants but the availability may be limited by binding to fiber or phytates.
2. Plant proteins are considered poor quality proteins because they lack a sufficient quantity or the proper ratio of one or more of the essential amino acids. The amino acid lacking in a protein is called the *limiting* amino acid. The quality of a plant protein may be improved if the limiting amino is supplied, either as an additive or by supplying another plant protein that has the amino acid in abundance. With the exception of gelatin, meat proteins are high quality proteins.
3. In general, legumes are limited in methionine and tryptophan; nuts in lysine and tryptophan; and grains and seeds in lysine.
4. An alkaline environment will increase the speed of rehydration of dried legumes but destroys thiamine. Acids have the opposite effect and, for this reason, should not be added until after the beans have softened.
5. The proteins in soy flour can be coagulated by heat and acid to form curds and whey. A milk-like product can be extracted from ground soybeans but lacks the high quality protein, calcium, and vitamin B_{12} content of cow's milk.
6. Meat analogs and TVP can be palatable and acceptable as substitutes or extenders of meat and meat products.

Exercise I: Nutritive Value of Legumes, Nuts, and Seeds

Calculate the nutritive value of the plant foods in Table 14–1.

TABLE 14–1   Nutritive Value of Legumes, Nuts, and Seeds

Plant Food	Nutritive Value[a]							
	Food Energy (Cal)	Fat (g)	Protein (g)	Carbo-hydrates (g)	Calcium (mg)	Iron (mg)	Thiamine (mg)	Ribo-flavin (mg)
LEGUMES[b] black-eyed peas								
kidney beans								
lentils								
lima beans								
navy beans								
peanuts								
pinto beans								
soybeans								
split peas								
NUTS almonds								
cashews								
pecans								
walnuts								
SEEDS pumpkin								
sesame								
sunflower								

[a] Per 1 c (250 ml).
[b] Cooked.

QUESTIONS

1. Name the nutrients that are found in high amounts in legumes: _____

   _____

   _____

   In nuts: _____

   In seeds: _____

2. Which of the above categories of plant foods have the highest protein content? _____

   _____ Would these be recommended as a source of protein for an individual

   on a weight reduction diet? _____

   Why or why not? _____

   _____

3. Which of the above plant foods are good sources of calcium? _____

   _____

   Of iron? _____

Exercise II: Combination of Plant Proteins

1. List the limiting amino acid(s) of the groups of plant foods listed in Table 14–2. Use either of the following.

   a. Table 25–3, "Calorie, Fiber, and Protein Content of Protein-Containing Plants with Their Respective Limiting Amino Acids" in J. Freeland-Graves and G. Peckham, *Foundations of Food Preparation*, New York, Macmillan, 1987, pg. 653.
   b. Orr, M. and B. Watt, "Amino Acid Content of Foods," *Home Economics Report 4*, Washington, D.C., U.S. Department of Agriculture, 1957.

2. Suggest one or more *plant* proteins that will complement the limiting amino acid of the food group.
3. Give 2 examples of recipes or food combinations that would result in a high quality protein.
4. Record results in Table 14–2.

TABLE 14–2   Combining Plant Proteins

Food Group	Limiting Amino Acid(s)	Supplementary Plant Protein	Food Examples
Grains			
Greens			
Legumes			
Soybeans			
Nuts			
Seeds			

QUESTIONS

1. How would the protein quality be affected if milk was used to supplement the limiting amino acid in each of the above food groups? _____

_____

2. Give examples of how animal protein combined with poor quality vegetable protein can "stretch" the value of plant protein. _____

_____

_____

Experiment I: Effect of pH on Rehydration of Dried Legumes

1. Pressure cook dried pinto beans that have been soaked overnight according to the recipe below with the following variations:

   a. None.
   b. Add 1/2 tsp (1 ml) baking soda to the water *before* cooking.
   c. Substitute 1/4 c (50 ml) chopped tomatoes for 1/4 c (50 ml) water *before* cooking. Do not add more tomatoes after cooking.

Pinto Beans

oil	1 tsp	5 ml	tomatoes, canned,	1/4 c	50 ml
onion, chopped	1 tsp	5 ml	coarsely chopped		
garlic, minced	dash		salt	dash	
water	3/4 c	180 ml	pepper	dash	
pinto beans	1/4 c	50 ml			

   a. Heat oil in a pressure saucepan over medium-high heat.
   b. Add onions and garlic. Sauté until soft.
   c. Add water and beans. Cover and close.
   d. Let the steam escape for a few seconds to make sure the vent is open; then cover vent with a gauge set at 15 lbs. Cook *14* minutes after the gauge first jiggles. Lower heat so that the gauge jiggles 1–2 times/minute.
   e. Remove pan from heat. Let it cool slowly for 5 minutes. Then instantly reduce pressure by placing it under cold running water in a sink until the hissing stops, 15–45 seconds. Check to make sure pressure is reduced by nudging gauge with a fork. If nothing happens, remove gauge with a fork and open.
   f. Add remaining ingredients and simmer 3–5 minutes.

2. Observe the exterior appearance of the beans. Cut a few beans in half and observe the interior. Taste for flavor and tenderness.
3. Record results in Table 14–3.

TABLE 14–3   Effect of pH on Rehydration of Dried Legumes

Treatment	Appearance		Tenderness	Flavor
	Exterior	Interior		
None				
Alkali				
Acid				

QUESTIONS

1. What effect did the addition of baking soda have on the appearance and tenderness of beans?

   _____

   _____

2. When might this effect be used to an advantage? _____

   _____

3. What is the nutritional effect of adding baking soda? _____

   _____

4. Why are tomatoes normally added at the end of the cooking period when cooking dried legumes?

   _____

   _____

Experiment II: Preparation of Dairy-Like Products from Vegetable Proteins

1. Prepare the following dairy-like products from soy beans:

Soy Milk

soy beans, soaked	2 c	500 ml	corn *or* soy oil	1 tsp	5 ml
overnight					
cheesecloth			honey	2 tsp	10 ml

   a. Bring 8 cups (1.5 liters) of water to boiling in a Dutch oven.
   b. Set up 2 double boilers. Start heating water to a boil.
   c. Rinse beans and drain. Divide into 2 parts.
   d. Preheat the blender with 1 c (250 ml) boiling water. Let stand 1 minute. Discard water.
   e. Place 1/2 of beans in blender. Add 3 c (750 ml) boiling water and liquify mixture in blender.
   f. Place mixture in top of double boiler and simmer 20 minutes, stirring often.
   g. Strain through triple thickness of cheesecloth in a colander. Discard cheesecloth but retain liquid.
   h. Repeat steps d–g.

i. Reserve 1 c (250 ml) of the liquid to serve as soy milk. Use the remaining milk to prepare tofu in one of the recipes that follow.
j. Mix honey and oil with with 1 c (250 ml) soy milk.
k. Chill and serve.

Note: If soy milk is to be used as a substitute for cow's milk, it must be fortified with 800 mg calcium carbonate and 5 mg vitamin B_{12}/quart (liter).

Tofu

	Salty		*Sweet*	
soy milk	3 c	750 ml	3 c	750 ml
salt	1 tsp	5 ml	1/4 tsp	1 ml
vinegar, white	1 Tbsp	15 ml		
lemon juice			3 Tbsp + 1 tsp	35 ml
cheesecloth				

a. Heat soy milk to boiling point in a Dutch oven.
b. Reduce heat and simmer 5 minutes. Remove from heat.
c. Using 1 c (250 ml) hot water, combine salt and vinegar with water for salty cheese; or salt and lemon juice with water for sweet cheese.
d. Pour approximately 1/3 of the vinegar– or lemon juice–water mixture into the soy milk; stir 5–6 times.
e. Pour another 1/3 c (80 ml) of the acid mixture evenly over soy milk. *Do not stir.* Cover. Let stand 3 minutes. (Curds should form.)
f. Pour remaining acid mixture evenly over soy milk. Slowly stir upper half of liquid 15 seconds.
g. Use slotted spoon to remove large curds. Place in a colander lined with triple thickness of cheesecloth. Discard liquid.
h. Strain remaining curds through a second colander lined with a triple thickness of cheesecloth. Discard liquid. Add curds to curds in first cheesecloth.
i. Fold cheesecloth over curds while still in colander. Press into a round shape and gently squeeze out the liquid. Place plate over curds in the colander and let stand 15 minutes.
j. Remove curds from colander. Place in cold water and unwrap. Lift out tofu, drain, and chill.

Note: Tofu may be stored in refrigerator for one week if covered with water that is changed daily.

2. Observe the appearance and texture of the products. Taste for flavor.
3. List some food uses of these products.
4. Record results in Table 14–4.

TABLE 14–4   Comparison of Dairy-Like Products from Vegetable Proteins

Product	*Appearance*	*Texture*	*Flavor*	*Food Use*
Soy milk				
Tofu				

QUESTIONS

1. Explain how a cheese can be made from a plant. _____

   _____

   _____

2. Why is calcium and vitamin B$_{12}$ usually added to commercial soy milk? _____

   _____

   _____

3. Is fortified soy milk equal in nutritive value to cow's milk? _____

   Explain. _____

   _____

   _____

Experiment III: Preparation and Comparison of Meat Analogs to Meats

1. Prepare and compare fried bacon to a bacon analog (available frozen).

   a. Fry bacon in skillet over medium-high heat. Drain on paper towels.
   b. Prepare bacon analog according to package directions.
   c. Observe appearance and texture. Taste for flavor and crispness.

2. Prepare and compare an appetizer made with sausage links to one made with a sausage link analog. Use the following recipe:

Sweet-Sour Sausage

sausage links	5		orange juice	2 Tbsp	30 ml
pineapple tidbits	1/4 c	50 ml	vinegar	1 Tbsp	15 ml
curry powder	1/8 tsp	0.5 ml	apricot jam	1/4 c	50 ml
ginger powder	1/8 tsp	0.5 ml	maraschino	1 Tbsp	15 ml
cornstarch	1-1/2 tsp	7 ml	cherries, chopped		
reserved pineapple syrup					

   a. Brown sausage links according to package directions. Cut in quarters crosswise.
   b. Drain syrup from pineapple tidbits and reserve.
   c. Combine curry powder, ginger, and cornstarch in a saucepan.
   d. Stir in reserved syrup, orange juice, vinegar, and apricot jam.
   e. Turn heat to medium-high and cook until thickened, stirring constantly.
   f. Add sausage links and cherries.

3. Observe appearance and texture. Taste for flavor.
4. Record results in Table 14-5.

TABLE 14-5   Comparison of Meat Analog to Meats

Product		Appearance	Texture	Flavor	Other Qualities
Bacon	Meat				
	Analog				
Sweet-Sour Sausage	Meat				
	Analog				

QUESTIONS

1. Can meat analogs be acceptable substitutes for meat? _____

   _____

2. Was there a difference between the real and imitation sausage link? _____

   _____

3. What nutritional benefits are there in eating meat analogs? _____

   _____

   Disadvantages? _____

   _____

Experiment IV: Use of Texturized Vegetable Protein as a Meat Extender

1. Rehydrate 1-1/2 oz (45 g) of dried texturized vegetable protein (TVP) by adding 1-1/2 oz (45 g) of water. Stir gently. Let stand covered 10 minutes.
2. Prepare one recipe of chili according to the recipe below for each of the following variations:

   a. none.
   b. add 2 oz (60 g) hamburger meat with the onoins. Sauté until brown.
   c. add 1 oz (30 g) hamburger meat with the onions. Sauté until brown. Add 1 oz (30 g) TVP with the tomatoes.
   d. add 2 oz (60 g) TVP with the tomatoes.

Chili Sin Carne

oil	2 tsp	10 ml	tomatoes, canned, coarsely chopped	1/2 c	125 ml
onions, chopped	1 Tbsp	15 ml			
green pepper, chopped	1 Tbsp	15 ml	cumin seed	1/8 tsp	0.5 ml
			salt	1/8 tsp	0.5 ml
garlic clove, minced	1/4		chili powder	1/4 tsp	1 ml
			cayenne pepper	dash	
kidney beans, canned	1/2 c	125 ml			

a. Heat oil in a small skillet.
b. Add onions, peppers and garlic. Sauté until lightly browned.
c. Add remaining ingredients. Bring to a boil; lower heat, cover, and simmer 30–45 minutes.

3. Observe appearance. Taste for texture, tenderness, and flavor.
4. Record results in Table 14–6.

QUESTIONS

1. Is it possible to tell from the appearance of tne products if TVP has been added? _____ _____ _____

2. Why would TVP be added to chili? _____ _____

3. How can TVP be made more palatable? _____ _____

TABLE 14–6 Use of Texturized Vegetable Protein as a Meat Extender in Chili

Ingredient Added	Appearance	Tenderness	Texture	Flavor
None				
Meat				
Meat + TVP				
TVP				

Experiment V: Preparation and Comparison of High Protein-Containing Plant Foods

1. Prepare and compare a variety of the recipes found in Applications.
2. Evaluate for palatability. Record results in Table 14–7.

TABLE 14–7 Comparison of High Protein-Containing Plant Foods

Product	Evaluation

APPLICATIONS

Hot Stir-Fried Tofu

broccoli, florets	1/2 c	125 ml	red pepper	1/4 tsp	1 ml
cauliflower, florets	1/2 c	125 ml	gingeroot, grated	1/2 tsp	2 ml
green onions,	2		*or*		
sliced diagonally			ginger, ground	1 tsp	5 ml
1/2 in. (1.3 cm)			tofu	3/4 c	180 ml
soy sauce	1–1/2 Tbsp	22 ml	oil	2 tsp	10 ml
water	1/4 c	50	pecans or walnuts	1/3 c	80 ml
cornstarch	1 tsp	5 ml	Mandarin oranges,	1/3 c	80 ml
sugar	1/2 tsp	2 ml	canned, drained		

1. Prepare vegetables if not previously prepared. Set aside.
2. Prepare sauce:

   a. Combine soy sauce, water, and cornstarch.
   b. Add sugar, red pepper, and ginger. Mix well. Set aside.

3. Drain tofu. Pat dry with paper towels. Cut into 1/2-in. (1.3 cm) cubes.
4. Heat 1 tsp (5 ml) oil in a heavy skillet or, preferably, electric wok over medium-high heat.
5. Stir-fry tofu until lightly browned, approximately 2 minutes. Make sure pieces remain intact and do not crumble. Remove to serving dish.
6. Add 1 tsp (5 ml) oil to skillet. Add vegetables and stir-fry 2–3 minutes. (Vegetables should still be crisp.) Remove to serving dish.
7. Add nuts. Stir-fry 1 minute.
8. Pour in sauce. Boil 1 minute, stirring constantly. If mixture becomes too thick, add additional water.
9. Return tofu and vegetables to skillet. Cover and cook 1 minute.
10. Stir in oranges. Heat through and serve immediately.

Curried Stir-Fried Tofu

curry powder	1-1/2 tsp	7 ml	almonds	1/4 c	50 ml
cumin	1/2 tsp	2 ml	raisins	1/4 c	50 ml
tumeric	1/2 tsp	2 ml	carrots, thinly	1/4 c	50 ml
mustard seed	1/2 tsp	2 ml	sliced diagonally		
cloves, ground	1/4 tsp	1 ml	yellow squash, thinly	1/4 c	50 ml
coriander, ground	1/4 tsp	1 ml	sliced diagonally		
chili powder	1/4 tsp	1 ml	broccoli florets	1/2 c	125 ml
salt	1/4 tsp	1 ml	green pepper, sliced	1/3	
ginger, ground	1/4 tsp	1 ml	red cabbage, shredded	3/4 c	180 ml
oil (divided)	1 Tbsp + 2 tsp	25 ml	vegetable bouillon	1/4 c	50 ml
margarine	1 Tbsp	15 ml	buttermilk	1/2 c	125 ml
onion, sliced	1/2		coriander (cilantro),	1 Tbsp	15 ml
tofu	3/4 c	180 ml	chopped (optional)		
peanuts	1/4 c	50 ml			

1. Measure spices and combine on wax paper.
2. Heat 1 Tbsp (15 ml) of oil and margarine in a skillet over low heat.
3. Add spices and the onion to oil. Sauté 15 minutes, stirring occasionally.
4. Drain tofu. Pat dry with paper towels. Cut into 1/2-in. (1.3 cm) cubes.
5. Add tofu, peanuts, almonds, and raisins to spices and stir-fry 5 minutes. Do not let the tofu crumble into small pieces.
6. Add remaining 2 tsp (10 ml) oil. Raise heat to medium. Add remaining vegetables except coriander; stir-fry 3 minutes.
7. Add vegetable bouillon; cover and cook 2–3 minutes.
8. Remove from heat; cool slightly.
9. Stir in buttermilk, sprinkle with coriander, and serve immediately.

Tofu Patties

oil (divided)	1 Tbsp + 1 tsp	20 ml	egg, beaten	1/2	
onion, minced	1-1/2 Tbsp	22 ml	whole wheat flour	2 tsp	10 ml
green pepper, chopped	1 Tbsp	15 ml	curry powder	1/2 tsp	2 ml
			soy sauce	2 tsp	10 ml
celery, chopped	1-1/2 Tbsp	22 ml	wheat germ	2 Tbsp	30 ml
tofu	1/2 c	125 ml			

1. Heat 1 tsp (5 ml) oil in a skillet over medium heat.
2. Add onion, green pepper, and celery, and sauté until soft.
3. Drain tofu. Pat dry with paper towels. Mash with fork in a bowl.
4. Mix sautéed vegetables with tofu, egg, whole wheat flour, curry powder, and soy sauce.
5. Form mixture into patties that are approximately 1/2-in. (1.3 cm) thick and 1-1/2 in. (3.8 cm) in diameter. Roll in wheat germ.
6. Heat remaining oil (1 Tbsp) in skillet over medium heat. Brown patties in oil, turning only once. Be careful because these patties easily burn.
7. Serve while still warm.

Lentils

lentils	1/2 c	125 ml	carrot, chopped	1/4	
vegetable bouillon	1-1/2 c	375 ml	margarine (divided)	1 Tbsp	15 ml
onion, chopped	2 Tbsp	30 ml	salt	1/8 tsp	0.5 ml
celery stalk, chopped	1/2		pepper	dash	

1. Place lentils, bouillon, vegetables, and 1/2 of the margarine in a saucepan.
2. Cover and bring to a boil. Simmer 30 minutes.
3. Pour into serving bowl. Place remaining margarine on top. Sprinkle with salt and pepper and serve hot.

Nut–Seed Burgers

coucous	1/4 c	50 ml	dry mustard	1 tsp	5 ml
almonds, peeled	2/3 c	160 ml	brown sugar	1 tsp	5 ml
peanuts	2/3 c	160 ml	cumin, ground	1 tsp	5 ml
sunflower seeds, hulled	2/3 c	160 ml	cayenne pepper	1/4 tsp	1 ml
			coriander, ground	1/4 tsp	1 ml
ketchup	1/4 c	50 ml	onion, minced	1/4 c	50 ml
garlic clove, crushed and chopped	1		green pepper, chopped	1/4 c	50 ml
vinegar, cider	1 Tbsp	15 ml	pita bread	4	
Worcestershire sauce	1 Tbsp	15 ml	Buttermilk Sauce	(see p. 200)	
chili powder	2 tsp	10 ml	Salsa	(see p. 200)	
monosodium glutamate	1 tsp	5 ml			

1. Pour 1/4 c (50 ml) hot water over coucous in a large bowl. Cover with aluminum foil and let set for 10 minutes until water is absorbed.
2. Coarsely chop almonds in a food processor.
3. Add peanuts to almonds and process until mixture clumps together and starts to leave the side of the container, approximately 2 minutes.
4. Add sunflower seeds and process 30 more seconds.
5. In a small bowl, combine ketchup, garlic, vinegar, Worcestershire sauce, chili powder, monosodium glutamate, dry mustard, brown sugar, cumin, cayenne pepper, coriander, onion, and green pepper.
6. Pour mixture over coucous. Add nut–seed mixture. Stir until well mixed.
7. Divide mixture into four parts. Shape each fourth into a patty.
8. Spray nonstick cooking spray on a nonstick frying pan.
9. Add patties, cover, and cook over medium heat until lightly brown on first side, approximately 1–2 minutes. Turn and continue cooking until brown on second side, approximately 2–3 minutes. *Watch carefully because these easily burn.*
10. Place each patty in the pocket of a pita bread. Pour 2 Tbsp (30 ml) Buttermilk Sauce (pg. 200) on top. Add 1/4 c (50 ml) Salsa (pg. 200) over sauce and patty and serve immediately.

Buttermilk Sauce

buttermilk	1/4 c	50 ml	salt	1/2 tsp	2 ml
lemon juice, fresh	2 Tbsp	30 ml	paprika	1/4 tsp	1 ml
cottage cheese	1/4 c	50 ml	green pepper	1/4	

1. Combine all ingredients except green pepper in a blender.
2. Blend until smooth on high speed.
3. Remove seeds and membranes from green pepper. Cut into chunks.
4. Add green pepper to blender. Blend just until green pepper is chopped.

Salsa

tomatoes, fresh, chopped	1 c (3)	250 ml	vinegar, cider	1-1/2 tsp	8 ml
			salt	1/2 tsp	2 ml
cucumber, small	1/2		pepper	dash	
onion, chopped	1/4 c	50 ml			
coriander (cilantro), chopped	2-1/2 Tbsp	38 ml			

1. Cut cucumber in half. Remove seeds with a spoon. Dice the remainder.
2. Combine all ingredients in a bowl and mix. Serve the same day.

Creole Lima Beans

baby lima beans, soaked overnight, 1/4 lb (125 g)	1 c	125 ml	seasoned salt	1/2 tsp	2 ml
			salt	dash	
			pepper	dash	
liquid	1-1/4 c	185 ml	brown sugar	2 tsp	10 ml
bacon slices*	2		Worchestershire sauce	1/4 tsp	1 ml
onion, chopped	1/4				
green pepper, chopped	1/4		tomatoes, canned, drained, coarsely chopped	1/2 c	125 ml
flour	1 tsp	5 ml			

1. Place the soaked lima beans and the liquid in the bottom of a pressure cooker. Use the liquid that the beans were soaked in plus tap water equal to 1-1/4 c (300 ml).
2. Cover and set gauge at 15 lbs. Cook for 25 minutes after the gauge first jiggles. Readjust heat so that the gauge jiggles 1-2 times/minute.
3. Prepare creole sauce:
   a. Fry bacon in a small skillet until crisp.* Remove and drain on paper towels. Crumble and set aside.
   b. Sauté onion and green pepper in hot fat over medium-high heat until soft.
   c. Add rest of ingredients and simmer 10 minutes over low heat, uncovered, to reduce sauce.
4. When beans have cooked for 25 minutes, remove pressure cooker from heat. Allow the cooker to cook slowly for 5 minutes. Then reduce pressure instantly by placing pan in sink under cold running water until hissing stops (15–45 seconds). Check to make sure pressure is reduced by nudging gauge with a fork. If nothing happens, remove gauge with a fork and open.
5. Pour lima beans into reduced creole sauce. Mix together and serve.

*Vegetarian: Use 3 Tbsp (45 ml) olive oil.

Black-Eyed Peas

black-eyed peas, canned	2/3 c	160 ml	whole wheat flour	1-1/2 Tbsp	22 ml
			salt	1/2 tsp	2 ml
broth from can	4 Tbsp	60 ml	chili powder	1/4 tsp	1 ml
olive oil	2 Tbsp	30 ml	margarine	1/4 tsp	1 ml
onion, chopped	1/3 c	80 ml			
garlic clove, minced	1				

1. Heat oil in a skillet over medium-high heat.
2. Sauté onion and garlic 5 minutes until lightly browned.
3. Stir in whole wheat flour and spices. Cover 1 minute until smooth and bubbly.
4. Add broth from can. Bring to a boil and cook 15 seconds.
5. Add peas and heat through.

(Courtesy of Oscar Mayer Foods Corp.)

15

Poultry

OBJECTIVES

The student should be able to:

1. Assess the nutritive value of poultry.
2. Cut up a chicken and bone the breast.
3. Describe the effect of age on the tenderness of poultry.
4. Evaluate the effect of the cooking method on the appearance and quality of poultry.
5. Prepare and compare dry and moist methods of cooking poultry.

FOOD SCIENCE PRINCIPLES

1. Poultry is similar to meat in its protein content but has fewer calories/serving. The fat content is generally lower than that of meats but may vary widely according to the species, age, and feeding practices. Poultry is a good source of the B vitamins: thiamine, riboflavin, and niacin. Livers are an excellent source of iron.
2. The tenderness of poultry is dependent on the age of the birds, the fat content, and the extent that the muscles have been exercised. Older birds have a more intense flavor, which is desirable for stewing.
3. Tender cuts of poultry may be cooked by all methods of cookery. Juicier meat results when plump birds are roasted. The lack of a strong flavor when stewing young poultry may be compensated for by the addition of a bouillon cube.
4. Less tender, older foul should be cooked by moist methods of cooking to tenderize the bird. These include pan- and oven-braising, simmering, and pressure cooking.

Exercise I: Calculation of Cost/Serving and Nutritive Value of Poultry

1. Calculate the nutritive value of poultry in Table 15–1.
2. Determine the cost/lb of poultry from supermarket ads or from a price list posted in the laboratory. Divide the cost/lb (500 g) by the number of servings/lb (500 g) to determine the cost/serving.
3. Record results in Table 15–1.

TABLE 15-1 Calculation of Cost/Serving and Nutritive Value of Poultry

Cooked Meat 3 oz (90 g)	Cost/lb (500 g)	Cost/ Serving	Food Energy (Cal)	Protein (g)	Fat (g)	Iron (mg)	Thia- mine (mg)	Ribo- flavin (mg)	Niacin (mg)
CHICKEN breast									
wing									
liver									
DUCK									
GOOSE									
TURKEY breast									
thigh									

QUESTIONS

1. Which type of poultry is the most expensive per lb (500 g)? _____
   Per serving? _____

2. Which species of poultry is the most caloric? _____
   Why? _____

3. What nutrient is found in high amounts in chicken livers? _____
   _____

4. In general, how does the nutritive value of poultry compare to that of beef? _____
   _____
   _____
   _____

Experiment I: Disjointing and Boning a Chicken

Select a whole broiler-fryer.

Observe or prepare a cut-up chicken and bone a chicken breast according to the directions in Figures 15–1 and 15–2:

1. Begin by cutting off legs. Cut skin between thighs and body of chicken.

2. Lift chicken and bend legs, grasping one leg with each hand. Bend legs until hip joints are loose.

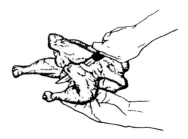

3. Remove leg from body by cutting from back to front as close as possible to the back bone.

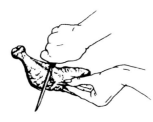

4. Separate thigh and drumstick. Locate joint by squeezing between thigh and drumstick. Cut through joint.

5. To remove wing from body, start cutting on inside of wing just over the joint. Cut down and around the joint. To make the wing lie flat, make a small cut on the inside of the large wing joint. Cut just deep enough to expose the bones. Repeat with wing on other side.

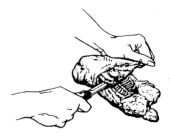

6. To cut the body into breast and back sections, place the chicken on neck end and cut from the tail along each side of back bone through rib joints to neck. Cut through the skin that attaches the neck-and-back strip to the breast. Place neck-and-back strip skin side up on cutting board. Cut into two pieces just above the spoon-shaped bones in the back. Another method is to separate the back from the breast by cutting between the breast and back ribs from the shoulder to the tail end. Bend the back away from breast to separate the shoulder joints.

7. Place breast skin side down on cutting board. Cut through white cartilage at the V of the neck.

8. Hold breast firmly with both hands and bend back both sides. Push up with fingers to snap out the breastbone. Cut breast in half lengthwise.

FIGURE 15–1 *How to cut up a chicken. (Courtesy of the National Broiler Council.)*

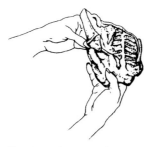
Bend and break keel bone.

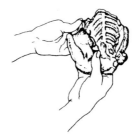
Run thumb between meat and keel bone.

Separate breast from rib cage.

Remove skin and trim.

FIGURE 15-2 *How to bone chicken breasts. (Courtesy of the National Broiler Council.)*

Experiment II: Effect of Age on the Tenderness of Poultry

Select a chicken part from a young broiler and an old stewing hen. Select the same part (leg, thigh, wing, breast) from each bird.

1. Broil chicken according to the following recipe:

Broiled Chicken

chicken part	1	
margarine	1–1/2 tsp	7 ml
salt	dash	
pepper	dash	

   a. Wash chicken and pat dry with paper towel.
   b. Position oven rack so that when chicken is placed on broiler pan, the top of the chicken is approximately 4–6 in. (10–15 cm) from the broiler.
   c. Melt margarine in saucepan or microwave 30 seconds in a small cup.
   d. Turn oven to broil.
   e. Place chicken on broiler pan skin side down. Brush with melted margarine.
   f. Broil approximately 10–20 minutes until brown, basting frequently.
   g. Turn chicken over with tongs. Do *not* pierce the meat. Broil 15 more minutes on second side.

    h. The chicken can be checked for doneness by piercing the meat and observing the color of t⬤ juices that run out. If they are clear, the chicken is cooked.

    i. Season and serve.

2. Remove chicken to a serving dish.
3. Observe appearance and texture. Taste for tenderness and flavor.
4. Record result in Table 15–2.

QUESTIONS

1. What effect did using a dry heat method have on the palatability of the less tender piece of chicken? _____

   _____

   Why? _____

   _____

2. Which chicken had the most "chicken" flavor? _____

   Why? _____

   _____

3. What would be the proper way to cook less tender cuts of poultry? _____

   _____

   _____ ⬤

4. Which type of chicken was the most tender? _____

   _____

Experiment III: Effect of Cooking Method on Appearance and Quality of Poultry

Select 3 chicken parts (3 legs, 3 thighs, or 3 breasts).

1. Preheat oven to 325°F (160°C).
2. Wash chicken and dry with a paper towel.
3. Melt 1/4 c (50 ml) margarine. Brush on chicken pieces. Sprinkle lightly with pepper and paprika.
4. Insert a meat thermometer into the thickest part of the muscle of each piece of chicken. Do not allow it to touch a bone. If the piece is too small, do not use thermometer; instead determine doneness with a fork.
5. Wrap 1 chicken piece in aluminum foil, dull side out. Leave top of thermometer exposed. Make sure the foil is sealed tightly around the bulb. Place in one side of an 8–9 in. (20–22.5 cm) pan.
6. Place second piece of chicken in a transparent browning bag. Tie and place in the other side of the pan with the chicken in step 5. Make sure thermometer is visible.
7. Place the third piece of chicken uncovered in a third 8 or 9 in. (20–22.5 cm) pan.
8. Place both pans in oven. Record time. (Alternative: Have 3 students bake each of the 3 pieces of chicken in separate pans or ovens.)
9. Bake 40–60 minutes until the thermometer reaches 185°F (85°C). If thermometers are not used bake until fork tender. Baste uncovered piece of chicken occasionally with margarine or drippings.
10. Remove each piece of chicken when the thermometer reaches the desired temperature. Record time.
11. Observe surface appearance, texture, and juiciness. Taste for tenderness and flavor. ⬤
12. Record results in Table 15–3.

TABLE 15–2   Effect of Broiling on Young and Old Poultry

Chicken	Surface Appearance	Texture	Flavor	Tenderness
Young broiler				
Old stewing hen				

QUESTIONS

1. Which method of cooking produced the brownest chicken? _____
   Why? _____
   _____

2. Which method of cooking produced the juiciest, most flavorful product? _____
   _____ Why? _____
   _____

3. What was the effect of wrapping chicken in foil? _____
   _____

4. How does cooking poultry in a bag compare to the other methods of roasting in terms of
   browning? _____
   Juiciness? _____
   Tenderness? _____
   Flavor? _____

TABLE 15–3   Effect of Cooking Method on Appearance and Quality of Chicken

Roasting Method	Roasting Time (minutes)	Surface Appearance	Texture	Juiciness	Tenderness	Flavor
Uncovered						
Wrapped in foil						
Browning bag						

Experiment IV: Preparation and Comparison of Dry and Moist Methods of Cooking Poultry

Select poultry to be prepared by dry and moist methods of cookery. Use either the basic method in each section or prepare a recipe which illustrates an application of the basic method.

1. Wash poultry and dry with a paper towel. Remove any inedible material.
2. Weigh the raw meat and record.
3. Prepare meats according to the basic method or selected recipe. Check with the laboratory teacher for instructions.
4. Keep a record of the preparation time.
5. Weigh the cooked meat and record. Calculate % cooking losses by the following formula:

$$\frac{\text{Raw weight} - \text{cooked weight}}{\text{Raw weight}} \times 100 = \%\ \text{cooking loss}$$

6. Observe appearance and juiciness. Determine tenderness by ease of penetration with a fork and ease of chewing. Taste for flavor.
7. Record results in Table 15–5.

Dry Methods of Cooking Poultry

Roasting

Use the basic method roasting to prepare roast chicken or roast guinea hen, or prepare Rock Cornish Game Hen á la Orange, p. 214.

Roasting Poultry–Basic Method

1. Preheat oven to 325°F (160°C).
2. Lightly rub cavity of bird with salt.
3. **Optional:** Fill cavity of bird *loosely* with a bread or rice stuffing. Heat will cause it to expand.
4. Fasten skin of neck to back with a wooden skewer. Tuck wings under back so that the tips are touching. Tie drumsticks to tail with a string.
5. Brush bird with melted margarine or butter.
6. Place bird breast side up on a rack in an uncovered shallow pan.
7. **Optional:** A meat thermometer can be placed in the center of the inner thigh muscle if the bird is large enough. Be certain that it does not touch a bone.
8. Place pan in oven and cook according to Table 15–4. Baste occasionally.
9. The bird is cooked when the leg moves easily up and down or the thermometer registers 180°F (82°C) to 185°F (85°C).
10. Remove from oven. Place on serving dish and cut string.
11. Salt and allow to stand a few minutes before carving.

TABLE 15-4   Timetable for Roasting Poultry at 325°F (160°C)[a]

Type of Poultry	Weight		Roasting Time
	lbs	kg	hours[b]
CHICKEN			
whole:[c]			
broiler-fryer	2-1/2–3-1/4	1.1–1.5	1-3/4–2-1/2
roaster	3-1/4–4-1/2	1.5–2	2–3
capon	5–8-1/2	2.3–3.9	3–4
Rock Cornish game hen	1–2	0.5–0.9	1-1/2–2
pieces	1/4–3/4	0.1–0.3	1–2-1/2
DUCK[c]	4–6	1.8–2.7	2-1/2–4
GOOSE	6–8	2.7–3.6	3–3-1/2
TURKEY			
whole[c]	6–8	2.7–3.6	3–3-1/2
	8–12	3.6–5.5	3-1/2–4-1/2
	12–16	5.5–7.3	4-1/2–5-1/2
	16–20	7.3–9	5-1/2–6-1/2
	20–24	9–10.9	6-1/2–7
halves, quarters	5–11	2.3–5	3–5-1/2
quarters, thighs, drumsticks	1–3	0.5–1.4	2–3-1/2
boneless turkey roasts[d]	3–10	1.4–4.5	3–4

[a] Adapted from "Poultry in Family Meals." *Home and Garden Bulletin No. 110*, Washington, D.C.: U.S. Department of Agriculture, 1982.
[b] Approximate time to reach 180°–185°F (82°–85°C) in thickest part of the meat. Stuffing should reach at least 165°F (74°C).
[c] Stuffed. Unstuffed poultry may require slightly less time.
[d] Turkey roasts should reach temperatures of 170°–175°F (77°–79°C) in the center.

Broiling

Select a young broiler. Use the method in Experiment II to prepare a quarter of a broiler chicken or half of a guinea hen, or, prepare Chicken Teriyaki, pg. 216.

Pan-Frying

Select a broiler or fryer. Use the basic method of pan-frying poultry to prepare fried chicken, capon or Rock Cornish game hen. (See Figure 15-3.)

Pan-Frying Poultry—Basic Method

1. Cut bird into serving pieces as shown in Experiment I.
2. Wash and dry with a paper towel.
3. **Optional:** Dip chicken pieces into a bag containing flour seasoned with salt and pepper. Shake off any excess flour. The pieces may then be further dipped in an egg-milk mixture and coated with bread crumbs.
4. Heat 1/4 c (50 ml) fat or oil in a *heavy* skillet over medium heat.
5. Add larger pieces of chicken to the pan, skin side down. Do *not* crowd pan. Gradually add smaller pieces.
6. Brown each side of the pieces of poultry.

FIGURE 15-3   Cooking breast slices of poultry by the basic method of pan-frying. (Courtesy of Oscar Mayer Foods Corp.)

7. Lower heat. Do *not* cover. Cook until tender for a total cooking time of 30–45 minutes.
8. Drain on paper towels to remove excess fat.

Deep Fat-Frying

See Batter-Fried Chicken, pg. 248.

Oven-Frying

Select a broiler or fryer. Use the basic method of oven-frying to prepare oven-fried chicken, capon, or Rock Cornish game hen.

Oven-Frying Poultry—Basic Method

1. Preheat oven to 400°F (200°C).
2. Follow steps 1–3 for the basic method of pan-frying poultry.
3. Add melted fat or oil to a baking pan to a depth of 1/8 in. (3 mm) deep.
4. Place pan with oil in the oven to preheat for 10 minutes.
5. Add chicken; cook skin down for 30 minutes.
6. Turn with tongs. Cook 20 to 30 minutes longer until tender.
7. Remove from oven and drain on paper towels.

Stir-Frying

See Ginger Lemon Stir-Fried Chicken, pg. 215.

Microwave Cooking

See Lemon Garlic Chicken, pg. 352.

Moist Methods of Cooking Poultry

Pan-Braising

Select a less tender, stewing fowl to illustrate tenderization by braising, or, select young, tender poultry for fast cooking. Use the basic method of pan-braising to prepare braised chicken or capon, or prepare Chicken Curry, pg. 216 or Chicken Paprika, pg. 217. (See Figure 15-4.)

Pan-Braising Poultry—Basic Method

1. Cut the bird into serving pieces as shown in Experiment I.
2. Wash chicken and dry with a paper towel.
3. **Optional:** Dip chicken pieces in a bag containing flour seasoned with salt and pepper. Shake off any excess flour.
4. Heat 2 Tbsp (30 ml) fat or oil in a heavy skillet over medium-high heat.
5. Add larger pieces of chicken to the pan, skin side down. Gradually add smaller pieces. Brown quickly on all sides. Do not allow the fat to burn or smoke.
6. Remove chicken from pan and place on a dish.
7. Drain off the fat from the skillet.
8. Place chicken back in pan. Add 1/4 c (50 ml) to 1 c (250 ml) water or liquid.
9. Cover and bring liquid to a boil.
10. Lower heat and simmer until tender, 1 to 2–1/2 hours. More liquid may be added if necessary to prevent sticking.
11. The cover may be removed during the last 30 minutes of the cooking time to crisp the skin.

Oven-Braising

Select a less tender, stewing fowl to illustrate tenderization by braising, or, select young, tender poultry for fast cooking. Use the basic method of oven-braising to prepare oven braised chicken or capon or, prepare Country Captain Chicken, pg. 217.

Oven-Braising Poultry—Basic Method

1. Preheat oven to 325°F (160°C).
2. Follow steps 1–8 for the basic method of pan-braising poultry. The bird may be left whole if desired. Aluminum foil may be used in place of a lid in step 9.
3. Place pan in oven.
4. Cook 1–2–1/2 hours.

Simmering (Stewing)

Select a less tender stewing fowl to illustrate tenderization by simmering or stewing, or, select young, tender poultry for fast cooking. Use the basic method of stewing or simmering to prepare stewed chicken, or prepare Chicken Fricassee with Dumplings, pg. 218.

FIGURE 15-4   *Cooking poultry by the basic method of braising. (Courtesy of Oscar Mayer Foods Corp.)*

Simmering (Stewing) Poultry—Basic Method

1. Follow steps 1 and 2 for the basic method of pan-braising poultry. The bird may be left whole if desired.
2. **Optional:** Follow steps 4–6 if bird is cut into pieces.
3. Place poultry in a heavy dutch oven. Add liquid or water to barely cover chicken pieces.
4. Bring to boil, cover, lower heat and simmer 45 minutes to 1 hour for tender poultry or 1-1/2–2 hours for less tender fowl.
5. Prepared vegetables may be added 45 minutes before the end of the cooking period. Vegetables should be added in this order: carrots, celery, onion, and potatoes. Add each vegetable separately and allow the liquid to boil for a few minutes before the next vegetable is added.
6. Seasonings, spices, wine, and herbs may be added when liquid is added to the poultry. Because the flavor of herbs and wine may be reduced with long cooking times, the stew may be "freshened" by the addition of more herbs or wine before the end of the cooking period.

Pressure Cooking

Use the method recommended of the instruction book for the pressure cooker or prepare Chicken Fricasee, pg. 218.

QUESTIONS

1. How many servings are there in a pound (500 g) of poultry? _____

2. What type of poultry is used in roasting? _____
   Why? _____

3. Why must the stuffing be *loosely* packed in the cavity? _____
   _____
   _____

4. What are the advantages of pan-frying poultry? _____
   _____

5. How does the final product from pan-frying compare to that of oven-frying? _____
   _____

6. Which method of braising, pan or oven, produces a more flavorful product? _____
   _____ Why? _____
   _____

7. Why are less tender fowl used for stewing if the cooking time must be doubled? _____
   _____
   _____

TABLE 15-5 Preparation and Comparison of Dry and Moist Methods of Cooking Poultry

Method of Cookery	Raw Weight (g)	Cooked Weight (g)	% Cooking Loss	Preparation Time (minutes)	Appearance	Tenderness	Flavor	Juiciness
DRY roasting								
broiling								
pan-frying								
deep fat-frying								
oven-frying								
stir-frying								
microwave cooking								
MOIST pan-braising								
oven-braising								
simmering (stewing)								
pressure cooking								

APPLICATIONS

Rock Cornish Game Hen á L'Orange

small guinea hen	1		margarine	1 Tbsp + 1 tsp	20 ml
onion slice	1		soy sauce	1 Tbsp + 1 tsp	20 ml
salt	dash		brown sugar	1/4 c	50 ml
paprika	dash		parsley flakes	2 tsp	10 ml
frozen or orange	1/2 c	125 ml	ginger, ground	1 tsp	5 ml
juice concentrate			water	1/4 c	50 ml
or			raisins	1/4 c	50 ml
small can frozen	1				
orange juice					

1. Preheat oven to 350°F (175°C).
2. Wash bird and pat dry with a paper towel. Sprinkle salt inside cavity.
3. Place the onion slice inside the cavity.
4. Arrange bird on a V-shaped roasting rack in a baking pan.
5. Sprinkle lightly with paprika.
6. Roast in the oven for 45 minutes/lb (500 g) or until the leg moves up and down easily. During the last 10 minutes of the roasting period, raise the oven temperature to 400°F (200°C).
7. Meanwhile, prepare orange sauce:

   a. Mix together the rest of the ingredients in a small saucepan.
   b. Bring to boil; lower heat and simmer 1 minute.
   c. Pour approximately half the sauce into a cup for basting.

8. Baste the bird with the orange sauce in the cup during the last 15 minutes of cooking.
9. When bird is cooked, remove from rack onto plate.
10. Warm sauce remaining in pan. Serve sauce separately with bird.

Nutty Rice Stuffing

margarine	2 tsp	10 ml	celery leaves,	2 Tbsp	30 ml
(divided)			chopped		
almonds, chopped	2 Tbsp	30 ml	rice	1/2 c	125 ml
celery, minced	1/4 c	50 ml	salt	1/4 tsp	1 ml
onion, chopped	1/4 c	50 ml	water, hot	1 c	250 ml
mushrooms, sliced	1/3 c	80 ml	chicken bouillon	1 tsp	5 ml
			powder		

1. Preheat oven to 350°F (175°C).
2. Melt 1 tsp (5 ml) margarine in a small skillet; add almonds and sauté over medium heat until golden. Set aside in a small dish.
3. Melt the remaining 1 tsp (5 ml) margarine in the same pan. Add celery and onions; sauté 3 minutes over medium-high heat.
4. Add mushrooms to the celery and onions; sauté 2 minutes.
5. Add celery leaves to the mushrooms, celery, and onions; sauté 1 minute.
6. Add rice and salt. Mix well with vegetables and sauté 3–5 minutes.
7. Add hot water, bouillon powder, and water; bring to a boil and pour mixture into a small casserole dish.
8. Cover tightly and bake 15–20 minutes until all the liquid has been absorbed.

Ginger Lemon Stir-Fried Chicken

chicken breasts, boned, skinned	2		broccoli florets	2 c	500 ml
			mushrooms, fresh	8 oz	250 g
garlic cloves	2		green onions	3	
lemon juice, fresh	2 Tbsp	30 ml	oil, divided	2 Tbsp	30 ml
soy sauce	3 Tbsp	45 ml	cornstarch	1 tsp	5 ml
ginger, fresh, grated	2 tsp	10 ml	coriander (cilantro), minced	1/2 tsp	2 ml
sesame seeds	1–1/2 tsp	7 ml	lemon slices	2	

1. Preheat oven to 450°F (230°C).
2. Cut chicken breasts into 1/2-in. (1.3 cm) thick strips.
3. Smash peeled garlic cloves in a garlic press.
4. Combine garlic, lemon juice, soy sauce, and ginger in a small bowl. Add chicken and marinate 20–30 minutes at room temperature.
5. Spread sesame seeds in a single layer on a baking sheet. Toast in oven until lightly browned, approximately 5–8 minutes. Watch carefully because these burn easily. Set aside.
6. Prepare vegetables:

   a. Cut broccoli florets into halves.
   b. Cut mushrooms into quarters.
   c. Slice entire green onions diagonally into 1-in. (2.5 cm) pieces.

7. Add 1/2 of oil (1 Tbsp or 15 ml) to heated electric wok or electric frying pan.
8. Drain chicken. Reserve marinade.
9. Measure remaining marinade, add enough water to equal 1/3 c (80 ml); stir in cornstarch. Set aside.
10. When oil sizzles, add chicken and stir-fry until it loses its pink color, approximately 1–2 minutes. *Do not overcook.* Remove chicken to plate and cover with aluminum foil to keep warm.
11. Add mushrooms to pan and stir-fry 1–2 minutes. Remove and add to chicken on plate.
12. Add remaining oil (1 Tbsp or 15 ml) to pan. When oil sizzles, add broccoli and green onion. Stir-fry 2–3 minutes until broccoli just starts to become slightly tender.
13. Add cornstarch–marinade mixture to pan. Return chicken and mushrooms to pan. Cook 1 minute until mixture thickens.
14. Immediately remove to serving platter. Sprinkle with toasted sesame seeds and cilantro. Garnish with lemon slices.

Chicken Curry

chicken	1/4		cinnamon	1/4 tsp	1 ml
margarine	2 tsp	10 ml	ginger, ground	1/8 tsp	0.5 ml
oil	2 tsp	10 ml	turmeric	1/8 tsp	0.5 ml
garlic clove, sliced	1		coriander, ground	1/2 tsp	2 ml
onion, sliced	1/2		cumin, ground	1/8 tsp	0.5 ml
cardamom seed, ground	1/8 tsp	0.5 ml	red pepper flakes	pinch	
			water		

1. Wash chicken and pat dry with a paper towel. Cut into 4 pieces.
2. Melt margarine and oil in a small skillet over medium heat.
3. Add garlic, onion, cardamom and cinnamon. Sauté approximately 5 minutes. Turn heat to medium high.
4. Add ginger, turmeric, coriander, cumin and red pepper. Sauté over low heat an additional 5 minutes. Turn heat to medium high.
5. Add chicken to skillet; coat thoroughly with the curry mixture. Fry 5–8 minutes being careful not to burn onions.
6. Add 1/4 c (50 ml) water. Cover and bring to boil; lower heat and simmer 20–25 minutes.

Lemon Basil Broiled Chicken

broiler-fryer	1/2		salt	3/4 tsp	3 ml
oil	1/4 c	50 ml	onion powder	1/2 tsp	2 ml
lemon juice, fresh	2 Tbsp	30 ml	paprika	1/4 tsp	1 ml
			garlic salt	1/8 tsp	0.5 ml
basil, fresh	1–1/2 tsp	7 ml	thyme	1/8 tsp	0.5 ml
or					
dried	1/2 tsp	2 ml			

1. Wash and dry chicken. Cut into small serving pieces.
2. Combine all ingredients in a heavy-weight plastic bag that seals tight.
3. Add chicken and coat with marinade.
4. Let chicken marinate at room temperature for a minimum of 30 minutes. (At home, marinate 6–8 hours in the refrigerator.)
5. Broil chicken according to the method in Experiment II.

Honey Teriyaki Chicken

broiler-fryer	1/2		ginger, fresh, grated,	1–1/2 tsp	7 ml
honey	3 Tbsp	45 ml	*or*		
lemon juice, fresh	2 Tbsp	30 ml	dried	1/2 tsp	2 ml
soy sauce	2 Tbsp	30 ml	garlic salt	1/4 tsp	1 ml

1. Wash and dry chicken. Cut into small serving pieces.
2. Combine all ingredients in a heavy-weight plastic bag that seals tight.
3. Add chicken and coat with marinade.
4. Let chicken marinate at room temperature for a minimum of 30 minutes. (At home, marinate 6–8 hours in the refrigerator.)
5. Broil chicken according to the method in Experiment II.

Chicken Paprika

chicken	1/4		salt	1/4 tsp	1 ml
onion	1/2		paprika	3/4 tsp	3 ml
butter	1 tsp	5 ml	chicken broth	3 Tbsp	45 ml
oil	1 tsp	5 ml	sour cream	1/4 c	50 ml

1. Wash and pat dry chicken with a paper towel.
2. Slice onion thinly.
3. Sauté onions in butter and oil in small frying pan over medium-high heat until golden.
4. Remove onions and set aside.
5. Add chicken to pan; fry until brown, approximately 10 minutes.
6. Sprinkle salt and paprika over chicken placed skin side up. Add onions back to pan.
7. Add chicken broth, cover, and simmer 30 minutes.
8. Remove chicken to serving dish.
9. Mix sour cream into remaining onions and juices in pan.
10. Heat 1–2 minutes. Do not boil.
11. Pour sauce over chicken and serve.

Country Captain Chicken

chicken	1/4		curry powder	1/4 tsp	1 ml
butter	1 tsp	5 ml	marjoram	1/4 tsp	1 ml
oil	1 tsp	5 ml	salt		
garlic clove	1/4		pepper		
onion	1/4		raisins	2 Tbsp	30 ml
green pepper	1/3		almonds	2 Tbsp	30 ml
tomatoes, canned, drained, coarsely chopped	1/2 c	125 ml			

1. Preheat oven to 400°F (200°C).
2. Fry chicken in butter and oil in frying pan over medium-high heat until brown.
3. Remove chicken and place in casserole dish with a cover.
4. Pour off and discard all but 1 Tbsp (15 ml) fat.
5. Mince garlic; chop onions; slice green pepper into long, thin strips.
6. Sauté garlic, onions and green peppers 3–4 minutes.
7. Add tomatoes, spices, and 1 Tbsp (15 ml) each of raisins and almonds.
8. Simmer 3 minutes.
9. Pour sauce over chicken in casserole dish.
10. Sprinkle with remaining raisins and almonds.
11. Cover and heat in oven 30 minutes.

Chicken Fricasee with Dumplings

margarine	1 Tbsp	15 ml	carrot	1		
chicken	1/2		celery stalk	1		
salt	1/2 tsp	2 ml	potato	2		
pepper	1/8 tsp	0.5 ml	onion	1/2		
bouillon cube, chicken	1		flour	1 Tbsp	15 ml	
			Dumpling batter	(see below)		

1. Cut up chicken into serving pieces. Wash and pat dry with a paper towel.
2. Melt margarine in the bottom pan of a pressure cooker over medium-high heat.
3. Add chicken to hot fat and brown on all sides. Do not allow the fat to smoke or burn.
4. Add 1 c (250 ml) hot water, bouillon cube, salt, and pepper to pan.
5. Cover and close. Turn heat to high.
6. Let steam escape a few seconds through the valve to make sure it is open. Place gauge set at 10 lbs over the valve. When the gauge first jiggles, readjust heat so that it will jiggle 1–4 times/minute.
7. Cook for 10 minutes after first jiggle.
8. Prepare vegetables: Slice carrots into 3/8 in. (9 mm) lengths. Slice celery stalk into 2 in. (5 cm) lengths. Quarter onion. Cut potatoes into 1 in. (2.5 cm) chunks.
9. When chicken has cooked 10 minutes, remove from heat and let stand 5 minutes to cool slowly.
10. Place in sink and run cold water over top of pressure cooker until hissing stops. The pressure should reduce within 15–45 seconds. Check to see if pressure has reduced by nudging the gauge with a fork. If nothing happens, remove gauge with a fork. Open pressure cooker.
11. Add vegetables. Repeat steps 5 and 6.
12. Cook 5 minutes after first jiggle.
13. Cool instantly by following step 10.
14. Drop dumpling batter (see below) by spoonfuls over chicken and vegetables.
15. Simmer 5 minutes, uncovered.
16. Cover pressure pan and close, but do not use gauge. Steam 5 more minutes without pressure gauge.
17. Prepare starch suspension. Mix 1 Tbsp (15 ml) flour in 2 Tbsp (30 ml) cold water.
18. Remove chicken, dumplings, and vegetables to serving bowl.
19. Bring remaining liquid in pan to boil. There should be approximately 1 c (250 ml) of liquid. Slowly add starch suspension while continuously stirring. Boil 1 minute, continuously stirring.
20. Pour gravy over chicken and vegetables. Serve hot.

Dumplings

flour, sifted	1/2 c + 3 Tbsp	215 ml	egg, beaten	1/2	
			milk	1/4 c	50 ml
baking powder	2 tsp	10 ml			
salt	1/2 tsp	2 ml			

1. Sift together flour, baking powder, and salt.
2. Mix egg and milk together until combined.
3. Combine flour and egg-milk mixtures. Stir until ingredients are just moistened.
4. Drop by spoonfuls *immediately* over simmering stew. Simmer 5 minutes.
5. Cover and let steam without pressure gauge for 5 more minutes.

Stuffed Chicken Breast

1 whole chicken breast, attached together to form 1 piece			salt	1/4 tsp	1 ml
			egg, beaten	1	
			lemon juice	1 tsp	5 ml
salt	dash		dry mustard	1/4 tsp	1 ml
bread crumbs	1/2 c	125 ml	margarine	1 tsp	5 ml
cream of mushroom soup, 10-3/4 oz can	1/4	75 g	Mushroom Sauce	(see below)	
celery, minced	2 Tbsp	30 ml			
Worchestershire sauce	3/4 tsp	3 ml			

1. Preheat oven to 375°F (190°C).
2. Debone whole chicken breast. Sprinkle inside with salt. Turn skin side down on a dish.
3. Mix remaining ingredients (except margarine) together in a bowl.
4. Place mixed ingredients on the open chicken breast.
5. Roll up each side so that they overlap in the center. Close with skewers. Roll up each end slightly to form a tight seal. Keep closed with a skewer on each end. Tie a piece of string like a shoelace to firmly tighten the skewers.
6. Place chicken breast skin side up in a baking dish. Brush with margarine.
7. Bake 40 minutes. Brush with mushroom sauce (see below) 15 minutes before the end of the cooking period.

Mushroom Sauce

cream of mushroom soup, 10-3/4 oz can	1/4	75 g	Kitchen Bouquet	1/2 tsp	2 ml
			onion juice	1/8 tsp	0.5 ml
margarine, melted	1 Tbsp	15 ml	pepper	dash	

Mix all ingredients together well.

(Courtesy of National Marine Fisheries Service,
U.S. Department of Commerce.)

16

Fish

OBJECTIVES

The student should be able to:

1. Assess the nutritive value and cost of fish.
2. Clean and dress a whole, fresh fish.
3. Describe the effect of heat and acid on the coagulation of fish protein.
4. Determine the effect of removing the shell prior to cooking on the quality of cooked shrimp.
5. Prepare and compare dry and moist methods of fish cookery.
6. Prepare and compare real and fabricated seafood.

FOOD SCIENCE PRINCIPLES

1. Fish are lower in fat and equal to (or higher) in protein content than meats or poultry. Shellfish are excellent sources of minerals and contain some carbohydrates. Generally, finfish are more economical than shellfish.
2. Fish muscle is more tender than that of meat because of the small quantity of connective tissue. Also, the collagen contains less hydroxylproline and is converted to gelatin at lower temperatures than meat. The proteins are easily coagulated with heat or acid. Hence, cooking times are short and the fish can be "cooked" by acid marination. Many populations in the world (Orientals, Spaniards, and Central and South Americans) prepare fish by marinating it in an acid solution, such as lemon or lime juice.
3. Peeling shrimp prior to cooking produces a product that is smaller in size, more ragged in appearance and texture, and has less flavor than shrimps cooked in the shell.
4. The delicate nature of fish requires that it be handled carefully during cooking. Fish is quickly cooked by both dry and moist methods of cookery. These include baking, broiling, pan-frying, oven-frying, deep-fat frying, poaching, and steaming. Fat is often added when fish is cooked by dry heat methods.
5. It is very important to cook fish to a just-done state, because beyond the point at which it flakes easily with a fork it will quickly dry out, shrink, toughen, and alter its flavor.

Exercise I: Calculation of Cost/Serving and Nutritive Value of Fish

1. Calculate the nutritive value of fish in Table 16-1.
2. Determine the cost/lb (500 g) of fish by visiting a supermarket or using a price list posted in the laboratory. Divide the cost/lb (500 g) by the number of servings/lb (500 g) to determine the cost/serving.
3. Record results in Table 16-1.

TABLE 16-1   Calculation of Cost/Serving and Nutritive Value of Fish

Raw Fish 4 oz (120 g) or Cooked Fish 3 oz (90 g)	Cost/lb (500 g)	Serving/ lb (500 g)	Cost/ Serving	Food Energy (Cal)	Protein (g)	Nutritive Value				
						Fat (g)	Carbo- hydrate (g)	Vit. A (g)	Cal- cium (mg)	Zinc (mg)
FINFISH flounder										
haddock										
halibut										
salmon										
sardines										
tuna										
SHELLFISH clams										
crab										
oyster										
scallops										
shrimp										

QUESTIONS

1. What types of fish are the most economical to buy? _____
_____

    The most expensive? _____

2. Is the nutritive value of the fish related to its cost? _____

3. What determines the price of a particular type of fish? _____
_____

4. What type of fish is considered to be a good source of minerals? _____
_____ Of Carbohydrates? _____

    Of vitamin A? _____

5. Do fish have a high fat content? _____ Protein content? _____
_____

6. How does the caloric value of fish compare to that of meats? _____
_____ Of poultry? _____
_____

Experiment I: Cleaning and Dressing a Whole, Fresh Fish

Purchase a whole fish that has *not* been scaled or cleaned. Select a species that will be appropriate for
use in the experiments and recipes prepared in the laboratory.

1. Observe or prepare a fish for filleting. Clean and dress the fish according to the directions and
illustrations in Figure 16–1.

Experiment II: Coagulation of Fish Protein by Heat and Acid

Select 7 oz (210 g) skinned, boneless fillets of fresh flounder or sole. If these fish are not available, any
bland fish may be substituted. Far better results will be obtained if fresh fish is used. Carefully inspect
the raw fish for worms or parasites.

1. Cut fish into 1/4 in. (0.6 cm) cubes.
2. Weigh out 2 groups of cubes of about 1/2 oz (15 g) and 1-1/2 oz (45 g) each. Set aside.
3. Place the rest of the fish cubes into a small bowl.
4. Pour 3 oz (6 Tbsp) (90 ml) of *fresh* lime juice (2 large limes) over the 5 oz (150 g) of fish cubes.
Make sure all the cubes are covered with lime juice. Stir occasionally to evenly distribute the lime
juice but do not damage the fish. Let it marinate 1 hour.
5. Bring a small amount of water to boil in a covered saucepan.
6. Place the 1-1/2 oz (45 g) of unmarinated, raw fish cubes into a steam basket and close.
7. Lower steam basket over (not touching) boiling water. Cover, and steam 8 minutes. Remove
from basket and refrigerate.

1

Scaling

Wash the fish. Place the fish on a cutting board and with one hand hold the fish firmly by the head. Holding a knife almost vertical, scrape off the scales, starting at the tail and scraping toward the head (fig. 1). Be sure to remove all the scales around the fins and head.

2

Cleaning

With a sharp knife cut the entire length of the belly from the vent to the head. Remove the intestines. Next, cut around the pelvic fins and remove them (fig. 2).

3

Removing the Head and Tail

Remove the head and the pectoral fins by cutting just back of the collarbone. If the backbone is large, cut down to it on each side of the fish (fig. 3).

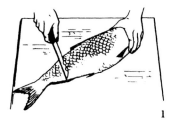

4

Then place the fish on the edge of the cutting board so that the head hangs over and snap the backbone by bending the head down (fig. 4). Cut any remaining flesh that holds the head to the body. Cut off the tail.

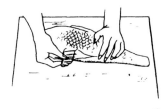

5

Removing the Fins

Next remove the dorsal fin, the large fin on the back of the fish, by cutting along each side of the fin (fig. 5). Then give a quick pull forward toward head and remove the fin with the root bones attached (fig. 5). Remove the ventral fin in the same way. Never trim the fins off with shears or a knife because the root bones at the base of the fins will be left in the fish. Wash the fish thoroughly in cold running water. The fish is now dressed or pan-dressed, depending on its size.

6

Cutting Steaks

Large size dressed fish may be cut crosswise into steaks, about an inch thick (fig. 6).

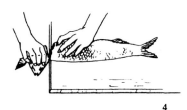

7

Filleting

With a sharp knife cut along the back of the fish from the tail to the head (fig. 7). Then cut down to the backbone just back of the collarbone.

8

Turn the knife flat and cut the flesh away from the backbone and rib bones (fig. 8).

9

Lift off the whole side of the fish or fillet in one piece (fig. 9). Turn the fish over and cut the fillet from the other side.

FIGURE 16–1 Cleaning and dressing a whole fish (Courtesy of National Marine Fisheries Service, U.S. Department of Commerce.)

8. Prepare the chili-tomato mixture from the recipes below for Ceviche.
9. At the end of 1 hour, weigh out 1 oz (30 g) of the marinated fish. Place on a plate.
10. Pour off all of the lime juice from the remaining 4 oz (120 g) of marinated fish. Use this fish to prepare Ceviche below.
11. Record results in Table 16–2.

Ceviche

fish fillet	4 oz	120 g	olive oil	2 Tbsp	30 ml
lime juice	1/4 c	50 ml	oregano	1/4 tsp	1 ml
tomato	1/2		salt	1/4 tsp	1 ml
chili serrano or jalapeno, canned	1/8		pepper	dash	

1. Marinated fish: Cut fish into 1/4 in. (0.6 cm) cubes. Pour lime juice over fish. Refrigerate and let marinate 4 hours.
2. Chili-tomato mixture:

   a. Remove seeds from tomato and chili.
   b. Dice tomatoes into 1/4 in. (0.6 cm) cubes.
   c. Dice chili into 1/8 in. (0.3 cm) cubes.
   d. Combine tomato, chili, olive oil, oregano, salt and pepper.

3. Ceviche: After pouring off lime juice, mix marinated fish and chili-tomato mixture. Let stand in the refrigerator for 1 hour to allow flavors to blend.

TABLE 16–2   Coagulation of Fish Protein by Heat and Acid

Coagulation of Protein	Preparation Time (minutes)	Color	Appearance	Texture	Taste
Uncooked, raw (1/2 oz; 15 g)					
Heat (1-1/2 oz; 45 g)					
Acid plain (1 oz; 30 g)					
Acid sauced (Ceviche) (4 oz; 120 g)					

QUESTIONS

1. Why does the raw fish that was marinated in lime juice appear to be cooked? _____
   _____

2. How does the marinated fish compare to the steamed fish? _____
   _____
   _____

3. What populations in the world prepare fish according to the marinated method? _____
   _____

   Why? _____
   _____

Experiment III: Effect of Cooking In and Out of the Shell on the Quality of Shrimp

Select 1/2 lb (250 g) fresh, green shrimp (in the shell).

1. Divide 1/2 lb (250 g) shrimp into 2 parts.
2. Peel 4 oz (125 g). Remove shell and tail. Make a shallow cut down the back of the shrimp to remove the sand vein (intestine). Rinse briefly in cold water. Pat dry with a paper towel. Weigh shrimp and record.
3. Rinse the unpeeled shrimp in cold water. Pat dry with a paper towel. Weigh and record.
4. Bring two pans of water, each containing 2 c (500 ml) water and 2 tsp (10 ml) of salt, to a boil.
5. Drop the peeled shrimp in 1 pan of boiling water. Bring to a boil again, cover; lower heat and simmer gently until just opaque (about 2 min.).
6. Repeat step 5 with the unpeeled shrimp.
7. Drain the shrimp and chill.
8. Prepare seafood cocktail sauce (recipe below).
9. Observe size and appearance of peeled and unpeeled shrimp.
10. Peel a few of the unpeeled shrimp. Compare them to the peeled shrimp for texture and flavor.
11. Record results in Table 16–3.
12. Serve with Seafood Cocktail Sauce.

Seafood Cocktail Sauce

chili sauce	1/4 c	50 ml	salt	dash
horseradish	2 tsp	10 ml	pepper	dash
lemon juice	1 tsp	5 ml		
hot red pepper sauce, drop	1			

1. Combine all ingredients and mix well.
2. Chill and serve.

TABLE 16-3   Effect of Cooking In and Out of the Shell on the Quality of Shrimp

Shrimp	Weight (g)		% Weight	Size	Appearance	Texture	Flavor
	Before Cooking	After Cooking					
Peeled							
Unpeeled							

QUESTIONS

1. What effect does peeling shrimp prior to cooking have on size? _____
_____

On appearance? _____

On texture? _____

2. Which method of cooking, in or out of the shell, produced the most intense seafood flavor?
_____ Why? _____
_____

3. What are the disadvantages of cooking shrimp in the shell? _____
_____
_____

4. Why do restaurants usually serve peeled shrimp? _____
_____

Experiment IV: Preparation and Comparison of Dry and Moist Methods of Fish Cookery

Select fish to be prepared by dry and moist methods of cookery. Use either the basic method in each section or prepare a recipe that illustrates an application of the basic method. (See Figure 16–2.)

1. Wash the fish if necessary. Remove any foreign material.
2. Prepare fish according to the basic method or the selected recipe. Check with the laboratory teacher for instructions.
3. Keep a record of the preparation time.
4. Observe appearance and juiciness. Smell odor. Determine tenderness by ease of flaking with a fork. Taste for flavor.
5. Record results in Table 16–4.

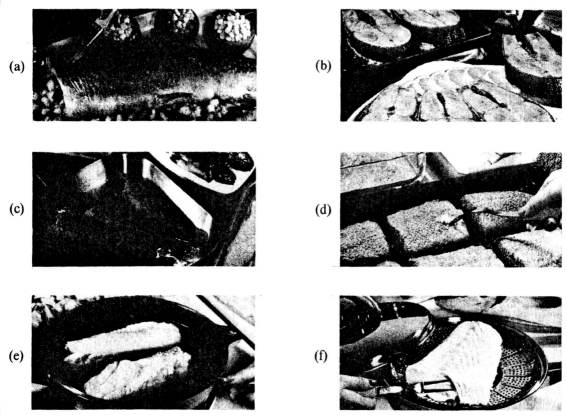

FIGURE 16-2 *Six basic methods of fish cookery: (a) Baking. (b) Broiling. (c) Pan-frying. (d) Oven-frying. (e) Poaching. (f) Steaming. (Courtesy of National Marine Fisheries Service, U.S. Department of Commerce.)*

Dry Methods of Fish Cookery

Baking

Select pan-dressed fish, fillets or steaks. Use the basic method to prepare baked pan-dressed fish, fillets or steaks, or, prepare Codfish Parmesan, pg. 234.

Baking Fish—Basic Method

1. Preheat oven to 350°F (175°C).
2. Whole fish: Clean, wash and dry with a paper towel.
   Fillets or steaks: Cut into serving pieces.
3. Sprinkle cavity and outer part with salt and pepper.
4. Whole Fish: Fill with bread, rice, seafood or vegetable stuffing.
5. Grease an uncovered roasting pan. Place fish in pan.
6. Melt butter or margarine; brush on fish.
7. Bake until fish flakes easily with a fork.
   Whole fish: 45–60 minutes.
   Fillets or steaks: 25–30 minutes.

Broiling

Select *thawed* or fresh fish at least 1 in. (2.5 cm) thick. Use the basic method of broiling fish to prepare broiled fillets, steaks, or pan-dressed fish, or, prepare Shrimp Scampi, pg. 234.

Broiling Fish—Basic Methods

1. Turn oven to broil.
2. Grease the rack of a broiler pan.
3. Cut fish into serving pieces and place skin side down on the broiler pan.
4. Melt butter, margarine or oil; brush on fish.
5. Place broiler pan 3–4 in. (7.5–10 cm) from broiler.
6. Broil 10–15 minutes until fish flakes easily with a fork. Baste occasionally. (Do not turn fish over when it is halfway done unless it is very thick. The bottom of the fish will coagulate from the heat of the broiler pan.)
7. Baste again and serve hot.

Pan-Frying

Select *thawed* or fresh pan-dressed fish, fillets, or steaks. Use the basic method to prepare fried pan-dressed fish, fillets or steaks, or prepare Trout Almondine, pg. 236.

Pan-Frying Fish—Basic Method

1. Cut fish into serving pieces.
2. Dip fish into an egg–milk mixture.
   Egg–milk mixture: 1 egg, 1 Tbsp (15 ml) milk, 1 tsp (5 ml) salt, 1/8 tsp (0.5 ml) pepper.
3. Roll fish into flour, or dry bread, cereal, or cracker crumbs.
4. Heat margarine, butter or oil to a 1/8 in. (3 mm) depth in a skillet over medium heat. Do not allow the fat to smoke or burn.
5. Add fish and fry 4–5 minutes until brown.
6. Turn carefully with a spatula. Fry another 4–5 minutes or until fish flakes easily with a fork.
7. Drain fish on paper towels.

Deep Fat Frying

See Fried Fish, pg. 249.

Oven Frying

Select fish fillets or steaks. Use the basic method of oven-frying to prepare oven-fried fillets or steaks.

Oven-Frying Fish—Basic Method

1. Preheat oven to 500°F (260°C).
2. Follow steps 1–3 for the basic method of pan-frying fish.
3. Grease a baking pan.
4. Arrange pieces of fish in pan.
5. Pour melted margarine, butter, or oil over fish.
6. Place pan in the middle of the oven.
7. Bake 10–15 minutes or until fish flakes easily with a fork.

Microwave Cooking

See Fish Veracruz, pg. 352.

Moist Methods of Fish Cookery

Poaching

Select *thawed* or fresh fillets or steaks. Use the basic method of poaching fish to prepare poached fillets or steaks, or, prepare New England Clam Chowder, pg. 236.

Poaching Fish—Basic Method

1. Cut fish into serving pieces.
2. Grease a 10 in. (25 cm) skillet.
3. Bring poaching liquid to a boil in the skillet. Suggested liquids are:

   a. Water: 3 c (500 ml) seasoned with 1/4 c (50 ml) lemon juice, sliced onion, 1 tsp (5 ml) salt, peppercorns, parsley, and 1 bay leaf.
   b. Milk
   c. White wine
   d. Milk and white wine

4. Add fish in a single layer.
5. Cover and simmer 5–10 minutes or until fish flakes easily with a fork.
6. Remove fish with spatula or slotted spoon.

Steaming

Select *thawed* or fresh pan-dressed fish, fillets, or steaks. Use the basic method of steaming fish to prepare steamed fish, fillets, or steaks.

Steaming Fish, Basic Method

1. Grease steamer rack. Place fish on steamer rack.
2. Bring the steaming liquid to a boil in a lightly covered saucepan or steaming pan. Suggested liquids are:

   a. Water: plain
   b. Water: seasoned with herbs and spices
   c. White wine

3. Lower rack into pan. Do not let liquid touch fish.
4. Cover and steam 5–10 minutes or until fish flakes easily with a fork.
5. Remove rack from pan. Remove fish carefully and chill.
6. Remove skin and bones. Use for recipes requiring cooked fish.

Simmering

Select shellfish such as shrimp or crab. Do not cook clams or mussels by this method. Use the basic method of simmering to prepare shrimp or crab cocktail.

Simmering—Basic Method

1. Bring a deep, large pan filled 1/3 with hot water to a boil.
2. Rinse shellfish thoroughly in cold, running water.
3. Add shellfish to rapidly boiling water, return to boil, immediately lower heat and stir. Watch carefully since water may boil out of the pan.
4. Simmer 1–2 minutes.
5. Drain immediately. If desired, rinse in running water to wash away scum.

TABLE 16–4   Preparation and Comparison of Dry and Moist Methods of Fish Cookery

Method of Cookery	Appearance	Juiciness	Odor	Tenderness	Flavor
Dry baking					
broiling					
pan-frying					
deep fat-frying					
oven-frying					
microwave					
MOIST poaching					
steaming					

QUESTIONS

1. Which method of cookery produced the juiciest product? _____

   Why? _____

   The best flavor? _____

2. Why is fat so often added to the dry methods of cooking fish? _____

   _____

   _____

3. Why does fish cook in such a short time compared to meats? _____

   _____

   _____

4. Why is the water seasoned or wine or milk used in place of water, when fish are poached or steamed? _____

   _____

   _____

Experiment V: Preparation and Comparison of Real Versus Fabricated Seafood Products

Select a form of seafood and its fabricated analog. Two suggestions are crab legs and imitation crab, or shrimp and fabricated shrimp. Purchase 1/2 lb (250 g) of each and keep a record of the cost.

1. Divide both the real seafood and its fabricated product into two parts.
2. Prepare one part of the real seafood and one part of the fabricated product according to the following recipes.

Sautéed Seafood

crab or shrimp, shelled	1/4 lb	125 g	paprika	dash	
			parsley, minced	1/4 tsp	1 ml
margarine	1–1/2 tsp	7 ml	lemon slice	1	
salt	dash				

a. Heat margarine in a small frying pan over medium-high heat until it sizzles. Do not allow the fat to smoke or burn.
b. Add shellfish to pan. Cook on one side until lightly browned, approximately 2–4 minutes.
c. Turn with spatula only once. Cook 1–2 minutes longer.
d. Remove from pan and sprinkle lightly with salt and paprika. Garnish with chopped parsley and serve with a lemon slice.

Seafood Salad

crab or shrimp, shelled	1/4 lb	125 g	dill, dried	1/4 tsp	1 ml
			onion, minced	2 tsp	10 ml
artichoke hearts, canned	2 (3 oz)	(90 g)	salt	1/8 tsp	0.5 ml
			pepper	dash	
mayonnaise	3 Tbsp	45 ml	celery,	1/4 c	50 ml
yogurt	1 Tbsp	15 ml	sliced 1/4-in.		
lemon juice, fresh	2 tsp	10 ml	(0.6 cm) thick		

a. *For shelled crab, crab analog, or shrimp analog:* Rinse the shellfish and cook by steaming over plain water according to the directions for the basic method of steaming, pg. 230.

For shrimp or crab in shell: Cook by simmering in plain water according to the directions for the basic method of simmering shellfish, pg. 230. Remove shell. If intestinal vein of shrimp is dark, remove vein with a knife and rinse again. Pat dry with paper towels.

b. Place cooked seafood in a single layer on a metal pan in the freezer to cool for 5–10 minutes. Remove seafood from freezer before ice crystals form. (At home, chill in the refrigerator.)

c. Coarsely chop seafood and artichoke hearts.

d. Combine mayonnaise, yogurt, lemon juice, dill, onion, salt, and pepper in a bowl.

e. Add celery, seafood, and artichokes to sauce and gently blend together.

3. Compare the real and fabricated seafoods for appearance, taste, odor, texture, and tenderness.
4. Compare the price of each type.
5. Record results in Table 16–5.

TABLE 16-5   Comparison of Real and Fabricated Seafood Products

Product	Appearance	Taste	Odor	Texture	Tenderness	Cost[a]
Sautéed seafood real						
fabricated						
Seafood salad real						
fabricated						

[a]Seafood portion only.

QUESTIONS

1. Describe how the real and fabricated seafoods differ: _____

_____

_____

_____ _____

2. What are fabricated seafoods used by many restaurants in preparing seafood salads? _____

_____

_____

APPLICATIONS

Codfish Parmesan

margarine	1/2 tsp	2 ml	Mozzarella cheese,	2 oz	60 g
codfish fillet	1/2 lb	250 g	grated		
tomato sauce	1-1/3 c	330 ml	Parmesan cheese,	2 Tbsp	30 ml
			grated		

1. Preheat oven to 350°F (175°C).
2. Grease a 8 in. (20 cm) baking dish with margarine.
3. Pour 1/3 c (80 ml) of tomato sauce into the bottom of the dish.
4. Place codfish fillet over tomato sauce.
5. Pour 2/3 c (160 ml) tomato sauce over fish. Spread with a spoon so that the entire fillet is covered.
6. Sprinkle the Mozzarella cheese evenly over the tomato sauce.
7. Pour the rest of the tomato sauce over the cheese.
8. Top with grated Parmesan cheese.
9. Place fish in oven. Bake 20 minutes.
10. Turn oven to broil.
11. Broil a few minutes until cheese turns brown and bubbly.
12. Let stand 5 minutes before serving.

Shrimp Scampi

shrimp	1/2 lb	250 g	garlic, minced	1/2 tsp	2 ml
butter or	2 Tbsp	30 ml	tarragon, dried	1/4 tsp	1 ml
margarine			parsley, dried	1/4 tsp	1 ml
olive oil	2 Tbsp	30 ml	salt	1/2 tsp	2 ml
lemon juice	1 tsp	5 ml	pepper	dash	
shallots or	1 Tbsp	15 ml			
green onions,					
minced					

1. Remove shell around body of shrimp, leaving tail section intact. Remove sand vein. Wash shrimp and pat dry with a paper towel.
2. Melt butter in a saucepan or microwave oven. Add remaining ingredients and mix well.
3. Add shrimp to butter and coat thoroughly. Pour into a pie plate or heat-resistant serving dish. Let shrimp marinate 15–30 minutes.
4. Turn oven to broil.
5. Broil shrimp 3 in. (7.5 cm) from heat until lightly browned, 5–7 minutes. Baste with sauce after 3 minutes.
6. Turn shrimp over. Broil another 5–7 minutes, basting every 2–3 minutes with sauce.
7. Serve hot in heat-resistant dish.

Broiled Fish with Garlic Salsa

fish steaks	1/2 lb	250 g	salt	dash
olive oil	3 Tbsp	45 ml	pepper	dash
lemon juice, fresh	1–1/2 Tbsp	22 ml	Garlic Salsa	
			lemon wedges	2
coriander (cilantro), minced	1 Tbsp	15 ml		

1. Rinse fish and pat dry with paper towels. Place in a shallow dish.
2. Combine oil, lemon juice, coriander, salt, and pepper in a bowl. Pour over fish and rub in.
3. Marinate 20–30 minutes.
4. Meanwhile, prepare Garlic Salsa (see the following recipe).
5. Drain fish and broil according to the Basic Method of Broiling Fish, pg. 228. Use the marinade as the basting sauce.
6. Transfer fish to serving platter. Cover with Garlic Salsa. Serve with lemon wedges.

Garlic Salsa

butter (divided)	1/4 c	50 ml	tomatoes, canned, drained, coarsely chopped	1 c	250 ml
red onion, chopped	2 Tbsp	30 ml			
garlic, minced	1–1/2 tsp	7 ml			
jalepẽno pepper, minced	1/2		salt	1/4 tsp	1 ml
			pepper	dash	
lemon juice, fresh	3/4 tsp	3 ml	coriander (cilantro), chopped	2 Tbsp	30 ml

1. Melt 1 Tbsp (15 ml) butter in a skillet over medium heat.
2. Add onion, garlic, and jalepeno pepper. Cook until onion is softened.
3. Add lemon juice, tomatoes, salt, and pepper. Cover and cook 10 minutes, stirring occasionally.
4. Mix in coriander.
5. Add remaining 3 Tbsp (45 ml) butter. Stir sauce only until butter melts. Serve sauce hot.

Bacon-Wrapped Scallops

sea scallops	1/2 lb	250 g	garlic powder	1/4 tsp	1 ml
flour	1/3 c	80 ml	milk	1/3 c	80 ml
salt	1 tsp	5 ml	egg, beaten	1/2	
paprika	1 tsp	5 ml	bacon	6–7 slices	
pepper	1/4 tsp	1 ml	toothpicks		

1. Preheat oven to 400°F (200°C).
2. Lightly grease a 9-in. (23 cm) glass pie plate.
3. Rinse scallops and pat dry with paper towels.
4. Prepare seasoned flour by combining flour, salt paprika, pepper, and garlic powder in a plastic bag.
5. Combine milk and egg in a small bowl.
6. Dip an individual scallop in the milk–egg mixture, then roll it in the seasoned flour.
7. Wrap each scallop with a piece of bacon that is cut to fit around the scallop. Secure it in place with a toothpick. Place scallop in pie plate.
8. Bake 25–25 minutes until bacon is crisp and scallop is cooked through.
9. Serve hot.

New England Clam Chowder

butter or margarine	2 Tbsp	30 ml	potatoes, cooked,	1 c	250 ml
onion, minced	3 Tbsp	45 ml	peeled, and diced		
celery, chopped	1/3 c	80 ml	salt	1/2 tsp	2 ml
celery leaves,	1 Tbsp	15 ml	white pepper	dash	
chopped			half and half	1-1/2 c	375 ml
minced clams,	1		*or*		
undrained can			milk and	1 c	250 ml
or			light cream	1/2 c	125 ml
shucked, (reserve	1/2 c	125 ml			
liquid)					

1. Melt 1 Tbsp (15 ml) butter in a heavy skillet over medium-high heat.
2. Add chopped celery and sauté 3 minutes. Do not allow the butter to brown, burn or smoke.
3. Add rest of butter, celery leaves, and onion. Sauté 3 minutes or until onion is soft.
4. Add liquid from canned minced clams or shucked clams, potatoes, salt and pepper.
5. Bring to boil; cover; lower heat and simmer 4-5 minutes.
6. Add clams and half and half. Simmer 3 minutes for canned and 5 minutes for fresh clams. Do not allow the mixture to boil.
7. Serve hot.

Trout Almondine

trout	1/2 lb	250 g
butter	2 Tbsp	30 ml
almonds	3 Tbsp	45 ml
lemon	1/8	

1. Wash trout and pat dry.
2. Heat butter in a skillet over medium heat. Do not allow the butter to smoke or burn.
3. Add trout and almonds; fry 4-5 minutes.
4. Turn fish over carefully with a spatula. Fry another 4-5 minutes or until fish flakes easily with a fork. Stir almonds so that they do not become too brown.
5. Carefully lift fish out of pan and place on serving dish.
6. Pour butter sauce and almonds over fish. Garnish with fresh lemon and serve.

(Courtesy of National Broiler Council.)

17
Fats and Oils

OBJECTIVES

The student should be able to:

1. Assess the nutritive value of fats and oils.
2. Distinguish the smoke points of fats.
3. Determine the effect of freshness, temperature, and type of fat on the quality of fried foods.
4. Prepare and compare foods fried in fat.

FOOD SCIENCE PRINCIPLES

1. Fats are essential in the diet as a source of linoleic acids, calories, and fat-soluble vitmains. Most vegetable oils contain polyunsaturated fats; animal fats have a large percentage of saturated fats.
2. The flavor of the fat used in cooking influences the flavor of the fried product. Butter and olive oil are highly valued for their flavor but their use is limited because of their high cost and low smoke point. Most have high smoke points but remain liquid when cool. This liquid state may impart a greasy feel to the surface of flour products such as doughnuts.
3. When fat is heated to its smoke point, its structure begins to break down and free fatty acids and acrolein are formed from glycerol. Acrolein is a substance irritating to the nostrils and eyes. Factors that decrease the smoke point of fats include:

   a. Presence of emulsifiers such as mono- and diglycerides in emulsified shortening.
   b. Repeated or prolonged use (heating) of the fat.
   c. Presence of food particles such as crumbs and egg coatings.
   d. Use of a wide, shallow pan that maximizes the surface area exposed to oxygen.
   e. Contamination by pans made of iron or copper, metals that accelerate oxidative rancidity of fats.

4. Foods should be cooked at temperatures below the smoke point of the fat but high enough to avoid a greasy product because low temperatures increase fat absorption. The absorption of fat also increases as the proportion of sugar, liquid, leavening, and fat in the food increases.
5. The browning of the outer portion of the food during frying is the result of sugars and proteins reacting via the Maillard reaction. The degree of browning is dependent on the time and temperature of frying and the chemical composition of the food, rather than the type of fat used.
6. The crispness created by frying is attributed to dehydration of the outer portion. The moisture loss is primarily responsible for the steam produced during frying. The void left by the moisture lost is filled by fat.

7. Used fat should be freshened by the addition of approximately 15–20% fresh fat. The life of a[n] can be increased by frying at temperatures below the smoke point, straining for contaminan[ts] after each use, cooling quickly, and storing in a cool, dark environment.

Exercise I: Nutritive Value and Cost of Fats and Oils

Calculate the nutritive value and cost of the fats and oils listed in Table 17–1.

TABLE 17–1   Nutritive Value of Fats and Oils

	Lipid	Water	Food Energy (Cal)	Nutritive Value/100 g					Cost (¢)
				Fat			Vitamin		
				Cholesterol (g)	Saturated (g)	Poly-unsaturated (g)	A	E	
Fat	beef								
	butter								
	hydrogenated								
	margarine								
Oil	coconut								
	corn								
	olive								
	soy								

QUESTIONS

1. Which of the above fats and oils have a relatively high water content? _____

   _____

   How will this affect their use in cooking? _____

   _____

2. Which fats or oils have a high degree of saturation? _____

   _____

3. Good sources of vitamin E include: _____

   _____

   of vitamin A: _____

4. What essential fatty acid do fats provide? _____

5. Do vegetable fats contain cholesterol? _____

6. Which fats or oils are the most expensive? _____

   The least expensive? _____

Experiment I: Determination of Smoke Points of Fats

1. Place 2 Tbsp (30 ml) of each of the fats and oils listed in Table 17-2 in 50 ml beakers. Set each beaker on the coil of an electric stove or over a bunsen burner. If any of the fats are solid at room temperature, gently heat until they melt.
2. Clamp a thermometer to a ring stand. Position the thermometer so that the bulb is in the center of the fat and not touching the sides or bottom.
3. Heat the fat over medium-high heat until the fat first smokes (*not* steams).
4. Record the smoke point of each fat in Table 17-2.

TABLE 17–2   Determination of Smoke Points of Fats

Fat	*Smoke Point °F(°C)*
Beef fat	
Butter	
Corn oil	
Hydrogenated fat	
Margarine	
Olive oil	

QUESTIONS

1. Which fats have the lowest smoke points? _____

   How will this affect their use in cooking? _____

   _____

2. Which fats have the highest smoke points? _____

   _____

Experiment II: Effect of Type of Fat on Quality of Fried Potatoes

1. Divide 5 (500 g) potatoes into 5 lots of 100 g each.
2. Prepare Home-Fried Potatoes according to the recipe below with each of the following fats. Note if the fats smoke during cooking.

   a. butter
   b. corn oil
   c. hydrogenated fat
   d. lard
   e. margarine

3. Observe surface appearance of each lot of potatoes. Taste for flavor.
4. Calculate the cost/Tbsp (15 ml).
5. Record results in Table 17-3.

Home-Fried Potatoes

white potato	1	100 g	salt	dash
fat	1-1/2 tsp	7 ml	pepper	dash
paprika	dash			

1. Scrub potato and remove sprouts. Peel and pat dry with a paper towel. Cut into 1 in. × 1 in. × 1/4 in. (2.5 cm × 2.5 cm × 0.6 cm) pieces or enough pieces for everyone in the class.
2. Heat fat in a small skillet over medium-high heat.
3. Add potatoes to fat when a drop of water sizzles when dropped into the hot fat. Sprinkle lightly with paprika.
4. Cover and cook potatoes 5-7 minutes until golden brown.
5. Turn over, season with salt and pepper, and cook 5-7 minutes more.
6. If potatoes have an excess of fat, briefly drain on paper towels.

TABLE 17-3   Effect of Type of Fat on Quality of Fried Potatoes

Fat	Cost/Tbsp (15 ml)	Appearance	Flavor	Did Fat Smoke?
Butter				
Corn Oil				
Hydrogenated fat				
Lard				
Margarine				

QUESTIONS

1. Which of the above fats produced the best quality potatoes? _____
   _____ Why? _____
   _____

2. How does the flavor of the fat influence the flavor of the potato? _____
   _____

Experiment III: Effect of Freshness of Fat on Quality of Fried Bread

1. Trim crusts off 3 slices of white sandwich bread that is slightly stale or frozen. Cut bread into 16 3/4 in. (1.8 cm) cubes. If there are more than 16 students in the class, use more bread.

2. Heat 1/4 c (50 ml) of each of the following fats in a small skillet over medium-high heat.

   a. fresh oil
   b. previously used oil (used for at least 5 hours and brought several times past the smoking point)
   c. 1/2 fresh oil; 1/2 previously used oil

3. When the temperature of the fat reaches 375°F (190°C), drop the bread cubes into each of the hot fats.

4. Turn the bread cubes over when they turn golden brown. When they are golden brown on both sides, remove the bread with a slotted spoon and drain on paper towels. Record the time that was required for the cubes to brown.

5. Observe appearance. Cut in half and observe crispness. Taste for flavor.

6. Record results in Table 17-4.

TABLE 17-4   Effect of Freshness of Fat on Quality of Fried Bread

Fat	Browning Time (seconds)	Appearance	Crispness	Flavor
Fresh				
Used				
Fresh + used				

QUESTIONS

1. How did the bread fried in fresh fat compare in quality to that fried in reused fat? _____

   _____

   Why? _____

2. What was the effect of adding fresh fat to the used fat? _____

   _____

Experiment IV: Preparations and Comparisons of Foods Fried in Fat

1. Prepare several of the recipes found in Applications. Obtain instructions from the laboratory instructor. Use either the basic method of shallow-fat frying or deep-fat frying.
2. Foods should be cut into uniform pieces. Coatings of flour, batter, or crumbs are optional.

Shallow-Fat Frying—Basic Method

   a. Heat a thin layer of fat, 1/8 in.-1/4 in. (3 mm-6 mm) over medium-high heat in a *heavy* skillet or electric fry-pan. The fat is hot enough when a drop of water added to the fat sizzles.
   b. Add the pieces of food a few at a time. Be careful not to crowd the pan. Do not allow the fat to smoke or burn.
   c. Cook the pieces of food until golden brown on one side and turn over.
   d. Season if desired and continue cooking until the second side is browned.
   e. Drain on paper towels and serve hot.

FIGURE 17-1 *The fryer basket is held over the fat for a few seconds to allow excess fat to drain off. (Courtesy of National Marine Fisheries Service, U.S. Department of Commerce.)*

Deep-Fat Frying—Basic Method

   a. Fill a deep, heavy skillet with a flat bottom or deep-fat fryer no more than 1/3 full with hydrogenated fat or oil.

   b. Clamp a deep-fat thermometer to the side of the pan so that the bulb is fully immersed in the fat.

   c. Preheat fat according to the recipe, usually 350-400°F (177-205°C). Higher temperatures will cause breakdown of the fat. Be extremely careful since hot oil can cause *severe* burns.

   d. Arrange absorbent paper on a counter. Do not place the paper near the hot burner of a stove.

   e. Place prepared food pieces in a basket. Do not overcrowd since too much food will lower the temperature of the fat. Cook several small batches instead. Lower basket into hot fat. Alternatively, pieces of food may be lowered into the hot fat with a slotted spoon or strainer. Dropping the pieces from a high distance may cause splattering.

   f. Stir small pieces of food occasionally. Turn large pieces over with tongs when browned on the first side. Cook until browned on second side.

   g. Raise basket and allow fat to drain for a few seconds over the hot fat. Turn on to absorbent paper. Alternatively, pieces of food may be removed with a slotted spoon or tongs when they are browned.

   h. Season if desired and serve hot.

   i. Cool fat to room temperature.

   j. Place cheesecloth in a funnel in the oil bottle or over the can of fat.

   k. Carefully pour fat through cheesecloth to remove contaminants. Discard dredges at bottom of pan.

Note: Do not throw darkened or obviously unusable fat down the drain. Use a special container designated by the instructor.

3. Observe surface appearance of fried foods. Cut into interior and observe extent of crispness. Taste for flavor.

4. Record observations in Table 17-5.

TABLE 17–5   Comparison of Foods Fried in Fat

Food	Appearance	Crispness	Flavor

Experiment V: Effect of Temperature in Deep-Fat Frying

1. Prepare Cheese Balls (recipe below).
2. Divide the balls into 3 groups. Use the basic method of deep fat frying in Experiment IV with the following temperatures for the fat for each group:

   a.   300°F (150°C)
   b.   365°F (185°C)
   c.   425°F (220°C)

3. Observe surface appearance. Cut in half and observe extent of crispness. Taste for flavor.
4. Record results in Table 17-6.

LE 17-6   Effect of Temperature in Deep-Fat Frying

Temperature		Surface Appearance	Crispness	Flavor
°F	°C			
300	150			
365	185			
425	220			

Cheese Balls

cheese, grated	1 c	250 ml	cayenne	dash	
flour	2 Tbsp	30 ml	dry mustard	1/4 tsp	1 ml
salt	1/4 tsp	1 ml	egg white	1-1/2	
paprika	1/8 tsp	0.5 ml	bread crumbs	1/4 c	50 ml

a. Mix together the cheese, flour, salt, paprika, cayenne, and dry mustard.
b. Beat egg whites with an electric beater until stiff.
c. Gently fold egg whites into cheese mixture. Let stand for 5 minutes.
d. Preheat fat.
e. Drop by rounded teaspoonfuls into the bread crumbs and coat.
f. Use a fork to lift the balls and drop into hot fat.
g. Fry until golden brown.
h. Drain on paper towels.

QUESTIONS

1. Which of the temperatures in Table 17-6 was the best for deep-fat frying? _____

_____

2. What was the problem in using the high temperature? _____

_____

How would this affect the storage life of the fat? _____

_____

3. What was the problem in using the low temperature? _____

_____

What might cause the temperature to fall to this level? _____

_____

APPLICATIONS

Stuffed Avocado with Creole Sauce

			Creole Sauce		
margarine	1 tsp	5 ml	brown sugar	2 tsp	10 ml
green onions, chopped	2 Tbsp	30 ml	salt	1/4 tsp	1 ml
ground beef	1/4 lb	120 g	pepper	dash	
raisins	2 Tbsp	30 ml	egg, beaten	1-1/2 Tbsp	22 ml
mixed nuts, chopped	1-1/2 Tbsp	22 ml	milk	1/4 c	50 ml
			flour	2 tsp	10 ml
avocado	1		flour	1/4 c	50 ml
egg, beaten	2 tsp	10 ml			

1. Prepare Creole Sauce (recipe below) and simmer.
2. Melt margarine in a small skillet over medium-high heat.
3. Add onions and sauté 2 minutes until soft.
4. Add ground beef and brown well. Pour off excess fat.
5. Mix in raisins and nuts and let mixture cool to lukewarm.
6. Peel avocado. Slice in half lengthwise. Remove seed. Increase the size of the hole left by scooping out more of the filling.
7. Combine scooped-out avocado meat, egg, brown sugar, salt, and pepper with meat mixture.
8. Preheat fat in a deep-fat fryer to 365°F (185°C). Follow the directions for the basic method of deep-fat frying, pg. 243.
9. Fill each avocado half with 1/2 the meat mixture.
10. Mix egg with milk and 2 tsp (10 ml) flour.
11. Dip avocado half in egg-milk mixture. Roll in flour.
12. Deep-fry a few minutes until golden brown.
13. Drain briefly on paper towels.
14. Serve on lettuce. Pour warm creole sauce over top.

Creole Sauce

olive oil	1 Tbsp	15 ml	Italian tomatoes, canned, drained, coarsely chopped	3/4 c	180 ml
green pepper, chopped	2 Tbsp	30 ml			
onion, chopped	2 Tbsp	30 ml	salt	1/4 tsp	
garlic, minced	1/4 tsp	1 ml	pepper	dash	1 ml

1. Put oil in saucepan over medium heat.
2. Add green pepper and onion. Gently sauté for five minutes or until onions are translucent.
3. Add garlic and sauté, stirring 30 more seconds.
4. Add chopped tomatoes, salt and pepper. Stir, gently simmer for 30 minutes, occasionally stirring.

ntucky-Fried Chicken

chicken wings	8		pancake mix	1/2 c	125 ml
butter	1/2 c	125 ml	paprika	1/4 tsp	1 ml
Italian salad	1 pkg.		sage	1/4 tsp	1 ml
dressing mix			thyme, crumbled	1/8 tsp	0.5 ml
flour	1-1/2 Tbsp	22 ml	pepper	dash	
salt	1/2 tsp	2 ml	milk	1/2 c	125 ml
lemon juice, fresh	2 Tbsp	30 ml			

1. Wash chicken. Break wing tip joint without breaking skin. Pat dry with paper towels.
2. Cream butter.
3. Mix in dry salad dressing mix, flour, salt, and lemon juice.
4. Coat chicken with salad dressing mixture. Marinate 20-30 minutes at room temperature. (At home, marinate 3-4 hours in the refrigerator.)
5. Combine pancake mix, paprika, sage, thyme, and pepper in a plastic bag.
6. Pour milk into a small bowl.
7. Preheat fat to 375°F (190°C).
8. Preheat oven to 350°F (175°C).
9. Dip each chicken piece into milk, then coat with pancake mixture in plastic bag. Shake off any excess. Save remaining milk.
10. Deep-fry 4 chicken wings at one time until they are browned according to the basic method of deep-fat frying, pg. 243.
11. Drain chicken wings briefly on paper towels, then place in a small, greased baking pan. Drizzle approximately 2 tsp (10 ml) of the remaining milk on *each* chicken piece.
12. Cover pan tightly with aluminum foil and bake 30 minutes.

Batter-Fried Chicken

chicken	1/2		celery salt	1/2 tsp	2 ml
chicken bouillon	1		salt	1/2 tsp	2 ml
cube			pepper	1/4 tsp	1 ml
flour	1/4 c	50 ml	thyme	dash	

1. Cut chicken into serving pieces. Wash.
2. Place chicken pieces and bouillon cube in a large saucepan. Cover with water.
3. Bring water to a boil. Cover, lower heat and simmer 20 minutes.
4. Drain through a colander. Pat dry with paper towels.
5. While chicken is cooking, prepare fritter batter (recipe below).
6. Preheat fat in a deep-fat fryer to 360°F (182°C) according to the basic method of deep-fat frying, pg. 243.
7. Mix together flour, celery salt, pepper, and thyme.
8. Roll chicken pieces in flour.
9. Dip pieces into fritter batter with tongs.
10. Fry 5-7 minutes until lightly browned.

Fritter Batter

flour	1/2 c	125 ml	milk	1/2 c	125 ml
baking powder	1/2 tsp	2 ml	egg	1/2	
salt	1/2 tsp	2 ml	oil	2 Tbsp	30 ml
pepper	1/8 tsp	0.5 ml			

1. Sift together flour, baking powder, salt, and pepper.
2. Beat milk, egg, and oil in a small bowl with a rotary beater.
3. Beat in flour mixture.

Hush Puppies

stone-ground cornmeal	1/2 c	125 ml	jalepaño, minced	1-1/2 tsp	7 ml
baking powder	1/4 tsp	1 ml	(optional)		
salt	1/4 tsp	1 ml	milk	2 Tbsp	30 ml
onion, minced	1 Tbsp	15 ml	egg, beaten	1/2	

1. Preheat fat to 370°F (188°C). Follow directions for the basic method of deep-fat frying, pg. 243.
2. Mix together the cornmeal, baking powder, and salt in a bowl.
3. Stir in onion and jalepaño.
4. Lightly beat milk and egg together.
5. Stir into cornmeal.
6. Shape into 3/4 in. (1.8 cm) balls.
7. Deep fry until golden brown.
8. Drain on paper towels.

nglish-Style Fried Fish

fish fillets	1/2 lb	250 g	pancake mix	1/2 c	125 ml
buttermilk	1/2 c	125 ml	club soda	1/2 c +	155 ml
lemon juice, fresh	1 tsp	5 ml		2 Tbsp	
flour			malt vinegar		

1. Rinse fish and pat dry with paper towels. Cut into serving pieces.
2. Observe consistency of the buttermilk.
3. Combine buttermilk and lemon juice in a shallow pie plate. Add fish and marinate 20-30 minutes at room temperature. (At home, marinate 2-3 hours in the refrigerator.)
4. Preheat fat to 350°F (175°C).
5. Coat fish with flour and set aside to dry.
6. Combine enough of the club soda with the pancake mix so that it has the same consistency as the buttermilk.
7. Dip fish into pancake batter. Shake off excess batter.
8. Deep-fry until the fish is browned according to the basic method of deep-frying, pg. 243. Do not overcook or the fish will be tough.
9. Drain briefly on paper towels and serve immediately. Sprinkle lightly with malt vinegar before eating.

Parmesan Zucchini Sticks

cchini	1/2 lb	250 g	Parmesan cheese	4 tsp	20 ml	
fritter batter	1/2 c	125 ml	salt	1/8 tsp	0.5 ml	× 2
flour	2 Tbsp	30 ml	pepper	1/8 tsp	0.5 ml	

1. Preheat fat to 375° (190°C).
2. Cut stem off zucchini and discard. Peel and cut in half crosswise. Cut each half into eighths lengthwise. If the seeds are big, cut them out and discard.
3. Prepare fritter batter (p. 248) and set aside.
4. Combine flour, cheese, salt, and pepper.
5. Roll zucchini in flour mixture.
6. Dip in fritter batter. Shake off excess.
7. Deep-fry according to the basic method of deep-frying, pg. 243, until golden brown.
8. Drain on paper towels and serve hot.

Buttermilk Cake Doughnuts

flour	2 c	500 ml	sugar	1/2 c	125 ml
baking powder	2 tsp	10 ml	buttermilk	1/3 c +	110 ml
baking soda	1/4 tsp	1 ml		2 Tbsp	
salt	1/4 tsp	1 ml	shortening, melted	2 Tbsp	30 ml
cinnamon	1/4 tsp	1 ml	vanilla	1/2 tsp	2 ml
nutmeg	1/8 tsp	0.5 ml	powdered sugar,		
egg, beaten	1		sifted	1/3 c	80 ml

1. Preheat fat to 375°F (190°C).
2. Sift together flour, baking powder, baking soda, salt, cinnamon, and nutmeg twice in a medium bowl.
3. Sprinkle flour on pastry cloth and the cloth sleeve of a rolling pin. Rub in.
4. Combine egg, sugar, buttermilk, shortening, and vanilla in a small bowl.
5. Gradually beat in wet ingredients to dry ingredients until just blended.
6. Gently pat dough to form a small ball. If dough is too moist, a little extra flour may be added so that the dough can be handled. Turn dough onto floured cloth.
7. Quickly and lightly, use short strokes to roll dough 1/2 in. (1/3 cm) thick.
8. Dip doughnut cutter into flour. Cut doughnuts. Remove with a spatula to wax paper. Let surface dry out for at least 15 minutes to reduce fat absorption.
9. Deep-fry doughnuts according to the basic method of deep-frying, pg. 243, approximately 1-1/2 minutes on each side.
10. Drain on paper towels. Cool slightly.
11. Roll in sifted powdered sugar in a plastic bag.

French Fries

baking (mealy potatoes)	1/2 lb	250 g
salt	2 tsp	10 ml
water	2 c	500 ml

1. Scrub potatoes and remove eyespots.
2. Cut into 1/3-1/2 in. (8-16 mm) slices. Trim the slices so that they are all the same width.
3. Dissolve salt in cold water. Add potatoes. Soak 20-30 minutes.
4. Drain with a colander. Pat dry with paper towels.
5. Deep-fry according to instructions on pg. 243 at 375°F (190°C).

(Courtesy of Hershey Foods Corp.)

18
Pastry

OBJECTIVES

The student should be able to:

1. Describe the effect of temperature and type of fat on pastry.
2. Discuss factors which affect the quality of pastry.
3. Demonstrate prevention of sogginess in pies.

FOOD SCIENCE PRINCIPLES

1. The flakiness of pastry is dependent on the type and consistency of the fat, the type of flour, the type and amount of liquid, extent and method of mixing, and the extent that the dough is rolled. Flakiness is not required for tenderness, as can be observed in oil pastry.
2. The type and quantity of fat will determine the flakiness, flavor, and color of pastry. Fats that can be used in making pastry are:

   a. *Lard:* This is the fat of choice in making pastry because it is more pliable over a range of temperatures than refrigerated butter, margarine, or hydrogenated fat.
   b. *Hydrogenated fat:* A satisfactory pastry is produced because of its plasticity, shortening power, and bland flavor.
   c. *Butter and margarine:* The water content (20%) of these fats necessitates that the amount of water in a recipe be reduced. Salt is omitted.
   d. *Oil:* Oil produces a mealy, tender pastry that is often dry and greasy rather than flaky.

3. The goal in making pastry is to form short strands of gluten with layers of fat trapped between them. Overmanipulation or rerolling pastry increases the length of gluten strands and creates a tough product. Pastry should never be stretched because the gluten strands shrink when coagulated.
4. Flakiness is caused by the development of "blisters" or holes when fat melts during baking. The melting fat is absorbed by the dough and leaves an opening. The moisture present in the melted fat, as well as the dough, vaporizes to steam, which leavens (puffs up) and increases the size of the opening. The structure becomes solid when the gluten strands coagulate from heat.

   Formation of large blisters is undesirable because they are unstable and prone to breaking. The tendency for large blisters is minimized by pricking the raw crust in order to create holes that permit steam to escape during baking. Blister size can also be reduced by placing a weight on the crust, such as dried beans or rice on aluminum foil.

5. The fragile egg proteins of custard pies cannot tolerate high oven temperatures. Lower temperatures, however, increase the sogginess of the crust. Sogginess can be minimized by prior baking t̶ set the crust, baking the crust and custard separately, or using a combination of high and low oven temperatures.

6. The top of a double-crust pie may trap the steam generated by the filling to produce a soggy crust. This can be minimized by cutting slits in the top crust, cooling the filling, or baking in a hot oven.

Experiment I: Effect of Temperature and Type of Fat on Pastry

1. Prepare 8 pastry wafers using the following ingredients. Vary the temperature and type of fat according to Table 18-1. Omit salt when the fat is margarine or salted butter.

Pastry Wafers

flour, sifted	1/4 c	60 ml	fat	1-1/2 Tbsp	22 ml
salt	1/8 tsp	0.5 ml	water	1-1/2-2 tsp	7-10 ml

2. Use steps 1-5 and 7 of the recipe for pie crust—Experiment II. Finish preparing the wafers by:

   a. Roll the dough using light, short strokes so that a 5 in. (13 cm) square can be cut from the dough.
   b. Cut the square in half from one direction and in quarters from the other so that there are 8 pastry wafers.
   c. Place the wafers on a baking sheet.
   d. Bake at 425°F (220°C) 8-10 minutes until lightly browned.

3. Observe appearance of the pastry wafers. Determine tenderness by ease of breaking. Observe flakiness. Taste for flavor.
4. Record results in Table 18-1.

TABLE 18-1   Effect of Temperature and Type of Fat on Pastry

Fat	Temperature	Appearance	Tenderness	Flakiness	Flavor
Butter	cold				
	room				
Lard	room				
Margarine	cold				
	room				
Oil	room				
Hydrogenated	room				

QUESTIONS

1. Which two fats produce the best quality pastry? _____
   _____

2. Describe what happens to the fat and water when pastry is baked. _____
   _____
   _____

3. What is the effect of varying the temperature of the fat? _____
   _____

Experiment II: Factors Affecting Quality of Pastry

1. Prepare pastry for six 6-in. (15 cm) pies. For 4 of the six 6-in. pie crusts, use the recipe for the 9-in. (23 cm) double-crust pastry. Use the following variations:

   a. unpricked
   b. pricking extensively with a fork on the sides, bottom, and inner edge
   c. stretching the dough
   d. rolling the dough thin, gathering the dough into a ball, and rerolling

   For the remaining 2 pie crusts, prepare two single crust pastries for 6-in. (15 cm) pies. Use the following variations:

   e. Substitute whole wheat flour for all-purpose white flour.
   f. Substitute milk for water.

2. Bake the pie shells for 8-10 minutes in a preheated 425°F (220°C) oven.
3. Observe color and appearance. Test for tenderness with a fork. Taste for flavor.
4. Record results in Table 18-2.

Pie Crust

	Single Crust				Double Crust			
	6 in. (15 cm)		9 in. (23 cm)		6 in. (15 cm)		9 in. (23 cm)	
flour	1/2 c	125 ml	1 c	250 ml	1 c	250 ml	2 c	500 ml
salt	1/4 tsp	1 ml	1/2 tsp	2 ml	1/2 tsp	2 ml	1 tsp	5 ml
fat	3 Tbsp	45 ml	1/3 c + 1 Tbsp	80 ml 15 ml*	1/3 c + 1 Tbsp	80 ml 15 ml*	2/3 c + 2 Tbsp	160 ml 30 ml*
ice water	1-1-1/2 Tbsp 15-22 ml		2-3 Tbsp 30-45 ml		2-3 Tbsp 30-45 ml		4-5 Tbsp 60-75 ml	

1. Rub flour into a pastry cloth and the sleeve of a rolling pin.
2. Mix together the flour and salt in a bowl.
3. Cut in fat until it is the size of peas. It will be necessary to occasionally scrape off the fat that accumulates on the pastry blender with a rubber spatula.

* Eliminate if lard is used as the fat.

4. Add water by drops while gently stirring the flour mixture with a fork. Stop adding water when the mixture leaves the sides of the bowl and starts to form a cohesive mass. The goal is to form hydrated dough with a minimal amount of gluten development. This can only be achieved if the dough is worked as little as possible.

5. Use a fork to help turn the dough onto a piece of waxed paper. Pick up the piece of wax paper and *gently* pat and squeeze to form a ball of dough. This should be done quickly and lightly without the dough touching the hands.

6. **Double-Crust Pie:** Divide the dough in half. Roll only 1 piece of dough at a time.

7. Place the ball of dough on the floured pastry cloth. *Gently* flatten the dough into a circle with the palm of the left hand while guiding the edge with the right. Avoid making cracks in the circle. Turn the dough over. Sprinkle lightly with flour.

8. Quickly using short, quick strokes, roll the dough evenly into a circle that extends 3/4 in. (1.9 cm) beyond the edge of the pie pan.

9. Gently pick up 1/2 of the pastry and fold in 1/2. Pick up 1/2 of the folded pastry and fold it in quarters. Lift completely from the pastry cloth.

10. Transfer the pastry to the pie pan and unfold. Do *not* stretch the pastry. Use the weight of the pastry to gently ease the dough into the inner edge of the pan.

11. **Single-Crust Pie:** Trim the pastry so that it extends 1/2 in. (1.3 cm) beyond the edge of the pan.

12. **Double-Crust Pie:** Trim the pastry at the edge of the pan. Repeat steps 7-10 with the other half of the dough for the top crust. Fill the pie with the desired filling. Unfold top crust over filling and trim so that it extends 1/2 in. (1.3 cm) beyond the edge of the pan.

13. Fold the overhanging crust under the pastry.

14. Trim the edge of the pastry by molding with a fork, spoon, or fingers.

15. **Baked Pie Shell:** Prick pastry extensively with a fork at sides, bottom, and inner edge. Bake 8-10 minutes at 425°F (220°C).

16. **Single-Crust Pie:** Add filling and bake according to the recipe.

17. **Double-Crust Pie:** Make several slits at least 1/4 in. (6 mm) long near the center of the top crust. Cover edge with a 2-3 in. (5-7.5 cm) strip of aluminum foil. Remove during the last 15 minutes. Bake according to the recipe.

TABLE 18-2   Factors Affecting Quality of Pastry

Variation	Color	Appearance	Tenderness	Flavor
Unpricked				
Pricked				
Stretched				
Rerolled				
Whole-wheat flour				
Milk				

1. Why are baked pie shells normally pricked before baking? _____

   _____

2. How does stretching the raw pastry affect the final product? _____

   _____

3. Why does rerolled pie crust become tough? _____

   _____

4. Describe the effect of substituting whole-wheat flour for all-purpose white flour? _____

   _____

   _____

5. Account for the difference in pie crust pastry when milk is substituted for water as the liquid.

   _____

   _____

Experiment III: Prevention of Sogginess in Single-Crust Pies

1. Prepare pastry for five 6-in. (15 cm) pies.
   a. Follow the recipe for the 9-in. (23 cm) double-crust pie.
   b. Divide the dough into 4 parts and roll the pastry according to the recipe. Place in 4 pans; do not prick these crusts.
   c. Prepare an additional, slightly thicker crust for a fifth pan using the following ingredients:

Thick Single-Pie Crust

	6 in. (15 cm)		9 in. (23 cm)	
flour	1/2 c + 2 Tbsp	155 ml	1-1/4 c	310 ml
salt	3/16 tsp	1 ml	1/2 tsp + 1/8 tsp	3 ml
fat	1/4 c + 1 tsp	55 ml	1/3 c + 2 Tbsp	110 ml
ice water	1 Tbsp + 3/4 tsp –		2 Tbsp + 1-1/2 tsp –	
	2 Tbsp	18-30 ml	3 Tbsp + 2 tsp	37-55 ml

2. Use one of the following treatments on each of the pie crusts:

   a. None
   b. Brush bottom crust with softened margarine.
   c. Set the pie shell by baking 5 minutes at 450°F (230°C). Prick the pie crust before baking.
   d. Set the pie shell by baking 5 minutes at 450°F (230°C). Cut a circle of aluminum foil the diameter of the bottom of the pan and place inside pastry. Spread 2 Tbsp (30 ml) dried beans on top of aluminum foil to keep the pastry weighted down while it is set by baking.
   e. Bake the pie crust and custard separately. Lightly grease outer sides of pie pan with fat. Place thick pie crust on outside of a pie pan upside down. *Gently* press crust to conform it to the shape of pan, but do not press edges into fluted rim. Trim off pastry so that it ends just above the beginning of the fluted rim. Bake 10-12 minutes at 450°F (230°C) until lightly browned.

3. Prepare custard using the following recipe:

Custard Pie*

milk	3 c	750 ml	sugar	1/2 c + 2 Tbsp	155 ml
eggs	4		vanilla	1 tsp	5 ml
salt	1/2 tsp	2 ml	nutmeg	dash	

    a. Preheat oven to 450°F (230°C).
    b. Scald the milk, measure, and allow to cool slightly. (This step is unnecessary if non-fat dry milk is used.)
    c. Beat the eggs until well blended with a rotary beater without creating a foam.
    d. Add the milk, salt, sugar, and vanilla to the eggs. Blend thoroughly.
    e. Pour mixture into pie crust.
    f. Sprinkle lightly with nutmeg.
    g. Bake 10 minutes at 450°F (230°C). Lower heat and bake 15-20 minutes at 350°F (177°C) or until the tip of a sharp knife inserted halfway between the center and the edge comes out clean.

4. Pour approximately 3/4 c (180 ml) into the pie crusts in 2a, b, c, and d, and bake as directed in the recipe.
5. Pour rest of the custard into a pie pan to within 1/2 in. (1.3 cm) of the rim.

    a. Place the pie pan inside a baking pan.
    b. Pour boiling water in the baking pan to a depth of 1/2 in. (1.3 cm).
    c. Bake 45-55 minutes at 350°F (177°C) or until the tip of a sharp knife inserted halfway between the center and the edge comes out clean.
    d. Allow the custard to cool in cold water until it is lukewarm.
    e. Rim the custard and carefully transfer it into the baked pie shell of 2e.

6. Allow the custard pies to cool. Cut out a 3-in. (7.5 cm) wedge and observe extent of sogginess of bottom crust.
7. Record results in Table 18–3.

TABLE 18–3   Prevention of Sogginess in Single-Crust Pies

Treatment	Ease of Preparation[a]	Extent of Sogginess[b]
None		
Brush with fat		
Set by baking and pricking		
Set by baking and weight		
Baked separately		

[a] Rate on a scale from 1-5; 1 = easiest.
[b] Rate on a scale from 1-5; 5 = soggiest.

* Double recipe for 7- or 8-in. (18 or 20 cm) pan and triple recipe for 9-in. (23 cm) pan.

QUESTIONS

1. Which of the above methods was most effective in preventing sogginess? _____
   _____ What is the disadvantage of this
   method? _____
   _____

2. Which of the above methods would be relatively easy, yet effective? _____
   _____

Experiment IV: Prevention of Sogginess in Double-Crust Pies

1. Prepare pastry for five 6 in. (15 cm) pies. Follow the recipe for double-crust pies in Experiment II.
2. Preheat 2 ovens, to 425°F (220°C) and 300°F (150°C).
3. Prepare apple pie filling for 3 of the 6 in. (15 cm) pies.

   a. Place filling in the 3 pies.
   b. Cover with top crust and seal around the edges. Cut slits in 2 of the 3 pie crusts Leave the third crust uncut.
   c. Bake the uncut pie and one of the slitted pies for 30-40 minutes at 425°F (220°C).
   d. Bake the other pie for 50-60 minutes at 300°F (150°C).

Apple Pie [6" (15 cm)]*

apples, peeled,	2	500 ml	cinnamon	1/8 tsp	0.5 ml
1/8 in. (3 mm) slices			nutmeg	1/8 tsp	0.5 ml
sugar	3 Tbsp	45 ml	lemon juice	1-1/2 tsp	7 ml
cornstarch	3/4 tsp	3 ml	margarine	1/2 tsp	2 ml
salt	dash				

   a. Prepare pastry for a 6 in. (15 cm) double-crust pie.
   b. Mix together the sugar, cornstarch, salt, cinnamon, and nutmeg.
   c. Sprinkle lemon juice over apple slices.
   d. Toss apples with dry ingredients.
   e. Place apple filling in pastry.
   f. Seal with top crust. Make slits in the top crust.
   g. Place a 2-3 in. (5-7.5 cm) of aluminum foil around edge of crust to retard browning. Remove during last 15 minutes of baking.
   h. Bake according to directions in the experiment. In nonlaboratory situations, bake at 425°F (220°C) for 40 minutes.

4. Prepare cherry pie filling for 2 of the 6 in. (15 cm) pies.

   a. Pour *hot* filling into pastry.
   b. Immediately seal with top crust and make slits.
   c. Bake 1 of the pies for 30 minutes at 425° F (220° C).
   d. Bake the other pie for 45 minutes at 300° F (150° C).

*Double recipe for 7- or 8-in. (18 or 20 cm) pan and triple recipe for 9-in. (23 cm) pan.

Cherry Pie [6" (15 cm)]*

cherries, canned, drained	1-1/2 c	375 ml	cornstarch	2-1/2 tsp	12 ml
			almond extract	2	
cherry juice	1/4 c	60 ml	drops		
sugar	1/2 c	125 ml	margarine	1 tsp	5 ml

    a. Prepare pastry for 6 in. (15 cm) pie.
    b. Dissolve sugar and cornstarch in cherry juice in a small saucepan. Bring to boil while stirring constantly.
    c. Add almond extract and heat until clear.
    d. Add cherries and coat well.
    e. Pour hot filling into pastry. In nonlaboratory situations allow the filling to cool to lukewarm.
    f. Dot with margarine.
    g. Seal with top crust. Make slits in top crust.
    h. Place 2–3 in. (5–7.5 cm) of aluminum foil around edge of crust to retard browning. Remove during last 15 minutes of baking.
    i. Bake according to direction in the experiment. In nonlaboratory situations, bake at 425°F (220°C) for 30 minutes.

5. Cool the pies as much as time will permit. Cut out a 3 in (7.5 cm) wedge of pie and observe sogginess of upper and lower crust.
6. Record result in Table 18–4.

TABLE 18–4   Prevention of Sogginess in Double-Crust Pies

Temperature		Slits	Sogginess of Crust	
Filling	Oven		Upper	Lower
Hot	hot	X		
	cool	X		
Cool	hot	X		
	hot			
	cool	X		

QUESTIONS

1. Which combination of filling and oven temperature produced the least soggy crust? _____ _____ The most soggy? _____ _____ Why? _____
_____
_____

2. Why are slits made in double-crust pies? _____
_____

*Double recipe for 7- or 8-in. (18 or 20 cm) pan and triple recipe for 9-in. (23 cm) pan.

APPLICATIONS

*Banana Cream Pie**

cornstarch	1-1/2 Tbsp	22 ml	egg yolk, beaten	1	
sugar	1/3 c	80 ml	margarine	1/2 tsp	2 ml
salt	1/8 tsp	0.5 ml	vanilla	1/2 tsp	2 ml
milk	1 c	250 ml	banana	1	

1. Prepare and bake pastry for a 6 in. (15 cm) single-crust pie.
2. Combine cornstarch, sugar, and salt in a saucepan.
3. Gradually stir in milk with a wooden spoon until well blended.
4. Bring to a boil, stirring constantly. Boil 1 minute.
5. Remove pan from heat.
6. Stir a small amount of the hot mixture into the egg yolk. Gradually add more of the mixture. Then slowly pour egg yolk mixture into the hot filling, stirring constantly.
7. Return pan to heat. Heat until the mixture thickens, stirring constantly.
8. Remove pan from heat.
9. Stir in margarine and vanilla until blended.
10. Cover and cool to room temperature in refrigerator.
11. Peel and slice bananas. Arrange in baked pie shell.
12. Pour custard over bananas.
13. Chill.

*Coconut Custard Pie**

flour	3 Tbsp	45 ml	egg yolk, beaten	1	
sugar	1/3 c	80 ml	margarine	1 tsp	5 ml
salt	1/4 tsp	1 ml	vanilla	1/2 tsp	2 ml
milk	1 c	250 ml	shredded coconut	1/2 c	125 ml

1. Preheat oven to 350°F (175°C).
2. Prepare and bake pastry for a 6 in. (15 cm) single-crust pie.
3. Combine flour, sugar, and salt in a saucepan.
4. Gradually stir in milk with wooden spoon until blended.
5. Bring the mixture to a boil, stirring constantly. Boil 1 minute.
6. Remove pan from heat.
7. Stir a small amount of the hot mixture into the egg yolk. Gradually add more of the mixture. Then slowly pour the egg yolk mixture into the hot filling, stirring constantly.
8. Return pan to heat. Heat until the mixture thickens, stirring constantly.
9. Remove pan from heat.
10. Stir in margarine and vanilla until blended. Cover.
11. Prepare meringue, pg. 263.
12. Add shredded coconut to the custard.
13. Pour custard into baked pie shell.
14. Spread with meringue. Seal to edges.
15. Bake 12–15 minutes until lightly browned.

*Double recipe for 7- or 8-in. (18 or 20 cm) pan and triple recipe for 9-in. (23 cm) pan.

Cream Cheese Pastry

butter	1/2 c	125 ml	apricot, mushroom,		
cream cheese	1/4 lb	125 g	or walnut filling		
salt	1/4 tsp	1 ml	egg yolk	1	
flour	1 c	250 ml	milk	2 tsp	10 ml

1. Cream butter until soft.
2. Add cream cheese and continue creaming until blended.
3. Blend in salt and flour to form a soft dough.
4. Chill in freezer while preparing filling. (At home, chill in the refrigerator.)
5. Prepare filling — see the following recipes. (If preparing apricot filling, do this first.)
6. Preheat oven to 350°F (175°C).
7. Flour surface of counter. Break dough in half. Leave remaining dough in refrigerator to continue chilling.
8. Roll out dough on floured surface until approximately 1/16 in. (0.15 cm) thick.
9. Cut dough in strips 2 in. (5 cm) wide. Cut strips into wedges.
10. Place a heaping teaspoonful of filling in the center of each wedge. Close tops by pressing tips together with your *washed* fingers.
11. Immediately before baking, combine egg yolk with milk. Brush tops of pastry with this mixture.
12. Bake approximately 20 minutes until lightly browned.

Apricot Filling

apricots, dried	1/4 lb	125 g	sugar	2-1/2 Tbsp	37 ml
water					

1. Place dried apricots in a small saucepan. Cover with water, cover pan, and bring to a boil.
2. Stir, lower heat, and let simmer 30 minutes until the apricots are soft and can be mashed against the side of the pan with the back of a spoon.
3. Drain apricots. Beat until smooth and creamy. Beat in sugar.

Mushroom Filling

margarine	1 Tbsp	15 ml	pepper	dash	
mushrooms, fresh,	1/4 lb	125 g	nutmeg	dash	
sliced	(1 c)	(250 ml)	flour	1 tsp	5 ml
onion, chopped	1/4 c	50 ml	sour cream	2 Tbsp	30 ml
lemon juice	1/2 tsp	2 ml	dill weed	1/8 tsp	0.5 ml
salt	1/4 tsp	1 ml			

1. Melt margarine over medium-high heat.
2. Add mushrooms and onions; cook until onion is softened.
3. Stir in lemon juice, salt, pepper, and nutmeg.
4. Blend in flour.
5. Combine sour cream and dill. Add mixture to mushrooms.
6. Allow filling to cool to room temperature before using. (Chill in freezer in laboratory to speed up the time required.)

Walnut Filling

walnuts	2/3 c	180 ml	milk or cream	2 tsp	10 ml
sugar	1 Tbsp + 1 tsp	22 ml			

1. Grind walnuts in a food processor, blender, or with a rolling pin between two sheets of wax paper.
2. Mix in sugar and milk or cream.

Chocolate Peanut Butter Pie *

sweet chocolate	2 oz	60 g	peanut butter chips	1/2 c	125 ml
gelatin	1-1/2 tsp	7 ml	egg white	1	
sugar	1/4 c	50 ml	sugar	1-1/2 tsp	7 ml
milk	3/4 c + 2 Tbsp	210 ml	whipped cream chocolate shavings		
egg yolk	1/2				
vanilla	1/2 tsp	2 ml			

1. Prepare Peanut Butter Chip Crust for a 6-in. (15 cm) pie.
2. Break chocolate in pieces and place in a bowl. Set aside.
3. Combine gelatin and sugar in a saucepan.
4. Add milk and stir until gelatin is dissolved.
5. Beat in egg yolk.
6. Cook over medium heat, stirring constantly, until gelatin dissolves and mixture lightly coats spoon. Do not boil.
7. Remove pan from heat. Stir in vanilla.
8. Pour 1/2 the mixture over the broken chocolate. Stir until melted.
9. Add peanut butter chips to the remaining hot mixture. Stir until melted.
10. Chill both mixtures in the refrigerator until the consistency of egg white.
11. Beat egg white until foamy. Gradually add sugar while continuing to beat. Beat until stiff peaks form.
12. Pour thickened chocolate into pie shell.
13. Combine egg white foam with peanut butter mixture. Spread over chocolate layer.
14. Chill.
15. Garnish with whipped cream, chocolate shavings, or peanut butter chips.

Peanut Butter Chip Crust *

peanut butter chips	1/3 c	80 ml	sugar	1 Tbsp	15 ml
graham cracker crumbs	1/2 c	125 ml	margarine, melted	2-1/2 Tbsp	37 ml

1. Chop peanut butter chips with knife or chopper.
2. Add to graham cracker crumbs and sugar. Mix well.
3. Toss with *cooled*, melted margarine.
4. Press into pie pan.
5. Chill.

*Double recipe for 7- or 8-in. (18 or 20 cm) pan and triple recipe for 9-in. (23 cm) pan.

Lemon Meringue Pie*

cornstarch	2 Tbsp	30 ml	egg yolk, beaten	1	
sugar	1/2 c	125 ml	margarine	1 Tbsp	15 ml
salt	dash		lemon juice	3 Tbsp	45 ml
water	1/2 c	125 ml	lemon rind, grated	1/2 tsp	2 ml

1. Prepare and bake pastry for a 6-in. (15 cm) single-crust pie.
2. Preheat oven to 400°F (200°C).
3. Combine cornstarch, sugar, and salt in a saucepan.
4. Stir in water with a wooden spoon.
5. Cook until the mixture boils, stirring constantly. Boil 1 minute.
6. Remove pan from heat.
7. Stir a small amount of the hot mixture into the egg yolk. Gradually add a little more of the mixture to warm the egg yolks. Then slowly pour egg yolk mixture into hot filling, stirring constantly.
8. Return to heat. Bring to a boil, stirring constantly. Boil 1 minute.
9. Remove pan from heat.
10. Stir in remaining ingredients.
11. Pour into baked pie shell.
12. Spread meringue over hot filling. Seal to the edge of the crust (See Figure 18-1).
13. Bake 10 minutes until lightly browned.

FIGURE 18-1 *Meringue should be spread to the edges of the crust to help hold it in place during baking. (Courtesy of Betty Crocker of General Mills, Inc.)*

* Double recipe for 7- or 8-in. (18 or 20 cm) pan and triple recipe for 9-in (23 cm) pan.

*Meringue**

egg white	1		sugar	2 Tbsp	30 ml
cream of tartar	1/8 tsp	0.5 ml	vanilla	1/8 tsp	0.5 ml

1. Combine egg white and cream of tartar in a deep bowl.
2. Beat with electric beater until foamy.
3. Gradually beat in sugar.
4. Continue beating until egg whites are stiff but not dry.
5. Blend in vanilla.

*Pecan Pie**

eggs, beaten	1-1/2		dark corn syrup	1/2 c	125 ml
sugar	1/3 c	80 ml	margarine, melted	3 Tbsp	45 ml
salt	1/4 tsp	1 ml	pecan halves	1/2 c	125 ml

1. Preheat oven to 375°F (190°C).
2. Prepare pastry for a 6 in. (15 cm) single-crust pie. Do not prick crust.
3. Beat eggs, sugar, salt, corn syrup, and margarine together with a rotary beater.
4. Stir in nuts.
5. Pour mixture into pie crust.
6. Bake 40 minutes until filling has set.

*Pumpkin Pie **

egg	1/2		ground cloves	1/8 tsp	0.5 ml
pumpkin,	1/2 c +	155 ml	nutmeg	1/8 tsp	0.5 ml
canned	2 Tbsp		ginger	1/8 tsp	0.5 ml
brown sugar	1/4 c	50 ml	salt	1/8 tsp	0.5 ml
sugar	1 Tbsp	15 ml	evaporated	1/2 c +	155 ml
cinnamon	1/2 tsp	2 ml	milk	2 Tbsp	

1. Preheat oven to 425°F (220°C).
2. Prepare pastry for a 6 in. (15 cm) single-crust pie. Do not prick crust.
3. Beat egg with a rotary beater.
4. Add remaining ingredients and blend thoroughly.
5. Pour into the pie shell.
6. Bake 4 minutes at 425°F (220°C). Lower heat and bake 20 minutes at 325°F (160°C) or until a knife inserted half-way between the center and the edge comes out clean.
7. Cool before serving.

* Double recipe for 7-or 8-in. (18 or 20 cm) pan and triple recipe for 9-in. (23 cm) pan.

(Courtesy of Hershey Foods Corp.)

19

Quick Breads

OBJECTIVES

The student should be able to:

1. Assess the nutritive value of flours.
2. Summarize the reactions of chemical leavening agents.
3. Describe factors affecting the quality of muffins and biscuits.
4. Prepare and compare a variety of quick breads.

FOOD SCIENCE PRINCIPLES

1. Flours are generally high in food energy and carbohydrates, and low in fat. The protein content varies according to the variety. The amount of iron and B vitamins present in the flour is dependent on the degree of processing of the grain and subsequent enrichment of the flour.
2. When an acid is added to baking soda in the presence of a liquid, carbon dioxide is quickly evolved. Any food substance that contains an acid such as sour milk (lactic), honey (formic) or molasses (aconitic), will cause this reaction.

   Baking powder is a mixture of baking soda and acid, with a dry dilutent such as cornstarch added to separate the mixture. Double-acting baking powders react first when a liquid is added, and second, when the liquid is heated. This retards the complete release of carbon dioxide until the mixture is heated.
3. Quick breads are baked products that are leavened by air, steam, and/or chemicals such as baking soda or powder. They are named quick because they are cooked quickly after mixing, rather than after fermentation as in yeast breads. Some factors affecting their quality include:

   a. *Type and amount of flour:* Flour provides gluten, the three-dimensional complex of hydrated proteins (glutenin and gliadin) in which starch grains are embedded. When heated to high temperatures, the proteins coagulate and form the structure of the product. Whole-wheat flour creates a product with a smaller volume because the germ has a detrimental effect on gluten development.

   b. *Leavening Agents:* Air, steam, and carbon dioxide are the three major leavening agents. Chemical agents such as baking soda and baking powder are added to muffins and biscuits to generate carbon dioxide, which makes them light and porous. Popovers and cream puffs are leavened primarily by steam.

    c. *Eggs:* Eggs provide leavening, color, shortening, flavor, and nutritive value to quick breads. Their emulsifying properties create an even distribution of shortening and a tender texture. In steam-leavened quick breads, the proteins of the eggs provide a firm structure.

    d. *Fat:* The addition of fat to a flour mixture produces a shorter or more tender dough, and aids in leavening.

    e. *Sugar:* Sugar tenderizes by interfering with gluten formation and by decreasing the uptake of water by the flour. It is also added for its sweetening, leavening, and browning ability.

    f. *Liquid:* Liqiuds serve as solvents for dry ingredients, hydrate proteins, gelatinize starch, leaven via steam, and are essential for the reaction of chemical leaveners.

    g. *Manipulation:* Manipulation, in the form of stirring or kneading, develops the gluten complex by allowing the protein molecules to slide past one another and form bonds. The extent of manipulation affects the volume, texture, and appearance of baked products. Insufficient manipulation produces products with low volume. In batters, excessive stirring creates products with long strands of gluten; these products are tough with peaked tops and tunnels. In doughs, excessive kneading results in a tough product that has a diminished volume due to broken gluten strands and loss of gas.

4. Flour mixtures can be classified as either batters or doughs. Batters can be subdivided into pour or drop batters. The approximate liquid:flour ratio is 2/3 to 1:1 for pour batters (pancakes, waffles) and 1:2 for drop batters (muffins). Doughs have a smaller proportion of liquid to flour, usually 1:3 for a soft dough (biscuits) and 1:6 to 8 for a stiff dough (pie crust).

5. The grain of a quick bread is a foam-like structure of small holes or pockets. These holes represent where carbon dioxide was evolved, water changed to steam, or air expanded during heating. An excessive amount of leavening or baking at too low a temperature causes the holes to enlarge or explode and the cells to thicken. Too little leavening agent or too much fat causes the holes to be small and the walls thin.

Exercise I: Nutritive Values of Flours

Calculate the nutritive values of the flours listed in Table 19–1.

TABLE 19–1   Nutritive Values of Flour

Flour	Nutritive Value/1 c (250 ml)							
	Food Energy (Cal)	Protein (g)	Fat (g)	Carbo-hydrate (g)	Iron (mg)	Thiamine (mg)	Riboflavin (mg)	Niacin (mg)
Corn								
Rye (medium)								
Soy (defatted)								
Wheat all purpose (sifted)								
all purpose, enriched (sifted)								
cake								
whole wheat								

QUESTIONS

1. Which of the above flours is highest in protein? _____ Lowest? _____

2. Explain how the protein content is related to the use of the product: _____
   _____
   _____

3. Which of the above flours is lowest in carbohydrates? _____
   Why? _____

4. Name 2 flours that are good sources of iron. a. _____ b. _____

5. Which flour has the lowest values for iron and vitamins? _____
   Why? _____
   _____

6. Why is all purpose flour enriched? _____
   _____

Experiment 1: Reaction of Chemical Leavening Agents

1. Label 8 *completely dry* custard cups 1-8.
2. Add 1/4 tsp (1 ml) of the following leavening agents to each of the custard cups.

> Custard cup No. 1: baking soda
> No. 2: baking soda + 1/4 tsp (1 ml) cream of tartar
> No. 3: double acting baking powder
> No. 4: baking soda
> No. 5: double acting baking powder
> No. 6: baking soda
> No. 7: baking soda
> No. 8: baking soda

3. Label the 6 other custard cups 9-14.
4. Place 1 tsp (5 ml) egg white into each of the custard cups 9-14. (It is not critical that the quantity of egg white in each custard cup be the same, only approximate.)
5. Add 1 Tbsp (15 ml) cold water into custard cups 9, 10, and 11. Stir with the edge of a knife; avoid making bubbles.
6. Pour the water-egg mixtures of custard cups 9, 10, and 11 into custard cups 1, 2, and 3, respectively. Gently stir each cup to mix. Observe reactions.
7. Add 1 Tbsp (15 ml) hot water into custard cups 12 and 13. Stir with the edge of a knife; avoid making bubbles.
8. Immediately pour the water-egg mixtures of custard cups 12 and 13 into custard cups 4 and 5, respectively. Gently stir each cup to mix. Observe reactions.
9. Add 1 Tbsp (15 ml) sour milk to custard cup 14. Mix with the edge of a knife; avoid making bubbles.
10. Pour the milk-egg mixture of custard cup 14 into custard cup 6. Gently stir cup to mix. Observe reactions.

11. Add 1 Tbsp (15 ml) honey to custard cup 7. Gently stir cup to mix. Observe reaction.
12. Add 1 Tbsp (15 ml) molasses to custard cup 8. Gently stir to mix. Observe reaction.
13. Record results in Table 19–2.

TABLE 19–2   Reactions of Leavening Agents

| Custard Cup No. | Leavening Agents | | Additive | Temperature of Additive | Observations |
	Baking Soda	Baking Powder			
1	X		water	cold	
2	X		cream of tartar & water	cold	
3		X	water	cold	
4	X		water	hot	
5		X	water	hot	
6	X		sour milk	room	
7	X		honey	room	
8	X		molasses	room	

QUESTIONS

1. What was the purpose of using egg white in custard cups 1-6 but not in 7 and 8?

_____

_____

2. Describe the reaction that occurs when acid is added to baking soda in the presence of water:

_____

_____

3. Explain the difference between baking soda and baking powder. _____

_____

_____

4. Why is the baking powder that was used in this experiment called "double-acting"? _____

_____

_____

5. What is the advantage of using double-acting baking powder rather than baking soda or single-acting baking powder? _____

_____

_____

6. Name an acid that is found in sour milk: _____

In honey: _____ In molasses: _____

7. Explain why the reactions of honey and molasses with baking soda do not begin immediately.

_____

_____

How could this be used to advantage in cooking? _____

_____

Experiment II: Factors Affecting the Quality of Muffins

1. Grease 14 muffin cups.
2. Label 7 small bowls, nos. 1-7 and 7 custard cups, nos. 1-7.
3. Prepare laboratory muffins according to the recipe below using the following variations:

> Bowl No. 1: standard recipe
> No. 2: substitute whole-wheat flour for white flour
> No. 3: omit baking powder
> No. 4: double the baking powder
> No. 5: omit egg
> No. 6: omit oil
> No. 7: omit sugar

4. Observe volume and shape.
5. Cut in half. Observe the grain (size and distribution of air cells). Taste for flavor and tenderness.
6. Record results in Table 19–3.

Laboratory Muffins (2)

flour	1/4 c	60 ml	sugar	3/4 tsp	3 ml
salt	1/8 tsp	0.5 ml	egg, beaten	1 tsp	5 ml
baking	1/2 tsp	2 ml	milk	2 Tbsp	30 ml
powder			oil	3/4 tsp	3 ml

a. Preheat oven to 425°F (220°C).
b. Sift together the dry ingredients, flour, salt, baking powder, and sugar, into each of the bowls. Make a well in the center of the dry ingredients in each bowl.
c. Blend the wet ingredients, eggs, milk, and oil, *thoroughly* in each of the 7 custard cups.
d. Pour the wet ingredients of each custard cup into the dry ingredients of the corresponding bowl. Stir *just to moisten;* the batter will be lumpy.
e. Pour each batter into 2 greased muffin cups, 1/2 full.
f. Bake 15-20 minutes.
g. Immediately remove from muffin cups to prevent sogginess.

TABLE 19-3   Factors Affecting the Quality of Muffins

Muffin Variation	Appearance			Tenderness	Flavor
	Volume	Shape	Grain		
Standard					
Whole-wheat flour					
— baking powder					
2x baking powder					
— egg					
— fat					
— sugar					

QUESTIONS

1. What was the difference between muffins made from whole-wheat and white flour? _____

_____

_____

What was the reason for these differences? _____

_____

2. How did the absence of baking powder affect the grain of the muffins? _____

_____

Why? _____

_____

3. What was the effect of adding excessive amounts of baking powder to the batter? _____

_____

_____

4. Describe how the absence of egg affects the quality of a muffin. _____

_____

5. Why is liquid fat added to muffins? _____

_____

6. What effect does sugar have on the color and crispness of muffins? _____

_____

7. What is the approximate liquid:flour ratio of a muffin batter? _____

Experiment III: Effect of Manipulation on the Quality of Muffins

1. Grease 6 muffin cups.
2. Prepare muffin batter using the recipe below.
3. Beat the batter with 5 strokes. Pour 1/4 c (50 ml) of the batter into a muffin cup.
4. Beat the batter an additional 10 strokes (for a total of 15). Pour 1/4 c (50 ml) of the batter into 2 muffin cups.
5. Beat the batter an additional 15 strokes (for a total of 30). Pour 1/4 c (50 ml) of the batter into 2 muffin cups.
6. Beat the remaining batter an additional 15 strokes (for a total of 45). Pour the batter into the last muffin cup.
7. Bake 15-20 minutes until golden brown.
8. Immediately remove muffins from the cups to prevent sogginess.
9. Observe surface appearance and shape. Measure the height with a ruler.
10. Cut each muffin in half. Observe the grain. Taste for flavor and tenderness.
11. Record results in Table 19-4.

Muffins (6)

flour	1 c	250 ml	egg, beaten	1/2	
salt	1/2 tsp	2 ml	milk	1/2 c	125 ml
baking powder	1-1/2 tsp	7 ml	oil	2 Tbsp	30 ml
sugar	2 Tbsp	30 ml			

a. Preheat oven to 425°F (220°C).
b. Sift together the dry ingredients, flour, salt, baking powder, and sugar. Make a well in the center of the ingredients.
c. Thoroughly blend the wet ingredients, eggs, milk, and oil.
d. Pour the wet ingredients into the well of the dry ingredients.

TABLE 19-4   Effect of Manipulation on the Quality of Muffins

Strokes	Height (in. or cm)	Appearance			Tenderness	Flavor
		Surface	Shape	Grain		
5						
15						
30						
45						

QUESTIONS

1. Describe the appearance of the batter that was understirred (5 strokes). _____

   _____

   Stirred to moisten ingredients (15 strokes). _____

   _____

   Overstirred. _____

   _____

2. Which of the muffins was the tallest? _____

   Why? _____

   _____

3. Describe the surface appearance and shape of an overstirred muffin. _____

   _____

   _____

4. Is it easy to overstir muffins? _____ Why? _____

   _____

5. In which muffins are there tunnels? _____

   _____ Why? _____

   _____

Experiment IV: Effect of Manipulation on the Quality of Biscuits

1. Lightly sprinkle flour on a pastry cloth or clean counter.
2. Prepare biscuit dough using the recipe below:
3. Cut off approximately 1/4 of the dough. Do not knead. Place it on the lightly floured pastry cloth and roll to form the size of 2 biscuits. Use a biscuit cutter to cut out 2 biscuits and place them on an ungreased baking sheet.
4. Place the remaining dough on the floured pastry cloth. Knead 10 strokes. Cut off approximately 1/3 of the dough and roll out 2 more biscuits.
5. Knead the remaining dough 10 more strokes. Divide the dough in half. Roll 1/2 of the dough to form 2 biscuits.
6. Knead the remaining dough an additional 30 strokes. Roll and cut 2 biscuits from the dough.
7. Bake 10-12 minutes until lightly browned.
8. Observe appearance. Measure the height with a ruler.
9. Cut 1 of each of the biscuits in half. Observe flakiness. Taste for tenderness and flavor.
10. Record results in Table 19-5.

Biscuits

flour	2 c	500 ml	shortening	1/4 c	50 ml
salt	1 tsp	5 ml	milk	3/4 c	180 ml
baking powder	1 Tbsp	15 ml			

a. Preheat oven to 425°F (220°C).
b. Sift together the flour, salt, and baking powder into a bowl.
c. Cut in the fat until the ingredients resemble coarse cornmeal.
d. Stir in enough milk until the mixture thickens into a soft dough.

TABLE 19-5   Effect of Manipulation on the Quality of Biscuits

Strokes	Height (in. or cm)	Appearance	Flakiness	Tenderness	Flavor
0					
10					
20					
50					

QUESTIONS

1. What is the optimal number of strokes to knead a biscuit? _____

2. Describe the effect of underkneading a biscuit: _____

   _____

   _____

3. What happens when a biscuit is overkneaded? _____

   _____

   _____

4. What is the approximate liquid:flour ratio in biscuit doughs? _____

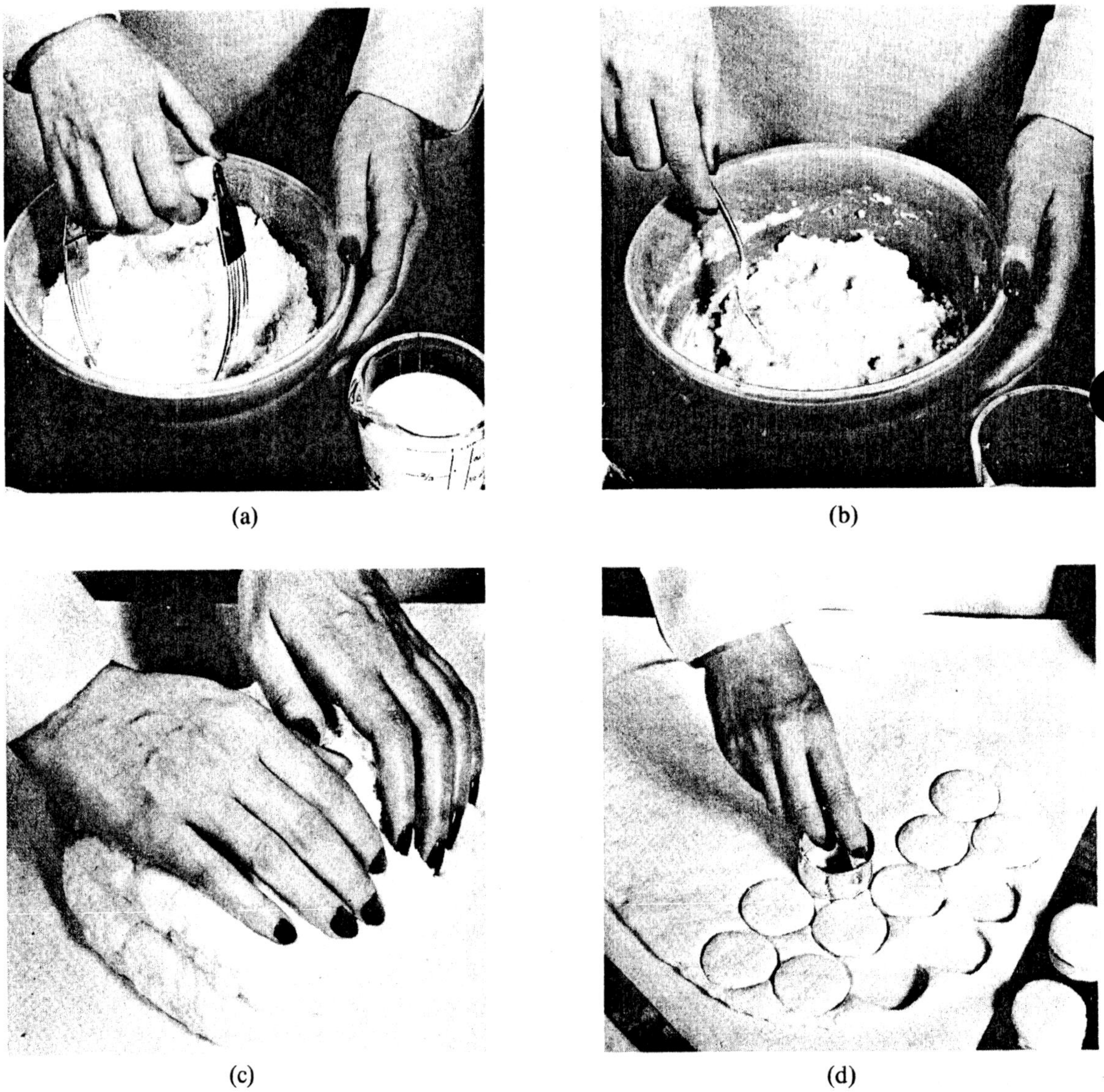

FIGURE 19-1   Preparation of biscuits. (a) Fat is cut into the flour until the mixture resembles coarse cornmeal. (b) Milk is stirred in to form a soft dough. (c) The dough is gently kneaded ten strokes. (d) Biscuits are cut from the rolled dough. (Courtesy of Wheat Flour Institute.)

Experiment V: Preparation and Comparison of Quick Breads Leavened by Steam

1. Prepare popovers according to the following recipe:

Popovers

eggs	3		instant flour	1 c	250 ml
whole milk	1 c	250 ml	salt	1/4 tsp	1 ml
margarine, melted	3 Tbsp	45 ml			

   a. Preheat oven to 450°F (230°C).
   b. Thoroughly grease 6 deep, straight-sided custard cups with hydrogenated shortening.
   c. Beat the eggs together with an electric mixer on slow speed.
   d. Add milk and the cooled, melted margarine. Beat until just blended, 20-30 seconds.
   e. Gradually beat in flour and salt for 30 seconds.
   f. Pour into heavily greased custard cups to within 1/4 in. (6 mm) of the top. Wipe off any spills with a paper towel.
   g. Set custard cups on a baking sheet. Place in oven.
   h. Bake 15 minutes at 450°F (230°C). Lower heat to 325°F (160°C) and bake an additional 30 minutes.
   i. Remove baking sheet from oven. Cut a slit in the top of each popover to allow steam to escape. Return popovers to the oven to become crisp, 5-10 minutes.

2. Prepare cream puffs according to the following recipe:

Cream Puffs

water	1 c	250 ml	flour	1 c	250 ml
margarine	1/2 c	125 ml	eggs	4	
salt	1/8 tsp	0.5 ml	vanilla pudding		

   a. Preheat oven to 450°F (230°C).
   b. Add water, margarine, and salt in a saucepan. Bring to a rolling boil.
   c. Stir in flour all at once. Combine stirring vigorously until mixture forms a ball, approximately 1 minute.
   d. Remove from heat and allow the mixture to cool slightly.
   e. Beat in the eggs, one at a time, until the mixture is smooth after each addition.
   f. Drop 1/4 c (50 ml) of the smooth batter 3 in. (7.5 cm) apart on an ungreased baking sheet.
   g. Bake 15 minutes at 450°F (230°C). Lower heat to 325°F (160°C) and bake an additional 25 minutes.
   h. Remove with spatula and cool away from a draft.
   i. Partially cut off tops. Remove loose strands of soft dough to create inner cavity.
   j. Fill with vanilla pudding or sweetened whipped cream. Replace tops.
   k. Keep refrigerated until served.

3. Observe appearance and volume. Taste for tenderness and flavor.
4. Record results in Table 19–6.

TABLE 19–6   Comparison of Quick Breads

Quick Bread	Volume	Appearance	Tenderness	Flavor
Popovers				
Cream puffs				

QUESTIONS

1. Explain why popovers and cream puffs rise without any baking soda, baking powder, or yeast.

   _____

   _____

2. What is the major difference in the ingredients between popovers and cream puffs? _____

   _____

   What effect does this have? _____

   _____

3. Why are so many eggs used in each recipe? _____

   _____

4. What is the purpose of baking at two different temperatures? _____

   _____

5. What is the approximate liquid:flour ratio of pour batters such as popovers? _____

APPLICATIONS

Banana Nut Bread

flour	1 c	250 ml	banana, mashed	1-1/2	
baking soda	1/2 tsp	2 ml	buttermilk	1-1/2 Tbsp	22 ml
salt	1/4 tsp	1 ml	egg white	1	
margarine	1/4 c	50 ml	cream of tartar	1/8 tsp	0.5 ml
sugar	1/2 c	125 ml	nuts, chopped	1/4 c	50 ml
egg yolk	1				

1. Preheat oven to 350°F (175°C).
2. Grease and flour a pup loaf pan, 5-1/2 in. × 3-1/4 in. (13.8 cm × 8 cm).
3. Sift together the flour, baking soda, and salt.
4. Cream the margarine. Gradually add sugar and cream until smooth.
5. Beat in the egg, banana, and buttermilk until smooth.
6. Whip egg white with cream of tartar with an electric mixer on medium speed until stiff peaks form.
7. Stir flour into the wet ingredients until well mixed.
8. Fold in egg white until just blended.
9. Stir in nuts.
10. Pour into loaf pan.
11. Bake 35-40 minutes or until a toothpick inserted in the center comes out clean.

Carrot Bread

oil	1/3 c	80 ml	carrots, sliced	1 c	250 ml
egg	1		whole wheat flour	1/3 c	80 ml
brown sugar	1/3 c	80 ml	all-purpose flour	1/3 c	80 ml
nutmeg	1/4 tsp	1 ml	baking soda	1/4 tsp	1 ml
cinnamon	3/4 tsp	3 ml	baking powder	3/4 tsp	3 ml
salt	3/4 tsp	3 ml			

1. Preheat oven to 375°F (190°C).
2. Grease a pup loaf pan, 5-1/2 in. × 3-1/4 in. (13.8 cm × 8 cm).
3. Place oil, egg, brown sugar, nutmeg, cinnamon, and salt in a blender.
4. Blend 5 seconds.
5. Gradually add carrots and blend just until carrots are grated.
6. Sift together the dry ingredients in a bowl.
7. Pour wet ingredients over dry ingredients and stir until blended.
8. Pour into a loaf pan.
9. Bake 40 minutes or until a toothpick inserted in the center comes out clean.
10. Remove from pan. Slice in 2 halves lengthwise so that sandwiches can be made.
11. Chill in freezer until cool. Do not let the bread form ice crystals.
12. Fill with Pecan-Cream Cheese Filling. Slice to make sandwiches.

Pecan-Cream Cheese Filling

cream cheese	3 oz	90 g	honey	1-1/2 Tbsp	22 ml
pecans, chopped	1/3 c	80 ml	lemon juice	2 tsp	10 ml

1. Soften cream cheese by creaming or soften in a microwave oven for 10 seconds.
2. Add remaining ingredients and mix well.

Coffee Cake

dark brown sugar	2-1/2 Tbsp	37 ml	margarine	1/4 c	50 ml
nuts, chopped	2-1/2 Tbsp	37 ml	sugar	1/4 c	50 ml
cinnamon	1/8 tsp	0.5 ml	egg, beaten	2 Tbsp	30 ml
flour	2/3 c	160 ml	sour cream	1/4 c	50 ml
baking powder	1/2 tsp	2 ml	vanilla	1/4 tsp	1 ml
salt	dash				

1. Preheat oven to 350°F (175°C).
2. Grease a pup loaf pan 5-1/2 in. × 3-1/4 in. (14 cm × 8 cm). Cut a piece of wax paper the size of the bottom of the pan. Place waxed paper in the pan. Grease wax paper. Sprinkle flour into pan to coat the fat; turn pan upside down and shake out excess flour. Set aside.
3. Mix together the brown sugar, nuts, and cinnamon. Set aside.
4. Sift together the flour, baking powder, and salt. Set aside.
5. Cream the margarine until soft.
6. Gradually beat in the sugar until smooth.
7. Beat in the egg, sour cream, and vanilla, blending thoroughly after each addition.
8. Mix the dry ingredients into the wet ingredients. Stir until blended.
9. Pour 1/2 of the batter into the pan. Sprinkle 1/2 of the topping over the batter.
10. Repeat step 9.
11. Bake 25-35 minutes or until a toothpick inserted in the center comes out clean.

Pancakes

egg, beaten	1/2		flour	1/2 c	125 ml
milk	1/2 c	125 ml	baking powder	1/2 tsp	2 ml
oil	1 Tbsp	15 ml	baking soda	1/4 tsp	1 ml
sugar	1-1/2 tsp	7 ml	salt	1/4 tsp	1 ml

1. Beat egg with a rotary beater.
2. Beat in milk, oil, and sugar until smooth.
3. Preheat griddle.
4. Add remaining ingredients and beat until well-blended.
5. Test the temperature of the griddle by sprinkling with a few drops of water. The drops should jump around. If the drops evaporate instantly, the griddle is too hot. If they sizzle, it is too cold.
6. Pour batter from a measuring cup onto hot griddle.
7. Turn pancakes when the pancake is set and bubbles form. Do not allow the bubbles to break.
8. Cook the other side until brown.
9. Serve with butter and pancake syrup.

Scones

flour	3/4 c	180 ml	margarine	2 Tbsp	30 ml
sugar	2 Tbsp	30 ml	raisins	2-1/2 Tbsp	37 ml
baking powder	3/4 tsp	3 ml	egg	1/2	
salt	1/8 tsp	0.5 ml	milk	1 Tbsp	15 ml

1. Preheat oven to 425°F (220°C).
2. Flour a pastry cloth and the sleeve of a rolling pin.
3. Grease a baking sheet.
4. Sift together the flour, sugar, baking powder, and salt into a bowl.
5. Cut in the margarine until the ingredients resemble coarse cornmeal.
6. Stir in raisins.
7. Beat together egg and milk. Add to flour mixture.
8. Mix gently until the mixture forms a soft dough.
9. Turn onto a floured cloth. Turn over.
10. Roll into a circle 1/2 in. (1.3 cm) thick.
11. Cut rounds with a floured biscuit cutter.
12. Place 2 in. (5 cm) apart on a baking sheet.
13. Bake 12-15 minutes until golden.
14. Cool on a wire rack 1-2 minutes before serving.
15. Serve with butter or margarine.

Pecan Waffles

flour	1 c	250 ml	milk	1/2 c	125 ml
salt	1/4 tsp	1 ml	margarine,	2 Tbsp	30 ml
baking powder	2 tsp	10 ml	melted		
egg whites	1-1/2		pecans,	1/4 c	50 ml
egg yolks	1-1/2		chopped		

1. Heat waffle iron.
2. Sift together flour, salt, and baking powder.
3. Beat egg whites with an electric beater until stiff.
4. Beat egg yolks until lemon-colored.
5. Add milk and melted margarine to egg yolks and blend.
6. Fold in egg whites and pecans.
7. Pour batter from a measuring cup into the center of a waffle iron.
8. Cook 5 minutes or until it stops steaming.
9. *Carefully* remove waffle and serve with butter and syrup.

(Courtesy of Hershey Foods Corp.)

20

Cakes and Cookies

OBJECTIVES

The student should be able to:

1. Classify the different types of cakes and cookies.
2. Compare the various methods of preparing cakes.
3. Identify factors that influence the quality of cakes.
4. Prepare and compare a variety of shortened cakes, sponge cakes, and cookies.

FOOD SCIENCE PRINCIPLES

1. Cakes are classified as *shortened* or *butter* cakes (made with fat), and *sponge* or *foam* cakes (m▊ without fat). Sponge cakes include angel food cake and yellow sponge cakes, such as jelly r▊ and lady fingers.
2. Cakes are prepared by the following methods:
   a. *Conventional mixing:* The fat is creamed until light and fluffy, the sugar is added gradually, and then eggs are creamed in. The dry ingredients are sifted together and then added in small amounts alternatively with the wet ingredients, with dry ingredients added last. If egg whites are separated from the yolks, they are beaten into a foam and folded into the batter at the end of mixing.
   b. *Conventional—meringue:* The separated egg whites are made into a meringue and folded in at the end of mixing.
   c. *Conventional—sponge:* The eggs are separated and about half the sugar is added to the egg whites. The mixture is beaten until foamy and stiff, and added to the batter at the end of mixing.
   d. *Quick mixing:* The dry ingredients are sifted together and the fat, liquid, and flavorings are added. The mixture is beaten vigorously, the eggs are added, and the mixture is beaten again.
   e. *Single-stage or dump:* All ingredients are combined together and are mixed until well-blended.
   f. *Pastry-blend:* The fat and flour are creamed together to produce a foam. A mixture of the remaining dry ingredients and one-half of the liquid is beaten in, followed by the addition of the eggs, and the remainder of the liquid.
3. Factors that affect the quality of cake include:

a. *Flour:* The best cakes are made from cake flour, a short patent, chlorinated flour. The protein content of the flour is low because cake structure is more dependent on starch gelatinization than on gluten formation. If all-purpose flour is used instead of cake flour, 2 Tbsp (30 ml) of cornstarch should be substituted for an equal quantity of all-purpose flour for each cup (250 ml) of all-purpose flour used.

b. *Liquid:* Liquid is essential to gelatinize the starch, to promote a small amount of gluten formation and to act as a solvent. Different forms of milk and acidic liquids are used as the liquid. Nonfat dry milk is often added for its enhancement of a golden crust via the Maillard browning reaction.

c. *Sugar:* Sugar tenderizes the crumb by competing with flour and delaying gelatinization of starch and formation of gluten. Powdered sugar should not be substituted for crystalline sugar because the sharp edges of sugar crystals help incorporate air during creaming. Substitution with honey produces a heavy cake with a dark crumb due to its reducing sugars.

d. *Leavening agents:* Smaller amounts of leavening agents are needed for cakes than for quick and yeast breads because the batter is weaker and less resistant to expansion. The use of a baking powder containing SAS-phosphate may result in a cake that is more alkaline and bitter than one made with baking soda and cream of tartar. However the greater loss of carbon dioxide before baking decreases the volume of the cake. The quantity of leavening agent used can be minimized by incorporating sufficient amounts of air during creaming, or by the addition of egg white foam at the end of mixing.

e. *pH:* Generally, cakes have the best flavor when the pH is slightly acidic or neutral. Too much acidity produces a tart and biting flavor, and an excessively fine, white crumb with a low volume; too much alkalinity produces a soapy and bitter flavor with a coarse and open yellow crumb. The exceptions are angel food cakes, which require an acid pH for functionality of egg-white proteins, and chocolate cakes, which require an alkaline pH for the characteristic color and flavor. A chocolate cake will have a cinnamon color at a pH of 5.5, a brown color at 7.0, and a reddish color at levels near 8. Acids in cake are donated by baking powder and foods such as sour milk, buttermilk, molasses, honey, chocolate, vinegar, lemon, and other fruits.

f. *Shortening:* The fat in a cake batter entraps air during creaming, physically interferes with the continuity of the starch and protein particles, and emulsifies liquid in the structure. Sufficient incorporation of fat produces a tender, moist cake with a good volume and long shelf-life. When chocolate is substituted for cocoa in chocolate cakes, a richer, more flavorful cake is produced because of the cocoa fat and flavors that are fat-soluble.

   Creaming is the process by which fat is mixed with a spoon to incorporate air. The ability of a fat to cream is dependent on the type of crystals that it contains. Hydrogenated fat creams well and results in a cake with a fine, even grain because of the small and numerous beta-prime crystals that it contains. Butter and margarine produce more tender cakes with a buttery flavor but they are expensive and have a lower creaming ability.

g. *Eggs:* Eggs act as an emulsifying agent, impart some leavening via incorporated air and liquid (that will turn to steam), and also contribute protein, color, and flavor.

4. Angel food cakes are basically a flour–sugar mixture that is folded into an egg-white foam. A high sugar content is necessary for tenderization because of the absence of fat. The foam must be beaten until stiff and handled carefully to prevent collapse of its fragile structure. Too little folding in creates a cake with coarse cells and uneven texture; too much creates a compact cake with a tough crumb.

   Cream of tartar is used as an acid in order to (a) whiten the batter through its effect on flavenoid pigments in egg whites and (b) improve the grain of the crumb by stabilization of proteins in the batter until it is set by heat. Too much acid produces a cake with a smooth volume and excessively moist crumb.

5. Yellow sponge cakes differ from angel food cakes in that the yolks as well as the whites are used and lemon juice is generally the acid ingredient. A high sugar content is necessary to reduce the toughening effect of the whole egg.

6. Chiffon cakes have oil as an ingredient but have several characteristics of sponge cakes. The egg whites are separated and beaten into a stiff foam. The other ingredients are combined by the muffin method and then batter is folded into the egg-white foam.

7. Cookies are similar to cake batters but have a decreased amount of liquid and an increased level of fat and egg. If the amount of liquid is too small for all the sugar to dissolve, an open texture is produced. All-purpose flour is used, rather than cake flour, because chlorination decreases the size of the cookie spread. The small quantity of leavening agents creates a crisp, compact product rather than one with soft texture and high volume.

Rerolling cookie dough develops gluten and creates a tougher product that is less crispy. Cookies can be classified as: drop, molded, rolled, refrigerator (icebox), pressed (bagged), and bar (sheet).

Experiment I: Comparison of the Method of Mixing on the Quality of Shortened Cakes

1. Prepare vanilla cake according to the recipe below using each of the following methods. Record the preparation time of each method.
2. Observe appearance of each cake. Measure height with a ruler. Cut cake in half. Observe grain. Taste and evaluate for tenderness and moisture.
3. Record results in Table 20–1.

TABLE 20–1   Effect of the Method of Mixing on the Quality of Shortened Cakes

Method of Mixing	Preparation Time (minutes)	Height (in. or cm)	Appearance	Grain	Tenderness	Moisture
Conventional						
Conventional–Meringue						
Conventional–Sponge						
Quick-Mixing						
Single-Stage						
Pastry-Blend						

Vanilla Cake

	4–5 in. (10–13 cm)*		8 in. (20 cm)	
cake flour, sifted	1/3 c	80 ml	1 c	250 ml
baking powder	1/2 tsp	2 ml	1–3/4 tsp	8 ml
salt	1/8 tsp	0.5 ml	1/2 tsp	2 ml
hydrogenated fat	1 Tbsp + 1 tsp	20 ml	1/4 c	50 ml
sugar	1/4 c	50 ml	3/4 c	180 ml
vanilla	1/8 tsp	0.5 ml	1/2 tsp	2 ml
egg, beaten	1 Tbsp	15 ml	1–1/2 Tbsp	22 ml
milk	2–1/2 Tbsp	38 ml	1/2 c	125 ml

   a. Arrange oven rack so that it is in center of oven. Preheat oven to 375°F (190°C).

   b. Cut a circle of wax paper big enough to line the bottom of the pan. Grease and flour pan. Shake out excess flour. Place wax paper in pan.

   c. Sift flour, baking powder, and salt together 2 times.

   d. Cream fat thoroughly in a small bowl.

   e. Gradually add sugar. Continue creaming until the mixture is light and fluffy and the crystals are dissolved.

   f. Cream in vanilla.

   g. Beat in egg until batter is smooth.

   h. Beat in approximately 1/3 of the flour mixture. Add approximately 1/2 of the milk. Beat until smooth.

   i. Beat in another 1/3 of the flour mixture until the batter is smooth.

   j. Add remaining milk. Beat batter until smooth.

   k. Add remaining flour mixture. Beat batter until smooth.

   l. Pour batter into pan. Use a rubber spatula to scrape all the batter out of the bowl. The pan should be no more than half full because the cake will double in volume. If there is too much batter, discard it.

   m. Place pan in the middle of the oven. If more than one cake is being baked, pans should be staggered so that air currents can flow equally around each pan.

   n. Bake 15–20 minutes for a small pan; 30–35 minutes for a large pan: or until a toothpick inserted in the center comes out clean (without batter clinging to it).

   o. Place pans on a cooling rack for 5 minutes to cool.

   p. Run edge of table knife around edge of pan. Place cooling rack on top of cake. Invert pan so that cake slips onto the rack. Gently peel off wax paper.

Conventional Mixing

   a. Follow recipe for vanilla cake.

Conventional–Meringue

   a. Separate 1 egg into the yolk and white. Discard 2/3 of the egg yolk and 2/3 of the egg white. The 1/3 egg yolk will be added in place of the 1 Tbsp (15 ml) egg in step g of the recipe for Vanilla Cake.

   b. With the remaining 1/3 of the egg white, prepare a meringue by beating the egg white with a wire whisk until soft peaks form. Add 1/2 Tbsp (8 ml) sugar and beat until peaks are stiff.

   c. Follow the recipe for Vanilla Cake. At the end of mixing (step k), fold in the meringue.

* 6-in. (15 cm) pie pan can be substituted.

Conventional–Sponge

a. Add 1/2 of the sugar (2 Tbsp or 30 ml) to 1 Tbsp (15 ml) egg. Set aside.
b. Follow steps a–f and h–k in the recipe for Vanilla Cake. In step e, only use 1/2 of the sugar (2 Tbsp or 30 ml).
c. Beat the sugar-egg mixture until it is foamy and stiff. Fold into batter. Follow remaining steps l–p.

Quick Mixing

a. Follow steps a–c in the recipe for Vanilla Cake.
b. Place the flour mixture in a small, deep bowl. Add shortening, sugar, vanilla, and milk to the dry ingredients.
c. Beat with an electric mixer for 30 seconds on low speed (25 strokes) to mix while constantly scraping the sides of the bowl with a spoon. Beat at high speed for 1-1/2 minutes (100 strokes).
d. Add eggs. Continue beating for an additional 2 minutes (150 strokes).
e. Follow steps l–p in the recipe.

Single-Stage (Dump)

a. Follow steps a and b in the recipe for Vanilla Cake.
b. Combine all ingredients in a small, deep bowl.
c. Beat at low speed for 30 seconds (25 strokes) to mix while constantly scraping the sides of the bowl with a spoon. Beat at high speed for 3 minutes (225 strokes).

Pastry Blend

a. Follow steps a and b in the recipe for Vanilla Cake.
b. Cream fat thoroughly.
c. Add flour and cream to produce a foam.
d. Beat in the remaining dry ingredients (baking powder, salt, sugar) and 1 Tbsp (15 ml) of the milk.
e. Beat in egg, vanilla, and the remaining milk (1-1/2 Tbsp or 23 ml) until batter is smooth.
f. Follow steps l–p in the recipe.

QUESTIONS

1. Which method of mixing was the fastest? _____

   What are the disadvantages of this method? _____

   _____

2. Which method of mixing produced the best volume? _____

   Appearance? _____

   Grain? _____

   Tenderness? _____

   Moisture? _____

Experiment II: Effect of Sugar on the Quality of Shortened Cakes

1. Prepare Vanilla Cake, pg. 283, using the conventional mixing method with each of the following variations:

   a. none (standard)
   b. minus sugar
   c. powdered sugar for crystalline sugar
   d. honey for crystalline sugar. Reduce milk to 1 Tbsp + 2 tsp (25 ml)

2. Observe appearance of each cake. Measure height with a ruler. Cut cake in half. Observe grain. Taste and evaluate for tenderness, moisture, and flavor.
3. Record results in Table 20–2.

QUESTIONS

1. What are the functions of sugar in shortened cakes? _____
   _____
   _____

2. Describe the effect of substituting powdered sugar for crystalline sugar. _____
   _____

   Why does this happen? _____
   _____

3. How does the substitution of honey for sugar affect the quality of a shortened cake? _____
   _____

4. Why was the amount of milk reduced when honey was used? _____
   _____

   What could be done in order to use honey as an ingredient? _____
   _____
   _____

TABLE 20–2   Effect of Sugar on the Quality of Shortened Cakes

Sugar	Height (in. or cm)	Appearance	Grain	Tenderness	Moisture	Flavor
Crystalline						
None						
Powdered						
Honey						

Experiment III: Some Ingredients Affecting the Quality of Chocolate Shortened Cakes

1. Prepare chocolate cakes according to the following recipe using the following variations:
   a. none (standard)
   b. all-purpose flour instead of cake flour
   c. 1 tsp (5 ml) baking powder for 1/4 tsp (1 ml) baking soda. Substitute regular milk for buttermilk
   d. an extra 1 tsp (5 ml) cream of tartar to the dry ingredients
   e. oil instead of hydrogenated fat
   f. minus eggs
   g. 1/4 oz (7g) chocolate instead of cocoa. Melt chocolate in microwave in bowl before use. Reduce baking soda to 1/8 tsp (0.5 ml) and add 1/16 tsp (0.25 ml) baking powder.

2. Observe appearance of each cake. Measure height with a ruler. Cut cake in half. Observe grain. Taste and evaluate for tenderness, moisture, and flavor.

3. Record results in Table 20–3.

TABLE 20–3   Effect of Some Ingredients on the Quality of Chocolate Shortened Cakes

Ingredient	Height (in. or cm)	Appearance	Grain	Tenderness	Moisture	Flavor
Standard						
All-Purpose flour						
Baking powder						
Extra acid						
Oil						
− Eggs						
Chocolate						

Chocolate Cake

	4-5 in. (10-13 cm)*		8 in. (20 cm)	
cake flour, sifted	1/4 c	60 ml	2 c	500 ml
cocoa	1 Tbsp + 1 tsp	20 ml	2/3 c	160 ml
baking soda	1/4 tsp	1 ml	1-1/2 tsp	7 ml
salt	1/8 tsp	0.5 ml	1 tsp	5 ml
shortening	1 Tbsp	15 ml	1/2 c	125 ml
sugar	3 Tbsp	45 ml	1-1/2 c	375 ml
vanilla	1/8 tsp	0.5 ml	1 tsp	5 ml
egg, beaten	1 Tbsp	15 ml	2	
buttermilk	3 Tbsp	45 ml	1-1/2 c	375 ml

a. Arrange oven rack so that it is in center of oven. Preheat oven to 375°F (190°C).
b. Cut a circle of wax paper big enough to line the bottom of the pan. Grease and flour pan. Shake out excess flour. Place wax paper in pan.
c. Combine 1/2 of the flour and the remaining ingredients in a small, deep bowl.
d. Beat at low speed for 30 seconds (25 strokes) to mix while constantly scraping the sides of the bowl with a spoon. Beat at high speed for an additional 3 minutes (225 strokes).
e. Add remaining flour. Beat batter until smooth.
f. Pour batter into pan. Use a rubber spatula to scrape all the batter out of the bowl. The pan should be no more than half full because the cake will double in volume. If there is too much batter, discard it.
g. Place pan in the middle of the oven. If more than one cake is being baked, pans should be arranged so that air currents can flow equally around each pan.
h. Bake 15–20 minutes for a small pan; 30–35 minutes for a larger pan; or until a toothpick inserted in the center comes out clean (without batter clinging to it).
i. Place pans on a cooling rack for 5 minutes to cool.
j. Run edge of table knife around edge of pan. Place cooling rack on top of cake. Invert pan so that cake slips onto the rack. Gently peel off wax paper.

QUESTIONS

1. How did the use of all-purpose flour rather than cake flour affect the quality of the cake? ____

   Account for the difference. _____

   What can be done if cake flour is not available? _____

2. What was the effect of adding baking powder rather than soda in a chocolate shortened cake?

   Of adding extra acid? _____

   Explain. _____

*A 6-in. (15 cm) pie pan can be substituted.

3. Is oil an adequate fat in shortened cakes? _____ Why or why not? _____

_____

4. What do eggs contribute to the quality of cakes? _____

_____

5. Describe how the use of chocolate rather than cocoa affects the quality of chocolate cakes.___

_____

_____

Experiment IV: Factors Affecting the Quality of Angel Food Cakes

1. Prepare angel food cake according to the following recipe with each of the following variations:
   a. none (standard)
   b. 1/2 the amount of sugar
   c. egg whites beaten only to the soft-peak, rather than to the stiff-peak, stage
   d. flour mixture is added all at one time by stirring, rather than in small amounts with folding in
   e. omit cream of tartar
   f. double amount of cream of tartar

2. Observe appearance of each cake. Measure height with a ruler. Cut cake in half. Observe grain. Taste and evaluate for tenderness, moisture, and flavor.

3. Record results in Table 20–4.

TABLE 20–4   Factors Affecting the Quality of Angel Food Cakes

Treatment	Height (in. or cm)	Appearance	Grain	Tenderness	Moisture	Flavor
Standard						
1/2 sugar						
Underbeaten egg-white foam						
Flour stirred in						
− acid						
2× acid						

Angel Food Cake

	Pup loaf pan		Standard tube pan	
cake flour, sifted	1/4 c	50 ml	1 c	250 ml
powdered sugar	1/4 c + 1 Tbsp	65 ml	1-1/2 c	375 ml
egg whites	1/4 c + 1 Tbsp	65 ml	1-1/2 c	375 ml
crystalline sugar	1/4 c	50 ml	1 c	250 ml
cream of tartar	3/8 tsp	2 ml	1-1/2 tsp	7 ml
salt	dash		1/4 tsp	1 ml
vanilla	3/8 tsp	2 ml	1-1/2 tsp	7 ml

a. Arrange oven rack so that it is at the bottom of the oven. Preheat oven to 375°F (190°C).
b. If using a pup loaf pan, place a piece of wax paper that has been cut to fit in the bottom of the pan.
c. Sift flour and powdered sugar together twice.
d. Beat egg whites until foamy with an electric beater on medium speed.
e. Add cream of tartar and salt.
f. Beat in crystalline sugar, 1 Tbsp (15 ml) at a time until egg whites are stiff and glossy but not dry. Add vanilla with the last addition of sugar.
g. Sift approximately 1/4 of the flour–sugar mixture into the stiff egg whites. Gently cut and fold mixture in with a rubber spatula until just blended. To fold, cut first through center to the bottom to the sides, then up. Rotate bowl 1/4 turn. Repeat if necessary until flour disappears into batter.
h. Repeat step g three times.
i. Pour into an ungreased pan. Cut mixture with spatula to remove large air pockets and to push batter to edge of pan.
j. Bake 20–25 minutes for pup loaf pan; 30–35 minutes for standard tube pan; or until the cracks feel dry and the cake springs back when touched.
k. Invert pan but do not remove cake.
l. Allow cake to cool to room temperature. Loosen sides by inserting the tip of a table knife or a spatula up and down the sides. Turn pan over and hit one side of pan against counter. The cake should slide out onto wax paper on a plate.

QUESTIONS

1. Why are large amounts of sugar needed in angel food cakes? _____

_____

2. Why should the egg-white foam be stiff before flour is added? _____

_____

3. What happens when flour is stirred in all at once rather than added in small amounts by folding?

_____

_____

4. What is the effect of insufficient acid? _____

_____

Too much acid? _____

_____

Explain. _____

_____

Experiment V: Preparation and Comparison of Sponge Cakes

1. Prepare and compare the following types of sponge cakes:

   a. Angel Food Cake, recipe pg. 289.
   b. Maple Nut Chiffon Cake, recipe pg. 299.
   c. Lemon Sponge Cake, recipe pg. 300.
   d. Jelly Roll, recipe pg. 301.

2. Observe appearance of each cake. Measure height with a ruler. Cut cake in half. Observe grain. Taste and evaluate for tenderness, moisture, and flavor.
3. Record results in Table 20–5.

TABLE 20–5   Factors Affecting the Quality of Sponge Cakes

Type of Cake	Height (in. or cm)	Appearance	Grain	Tenderness	Moisture	Flavor
Angel Food						
Chiffon						
Yellow Sponge						
Jelly Roll						

QUESTIONS

1. Explain the difference between an angel food cake and a yellow sponge cake. _____
   _____

2. How does a chiffon cake differ from both of the above cakes? _____
   _____

   How is it similar? _____
   _____

3. Why is fat not added to sponge cakes? _____
   _____

3. Why is lemon juice or cream of tartar added to sponge cakes? _____
   _____

Experiment VI: Preparation and Comparison of Cakes and Cookies

1. Select a variety of cakes or cookies to be prepared from the recipes found in Applications.
2. Identify the general type of baked good, and for cakes, the method of mixing.
3. Observe appearance of each baked good. Cut it in half. Observe grain. Taste and evaluate for tenderness, moisture, and flavor.
4. Record results in Table 20–6.

TABLE 20–6   Comparison of Cakes and Cookies

Type	Method of Mixing	Appearance	Grain	Tenderness	Moisture	Flavor

Experiment VII: Effect of the Type of Fat and Rerolling on the Quality of Cookies

1. Prepare vanilla cookies according to the following recipe using the following types of fat:
   a. butter
   b. margarine
   c. 50% butter; 50% margarine
   d. hydrogenated fat
   e. oil

2. Reroll the leftover dough for each variation and cut cookies of a slightly different shape so that they can be identified after baking.
3. Calculate the cost/recipe using each type of fat.
4. Compare the appearance of each type of cookie. Measure size of spread with a ruler. Taste and evaluate for crispness, flavor, and chewiness.
5. Record results in Table 20–7.

TABLE 20–7   Effect of the Type of Fat and Rerolling on the Quality of Cookies

Type of Fat	Rerolled	Cost/ Recipe ($)	Size of Spread (in. or cm)	Crispness	Flavor	Chewiness
Butter	No					
	Yes	X				
Margarine	No					
	Yes	X				
Butter and margarine	No					
	Yes	X				
Hydrogenated fat	No					
	Yes	X				
Oil	No					
	Yes	X				

Vanilla Cookies

flour	3/4 c + 2 Tbsp	210 ml	sugar	1/4 c + 2 Tbsp	90 ml
baking powder	1/4 tsp	1 ml	egg, beaten	1/4	
salt	1/8 tsp	0.5 ml	vanilla	1/4 tsp	1 ml
fat	1/4 c	60 ml			

a. Sift together the flour, baking powder, and salt.
b. Cream fat. Add sugar gradually and continue to beat until light.
c. Add eggs and blend thoroughly. Beat in vanilla.
d. Add flour mixture to wet ingredients. Mix well.
e. Chill thoroughly.
f. Preheat oven to 400°F (200°C).
g. Grease a cookie sheet.
h. Lightly flour a pastry cloth and the sleeve of a rolling pin.
i. Turn dough onto a piece of waxed paper. Pick up the wax paper and without touching the dough with the hands, gently squeeze into a ball.
j. Turn dough onto lightly floured cloth.
k. Press the ball down with the palms of the hand.
l. Quickly and lightly, use short strokes to roll dough as thin as possible.
m. Cut out cookies with a floured cookie cutter.
n. Place cookies on greased baking sheet.
o. Bake 6–10 minutes until lightly browned.

QUESTIONS

1. What effect does fat have on the quality of cookies? _____
_____

2. What fat should *not* be used in making cookies? _____
Why? _____
_____

3. Which type of fat produces the best quality cookie? _____
The most expensive? _____ . Suggest a way to reduce the cost.
_____

4. Describe the effect that rerolling the dough has on cookie quality. _____
_____
Why does this happen? _____
_____

Experiment VIII: Preparation and Comparison of Different Methods of Making Cookies

1. Prepare several of the following recipes, which illustrate the different methods of making cookies.

FIGURE 20-1   Three common types of cookies (clockwise from top): drop, refrigerator, and bar. (Courtesy of Hershey Foods Corp.)

Drop

Chocolate Chip Cookies

flour	3/4 c	180 ml	sugar	1/4 c	50 ml
baking soda	1/4 tsp	1 ml	egg	1/2	
salt	1/4 tsp	1 ml	vanilla	1/2 tsp	2 ml
margarine	1/4 c	50 ml	nuts, chopped	1/4 c	50 ml
brown sugar	1/4 c	50 ml	chocolate chips	2 oz	60 g

   a. Preheat oven to 375°F (190°C).
   b. Sift together the flour, baking soda, and salt in a bowl. Set aside.
   c. Cream the margarine.
   d. Add the sugars, egg, and vanilla, beating well after each addition.
   e. Add the flour mixture to the wet ingredients. Stir until blended.
   f. Stir in nuts and chocolate chips.
   g. Drop by rounded teaspoonfuls onto a baking sheet 2 in. (5 cm) apart.
   h. Bake 8–10 minutes.
   i. Cool for 1 minute before removing from baking sheet with a spatula.

Molded

Peanut Butter Cookies

flour	1/2 c + 2 Tbsp	155 ml	margarine	2 Tbsp + 2 tsp	40 ml
baking soda	1/4 tsp	1 ml	chunky peanut butter	1/4 c	50 ml
baking powder	1/4 tsp	1 ml	brown sugar	1/4 c	50 ml
salt	1/8 tsp	0.5 ml	sugar	1/4 c	50 ml
			egg, beaten	1/2	

a. Sift together flour, baking soda, baking powder and salt.
b. Cream margarine. Add peanut butter. Cream thoroughly.
c. Gradually cream in sugars until thoroughly mixed.
d. Beat in egg. Mix well.
e. Gradually beat in flour mixture. Blend well.
f. Cover with wax paper.
g. Chill thoroughly.
h. Preheat oven to 375°F (190°C).
i. Grease a baking sheet with margarine.
j. Shape chilled dough into 1 in. (2.5 cm) balls.
k. Place 3 in. (7.5 cm) apart on baking sheet.
l. Dip a fork in flour. Shake off excess flour. Flatten balls of dough to form a crisscross.
m. Bake 10-12 minutes.
n. Let cookies rest 1 minute on baking sheet before removing with a spatula.

Rolled

Cream Cheese Cookies

flour	1/2 c	125 ml	sugar	1 Tbsp	15 ml
baking powder	1/8 tsp	0.5 ml	nuts, chopped	1 Tbsp	15 ml
butter	1/4 c	60 ml	sugar	2 tsp	10 ml
cream cheese	2 oz	60 g	cinnamon	1/4 tsp	1 ml

a. Sift together flour and baking powder.
b. Cream butter thoroughly. Add cream cheese and cream until well blended.
c. Gradually beat in sugar until smooth.
d. Stir flour in mixture. Mix well.
e. Cover with wax paper.
f. Chill thoroughly.
g. Mix together nuts, cinnamon, and sugar.
h. Preheat oven to 375°F (190°C).
i. Lightly flour a pastry cloth and the sleeve of a rolling pin.
j. Pick up chilled dough with wax paper. Do not touch with hands. Pat gently into a ball.
k. Turn ball of dough onto floured cloth.
l. Press down with the palm of one hand to flatten dough.
m. Quickly and lightly, use short strokes to roll dough 1/8 in. (3 mm) thick.
n. Cut dough into shapes using a cookie cutter.
o. Sprinkle a little of the nut mixture on each cookie.
p. Bake 8-12 minutes until lightly browned.
q. Remove with a spatula.

Refrigerator

Cinnamon Crisps

flour	1 c + 2 Tbsp	280 ml	shortening	1/4 c	50 ml
baking soda	1/4 tsp	1 ml	sugar	1/4 c	50 ml
salt	1/4 tsp	1 ml	brown sugar	1/4 c	50 ml
cinnamon	1/2 tsp	2 ml	egg, beaten	1/2	
cloves, ground	1/4 tsp	1 ml	milk	1 Tbsp	15 ml
nutmeg	1/4 tsp	1 ml	nuts, finely	1/4 c	50 ml
butter	1/4 c	50 ml	chopped		

1. Sift together flour, baking soda, salt, cinnamon, cloves, and nutmeg. Set aside.
2. Cream butter and shortening until light and fluffy.
3. Gradually beat in sugars.
4. Beat in egg until smooth. Add milk and blend well.
5. Add dry ingredients to egg mixture. Mix until well blended.
6. Stir in nuts.
7. Place dough on a sheet of wax paper. Using the wax paper, shape into a cylinder approximately 2 in. (5 cm) in diameter. If the dough is too sticky to handle, place it in the wax paper in the freezer for 10 minutes until it becomes easy to handle.
8. Chill in freezer until cold throughout, approximately 20-25 minutes. (At home, chill in the refrigerator.)
9. Meanwhile, preheat oven to 375°F (190°C).
10. When dough is chilled, slice cylinder into 1/4-in. (0.6 cm) slices. Place on cookie sheet, approximately 1 in. (2.5 cm) apart.
11. Bake 7-8 minutes until lightly browned.
12. Wait 1 minute before removing cookies from the pan with a spatula.

Pressed

Spritz

margarine	1/4 c	60 ml	flour	1/2 c +	140 ml
sugar	2 Tbsp	30 ml		1 Tbsp	
egg yolk	1/2		salt	1/8 tsp	0.5 ml
almond extract	1/4 tsp	1 ml	candied cherries	15	

a. Preheat oven to 400°F (200°C).
b. Cream margarine.
c. Gradually add sugar. Cream thoroughly.
d. Beat in egg yolk. Add almond extract.
e. Stir in flour and salt. Mix well.
f. Place dough in cookie press.
g. Shape into cookies on baking sheet.
h. Press a candied cherry in the middle of each cookie.
i. Bake 6-8 minutes until set. Do not brown.
j. Remove with a spatula.

Bar

Brownies

flour	1/3 c	80 ml	egg, beaten	1 oz	30 g
baking powder	1/4 tsp	1 ml	sugar	1/2 c	125 ml
salt	1/8 tsp	0.5 ml	vanilla	1/2 tsp	2 ml
margarine	2 Tbsp + 2 tsp	40 ml	walnuts, chopped, coarsely	1/4 c	50 ml
unsweetened chocolate	1 oz	30 g			

  a. Preheat oven to 350°F (175°C).
  b. Grease a 6-in. (15 cm) square pan with margarine. Line bottom with waxed paper.
  c. Sift together the flour, baking powder, and salt.
  d. Melt margarine and chocolate over low heat or in a microwave oven.
  e. Add sugar to egg. Beat until smooth.
  f. Add vanilla. Beat until smooth.
  g. Add margarine and chocolate to egg mixture. Blend well.
  h. Stir in flour mixture.
  i. Mix in nuts.
  j. Spread in pan.
  k. Bake 20-25 minutes.
  l. Cool in pan. Cut into squares.

Compare the different types of cookies for size, appearance, and texture. Taste for tenderness and flavor.

Record results in Table 20–8.

TABLE 20–8 Comparison of Different Methods of Making Cookies

Method	Size	Appearance	Texture	Tenderness	Flavor
Drop					
Molded					
Rolled					
Refrigerator					
Pressed					
Bar					

QUESTIONS

1. Which of the above methods was the easiest? _____
   The most time-consuming? _____

2. Why do several of the methods require chilling before handling? _____
   _____
   _____

3. Which of the above doughs was the stiffest? _____
   Why? _____
   _____

APPLICATIONS

Maple Nut Chiffon Cake

cake flour	1/2 c + 1 Tbsp	140 ml	water	3 Tbsp	45 ml
sugar (divided)	3 Tbsp	45 ml	maple flavoring	1/2 tsp	2 ml
baking powder	3/4 tsp	3 ml	egg whites	2	
salt	1/4 tsp	1 ml	cream of tartar	1/8 tsp	0.5 ml
brown sugar	3 Tbsp	45 ml	nuts, finely	1/4 c	50 ml
oil	2 Tbsp	30 ml	chopped		
egg yolk	1				

1. Preheat oven to 350°F (175°C).
2. Sift together flour, 1 Tbsp (15 ml) sugar, baking powder, and salt twice.
3. Add brown sugar to flour mixture in a bowl. Stir until well mixed. Make a well in the center of the mixture and set aside.
4. Combine oil, egg yolk, water, and flavoring. Set aside.
5. Whip egg whites on medium speed with an electric blender in a medium deep bowl until foamy. Add cream of tartar.
6. Gradually beat in remaining 2 Tbsp (30 ml) sugar on high speed until the egg whites form stiff peaks. Set aside.
7. Add oil-egg yolk mixture into the center of the dry ingredients. Mix until batter is smooth.
8. Pour batter over egg whites. Fold in until mixture is the same color throughout.
9. Fold in nuts.
10. Pour batter into 2 ungreased pup loaf pans, 5-1/2 in. × 3-1/4 in. (13.8 cm × 8 cm). *Do not fill pans more than half-full.* Discard any excess batter.
11. Bake 25 minutes or until cakes spring back when lightly touched with a finger.
12. Remove pan from oven and invert over a cake rack. Let cool to room temperature before removing cake from pan with a spatula.

Lemon Sponge Cake

cake flour	1/3 c	80 ml	egg yolks	2		
salt	1/8 tsp	0.5 ml	lemon rind, grated	1 tsp	5 ml	
egg whites	2		lemon juice, fresh	1 tsp	5 ml	
cream of tartar	1/8 tsp	0.5 ml	(divided)	+ 4 tsp	20 ml	
sugar	1-1/2 Tbsp	22 ml	powdered sugar			
(divided)	+ 1/4 c	50 ml				
	+ 1/4 c	50 ml				

1. Preheat oven to 350°F (175°C).
2. Sift together flour and salt. Set aside.
3. Beat egg whites in a deep medium bowl with an electric mixer on medium speed until foamy. Add cream of tartar.
4. Gradually beat in 1-1/2 Tbsp (22 ml) sugar on high speed until egg whites form stiff peaks. Set aside.
5. Beat the egg yolks with an electric mixer on high speed until thick and lemon-colored, approximately 4-5 minutes. Stir in lemon rind and 1 tsp (5 ml) of the lemon juice.
6. Gradually beat in 1/4 c (50 ml) of sugar into the egg yolks. Set aside.
7. Sift 1 Tbsp (15 ml) of the flour into the egg yolks. Gently fold flour in until it is just blended.
8. Repeat step 7 until all the flour is added.
9. Pour batter over the stiff egg whites. Fold in until color is even.
10. Pour batter into 2 ungreased pup loaf pans, 5-1/2 in. × 3-1/4 in. (13.8 cm × 8 cm). *Do not fill pans more than one-half full.* Discard any excess batter.
11. Bake 25-35 minutes or until cakes spring back when lightly touched with a finger.
12. Remove pan from oven and invert over a cake rack. Let cool to room temperature before removing cake from pan with a spatula.
13. Mix 4 tsp (20 ml) lemon juice with 1/4 c (50 ml) sugar. It is not necessary for all the sugar to dissolve. Dribble mixture evenly over tops of cakes.
14. When lemon juice has soaked into the cake, sift powdered sugar over top and serve.

Jelly Roll

powdered sugar			vanilla	1 tsp	5 ml
cake flour	1 c	250 ml	water	1/4 c	50 ml
baking powder	1 tsp	5 ml	jelly or jam	3/4 c	180 ml
salt	1/4 tsp	1 ml	*or*		
eggs	3		Almond Cherry Filling		
sugar	1 c	250 ml			
(divided)					

1. Preheat oven to 375°F (190°C). Place rack 1 shelf above the center of the oven.
2. Place jelly roll pan on waxed paper. Draw a line around the base of the pan. Cut a rectangle that is the size of the bottom of the pan and place in pan.
3. Heavily grease the wax paper and the sides of the pan with shortening.
4. Spread a pastry towel on the counter. Sift powdered sugar over an area that is the size of the bottom of the pan. Gently rub it in to form a smooth surface.
5. Sift together the flour, baking powder, and salt twice. Set aside.
6. Separate eggs into whites and yolks.
7. Beat egg whites in a deep bowl with an electric mixer on high speed until foamy. Gradually beat in 1/2 c (125 ml) sugar. Beat until stiff peaks form.
8. Beat egg yolks in a deep bowl with an electric mixer on high speed until they are thick and lemon-colored. Gradually beat in 1/2 c (125 ml) sugar.
9. Add vanilla to egg yolks. Blend with mixer on slow speed.
10. Add water to egg yolks. Blend in with mixer on slow speed.
11. Gradually add flour mixture while beating with mixer on slow speed. Stop beating as soon as the batter is smooth.
12. Fold egg yolk mixture into egg whites until batter is blended.
13. Pour batter into jelly roll pan. Use a rubber spatula to spread batter evenly to the sides and corners.
14. Bake 10-12 minutes. Do not allow the cake to become too brown or hard at the edges.
15. Remove from oven and run a metal spatula along the sides of the pan.
16. Cool slightly; remove waxed paper.
17. Trim off browned edges. Do not trim the ends.
18. Pick up both edges of the towel and roll the cake up from the narrow end. Continue rolling by holding up the towel but do not crush or squeeze the cake as it is rolled. It is easier if the rolling is done quickly.
19. Keep the cake rolled in the towel on a rack until it is completely cool.
20. Unroll cake. Remove towel.
21. Spread jelly, jam, or Almond Cherry Filling (see the following recipe) on cake. If jelly is used, it should be softened before use by beating it lightly with a fork.
22. Roll up cake. Place seam side down on plate. Sprinkle with powdered sugar.

Almond Cherry Filling

almonds, slivered	1/3 c	80 ml	heavy cream	1-1/2 c	375 ml
maraschino cherries	1/3 c	80 ml	powdered sugar	3 Tbsp	45 ml

1. Preheat oven to 475°F (245°C). Chill beaters, bowl, and cream in the freezer.
2. Toast almonds in the oven in a single layer on a cookie sheet for approximately 5 minutes until they just begin to turn light brown. Watch carefully because these burn easily.
3. Immediately remove almonds from the oven and onto a plate. Cool in freezer in a single layer until room temperature.
4. Meanwhile, rinse cherries and dry thoroughly with a paper towel. Chop coarsely and set aside.
5. Whip the chilled cream in a deep bowl with an electric mixer on high speed until it has the appearance of whipped cream. Do not overbeat because only a few extra seconds can irreversibly break the emulsion and convert the cream into butter.
6. Fold in sugar, almonds, and cherries.

Sour Cream Nut Cake

brown sugar	3 Tbsp	45 ml	baking soda	1/4 tsp	1 ml
nuts, chopped	3 Tbsp	45 ml	salt	1/8 tsp	0.5 ml
cinnamon	1/8 tsp	0.5 ml	margarine	1/3 c	80 ml
flour	3/4 c + 2 Tbsp	210 ml	egg	1	
			sour cream	1/3 c	80 ml
baking powder	3/4 tsp	3 ml	vanilla	1/4 tsp	1 ml

1. Preheat oven to 350°F (175°C).
2. Grease a pup loaf pan 5-1/2 in. × 3-1/4 in. (13.8 cm × 8 cm).
3. Mix together the brown sugar, nuts, and cinnamon for a topping. Set aside.
4. Sift together the flour, baking powder, baking soda, and salt. Set aside.
5. Cream the margarine until soft.
6. Beat in the egg, sour cream, and vanilla, blending thoroughly after each addition.
7. Pour the wet ingredients into the flour mixture. Stir until blended.
8. Pour 1/2 of the batter into the pan. Sprinkle 1/2 of the topping over the batter. Repeat.
9. Bake 25-35 minutes or until a toothpick inserted in the center comes out clean.

Sour Cream Spice Cake

cake flour	2-1/4 c	560 ml	eggs	3	
cinnamon	2 tsp	10 ml	butter, melted	1 c	250 ml
nutmeg	1 tsp	5 ml	sour cream	1 c	250 ml
baking powder	1 tsp	5 ml	vanilla	1 tsp	5 ml
baking soda	3/4 tsp	3 ml	Orange Butter		
cloves, ground	1/2 tsp	2 ml	Cream Frosting		
salt	1/4 tsp	1 ml	walnuts		
sugar	1-2/3 c	410 ml			

1. Preheat oven to 350°F (175°C).
2. Grease and flour two 9-in. (22.5 cm) cake pans.
3. Sift together the flour, cinnamon, nutmeg, baking powder, baking soda, cloves, and salt.
4. Stir in sugar.
5. Beat together the eggs, butter, sour cream, and vanilla.
6. Pour into dry ingredients. Mix well.
7. Pour batter into pans.
8. Bake 25-30 minutes or until a toothpick inserted in the center comes out clean.
9. Cool.
10. Frost with Orange Butter Cream Frosting (see the following recipe).
11. Garnish with walnuts.

Orange Butter Cream Frosting

butter	3 Tbsp	45 ml	orange juice	2 Tbsp	30 ml
egg yolk	1/2		lemon juice	3/4 tsp	3 ml
confectioners' sugar	2 c	500 ml			

1. Cream butter until soft.
2. Beat in egg yolk until smooth.
3. Add sugar gradually, beating until well blended.
4. Combine juices; blend in amount necessary for a spreading consistency.

Crisp Oatmeal Cookies

oatmeal	1 c	250 ml	margarine	1/3 c	80 ml
nuts, chopped	1/3 c	80 ml	egg	1	
raisins	1/3 c	80 ml	sugar	1/3 c	80 ml
flour	1/2 c	125 ml	brown sugar	1/3 c	80 ml
salt	1/4 tsp	1 ml	cinnamon	1/4 tsp	1 ml
baking soda	1/4 tsp	1 ml	vanilla	1/2 tsp	2 ml

1. Preheat oven to 350°F (175°C). Grease 2 cookie sheets.
2. Mix oatmeal, nuts, and raisins together. Set aside.
3. Sift together flour, salt, and soda. Set aside.
4. Cream margarine. Add sugars. Beat until well blended.
5. Add egg, cinnamon, and vanilla to margarine-sugar mixture. Stir until thoroughly blended.
6. Fold flour mixture into wet ingredients.
7. Add oatmeal, nuts, and raisins, stir until mixed well.
8. Drop by rounded teaspoonfuls onto a greased baking sheet 1 in. (2.5 cm) apart.
9. Bake for 10-12 minutes.

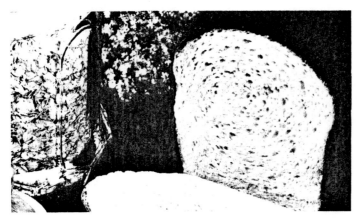

(Courtesy of Wheat Flour Institute.)

21
Yeast Breads

OBJECTIVES

The student should be able to:

1. Determine the effect of temperature and food source on the fermentation of yeast.
2. Describe factors affecting gluten and dough development.
3. Evaluate the effect of flour type on the quality of yeast breads.
4. Prepare and compare yeast breads and rolls.
5. Describe the scientific principles involved in the preparation of bread.

FOOD SCIENCE PRINCIPLES

1. In yeast breads, yeast acts as a leavening agent by producing *zymase,* an enzyme that convert glucose and fructose into carbon dioxide, alcohol, and other flavor components. The carbon dioxide serves to inflate the dough and produces a light, airy baked product. Yeast also produces a number of other chemicals that contribute to the unique flavor of the dough and brings about changes (maturing or ripening) in the structure of gluten.
2. The type of yeast used may be active-dry, instant, compressed, a sour starter, or a liquid yeast. Active-dry yeast is the most popular because of its long storage life. It should be rehydrated in warm water—110-115°F (43-46°C)—before use. Temperatures higher than 140°F (60°C) kill the yeast and those lower than 100°F (38°C) cause glutathione to be leached from the cells. Glutathione is a detrimental substance that limits gluten development by decreasing formation of disulfide bonds.

   Instant yeast is a newer, more soluble form of dry yeast that does not have to be rehydrated before use; it can be added directly to the dry ingredients. When instant yeast is added to the dry ingredients, the temperature of the liquid can be as high as 125°F (51°C) because the flour mixture quickly cools. Compressed yeast should be softened for a *short* period of time in warm water (80-85°F or 27-30°C) before combining with the dry ingredients.
3. The fermentation of yeast is dependent on the environmental temperature and the food source. Optimal temperatures for yeast growth are 86-95°F (30-35°C) but temperatures of 80-85°F (27-30°C) are more practical at home. Fermentation is slow below 75°F (24°C); above 98°F (37°C), the dough may rise before it has a chance to mellow.

   The sugars, glucose, fructose, sucrose, and maltose, are used by yeast as food. In the absence of sugar, glucose can be slowly hydrolyzed from flour by the yeast. Yeast cannot use lactose (milk sugar) as a food.

304

4. Factors affecting gluten and dough development include:

a. *Protein:*   The protein content of flour determines its water-absorption ability and its gluten-formation potential. High protein flour from wheat produces a strong, elastic gluten. Flours from soft wheat such as cake flour do not have a sufficient amount of protein to develop strong gluten and are not suitable in bread making. The protein in rye, corn, and soy flour does not produce an elastic dough that stretches with fermentation; thus wheat flour must be added to increase its volume.

b. *Liquid:*   Liquids hydrate the yeast, the proteins for gluten formation and the starch for gelatinization, as well as act as a solvent for salt and sugar. The amount used depends on the absorptive capacity of the gluten-forming proteins in the flour. Strong- or high-protein flours absorb more liquid than do soft- or low-protein flours. Too little liquid produces a stiff dough that creates a loaf with a small volume and thick cell walls. Too much liquid does not permit adequate gluten development.

Liquids used in yeast bread include water, potato water, and milk. Potato water is ideal because it contains starch that already has been gelatinized; this starch is readily degraded by amylases present in the flour. Small amounts of potato in yeast bread produce a moist crumb but large amounts interfere with gluten formation.

Milk is often added for its browning and moisture-retaining properties. It must be scalded before use in order to inactivate enzymes and to kill bacteria that interfere with regeneration of yeast. Unscalded milk produces a dough that softens during fermentation and a bread with a decreased volume, open grain, and coarse texture. Scalding is unnecessary if non-fat dry milk is used because it has already been heat-treated during processing.

c. *Sugar:*   Wheat flour naturally contains 1-2% sugars and more are produced by the amylases during fermentation. Added table sugar is not essential in bread dough but its addition initiates rapid growth of yeast. The high sugar content of sweet breads increases the time required for fermentation and proofing. Too much sugar (>10%) hinders fermentation and produces a loaf with a small volume.

Sugars that are not used by yeast for food (particularly lactose) contribute to the browning of the crust during baking. When heated, sugars react with free amino acids formed during fermentation to produce the brown color of the Maillard reaction. Sugar also acts as a solvent and competes with wheat proteins for water; it has a tenderizing effect in that it slows the development of gluten.

d. *Salt:*   Salt is added for flavor and its ability to allow proteins to stretch without breaking. Absence of salt results in a sticky dough and a bread with a coarse, crumbly texture and bland flavor. Too much salt retards fermentation of yeast.

e. *Fat:*   Fat is an optional ingredient that increases the tenderness of the bread by physically shortening gluten strands. It also aids in browning and decreases staling. The fat naturally present in flour is believed to increase the volume of bread by sealing holes in the gluten framework as it stretches around gas cells. Solid fat produces a superior bread compared to liquid oil.

f. *Egg:*   Egg is an optional ingredient that produces a rich crumb and brittle crust.

5. Bread is prepared in the following steps:

a. *Hydrating and solubilizing flour particles and yeast:*   When water is added initially, a sticky, plastic mass is formed.

b. *Manipulation via stirring, beating, or kneading:* Manipulation transforms the sticky inelastic mass into a smooth, dry, and elastic dough that is capable of retaining gas and water vapor during fermentation. A mature or ripe dough has an optimal balance of extensibility and resistance with its maximum gas retaining capability. Undermixed or overmixed doughs are either too extensible or resistant, and produce coarse, compact breads.

c. *Fermentation:* During fermentation, the yeast cells transform available sugars into carbon dioxide and alcohol. Also, amylase and protease enzymes degrade the flour, gluten becomes more elastic, the acidity increases, and volume increases. The time required for fermentation is dependent on the type of flour, room temperature, and the concentrations of yeast, sugar, and salt. High temperatures create a sticky dough that is hard to handle and facilitates growth of bacteria that produce undesirable flavors. Underfermented breads are coarse, small, and compact; overfermented breads are coarse, small, pale in color (due to depletion of sugar by yeast), and often have a sour odor (due to overproduction of lactic acid).

d. *Punching down:* Gently pushing the dough down after it has doubled in bulk during fermentation releases excess gas and deters the size of the air holes from becoming too big and the grain uneven. It also prevents the films of gluten from overstretching and redistributes the nutrients and heat.

e. *Proofing:* Proofing is the final rising after the dough has been shaped. Insufficient proofing causes the product to tear along its sides during the first few minutes of oven spring. Overproofing creates a bread with large holes and crumbly texture.

f. *Baking: Oven spring* is the considerable increase in volume that occurs during the first 10-12 minutes of baking. It is the result of the rapid expansion of gases with heating, increased fermentation of yeast, increased enzyme activity, and softening of the gluten as the temperature rises. Inadequate fermentation produces a poor oven spring and a small loaf. Too much oven spring results in a loaf with a flat top that balloons over the sides of the pan, and a crumb with a moth-eaten appearance. It may be caused by too low an oven temperature, insufficient salt, or overfermentation.

   At a temperature of 140°F (60°C), starch granules begin to gelatinize and yeast are killed. As the temperature continues to increase, enzyme activity ceases and gluten proteins coagulate. The combination of coagulated gluten and partially gelatinized starch form the semi-rigid, self-supporting structure of bread.

Experiment I: Effect of Temperature and Food on the Fermentation of Yeast

1. Label 9 custard cups 1-9.
2. Pour 1/4 c (50 ml) of the following liquids into the appropriate custard cups:

   Cup 1: ice water
       2: ice water
       3: lukewarm water
       4: lukewarm water
       5: lukewarm water
       6: lukewarm water
       7: boiling water
       8: boiling water
       9: lukewarm milk

Add the following foods to the appropriate custard cup:

Cup 1: —
    2: 1 tsp (5 ml) sugar
    3: —
    4: 1 tsp (5 ml) sugar
    5: 1 tsp (5 ml) sugar + 1/2 tsp (2 ml) salt
    6: 1 tsp (5 ml) flour
    7: —
    8: 1 tsp (5 ml) sugar
    9: —

3. Add 1/2 tsp (2 ml) dry yeast to each custard cup. Stir until completely dissolved.
4. Observe appearance at the end of 25 minutes and 50 minutes.
5. Record results in Table 21–1.

TABLE 21–1   Effect of Temperature and Food on the Fermentation of Yeast

Liquid	Temperature	Food	Appearance	
			25 min.	50 min.
	Cold	—		
	Cold	Sugar		
	Lukewarm	—		
	Lukewarm	Sugar		
Water	Lukewarm	Sugar + salt		
	Lukewarm	Flour		
	Hot	—		
	Hot	Sugar		
Milk	Lukewarm	—		

QUESTIONS

1. What is the optimal temperature to rehydrate dry yeast? _____
_____ Why? _____
_____

2. What effect did the addition of sugar to the liquid have on the fermentation of yeast?

_____

Why? _____

_____

3. What was the effect of adding salt? _____

Why? _____

_____

4. How did flour compare to sugar as a food for yeast? _____

_____

_____

What is the reason for this difference? _____

_____

_____

5. Is milk a suitable liquid for the rehydration and fermentation of yeast? _____

Why or why not? _____

_____

_____

Experiment II: Formation of Gluten Balls from Flours

1. Measure 100 g of the following flours:

   a. all-purpose
   b. bread
   c. cake
   d. rye
   e. whole-wheat

2. Add 3-4 Tbsp (45-60 ml) water to each of the flours to make a stiff dough.
3. Let the doughs rest for 5 minutes to allow the flour to hydrate.
4. Knead each dough 10 minutes until it is smooth and elastic.
5. Wrap each dough in a double-thickness piece of cheesecloth.
6. Place each dough in a bowl of cold water and let it soak 5 minutes. Wrap dough in cheesecloth.
7. Preheat oven to 450°F (230°C).
8. Place ball in palm of hand and squeeze hard to extract the starch.
9. Continue kneading under cold running water until all the starch has been extracted, approximately 10 minutes. Check to make sure all the starch has been dissolved by placing the ball in a bowl of cold water and kneading. If the water remains clear, the starch has been completely extracted.
10. Squeeze out as much water as possible. Blot on paper towels until ball is *completely dry*. Test the elasticity of the dough by *gently* pulling the strands.
11. Shape the strands into a ball and weigh. Measure height with a ruler.
12. Place each gluten ball on a greased cookie sheet far enough apart to allow room for expansion.

13. Bake 10-20 minutes at 450°F (230°C). Lower heat to 300°F (150°C).
14. Weigh baked gluten balls and measure height.
15. Observe surface appearance. Cut in half. Observe interior appearance and texture.
16. Record results in Table 21-2.

QUESTIONS

1. Which flour produced the largest gluten ball? _____

   The smallest? _____ Why? _____

   _____

   _____

2. How could the lack of gluten development be used as an advantage? _____

   _____

   _____

3. Why is it necessary for gluten strands to be elastic when baking? _____

   _____

   _____

4. Which flour had the most expansion of its gluten ball when baked? _____

   The least? _____

   Why? _____

   _____

5. Which of the flours below would be most suitable for making bread? _____

   _____

TABLE 21-2   Comparison of Gluten Balls Formed from flours

Flour	Weight (g)		Height (in. or cm)		Elasticity	Appearance		Texture
	Raw	Baked	Raw	Baked	Raw	Surface	Interior	
All-purpose								
Bread								
Cake								
Rye								
Whole-wheat								

Experiment III: Factors Affecting Gluten Development

1. Prepare 6 baked gluten balls using 100 g all purpose flour according to steps 2-15 in Experiment II. Prepare a standard gluten ball* and add the following variations at the beginning of the recipe:

   a. + 1/4 tsp (1 ml) salt
   b. + 1/2 tsp (2 ml) sugar
   c. + 1 tsp (5 ml) fat
   d. + 1 tsp (5 ml) egg
   e. substitute 2 Tbsp (30 ml) milk for 2 Tbsp (30 ml) of the water

2. Record results in Table 21-3.

QUESTIONS

1. How does salt affect gluten development? _____

   _____

2. Why are sugar and fat added to bread? _____

   _____

3. What would be the effect of adding milk to a bread dough? _____

   _____

4. Explain the effect of eggs on gluten development. _____

   _____

TABLE 21-3   Factors Affecting Gluten Development

Variation	Weight (g)		Height (in. or cm)		Elasticity	Appearance		Texture
	Raw	Baked	Raw	Baked	Raw	Surface	Interior	
Standard								
+ salt								
+ sugar								
+ fat								
+ egg								
+ milk								

* If a gluten ball from all-purpose flour is prepared in Experiment II, use it as the standard rather than making a duplicate.

Experiment IV: Comparison of Flours in Making Bread *

1. Grease 6 pup loaf pans, 5-1/2 in. × 3-1/4 in. (13.8 cm × 8 cm) and 6 bowls.

   Note: Regular sized loaf pans can be used if the recipe is tripled. However this will produce a large quantity of bread.

2. Use the Straight Dough Method to prepare breads from the following flours:

   a. all-purpose
   b. bread
   c. cake

3. Use the Sponge Method to prepare breads from the following flours:

   a. whole-wheat
   b. 40% whole-wheat; 60% all-purpose
   c. rye

4. Measure height of baked breads. Observe appearance.
5. When the bread has cooled, cut a slice. Note the texture. Taste for lightness and flavor.
6. Record results in Table 21-4.

*Laboratory** Bread, Straight Dough Method*

yeast	1 tsp	5 ml	sugar	1 Tbsp	15 ml
water	1/4 c	60 ml	flour	1 c	250 ml
shortening	1 Tbsp	15 ml	flour, all-purpose	2 Tbsp	30 ml
NFDM, reconstituted	3 Tbsp	45 ml	margarine, melted	—	—
salt	1/4 tsp	1 ml			

1. Dissolve yeast in warm water, 105-115°F (40-46°C).
2. Add shortening, lukewarm NFDM, salt, sugar, and 1/3 of the flour. Beat until smooth by hand or 2 minutes with an electric dough hook.
3. Add enough of the remaining flour to form a dough that can be handled. Let the dough rest 5 minutes.
4. Sprinkle 1 Tbsp (15 ml) all-purpose flour on a pastry cloth or a clean counter.
5. Turn dough onto lightly floured counter. Knead 6-8 minutes by hand until dough is smooth and elastic. Knead by flattening dough, pushing with palms of hands, folding over, and rotating. Avoid adding more flour unless dough is too sticky to handle. Alternatively, the dough may be kneaded by an electric dough hook for 5 minutes. Finish kneading with a few strokes by hand.
6. Place dough in a greased bowl and turn over by sliding to expose the greased side.
7. Place bowl of dough in warm water, 90-110°F (31-43°C).
8. Cover dough with a towel that has been dipped in warm water and squeezed until damp.
9. Let dough ferment 30 minutes.
10. Remove dough from bowl and "punch down" by kneading 5 strokes.
11. Return to bowl in warm water, cover, and ferment another 30 minutes.
12. Place dough on lightly floured counter. Roll into a rectangle as wide as the pan is long and 2 times as long as the length of the pan. Roll the dough from the short side into a loaf. Press each end to seal and fold under the loaf.

---

*The time expenditure in this experiment makes it practical *only* in 3-hour labs.
**Under nonlaboratory conditions, the first fermentation time is 1-1/2 hours and the bowl of dough is placed in a warm room rather than in warm water.

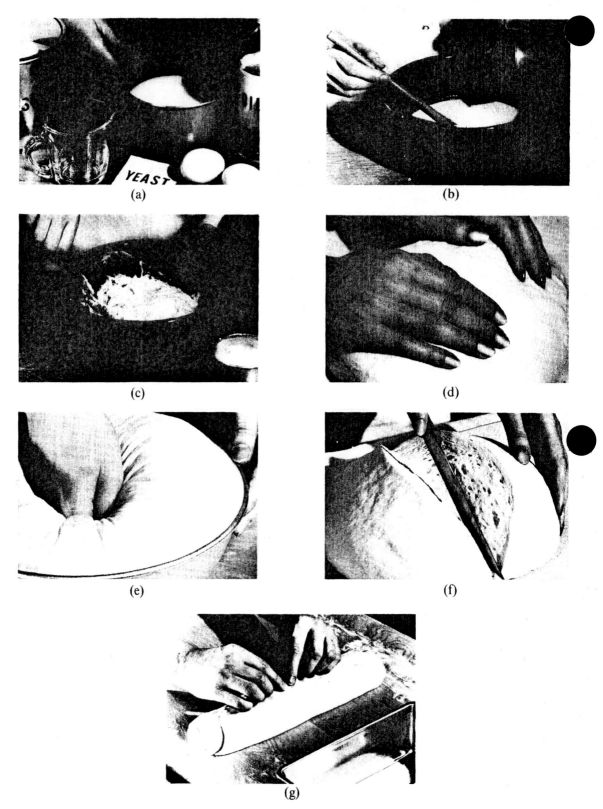

FIGURE 21-1   Preparation of bread by the straight dough method. (a) The ingredients are assembled. (b) and (c)
Enough flour is added to form a dough that leaves the side of the bowl. (d) The dough is kneaded until smooth and
elastic. (e) After the dough doubles its volume from rising, it is punched down to redistribute nutrients and heat.
Notice the bubbles of gas caused by the fermentation of yeast as the dough is cut. (g) The dough is rolled and shaped
into a loaf before it is placed in the pan for proofing. (Courtesy of Wheat Flour Institute.)

13. Place loaf, seam side down, into a greased pan.
14. Brush with melted margarine.
15. Let loaf rise until doubled, approximately 40 minutes.
16. Preheat oven to 425°F (220°C).
17. Place pan in center of the oven. If baking more than 1 loaf, evenly distribute pans. Do not allow the pans to touch each other or the sides of the oven.
18. Bake until a deep, golden brown, 20-30 minutes. Check for doneness by tapping top crust with knuckle. A hollow sound indicates that the loaf is done.
19. Remove loaf from pan. Brush with melted margarine.

Laboratory Bread, Sponge Method

a. Follow steps 1 and 2 for the straight dough method except add the NFDM later in step 3.
b. Follow Steps 7 and 9.
c. Follow steps 3-9 and 12-19. Be sure to add the NFDM at the beginning of step 3.

TABLE 21–4   Comparison of Flours in Making Bread

Flour	Height (in. or cm)	Appearance	Texture	Lightness	Flavor
All-purpose					
Bread					
Cake					
Whole-wheat					
Whole-wheat + all-purpose					
Rye					

QUESTIONS

1. Which flour produced the best quality loaf of bread? _____
   The poorest quality? _____ Why? _____
   _____
   _____

2. Which flour could best substitute if bread flour were not available? _____
   _____

3. How did the addition of all-purpose flour to whole-wheat flour affect the quality of the bread?
   Why? _____
   _____

4. How could the rye bread be made into a lighter product? _____
   _____

5. Explain the difference in nutritive value between whole-wheat bread and white bread. _____
   _____
   _____
   _____

6. Define oven spring. _____
   _____
   Describe the factors that influence it. _____
   _____
   _____

7. Explain scientifically what happens in the basic steps of preparing yeast breads: _____
   _____
   Hydration: _____
   _____
   Manipulation: _____
   _____
   Fermentation: _____
   _____
   Proofing: _____
   _____
   Baking: _____
   _____

Experiment V: Preparation of Refrigerator Rolls

The potato dough in this experiment may be prepared up to 5 days in advance by a laboratory aide for the first laboratory of the week. The quantity to prepare will be determined by the number of roll variations desired in step 3. Each student should then prepare more dough to be used by the next laboratory.

1. Each unit performing this experiment should prepare the recipe for refrigerator dough below.

Refrigerator Dough

yeast, dry	3/4 tsp	3 ml	oil	2 Tbsp	30 ml
water	1/3 c	80 ml	egg, beaten	1/2	
sugar	2 Tbsp	30 ml	potatoes, mashed	1/4 c	60 ml
salt	1/4 tsp	1 ml	flour	1-1/2–1-3/4 c	375-430 ml

   a. Dissolve yeast in warm water, 105-115°F (40-46°C).
   b. Add sugar, salt, oil, egg, potatoes, and 1/3 of the flour to the yeast. Beat until smooth.
   c. Add enough of the remaining flour to form a dough that can be handled.
   d. Sprinkle flour onto a pastry cloth or a clean counter.
   e. Turn dough onto counter and knead 5-6 minutes or until smooth and elastic. Knead by flattening dough, pushing with palms of hands, folding over, and rotating. Avoid adding more flour unless dough is too sticky to handle.
   f. Place dough in a greased bowl and turn over by sliding to expose the greased side.
   g. Cover with a damp towel.

2. Place the freshly prepared dough in the refrigerator for the next day's laboratory. Cover all doughs with a dampened cloth. If the next laboratory is on the same day, leave the dough at room temperature. Obtain previously prepared dough from the instructor.
3. Prepare rolls using one of the following variations:

   a. Bowknots
   b. Butterscotch Pecan Rolls
   c. Crescents
   d. Cloverleaf
   e. Fan Tans

4. Place small rolls 1 in. (2.5 cm) apart and large rolls 2 in. (5 cm) apart on greased baking sheets.

Bowknots

   a. Divide dough into pieces the size of walnuts.
   b. Roll the piece of dough between the palms of the hands to form a 4-5 in. (10-12.5 cm) cylinder.
   c. Loosely tie the dough cylinder into a knot.

Butterscotch Pecan Rolls

brown sugar	1/4 c	50 ml	margarine, melted	2 Tbsp	30 ml
margarine, melted	2 Tbsp	30 ml	sugar	1/4 c	50 ml
corn syrup	1 Tbsp	15 ml	cinnamon	1/2 tsp	2 ml
pecan halves	1/4 c	50 ml			

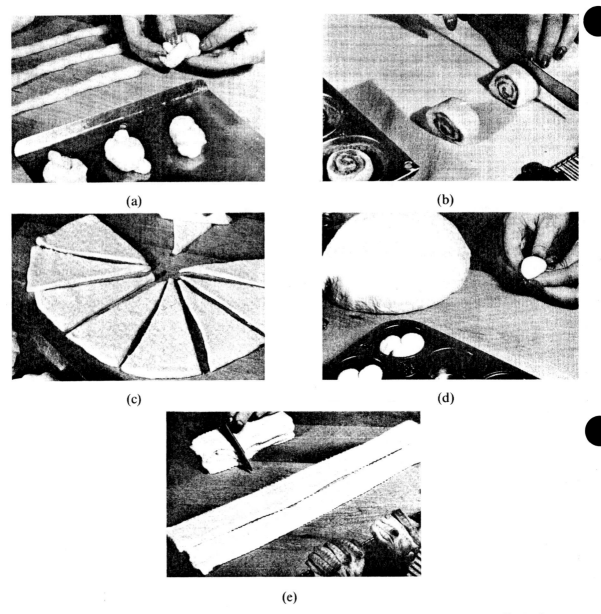

(a)

(b)

(c)

(d)

(e)

FIGURE 21-2   Shaping the dough into refrigerator rolls. (a) Bow knots. (b) Butterscotch pecan rolls. (c) Crescents. (d) Cloverleaf rolls. (e) Fan tans. (Courtesy of Wheat Flour Institute.)

a. Sprinkle brown sugar into 6 muffin cups. Drizzle corn syrup mixed with melted margarine over brown sugar. Sprinkle with pecan halves.
b. Roll dough into a rectangle, 1/4 in. × 8 in. × 8 in. (0.6 cm × 20 cm × 20 cm).
c. Brush dough with melted margarine.
d. Mix sugar and cinnamon together. Sprinkle over margarine on dough.
e. Roll up into a jelly roll, sealing the edge.
f. Cut into slices, 1-1/2 in. (3.8 cm) thick.
g. Place the slice, cut side down, into muffin cup.

Crescent Rolls

    a. Roll dough into a circle 1/4 in. (6 mm) thick.
    b. Brush with melted margarine.
    c. Cut into pie-shaped pieces.
    d. Roll up dough, beginning at the wide end.
    e. Place rolls with points underneath on greased baking sheet. Curve slightly.

Cloverleaf Rolls

    a. Divide dough into 1-in. (2.5 cm) smooth balls.
    b. Place 3 balls in a greased 2-in. (5 cm) muffin cup.
    c. Brush with melted margarine.

Fan Tans

    a. Roll dough into a rectangle, 6 in. $\times$ 4 in. (15 cm $\times$ 10 cm).
    b. Brush with melted margarine.
    c. Cut into 4 strips crosswise, 1-1/2 in. (3.8 cm) wide.
    d. Stack strips of dough on top of each other.
    e. Cut into 6 pieces, 1 in. (2.5 cm) wide.
    f. Place the piece, cut side down, into greased muffin cups.
    g. Brush with melted margarine.

5. Let all rolls rise until doubled, approximately 45 minutes.
6. Bake the rolls in a preheated oven at a temperature of 350°F (175°C) for 15-20 minutes until they are golden brown. Do not bake until they harden.
7. Observe appearance. Taste for lightness and flavor.
8. Record results in Table 21–5.

TABLE 21–5   Preparation and Comparison of Refrigerator Rolls

Roll Variation	*Appearance*	*Lightness*	*Flavor*
Bowknots			
Butterscotch Pecan Rolls			
Crescents			
Cloverleaf			
Fan Tans			

QUESTIONS

1. Why were potatoes added to the dough? _____
_____

2. Which of the above rolls would be ideally suited for a continental breakfast?
_____ Why? _____
_____

APPLICATIONS

Cheese Bread

milk	2 Tbsp +	40 ml	water	1/4 c	60 ml
	2 tsp		flour	1 c	250 ml
sugar	1 tsp	5 ml	cheddar cheese,	1/2 c	125 ml
salt	1/4 tsp	1 ml	grated		
dry yeast	1 tsp	5 ml			

1. Scald milk in a saucepan. Remove from heat. Stir in sugar and salt until dissolved. Cool to 115°F (46°C).
2. Dissolve yeast in warm water, 105-115°F (40-46°C).
3. Pour in milk-sugar mixture and blend.
4. Stir in 2/3 of the flour. Mix well.
5. Add remaining flour and cheese. Mix until well blended.
6. Follow steps 4-15 for the Straight Dough Method of Laboratory Bread, pg. 311.
7. Bake 30-40 minutes at 375°F (170°C).
8. Remove loaf from pan. Brush with melted margarine.

French Bread*

flour	1-3/4 c–	430-460 ml	sugar	3/4 tsp	3 ml
	1-7/8 c		salt	3/4 tsp	3 ml
yeast	1-1/4 tsp	7 ml	cornmeal		
water	1/2 c +	155 ml	egg white	1/2	
	2 Tbsp		water	1 tsp	5 ml
shortening	3/4 tsp	3 ml			

1. Combine 3/4 c (180 ml) of the flour and the yeast in a large bowl.
2. Heat water, shortening, sugar, and salt in a saucepan until lukewarm 115-120°F (46-49°C), stirring constantly.
3. Pour over dry mixture. Blend with an electric mixer on low speed for 30 seconds. Scrape bowl as needed.
4. Turn mixer to high speed, beat 3 minutes.
5. Follow steps 3-10 for the Straight Dough Method of Laboratory Bread, pg. 311.
6. Roll into a rectangle, 6 in. × 9 in. (15 × 22.5 cm). Roll up tightly from the long side. Seal at the seam. Taper the ends and seal.
7. Grease a baking sheet. Sprinkle with cornmeal.
8. Place loaf, seam side down, on cornmeal.
9. Slash tip diagonally, 1/8-1/4 in. (3-6 mm) deep every 2 in. (5 cm).
10. Beat egg white until foamy. Stir in water.
11. Brush egg white on top and sides of loaf.
12. Cover. Let rise until double, 50 minutes.
13. Preheat oven to 375°F (190°C).
14. Bake 20 minutes until light brown. Brush with egg white.
15. Bake 20 minutes longer.
16. Remove from baking sheet and cool.

*Recommended *only* for 3-hour laboratories.

Onion-Caraway Bread

yeast	1-3/4 tsp	8 ml	cottage cheese	1 c		250 ml
water	1/4 c	50 ml	caraway seed	1 tsp		5 ml
sugar	1 Tbsp	15 ml	salt	1/4 tsp		1 ml
oil	1 Tbsp +	25 ml	baking soda	1/4 tsp		1 ml
	2 tsp		beef bouillon	1/2 tsp		2 ml
onion, minced	2/3 c	160 ml	flour	1-1/2–2 c		375-500 ml

1. Follow step 1 for the Straight Dough Method of Laboratory Bread, pg. 311.
2. Add sugar to yeast.
3. Heat oil in a small skillet over medium-high heat. Add onion and sauté until soft. Cool slightly.
4. Beat together the onions and oil, cottage cheese, caraway seed, salt, baking soda and beef bouillon.
5. Follow steps 3-19 of the Straight Dough Method. Divide dough in half in step 12 to make 2 loaves of bread rather than 1.

Pumpernickel Bread

yeast	2-1/2 tsp	12 ml	salt	dash	
water	1/2 c	125 ml	rye flour	1 c	250 ml
molasses	1-1/2 Tbsp	37 ml	all-purpose flour	3/4-1 c	180-250 ml
shortening	2 tsp	10 ml	corn meal		
caraway seeds	1 tsp	5 ml			

1. Follow step 1 for the Straight Dough Method of Laboratory Bread, pg. 311.
2. Add molasses, shortening, caraway seed, salt, rye flour, and 1/4 of the all-purpose flour. Beat until smooth by hand or 2 minutes with an electric dough hook.
3. Follow steps 3-11 of Straight Dough Method.
4. Shape into a ball.
5. Grease a baking sheet. Sprinkle with cornmeal.
6. Place the ball of dough on the cornmeal.
7. Cover. Let rise until double, 30 minutes.
8. Preheat oven to 375°F (190°C).
9. Bake 30-35 minutes until well browned. A chewy crust can be obtained by brushing with warm water several times during the last 10-15 minutes of the baking period.
10. Remove from baking sheet and cool.

Wheat Germ Bread

yeast	1-1/4 tsp	6 ml	molasses	2 Tbsp	30 ml
water	2 Tbsp	30 ml	wheat germ	1/4 c	50 ml
sugar	1-1/2 tsp	7 ml	whole wheat flour	1/2 c	125 ml
salt	3/4 tsp	3 ml	white flour,	3/4 c	180 ml
oil	1 Tbsp + 1 tsp	20 ml	unsifted		

1. Follow step 1 for the Straight Dough Method of Laboratory Bread, pg. 311.
2. Add sugar, salt, oil, molasses, wheat germ, and whole wheat flour. Beat until smooth by hand or 2 minutes with an electric dough hook.
3. Follow steps 3-19 of the Straight Dough Method.

Garlic Bread

French or Italian bread, loaf	1/2	200-250 g
butter	1/4 c	60 ml
garlic cloves, minced	2	
salt	1/4 tsp	1 ml

1. Preheat oven to 425°F (220°C).
2. Slice bread into pieces 1 in. (2.5 cm) thick.
3. Melt 2 Tbsp (30 ml) of the butter in a heavy skillet over medium-low heat.
4. When the butter sizzles, add the minced garlic.
5. Sauté until golden brown. Stir occasionally. Do not allow the butter to *brown* or smoke. If the butter becomes too hot, lift the pan off the burner for a few seconds and swirl.
6. Add remaining 2 Tbsp (30 ml) butter and melt.
7. Add salt and mix.
8. Dip both sides of bread into the garlic butter.
9. Place coated bread on a cookie sheet.
10. Set pan in hot oven for 4 minutes for soft bread, 6 minutes for hardened bread.
11. Serve while hot.

Herb Crisps

white bread, slices	3		tarragon	1/4 tsp	1 ml
			chervil	1/4 tsp	1 ml
butter or margarine	1/4 c	50 ml	parsley	1/8 tsp	0.5 ml
			thyme	1/8 tsp	0.5 ml
lemon juice	1/2 tsp	2 ml	salt	dash	
chives or green onions, minced	1/4 tsp	1 ml	garlic clove, crushed	1/2	

1. Preheat oven to 350°F (175°C).
2. Cut bread diagonally into 4 pieces.
3. Cream butter until soft. Cream in lemon juice until well mixed.
4. Cream in remaining ingredients.
5. Spread herb butter on both sides of the bread slices.
6. Place on baking sheet.
7. Bake 15-20 minutes until lightly browned and crisp.

Raised Doughnuts

milk	1/4 c + 2 Tbsp	90 ml	sugar	2 Tbsp	30 ml
			salt	1/2 tsp	2 ml
yeast	1-1/2 tsp	7 ml	shortening	2 Tbsp	30 ml
water	1/4 c	60 ml	egg, beaten	1/2	
flour	1-1/2 c	375 ml			

1. Scald milk and let cool to lukewarm.
2. Dissolve yeast in warm water, 105-115°F (40-46°C).
3. Stir in 1/2 of the flour, sugar, salt, shortening, and egg. Beat until mixture is smooth.
4. Follow steps 3-12 for the Straight Dough Method of Laboratory Bread, pg. 311.
5. Turn dough onto floured cloth.
6. Quickly and lightly, use short strokes to roll dough 3/8 in. (9 mm) thick.
7. Cut doughnuts with a floured doughnut cutter.
8. Let rise on counter, uncovered, for 30 minutes.
9. Pour oil or hydrogenated fat to a depth of 3 in. (7.5 cm) in a deep-fat fryer or a deep saucepan. The pan should not be filled more than 1/3 full. Clamp a deep-fat thermometer to the pan so that the bulb is immersed in the fat.
10. Preheat fat to 375°F (190°C).
11. Remove doughnuts with a spatula and slide into hot fat.
12. Turn doughnuts over as they rise to the surface. Fry 2-3 minutes.
13. Remove from fat by a fork slipped through the hole. Do not pierce doughnut.
14. Drain on paper towels.
15. Roll doughnuts in sugar.

Pretzels

yeast	1-1/2 tsp	7 ml	salt	1/4 tsp	1 ml
milk	1/2 c	125 ml	caraway seed	1-1/2 tsp	7 ml
sugar	1/8 tsp	0.5 ml	egg, beaten	1/2	
margarine	1 Tbsp	15 ml	coarse salt	1 tsp	5 ml
flour	1-1/2 c	375 ml			

1. Heat milk to lukewarm, 105-115°F (40-46°C) in a small saucepan.
2. Dissolve yeast and 1 Tbsp (15 ml) sugar in the milk in a bowl.
3. Cover and set the bowl in warm water 90-110°F (31-43°C) for 15 minutes.
4. Add margarine to the warm milk. Stir until heated. It may be necessary to return the milk to the heat to keep it lukewarm but do not heat the milk too much.
5. Warm a mixing bowl by running hot water over it. Dry thoroughly.
6. Sift the flour and salt into the warmed bowl. Stir in 1 tsp (5 ml) of the caraway seed.
7. Make a well in the center of the flour. Pour in yeast and margarine with the milk.
8. Mix the dough until the flour comes away from the sides of the bowl.
9. Follow steps 3-9 for the Straight Dough Method of Laboratory Bread, pg. 311.
10. Turn dough onto floured cloth. Knead 4 minutes.
11. Form the dough into a cylinder 6 in. (15 cm) long. Cut into 24 equal pieces with a knife.
12. Roll each piece between the palms of the hands to form a cylinder approximately 6 in. (15 cm) long.
13. Preheat oven to 375°F (190°C).
14. Grease a baking sheet.
15. Place each piece on a counter. Curve the ends towards yourself.
16. Form a pretzel shape by curving the ends back towards, then past, the center of the roll and crossing halfway in between and twisting. Bend ends back towards center and seal to curve of loop
17. Bring 1 qt (1 l) of water to boil over high heat.
18. Carefully drop dough into boiling water, a few pieces at a time. Boil 1 minute or until they rise to the surface.
19. Remove pretzels with a slotted spoon. Drain in a colander.
20. Place on baking sheet.
21. Brush with beaten egg. Sprinkle with the coarse salt and remaining caraway seeds.
22. Bake 15 minutes until golden brown.
23. Remove pretzels with a spatula and place on a rack to cool.

(Courtesy of American Dairy Association.)

22

Sugars and Frozen Desserts

OBJECTIVES

The student should be able to:

1. Discuss the similarities between candies and frozen desserts.
2. Measure the relationship between boiling point and sugar concentration of a sugar syrup.
3. Describe the factors that influence the rate or size of crystal growth.
4. Explain the formation and function of invert sugar.
5. Demonstrate and explain caramelization.
6. Describe the factors that affect the quality of frozen desserts.
7. Classify, prepare, and compare candies and frozen desserts.

FOOD SCIENCE PRINCIPLES

1. Candy is a network of sugar crystals suspended in a supersaturated solution. Frozen desserts consist of ice crystals surrounded by a sugar syrup. The size of crystal growth in both is limited by the presence of interfering agents and agitation. Texture is dependent on the size, shape, and arrangement of the crystals.
2. The concentration of sugar in a sugar syrup can be determined by measuring its boiling point because the boiling point is raised 0.94°F (0.52°C) for every mole of sugar (342 g for sucrose) dissolved in 1 liter of water. However, interfering agents, barometric pressure, and altitude can also alter the boiling point.
3. The doneness of candy can be measured by (a) the temperature of the syrup via a thermometer or (b) the cold water test, which measures the consistency of the syrup when dropped in cold water.
4. Factors affecting the size or rate of crystal growth include:

   a. *Interfering agents:* Interfering agents are impurities in a sugar syrup that physically interfere with the size or rate of crystal growth. These are deliberately added to produce a smooth texture. Examples are cream, milk solids, egg white, gelatin, chocolate, cocoa, invert sugar, sucrose, and glucose. These ingredients provide fat, protein, air, dextrins, and simple sugars that surround or coat the crystals and impede further growth.

b. *Concentration of the sugar solution:* Crystallization only occurs if a sugar solution is supersaturated. A *supersaturated* solution is one in which the concentration of sugar dissolved is greater than it normally would be at a certain temperature. It can be accomplished by heating a sugar syrup to a high temperature so that large amounts of sugar will dissolve, then slowly letting it cool without agitation. Any agitation, contact with rough surfaces, or seeding from dust or extra sugar crystals can initiate crystallization.

Candies are cooked in order to boil away the water so that a supersaturated solution is formed. The concentration of the solution is a major factor influencing the characteristics of candy. Once the correct concentration has been reached, the candy syrup must immediately be removed from heat to prevent further water loss.

c. *Temperature:* Heating a sugar solution to the proper temperature is critical because the temperature of a sugar syrup is an index of its concentration. The correct concentration of supersaturation ensures that crystallization will be rapid and small crystals will form. Small crystals are desirable because they contribute to a smooth texture.

It is also critical to cool the syrup to the proper temperature before agitation begins. If the syrup is beaten while still hot, large crystals form because of the rapid movement of molecules. If the solution is cooled properly before agitation, tiny crystals form all at once, and a creamy texture is created.

d. *Agitation:* Agitation incorporates air, promotes the formation of many crystal nuclei by redistributing impurities, and breaks up large crystals. Agitation should begin only after candies have cooled to a certain temperature and must continue until crystallization is complete. Otherwise, already formed crystals will continue to grow and create a grainy product.

5. Invert sugar is an equimolar mixture of glucose and fructose that is formed when sucrose (table sugar) is heated in the presence of an acid or the enzyme invertase. Some acids used in candies to produce invert sugar are cream of tartar, vinegar, and molasses (in brown sugar). Because the formation of invert sugar is dependent on cooking time, too long a cooking time produces too soft a candy and too little creates a coarse and grainy product.

6. Caramelization is a nonenzymatic browning that occurs when sugar is decomposed by heating to 338°F (170°C). Organic acids are formed as the sugar decomposes. In the preparation of peanut brittle, baking soda is added to caramelized sugar to react with the organic acids. The reaction of the soda and acids produces bubbles of carbon dioxide that form the characteristic holes of the brittle.

7. Candies can be classified as crystalline (fondant, fudge, panocha, divinity), noncrystalline, or other (nougat, taffy). Noncrystalline candies can be chewy (caramels), hard (brittles), or aerated (marshmallow, gum drops).

8. Frozen desserts can be classified as ice cream (French, American or plain, Philadelphia), ice milk, imitation (mellorine, frozen tofu), water ices, sherbets, and stiff-frozen (mousses, parfait). French ice cream has eggs added for thickening and Philadelphia ice cream is uncooked. Ice milk contains milk instead of cream. Mellorine has vegetable fat substituted for milk fat. Frozen tofu contains tofu or soy bean protein, high-fructose corn sweetener, and corn oil. Sherbets have milk, cream, or egg whites. Still-frozen desserts have large amounts of whipped cream, gelatin, or egg whites.

9. Factors affecting the quality of frozen desserts include:

a. *Sugar:* High concentrations of sugar are used because the flavor of a frozen dessert is not as pronounced as that at room temperature. Also, sugar lowers the freezing point of water; one mole of sucrose decreases it 3.35°F (1.86°C). Too much sugar lowers the freezing point too much and decreases overrun.

b. *Milk solids:* Nonfat milk solids are added to ice cream to give it more body and to promote a smooth texture. Too many nonfat milk solids create a sandy texture because lactose is relatively insoluble and easily precipitates into large crystals that can be felt by the tongue. Milk solids can also be added through use of evaporated milk.

c. *Fat:* Fat creates a rich body and a smooth texture in a frozen dessert. The amount of fat is limited because too much creates too hard a product.

d. *Emulsifiers and stabilizers:* These compounds promote a smooth texture by incorporation of air, restrict crystal growth, and stabilize foam structure during storage. Gelatin and egg yolk are used in home cookery.

Note: The temperatures reached in sugar cookery are much higher than that of boiling water and can cause severe burns. Please be careful.

Experiment I: Calibration of a Candy Thermometer.

1. Fill a small saucepan 1/2 full with hot water. Place over high heat.
2. Clamp a candy thermometer to the saucepan so that the bulb is immersed in the water. Do not allow the bulb to touch the sides or bottom of the pan.
3. Bring the water to a boil.
4. Record the temperature at which the water boils.
5. If the recorded temperature is below 212°F (100°C), subtract it from 212°F (100°C). Record the number of degrees. Add this number to all future temperatures.
6. If the recorded temperature is above 212°F (100°C), subtract 212°F (100°C) from the number. Record the number of degrees. Subtract this number from all future temperatures.

No. of degrees to add: _____   ~~5°~~   207°

to subtract: _____

Experiment II: Determination of the Stages of Sugar Cookery

1. Calibrate a candy thermometer.
2. Dissolve 1 c (250 ml) sugar and 1/2 c (125 ml) hot water in a deep saucepan. Add 1 drop of red food coloring.
3. Clamp a candy thermometer to the saucepan so that the bulb is immersed in the syrup. Do not allow the bulb to touch the sides or bottom of the pan.
4. Bring the mixture to a boil over high heat.
5. Spread a lightly greased sheet of aluminum foil on a cookie sheet.
6. Arrange 7 custard cups filled with cold water in a line along the foil. An ice cube may be added to each cup to keep the water cold.
7. Perform the following procedures when the thermometer reaches the temperatures listed in Table 22–1.

a. Remove 1/4 tsp (1 ml) of the liquid and drop it into cold water.
b. Remove 1/4 tsp (1 ml) of the liquid and drop it on the aluminum foil on a cookie sheet.

8. Observe appearance and feel texture.
9. Determine the name of the test for each stage of sugar cookery from your textbook.
10. Record results in Table 22–1.

TABLE 22–1   Stages of Sugary Cookery

Temperature		Test	Description of Sugar Mixture	
°F	°C		Water	Foil
232	111			
236	113			
246	119			
252	122			
272	133			
302	150			
322	161			

QUESTIONS

1. Why are the above tests for sugar cookery important? _____

_____

2. List the candies that are cooked to the approximate temperatures of:

   236°F (113°C) _____   272°F (133°C)_____

   246°F (119°C) _____   302°F (150°C)_____

   252°F (122°C) _____

Experiment III: Effect of Agitation and Temperature on Crystallization

1. Calibrate a candy thermometer.
2. Prepare chocolate fudge according to the recipe below with the following variations:

   a.   none
   b.   beat fudge while still hot
   c.   do not beat fudge

3. Observe appearance, texture, and firmness of each fudge.
4. Record results in Table 22–2.

Chocolate Fudge

sugar	1-1/2 c	375 ml	corn syrup	1-1/2 tsp	7 ml
milk	1/2 c +	140 ml	salt	dash	
	1 Tbsp		margarine	1 Tbsp +	22 ml
unsweetened	1-1/2 oz	45 g		1-1/2 tsp	
chocolate			vanilla	3/4 tsp	3 ml

a. Grease three 6 in. (15 cm) glass pie pans.
b. Mix sugar, milk, chocolate, corn syrup, and salt in a saucepan.
c. Clamp a candy thermometer to the pan so that the bulb is immersed in the mixture.
d. Cook over medium heat, stirring with a wooden spoon, until mixture is well blended.
e. When the mixture begins to steam, cover with a lid for 2 minutes to allow the steam to "wash down" any crystals adhering to the sides of the pan. It may be necessary to remove the crystals with a damp cheesecloth wrapped around a fork. Uncover.
f. When mixture reaches 234°F (112°C), remove pan from heat.
g. Pour 1/3 of the mixture into each of the 3 pie pans.
h. Add 1/3 of the margarine on top of the fudge. Do not stir in. (For this experiment, add 1/3 of the margarine, 1-1/2 tsp (7 ml) on top of each of the fudges.)
i. Cool undisturbed, until mixture reaches 120°F (49°C).
j. Add vanilla, 1/4 tsp (1 ml) to each of the fudges. Stir in vanilla but do not beat.
k. Beat fudge 5-10 minutes with a wooden spoon.
l. Spread evenly in greased pan and chill.

TABLE 22–2 Effect of Agitation and Temperature on Crystallization

Procedure	Appearance	Texture	Firmness
Beaten hot			
cool			
Unbeaten			

QUESTIONS

1. Why are crystalline candies beaten? _____

   _____

   _____

2. Which of the above procedures produced the best quality fudge? _____

   _____ Why? _____

   _____

3. Explain how the temperature at which a candy is beaten influences the firmness of the final

   product. _____

   _____

   _____

Experiment IV: Effect of Temperature on Amorphous Candy

1. Calibrate a candy thermometer.
2. Prepare butterscotch according to the recipe below. Remove samples at the following temperatures and drop onto a greased sheet of aluminum foil.

   a. 268°F   131°C
   b. 278°F   136°C
   c. 288°F   142°C
   d. 298°F   148°C

3. Observe appearance, texture, and firmness of candy.
4. Record results in Table 22–3.

Butterscotch

brown sugar	1 c	250 ml	margarine	3 Tbsp	45 ml
corn syrup	2 Tbsp	30 ml	salt	dash	
water	1/2 c	125 ml			

a. Combine all ingredients in a heavy saucepan.
b. Heat over high heat to a boil, stirring as little as necessary.
c. Cover and let the steam "wash down" any crystals adhering to the sides of the pan.
d. Heat until thermometer reaches 288°F (142°C).
e. Remove from heat and drop by teaspoonfuls onto greased aluminum foil.

TABLE 22-3   Effect of Temperature on Amorphous Candy

| Temperature | | Appearance | Texture | Firmness |
°F	°C			
268	131			
278	136			
288	142			
298	148			

QUESTIONS

1. Why are amorphous candies heated to higher temperatures than crystalline candies? _____

_____

_____

2. What temperature is most optional for preparing butterscotch candy? _____

_____

Experiment V: Effect of Interfering Agents on Crystallization

1. Calibrate a candy thermometer.
2. Dissolve 1/2 c (125 ml) sugar in 1/4 c (60 ml) hot water in a deep saucepan. Mix in the following interfering agents to each sample:

   a.   none
   b.   2 tsp (10 ml) corn syrup
   c.   2 tsp (10 ml) fat
   d.   1/8 tsp (0.5 ml) cream of tartar

3. Clamp a candy thermometer to the saucepan so that the bulb is immersed in the mixture.
4. Bring the mixture to a boil over high heat. Stir occasionally but only at the beginning of heating.
5. When the temperature reaches 236°F (113°C), remove the pan from the heat.
6. Do not disturb the pan until the fondant drops to a temperature of 110°F (44°C).
7. Vigorously beat 10-20 minutes. Knead until the mixture is smooth.
8. Observe appearance, texture, and firmness.
9. Record results in Table 22–4.

TABLE 22–4   Effect of Interfering Agents on Crystallization

Interfering Agent	Appearance	Texture	Firmness
None			
Corn syrup			
Fat			
Cream of tartar			

QUESTIONS

1. Explain why corn syrup interferes with the crystallization of sugar. _____

   _____

   _____

2. How does the presence of fat affect crystallization? _____

   _____

3. What reaction does the addition of cream of tartar have? _____

   _____ Why? _____

   _____

4. What would have happened to the candy to which cream of tartar was added if the cooking had

   been prolonged? _____

   Why? _____

Experiment VI: Preparation and Comparison of Candies

1. Select a variety of candies to be prepared from Applications.
2. Compare the candies for type (crystalline, noncrystalline), interfering agents, and final cooking temperature.
3. Observe appearance. Evaluate texture. Taste for flavor.
4. Record results in Table 22–5.

TABLE 22-5 Comparison of Candies

Candy	Type	Interfering Agents	Final Cooking Temperature	Appearance	Texture	Flavor

QUESTIONS

1. Describe the difference in texture between crystalline and noncrystalline candies. _____

   _____

   Why does this difference occur? _____

   _____

2. What type of effect did fat have as an interfering agent? _____

   _____

3. Explain why each candy must be heated to a specific final cooking temperature. _____

   _____

4. What relationship was found between the presence of interfering agents and final cooking

   temperature? _____

   _____

5. If peanut brittle was made, explain how the bubbles developed in the structure. _____

   _____

   _____

   _____

Experiment VII: Preparation and Comparison of Frozen Desserts

1. Prepare one or more of the frozen desserts that follow.
2. Save a small portion of the unfrozen dessert for tasting.
3. Calculate cost/serving. List the type of interfering agents present.

4. Observe appearance and texture of frozen dessert. Taste the unfrozen sample and frozen desse[...] for flavor.
5. Record results in Table 22–6.

Stir-Frozen

French Vanilla Ice Cream (1 quart or liter)

sugar	3/4 c	180 ml	milk	1 c	250 ml
salt	1/4 tsp	1 ml	vanilla	1-1/2 Tbsp	22 ml
egg yolks	3		heavy cream	2 c	500 ml

1. Combine sugar, salt, egg yolk, and milk in a saucepan. Stir to dissolve sugar.
2. Clamp a candy thermometer to the side of the pan. Be sure that the bulb is immersed in the liquid and does not touch the bottom or sides of the pan.
3. Cook over medium heat while stirring until mixture reaches 180°F (82°C).
4. Remove pan from heat and pour mixture into a small, shallow metal baking pan. Place in freezer to chill but do not allow it to freeze. (At home, chill in the refrigerator.)
5. Place metal ice cream can in freezer to chill.
6. Remove chilled egg mixture from freezer and mix in vanilla and cream.
7. Pour chilled mixture into metal can. Do not fill can more than two-thirds full.
8. Place beater in pan. Cover with top and place in ice cream tub. Make sure that the can is centered in the tub. Attach motor and lock can into place.
9. Plug motor in and the can will begin to move. Pack approximately 3 in. (7.5 cm) *crushed* ice in the pan. Sprinkle with approximately 1/2 c (125 ml) *rock* salt.
10. Continue adding layers of ice and salt in these proportions until it reaches the top of sides of t[...] can. When tub is half full, pour 1 c (250 ml) of cold water over the ice and salt mixture to shorten the freezing time. When tub is filled, pour in another cup of cold water.
11. If necessary, more ice and salt can be added if level of mixture decreases as the ice melts. *But do not add ice or salt over the top of the can.*
12. Let motor run 20-30 minutes until mixture is the consistency of mush. (If using a hand-cranked ice cream maker, crank it slowly at first until mixture is evenly chilled. Then crank faster and continuously until crank can no longer be turned with ease.)
13. Remove motor unit and wipe off all salt and ice from the top of the can. Remove top and take out beater. Scrape the ice cream from the beater with a rubber spatula and return ice cream to pan.
14. *Ripening and hardening:* Replace top of pan and insert cork. Allow ice cream to ripen and harden by packing more ice and salt in the freezer until can and top are completely covered. Cover freezer with heavy towel or newspaper and let set until ready to serve. The mixture will freeze hard. After removal of pan for serving, be sure to wipe off the ice and salt from the can before opening.

Vanilla Ice Milk (1 quart or liter)

egg	1		milk	2-1/2 c	625 ml
sugar	1/2 c + 2 Tbsp	155 ml	vanilla	2 tsp	10 ml
salt	1/8 tsp	0.5 ml			

1. Place metal ice cream can, beaters, and medium deep bowl in freezer to chill.
2. When beaters are chilled, place egg in chilled deep bowl and beat with electric mixer on high speed until thickened.

3. Gradually beat in sugar and beat until thick.
4. Add remaining ingredients and mix well.
5. Follow steps 7-14 for making French Vanilla Ice Cream.

Vanilla Frozen Custard (1 pint or 500 ml)

sugar	1/4 c + 2 Tbsp	80 ml	egg, beaten	1	
flour	1 Tbsp	15 ml	heavy cream	1 c	250 ml
salt	1/8 tsp	0.5 ml	vanilla	2 tsp	10 ml
milk	1 c	250 ml			

1. Combine sugar, flour and salt in a small saucepan. Mix well.
2. Gradually add in milk and beat until blended.
3. Cook mixture on medium heat, stirring constantly, until it just begins to boil and thicken. Remove pan from heat and reduce heat to low.
4. Stir approximately 1 Tbsp (15 ml) into beaten egg. Mix well.
5. Repeat step 4 three times until egg is warmed.
6. Replace pan back on burner. Slowly pour warmed egg mixture back into pan while stirring continuously.
7. Cook and stir 1 minute.
8. Follow steps 4-14 for making French Vanilla Ice Cream.

Lemon Sherbet (1 quart or liter)

half and half	2 c	500 ml	lemon rind, finely grated	2 Tbsp	30 ml
sugar	1 c	250 ml			
lemon juice, fresh	1/3 c	80 ml			

1. Place metal can in freezer to chill.
2. Mix half and half and sugar in a bowl until dissolved.
3. Stir in lemon juice and rind.
4. Follow steps 7-14 for making French Vanilla Ice Cream. Use an extra tablespoon (15 ml) of salt for each 3 in. (7.5 cm) of ice.

Orange Sherbet with Egg White (1 quart or liter)

ice water	1-1/4 c	300 ml	salt	dash	
orange juice	1/4 c	50 ml	sugar	1/2 c	125 ml
orange rind, finely grated	1 Tbsp	15 ml	boiling water	1/4 c	50 ml
			egg white	1/2	

1. Place metal can in freezer to chill.
2. Combine ice water (water only—no ice), orange juice, orange rind, and salt in a bowl.

3. Follow steps 7-13 for making French Vanilla Ice Cream. Use an extra tablespoon (15 ml) of s[...] for each 3 in. (7.5 cm) of ice.
4. Meanwhile, dissolve sugar in boiling water in a saucepan. Bring to a boil over high heat until the mixture reaches a temperature of 230°F (110°C) or forms a thread when 1/4 tsp (1 ml) is dropped into ice water. Remove pan from heat.
5. Beat the egg white with an electric beater until stiff.
6. Slowly pour syrup into egg white and blend gently.
7. Quickly add egg-white mixture to frozen orange mush in the freezer.
8. Follow step 14 for making French Vanilla Ice Cream.

Grape Ice (1 pint or 500 g)

boiling water	1/4 c	50 ml	ice water	3/4 c	180 ml
sugar	1/2 c	125 ml	lemon juice	1-1/2 tsp	7 ml
salt	dash		grape juice	1/2 c	125 ml

1. Place metal can in freezer to chill.
2. Combine sugar and salt with boiling water in a bowl. Stir to dissolve as much as possible.
3. Add ice water (water only—no ice). Stir and place in freezer to chill.
4. Remove chilled liquid from freezer and add lemon and grape juice.
5. Follow steps 7-14 for making French Vanilla Ice Cream. Use 2/3 c (180 ml) rock salt for every 3 in. (7.5 cm) crushed ice.

Still-Frozen

Chocolate Mousse

egg yolks	2		sugar	1/4 c +	90 ml
sugar	2 Tbsp	30 ml		2 Tbsp	
milk	1/4 c	50 ml	vanilla	1/2 tsp	2 ml
water	1/4 c	50 ml	heavy cream,	1 c	250 ml
baking chocolate	1 oz	30 g	chilled		

1. Bring water to boil in the bottom half of a double boiler.
2. Blend egg yolks, sugar, and milk in the top pan of a double boiler. Place over bottom pan but do not allow the water to touch the bottom of the top pan.
3. Cook custard 20 minutes or until the mixture coats the back of a spoon.
4. Melt chocolate in water in a bowl in the microwave oven or in a saucepan over low heat.
5. Mix in remaining sugar with the chocolate.
6. Slowly pour custard into chocolate mixture.
7. Blend well and chill.
8. Add vanilla to cream. Whip with an electric beater.
9. Fold into chilled chocolate mixture.
10. Pour into parfait glasses.
11. Freeze.

TABLE 22-6   Comparison of Frozen Desserts

Dessert	Cost/ 1/2 c Serving (125 ml)	Interfering Agents	Appearance	Texture	Flavor	
					Frozen	Unfrozen
Ice Cream						
Ice Milk						
Frozen Custard						
Sherbet milk						
egg white						
Ice						
Still-frozen (mousse)						

QUESTIONS

1. What was the function of the eggs in French Vanilla Ice Cream? _____

   _____

2. What difference in taste did you notice between the unfrozen and frozen desserts? _____

   _____

   Why? _____

3. What effect did the substitution of milk for heavy cream have on the quality of the frozen dessert?

   _____

   _____

4. Why are egg whites sometimes added to sherbets? _____

   _____

5. Explain the difference between a sherbet and an ice. _____

   _____

   _____

6. What prevents the mousse from freezing solid? _____

   _____

7. What similarities are there between candies and frozen desserts? _____

   _____

   _____

   _____

APPLICATIONS

Caramels

sugar	1 c	250 ml	light cream	1 c	250 ml
corn syrup	1/2 c	125 ml	vanilla	1/2 tsp	2 ml
margarine	1/4 c	60 ml			

1. Grease a 7-in. (17.5 cm) square pan.
2. Combine sugar, corn syrup, margarine, and half the cream in a deep saucepan.
3. Clamp a candy thermometer to the pan so that the bulb is immersed in the mixture.
4. Heat to boiling over medium heat, stirring constantly. Stir in remaining cream.
5. Continue cooking until mixture reaches the firm-ball stage, 246°F (119°C). Stir occasionally.
6. Remove pan from heat.
7. Pour in greased pan.
8. Allow to cool.
9. Loosen with a knife and invert onto wax paper. If the caramels do not fall out easily, warm bottom of the pan slightly. Try again.
10. Cut with large knife or scissors into squares.

Divinity

sugar	1 c	250 ml	cream of tartar	1/8 tsp	0.5 ml
light corn	1/4 c	60 ml	vanilla	1/2 tsp	2 ml
syrup			nuts, chopped	1/4 c	60 ml
water	1/4 c	60 ml			
egg white	1				

1. Combine sugar, corn syrup, and water in a saucepan.
2. Clamp a candy thermometer to the pan so that the bulb is immersed in the mixture.
3. Turn heat to high.
4. Cover for 2 minutes when mixture begins to steam so that the steam can "wash down" any crystals adhering to the sides of the pan. Uncover.
5. Meanwhile, beat egg whites and cream of tartar with an electric mixer until stiff.
6. Continue heating mixture until it reaches the hard-ball stage, 262°F (128°C).
7. Remove pan from heat.
8. Pour hot syrup in a thin stream over egg whites, beating continuously.
9. Cool for several minutes. Beat in vanilla.
10. Continue beating until mixture holds its shape and becomes dull.
11. Fold in nuts.
12. Grease a spoon with margarine.
13. Drop from a teaspoon onto waxed paper. Swirl on top with the tip of the spoon.

Lollipops

sugar	1/2 c	125 ml	water	1/4 c	60 ml
corn syrup	2 Tbsp + 2 tsp	40 ml	flavoring		
			coloring		
			paper sticks		

1. Grease a baking sheet or a piece of aluminum foil with margarine.
2. Combine sugar, corn syrup, and water in a saucepan.
3. Clamp a candy thermometer to the pan so that the bulb is immersed in the liquid.
4. Cook over medium-low heat until the mixture reaches the hard-crack stage, 310°F (154°C). Stir as *little* as possible. Before the mixture reaches this temperature, wipe away any sugar crystals adhering to the sides of the pan with a fork covered with a damp cheesecloth.
5. Remove pan from heat. Stir in the amount of coloring or flavoring that clings to the end of a toothpick.
6. Use a metal spoon to drop rounds of the candy onto a greased baking sheet.
7. Quickly press in sticks.
8. Remove lollipops from the greased sheet with a spatula before they completely harden.

Marshmallows

gelatin	1 Tbsp	15 ml	water	1/4 c	60 ml
cold water	1/3 c	80 ml	vanilla	1/8 tsp	0.5 ml
sugar	1 c	250 ml	confectioners' sugar		
salt	dash				

1. Dust a 8 in. (20 cm) square pan with confectioners' sugar.
2. Sprinkle gelatin over cold water in a bowl. Stir until dissolved.
3. Combine sugar, salt and water in a saucepan.
4. Clamp a candy thermometer to the pan so that the bulb is immersed in the liquid.
5. Cook over high heat until the mixture reaches the soft-ball stage, 236°F (113°C).
6. Remove pan from heat.
7. Pour hot syrup in gelatin. Beat until the foam holds its shape.
8. Blend in vanilla.
9. Pour in pan allow to cool.
10. Cut marshmallow into cubes. Roll in confectioners' sugar.

Peanut Brittle

boiling water	1/4 c	60 ml	margarine	1 Tbsp	15 ml
sugar	1 c	250 ml	salt	1/2 tsp	2 ml
light corn	1/2 c	125 ml	vanilla	1/2 tsp	2 ml
syrup			baking soda	1/2 tsp	2 ml
raw peanuts	3/4 c	180 ml			

1. Grease a piece of heavy aluminum foil or a baking sheet.
2. Combine water, sugar, and corn syrup in a saucepan.
3. Clamp a candy thermometer to the pan so that the bulb is immersed in the mixture.
4. Bring mixture to a boil over high heat, stirring occasionally.
5. Continue cooking until the mixture reaches the soft-ball stage, 234°F (112°C).
6. Stir in peanuts and margarine.
7. Cook until mixture reaches 300°F (149°C), stirring constantly. Do not allow the mixture to burn.
8. Remove pan from heat. Blend in salt and vanilla.
9. Stir in baking soda thoroughly.
10. Pour into greased foil. Quickly pull to form a thin sheet.
11. Cool.
12. Break into pieces.

Pralines

sugar	1/2 c	125 ml	salt	1/8 tsp	0.5 ml
brown sugar	1/2 c	125 ml	margarine	1 Tbsp	15 ml
light cream	1/4 c	60 ml	pecan halves	1/2 c	125 ml

1. Grease a baking sheet or piece of aluminum foil.
2. Combine sugars, cream, and salt in deep saucepan.
3. Clamp a candy thermometer to the pan so that the bulb is immersed in the mixture.
4. Cook over medium heat to the thread stage, 230°F (110°C). Stir constantly.
5. Stir in margarine and pecans until mixture drops to 226°F (108°C). *[handwritten: 225 221]*
6. Remove pan from heat.
7. Allow to cool 5 minutes.
8. Use a wooden spoon to beat candy until it thickens and just coats the nuts.
9. Drop by rounded tablespoons onto a greased sheet.

Taffy

sugar	1 c	250 ml	cream of tartar	1/8 tsp	0.5 ml
light corn syrup	1/4 c	60 ml	vanilla	1/2 tsp	2 ml
water	1/4 c	60 ml	coloring		

1. Grease a baking sheet or a piece of aluminum foil.
2. Combine sugar, corn syrup, water, and cream of tartar in a deep saucepan.
3. Clamp a candy thermometer to the pan so that the bulb is immersed in the mixture.
4. Heat over medium heat until the mixture reaches the hard-ball stage 265°F (129°C). Stir occasionally.
5. Remove pan from heat.
6. Stir in vanilla and the amount of coloring that clings to an end of a toothpick.
7. Pour mixture onto greased sheet.
8. Cool until the taffy can be touched without burning the hands.
9. Grease the hands. Pull until light in color, stiff, and satiny.
10. Pull into strips 1/2 in. (1.3 cm) wide. Cut into 1 in. (2.5 cm) pieces with scissors.
11. Wrap pieces in waxed paper to hold their shape.

Toffee

sugar	1/2 c	125 ml	salt	dash	
corn syrup	1-1/2 tsp	7 ml	slivered almonds, chopped fine	1/4 c	60 ml
water	2 Tbsp	30 ml			
butter	1/3 c	80 ml	milk chocolate	2 oz	60 g

1. Grease two 6 in. (15 cm) glass pie pans or casseroles.
2. Combine sugar, corn syrup, water, butter, and salt in a saucepan. Stir until sugar is dissolved.
3. Clamp a candy thermometer to the pan so that the bulb is immersed in the liquid.
4. Cook over high heat until the mixture reaches the hard-crack stage, 300°F (149°C), stirring constantly.
5. Remove pan from heat. Stir in almonds.
6. Pour into greased dishes.
7. Cool.
8. Melt chocolate in a microwave oven or a saucepan over low heat. Spread on cooled candy.
9. Break into serving pieces.

Strawberry Frozen Yogurt (1 pint or 500 g)

gelatin, unflavored	1 tsp	5 ml	red food color	1 drop	
cold water	2 Tbsp	30 ml	salt	dash	
yogurt	10 oz	300 g	vanilla	1/2 tsp	2 ml
sugar	1/4 c	50 ml	strawberries frozen	4 oz	120 g
evaporated milk	1/4 c	50 ml	in sugar, thawed		

1. Place metal can in freezer to chill.
2. Add gelatin to cold water and stir to dissolve. Let set 1 minute.
3. Pour off any liquid that has collected on top of the yogurt.
4. Combine gelatin with yogurt and remaining ingredients. Mix well.
5. Follow steps 7-14 for making French Vanilla Ice Cream, pg. 332.

(Courtesy of Amana Refrigeration, Inc.)

23
Microwave

OBJECTIVES

The student should be able to:

1. Determine the heat pattern in a microwave oven.
2. Describe the effect of density and food composition on heat transfer and absorption of microwaves.
3. Describe the differences in the texture, flavor, and moisture of foods reheated by either the microwave oven or conventional methods.
4. Discuss the importance of rest periods when defrosting food with microwave energy.
5. Compare conventional baking vs. microwave baking for volume, shape, grain, color, texture, and flavor.
6. Describe the effects of browning on flavor development.
7. Discuss the importance of the appropriate covering for microwave-cooked foods.
8. Explain the reasons for using the low-power settings of the microwave oven.

FOOD SCIENCE PRINCIPLES

1. The uneven distribution of microwaves generated in a microwave oven causes foods to heat up unevenly. Unless the food is rotated and stirred, hot spots and subsequent overcooking of these areas will occur.
2. The density and composition of a food will determine its rate of heating by microwaves. Porous foods transfer microwaves more quickly than do dense foods. Sugar and fats in foods absorb microwaves quickly; their concentrated presence in foods can cause them to heat up evenly.
3. Foods reheated by microwave energy are superior in flavor, texture, and moisture and easier to prepare than those reheated by conventional methods. Stale baked goods and other starchy foods taste freshly cooked when reheated in a microwave oven.
4. Foods can be easily defrosted in a short period of time by microwave energy. The unequal distribution of microwaves will cause hot spots to occur when the food is defrosting. This can be avoided by alternating microwaves with short rest periods to allow even heat distribution through conduction.
5. Successful cakes can be baked in the microwave oven.

   a. The lack of browning and crust formation can be compensated by using dark colored cake mixes and/or frosting. Frosting will also hide flaws in the shape of the product.

b. Volume is greater in the microwave-baked cake. This is the result of greater expansion steam, which causes larger air bubbles in the grain and a coarse crumb.

c. The incorporation of more air in the microwave-baked cake decreases the intensity of the color.

d. Conventionally baked cakes have a higher moisture content.

6. Browning meats increases the flavor but decreases the tenderness. Meats become tougher as a result of extensive coagulation of the proteins. In the absence of browning, dark-colored sauces can be successfully used to add color as well as flavor to meat.

7. Microwave-cooked meats lose much more moisture than do meats cooked by conventional methods.

8. Microwave cookery is much faster and easier than conventional cookery and requires fewer utensils.

9. Foods with a high water content must be cooked in a tightly sealed casserole to avoid excessive moisture loss.

10. Delicate foods that curdle easily when subjected too quickly to heat can be successfully cooked in a microwave oven with reduced power settings. Reduced power settings are also used to prolong the time of cooking in order to allow time for flavor development and to tenderize meats.

Note: All experiments are designed to be conducted with the highest setting on the microwave oven, unless otherwise noted.

Experiment I: Determination of Heat Patterns

egg white   8 Tbsp   120 ml

1. Thoroughly blend egg whites with fork.
2. Place 1 Tbsp (15 ml) egg white into each of 8 custard cups.
3. Set custard cups in microwave oven equidistant from each other.
4. Microwave 45 seconds.
5. Record heat distribution pattern in Figure 23–1.

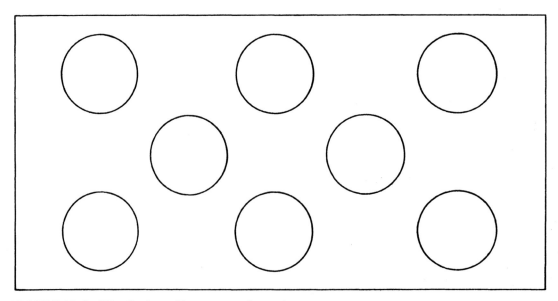

FIGURE 23–1   Distribution-of-heat pattern in a microwave oven.

QUESTIONS

1. Describe the difference in the pattern of coagulation of the egg whites. _____
   _____
   _____

2. Why does this occur? _____

3. How will this influence cooking? _____
   _____

4. What can be done during cooking in order to compensate for this variation? _____
   _____
   _____

Experiment II: Effect of Density and Food Composition on Heat Transfer and Absorption

A. Density

egg whites	8
identical plastic glasses	2

microwave thermometers 2

1. Place 2 egg whites in a 12-oz (375 ml) or larger plastic glass. Arrange 1 microwave thermometer in the middle of the egg whites.
2. Whip 2 other egg whites with an electric beater until stiff peaks form.
3. Transfer the egg-white foam into the other plastic glass. Use a spatula to cut through the foam and push it down so that no large air holes remain. Arrange the other microwave thermometer in the middle of the egg-white foam.
4. Place both glasses in the microwave oven. Make sure that the glasses are equidistant from the walls and each other, and the markings on the thermometers are clearly visible.
5. Microwave until one temperature reaches 160°F (71°C). Immediately observe other temperature and simultaneously stop the oven.
6. Record final temperatures in Table 23-1.
7. Repeat.

B. Food Composition

microwave thermometers	2
jelly doughnuts or non-iced cream-filled snack cakes	4

1. Place 2 jelly doughnuts on 2 separate plates.
2. Insert one thermometer into center of jelly inside the first doughnut. Insert second thermometer into the second doughnut so that it does not touch the jelly.
3. Place plate in the microwave oven. Make sure that the plates are equidistant from the walls and each other and that the markings on each thermometer can be read easily.
4. Microwave until one temperature reaches 160°F (71°C). Immediately observe other temperature and simultaneously stop the oven.
5. Record final temperatures in Table 23-1.
6. Repeat.

TABLE 23-1   Comparison of Density and Varying Food Composition on Heat Transfer and Absorption

Comparison	Final Temperature (°F or °C)		
	Test 1	Test 2	Average
Density Egg white			
Egg-white foam			
Composition Jelly (cream)			
Doughnut (cake)			

QUESTIONS

1. Which heated up the fastest, the thick egg white or the foam? _____
   Why? _____

   _____

2. Which heated up the fastest, the jelly (cream) or the surrounding doughnut (cake)? ____
   Why? _____

   _____

3. How can the results of this experiment be applied to cooking? _____

   _____

   _____

4. What dangers are there in eating jelly doughnuts (cream-filled cakes) that have been heated up in
   microwave ovens? _____

   _____

Experiment III: Reheating of a Starchy Vegetable

2 small, unpeeled, cooked, chilled potatoes

1. Peel chilled potatoes.
2. Place one in a saucepan filled with a small amount of simmering water.
3. Cover and simmer until potato is warmed.
4. Meanwhile, place the other potato on a paper towel in the microwave oven.
5. Microwave 30-45 seconds until potato is warm.
6. Cut each potato in half while still warm. Taste and compare.
7. Record results in Table 23-2.

TABLE 23–2 Comparison of a Conventional and Microwave-Heated Potato

Comparison	Reheating	
	Conventional	Microwave
Texture		
Moisture		
Flavor		
Ease of preparation		

Experiment IV: Reheating Baked Goods

5 pieces of bread or cake, slightly stale

1. Preheat oven to 400°F (200°C).
2. Reserve one of the pieces for comparison.
3. Wrap one piece in aluminum foil and place in oven. Also place an unwrapped piece in the oven. Heat until warm. Record time required for reheating.
4. Wrap one piece of bread or cake loosely with a paper towel. Place the wrapped piece and another unwrapped piece in the microwave oven. Microwave 15 seconds until warm.
5. Taste all pieces of bread or cake while still warm. Compare to unheated piece.
6. Record results in Table 23–3.

TABLE 23–3 Comparison of Wrapped and Unwrapped Reheated Baked Goods

Comparison	Baked Goods				
	Stale	Reheated			
		Conventional		Microwave	
		Unwrapped	Wrapped	Unwrapped	Wrapped
Time (minutes)					
Tenderness					
Moisture					
Taste					

QUESTIONS

1. Why does microwave reheating of stale baked goods produce a softer product than conventional methods? _____

_____

2. Which method — conventional or microwave — produces a better product? _____

_____

3. Should stale baked goods be wrapped when reheated in a conventional oven? _____
   Why or why not? _____

4. Should stale baked goods be wrapped when reheated in a microwave oven? _____
   Why or why not? _____

Experiment V: Defrosting

2 meat balls, solidly frozen

1. Place 1 meat ball on a plate in the center of the microwave oven.
2. Microwave on defrost setting 1 minute 30 seconds or until ice crystals no longer appear. (If oven does not have a defrost setting, alternate between 15 seconds cooking and 15 seconds resting). Remove and cut in half.
3. Place the other meat ball on a plate in the microwave oven.
4. Microwave at highest setting for 1 minute 30 seconds. Remove and cut in half.
5. Record results in Table 23–4.

Note: If the first meat ball takes longer than 1 minute 30 seconds to defrost, record the time that it does take and use that time for the second meat ball.

TABLE 23–4   Comparison of Defrosting Methods in a Microwave Oven

Comparison	Microwave Setting	
	High	*Defrost*
Color		
Texture		
Evenness		
Moisture		

Experiment VI: Baking

chocolate cake mix 1/2 box   9.3 oz   264 g

1. Preheat conventional oven to 325°F (160°C).
2. Grease one 6-in. (15 cm) glass dish; line the bottom of 2 other dishes that are the same size with wax paper.
3. Prepare cake mix according to label directions.
4. Pour equal amounts of batter, approximately 2/3 c (160 ml), into the dishes *but do not fill more than one-half full.*
5. Bake the batter poured into the greased dish in the conventional oven for 25-30 minutes or until a toothpick inserted into the center comes out clean. Invert onto a plate.
6. Let the batter poured into the wax paper-lined dishes stand 15 minutes. Then tap gently to remove large air bubbles.
7. Cover both dishes loosely with a paper towel. Place one dish in microwave oven on an inverted plate and microwave 2 minutes; turning dish halfway through baking period.
8. The cake may look too moist; check for doneness with a toothpick. Remove paper towel and let cool for 5 minutes before removing from a dish.
9. Place other dish on a microwave oven rotator in the microwave oven. (Make sure rotator is wound up before using if this is necessary.) Microwave 2 minutes.
10. Repeat step 8.
11. Unpeel wax paper from cakes. Cut all cakes in half with serrated knife. Observe appearance and taste for flavor, tenderness, and moisture.
12. Record results in Table 23–5.

TABLE 23–5   Comparison of Conventional and Microwave-Baked Cakes

Comparison	Method of Baking		
	Conventional	Microwave Oven	
		Stationary	Rotating
Volume			
Shape			
Grain			
Color			
Tenderness			
Flavor			
Moisture			
Crust formation			

QUESTIONS

1. What are the disadvantages of cakes baked in a microwave oven? _____

   _____

2. What can be done to compensate for the difference in appearance? _____

   _____

Experiment VII: Flavor Development from Browning

4 hamburger patties,	1 lb	500 g
1/2 in. (1.3 cm) thick		
kitchen bouquet	1/4 tsp	1 ml
fat	1/2 tsp	2 ml
salt		

1. Cook hamburgers until done by each of the following three methods: Keep a record of the time required for each method.

Conventional Skillet

    a.   Melt 1/2 tsp (3 ml) fat in skillet over medium heat.
    b.   Brown hamburger on both sides for approximately 8-10 minutes, turning only once.

Microwave Plus Browning Sauce

    a.   Brush hamburger with browning sauce.
    b.   Microwave 1 minute 30 seconds; rotate dish and turn over once during cooking period.

Microwave Only

    a.   Repeat above procedure eliminating browning sauce.

Microwave Browning Skillet

    a.   Preheat browning skillet in microwave oven according to manufacturer's directions. Do not use cover for this experiment.
    b.   Place hamburger in dish, microwave 1-2 minutes; turn over only once during cooking period.

2. Salt all hamburgers. Observe appearance, cut in half and taste while still warm.
3. Record results in Table 23-6.

TABLE 23–6   Evaluation of Browning in the Microwave Oven

Evaluation	Cooking Method			
	Conventional Skillet	Microwave Skillet	Microwave Only	Microwave Plus Browning Sauce
Appearance				
Color				
Texture				
Tenderness				
Flavor				
Moisture				
Time (minutes)				
Extent of spattering fat				

QUESTIONS

1. What are the advantages of using the conventional skillet? _____

   _____

   The microwave skillet? _____

   _____

   Just the microwave oven? _____

   _____

Experiment VIII: Effect of Covering on Cooking Broccoli

broccoli   3 stalks
water   1/4 c   50 ml

1. Wash broccoli and trim off woody ends.
2. Cut stalks in 4 pieces lengthwise so that each piece is no smaller than 1/2 in. × 1 in. (1.3 cm × 2.5 cm) × length of stalk.
3. Place 4 of the pieces on a plate in a circle with the flowers in the middle. Cover loosely with wax paper. Microwave 3 minutes.
4. Repeat step 3 above except cover tightly with plastic wrap. (Do not use heat-resistant type.)
5. Place the other 4 pieces in a casserole dish with 1/4 c (50 ml) water. Cover with a tight lid and microwave 3 minutes. Rearrange pieces once.
6. Let broccoli stand 3 minutes before tasting.
7. Observe appearance. Taste for tenderness and flavor.
8. Record results in Table 23–7.

TABLE 23–7   Comparison of Effect of Covering on Cooking Broccoli

Comparison	Covering		
	Wax Paper	Plastic Wrap	Tight Lid
Appearance			
Color			
Tenderness			
Flavor			

QUESTIONS

1. What happened to the plastic wrap? _____

    Why did this happen? _____

    _____

2. Which of the coverings produced the best product? _____

    Why? _____

    _____

3. Discuss the effect of not rearranging the broccoli that was cooked without a covering. _____

    _____

    _____

Experiment IX: Effect of Full and Reduced Power Settings of the Microwave Oven on the Quality of Custard

Custard

milk	1 c	250 ml	vanilla	1/2 tsp	2 ml
eggs	2		salt	dash	
sugar	2 Tbsp	30 ml			

1. Scald milk in a 2-c (500 ml) measuring cup by microwaving in the oven for 1-1/2 minutes. Let cool slightly.
2. Combine remaining ingredients in a bowl and beat until blended with a wire whisk.
3. *Gradually* stir the hot milk into the egg-sugar mixture while continuing to stir.
4. Pour equal amounts into four custard cups.
5. Place 2 cups in the microwave oven and microwave at low power (3 or 30%) 6 minutes (700 watts) or 7 minutes (650 watts). The custard will still be slightly soft in the center but will set upon standing. (Do not overcook because the custard will curdle.) Remove from oven.

6. Cover cups with a paper towel and an inverted small plate. The paper towel will absorb excess moisture during cooling.

7. Place remaining 2 cups in the oven and microwave at full power (10 or 100%) 2 minutes (700 watts) or 2 minutes 15 seconds (650 watts).

8. Repeat step 6 above.

9. When custard has cooled, remove covering. Rim the custard with a knife. Place saucer inverted over custard, hold together and turn upside down so that custard falls onto plate. Cut in half and observe appearance. Taste one half for flavor and texture.

10. Record results in Table 23-8.

QUESTIONS

1. What was the effect of reducing the powder setting on the quality of the custard? _____

_____

2. Why was custard used as the food product in this experiment? _____

_____

_____

3. List some other cooking situations in which reduced microwave power settings are used. _____

_____

_____

TABLE 23–8   Effect of Full and Reduced Power Settings of the Microwave Oven on the Quality of Custard

Comparison	Power Setting	
	Full	Reduced
Appearance		
Texture		
Flavor		

APPLICATIONS

Lemon Garlic Chicken

chicken breast	1		black pepper	dash	
butter	1 Tbsp	15 ml	parsley, minced	1/4 tsp	1 ml
garlic clove, minced	1/2		salt	dash	
			bread crumbs	2 tsp	10 ml
lemon juice	2 tsp	10 ml	lemon slice	1	

1. Remove skin, fat, and bone from chicken breast and discard.
2. Place butter and garlic in a small baking dish. Cover loosely with wax paper and microwave 2 minutes.
3. Add lemon juice, black pepper, and parsley to butter mixture.
4. Add chicken. Coat well and let chicken marinate for a minimum of 20 minutes in order for flavors to combine.
5. Cover loosely with wax paper. Microwave 45 seconds. Turn chicken over and check to see if any traces of pink remain in the meat. If meat is still pink, microwave 15 seconds more. If any small pieces of meat are cooked, remove them to a serving dish. Continue microwaving at 15-second intervals until meat is white. Do not overcook.
6. Sprinkle with salt and remove chicken to serving dish.
7. Add bread crumbs to butter mixture; microwave uncovered 15 seconds.
8. Spread mixture over chicken, cover with lemon slice, and serve immediately.

Fish Veracruz

garlic clove, minced	1/2		green pepper, minced	1 Tbsp	15 ml
paprika	1/4 tsp	1 ml	tomatoes, canned, drained and coarsely chopped	1/2 c	125 ml
oregano	1/8 tsp	0.5 ml			
black pepper	dash				
onion, minced	1 Tbsp	15 ml	fish fillet	1/2 lb	225 g

1. Combine all ingredients except fish in a glass casserole.
2. Microwave 3 minutes.
3. Coat fish with tomato mixture and cover loosely with wax paper.
4. Microwave 4 minutes.
5. Let stand covered 2 minutes before serving.

Stuffed Zucchini

zucchini	1		bread crumbs,	2 Tbsp	30 ml
margarine	2 Tbsp	30 ml	Italian flavored		
onion, minced	2 Tbsp	30 ml	salt	dash	
green pepper,	2 tsp	10 ml	cheese, grated	2 Tbsp	30 ml
minced			(optional)		
tomato, chopped	1/3				

1. Cut zucchini into halves lengthwise.
2. Scoop out center, leaving a shell no more than 1/2 in. (1.3 cm) thick. Coarsely chop the removed squash.
3. Place margarine in small bowl or baking dish and microwave 30 seconds until margarine has melted.
4. Add onion and green pepper and sauté in microwave oven for 3 minutes.
5. Stir in tomatoes and chopped zucchini. Sauté 1 minute.
6. Add bread crumbs, mix gently and spoon into zucchini shells.
7. Place shells on serving platter and microwave 5 minutes, rotating plate a few times.
8. Sprinkle with grated cheese and serve.

Stuffed Baked Potato

baking potato	1		salt	dash	
milk	2-3 Tbsp	30-45 ml	pepper	dash	
sour cream	1 Tbsp	15 ml	cheese, grated	1 Tbsp	15 ml
margarine	2 tsp	10 ml	paprika	dash	
chives, or	1/2 tsp	2 ml			
green onion,					
chopped					

1. Scrub potato and prick several times with a fork.
2. Place on a paper towel in the microwave oven.
3. Microwave 6 minutes; rotating and turning every few minutes.
4. Cut in half and scoop out center without breaking shell.
5. Mix together the potato, milk, sour cream, margarine, chives, salt and pepper.
6. Fill shells, top with cheese and sprinkle with paprika.
7. Microwave until cheese melts.

Baked Apple

baking apple	1		butter	1/2 tsp	2 ml
brown sugar	1 Tbsp	15 ml	cinnamon	dash	

1. Wash and core apple; place in a casserole dish.
2. Place brown sugar and margarine in core and sprinkle with cinnamon.
3. Microwave 3 minutes.
4. Spoon liquid in custard cup back into core of apple.
5. Let stand 3 minutes.

(Courtesy of Lenox China Crystal.)

24

Meal Management

OBJECTIVES

The student should be able to:

1. Plan a palatable, nutritious menu for a day.
2. Evaluate the nutritional adequacy of a menu.
3. Develop a work schedule and meal service plan.
4. Prepare and evaluate a well-balanced meal.

PRINCIPLES

1. The preparation of a meal requires knowledge of management concepts in order to effectively resources such as time, money, personnel, and equipment. The ability to create a meal will depen on the following skills of the meal manager:

   a. *Technical:* Technical skills are the physical skills involved in cooking, such as preparing a gravy to avoid lumps.
   b. *Human:* Human skills are the ability to communicate and build cooperation with other individuals so that tasks may be assigned and coordinated.
   c. *Conceptual:* Conceptual skills involve the ability to see the meal as a whole unit, including planning the menu, buying and storing foods, using the kitchen and its equipment, planning correct methods of preparing food, determining the proper type of table arrangement and meal service, and organizing clean-up.

2. Menus should be planned with the following considerations: economics, palatability, satiety, practicality, time, nutritive value, and service of food.

3. A rough estimate of the nutritional adequacy of a menu can be obtained by comparing it to the Basic Food Groups. These groups and the primary nutrients that they provide are:

   a. *Meat:* protein, niacin, iron, thiamin, zinc
   b. *Milk:* calcium, riboflavin
   c. *Grains:* carbohydrates, thiamin, iron, niacin
   d. *Fruit-Vegetable:* vitamin A, vitamin C, fiber
   e. *Others:* carbohydrates, fats, calories

4. A more precise determination of nutritional adequacy requires calculation of individual nutrients using nutrient composition tables. Values of individual nutrients are compared to the Recommended Dietary Allowances (RDAs) according to the age and sex of the person. Levels above two-thirds the RDA for a specific nutrient are considered adequate for an individual.

5. A work schedule should be developed so that all tasks are done on time and the food is served hot.
6. Prior arrangement of meal service and table setting is necessary to avoid last minute confusion.

Exercise I: Menu Planning

1. Plan a menu for an entire day for 2 adults. Each of the meals should contain at least 4 items, including 1 product made from scratch. Select one of the meals to prepare in class.
2. Use the following considerations in planning the menu:

   a. *Economics*

      1. Cost/day _____
      2. Cost/person _____
      3. Cost/meal _____

   b. *Palatability:*

      1. Size and shape: varied, original
      2. Texture: contrasting, interesting, varied
      3. Color: varied, contrasting, *not* clashing
      4. Flavor: well seasoned, compatible
      5. Temperature: at least 1 hot dish and 1 cold dish
      6. Preparations: at least 1 different type of food preparation
      7. Creativity: unusual, exciting
      8. Degree of doneness: appropriate for each food item

   c. *Satiety:*

      1. Portion size: standard

   d. *Practicality:*

      1. Availability and adaptability: season, geographical location
      2. Religious beliefs
      3. Cultural and ethnic preferences
      4. Food allergies and special diets
      5. Individual food preferences and schedules of eaters

   e. *Time:*

      1. Time limit for preparation and serving:_____
      2. Use of convenience foods, prepreparation, labor-saving equipment, disposable items, and extra help.

   f. *Nutritive value:*

      1. Basic Food Groups: Exercise II
      2. Optional: Comparison of Nutritive Value to RDAs: Exercise III

   g. *Service of food:*

      1. Attractive table appearance
      2. Correct table setting arrangement
      3. Appropriate type of meal service
      4. Efficient service

3. Write the menu for the entire day in Table 24–1. Place a star by the meal that will be prepared by the student in class. Also write out a more detailed menu for the meal that will be prepared providing as much information as possible (such as fresh vs. frozen broccoli).

Exercise II: Comparison of the Menu to the Basic Food Groups

1. Record the name and serving size/person of the foods listed in the menu prepared for the entire day.
2. Compare the results to the recommended servings listed in Table 24–2, pg. 360.

QUESTIONS

1. List the major nutrients provided by each of the Basic Food Groups:

   Meat: _____

   Milk: _____

   Grains: _____

   Fruits-Vegetables: _____

   Others: _____

2. What substitute foods could you have used in your menu that still fulfilled the classifications of the Basic Food Groups but were lower in cost? _____

   _____

   _____

   Lower in calories? _____

   _____

   _____

Exercise III: Comparison of Nutritive Value of Menu to RDA

1. Combine any foods which are the same in the planned menu, e.g. milk in beverage and milk in pancakes. It may be helpful to use the foods that have already been listed in Table 24–2. List all foods in the menu in Table 24–3, pg. 361.
2. Calculate the nutritive value of the day's menu.
3. Compare the total values for the day to the Recommended Daily Allowance (RDA) listed in the table.
4. Check the appropriate box if the values are less than 2/3 or 1/3 of the RDA.
5. Determine % of calories for protein, fat, and carbohydrate by the following method.

   a. _____ g protein $\times$ 4 cal/g   = _____ $\div$ _____ calories $\times$ 100 = _____ %

   b. _____ g fat $\times$ 9 cal/g   = _____ $\div$ _____ calories $\times$ 100 = _____ %

   c. _____ g carbohydrate $\times$ 4 cal/g = _____ $\div$ _____ calories $\times$ 100 = _____ %

QUESTIONS

1. Which nutrients in the menu were most limited in terms of percentages of the RDAs? _____
   _____

   Suggest other food sources of these nutrients. _____
   _____

2. Which nutrients appear to be found in abundant quantities in our diet? _____
   _____
   _____

3. What is the advantage of determining nutritional adequacy by comparison to the RDAs rather
   than the Basic Food Groups? _____
   _____

   The disadvantage? _____
   _____

Exercise IV: Preparation of Market and Equipment Order

1. List in Table 24–4, pg. 362, all foods needed for the meal to be prepared in class. Do not duplicate
   any food listing.
2. List any special equipment that will be needed in the preparation or serving of the meal that is not
   normally found in the kitchen, for example, fondue set, meat skewers.

QUESTIONS

1. What labor saving devices did you plan on using? _____
   _____

2. What would you have liked to use that was not available in the laboratory ? _____
   _____

3. What convenience foods or preprepared foods could have been used in your menu if it were made
   at home? _____
   _____

Exercise V: Preparation of Work Schedule for Laboratory Meal

1. Itemize the tasks that will need to be done and the estimated time required for each in Table 24–5.
   Include food preparation, cooking, chilling, table setting, serving, and clean-up time.
2. Rewrite the tasks above in Table 24–6 in the *descending* order of time required.
3. Decide on a starting time for each task and assign the task to a person. Rewrite the tasks and add
   the starting times in Table 24–7.
4. Write menu and recipes on file cards for easy reference during meal preparation.

QUESTION

Explain why tasks were rewritten in descending order of time required. _____

_____

_____

Exercise VI: Meal Serving Plan and Table Appointment Order

1. Decide on the appropriate type of service for the meal that is planned. Record in the Meal Service Plan on pg. 366.
2. Diagram an individual cover for the meal in Table 24–8. Include mats, napkins, dishes, cups, glasses, and flatware. Assign each item a number and fill in the key to the diagram.
3. Diagram in the Meal Service Plan the table arrangement. Include the placement of the covers, serving pieces, centerpieces, and accessories.
4. Fill in the Table Appointments Order, Table 24–9. Include all items that will be needed for tablesetting.

QUESTIONS

1. Define *cover*. _____

_____

2. List any table setting items that could have been used but were not available. _____

_____

3. List the type of meal service to be used. _____

   Explain your choice. _____

_____

Exercise VII: Meal Evaluation

Use the Meal Evaluation Form (Table 24–10) on pg. 368 as a guide to understanding how the grade will be determined. Plan ahead so that all of these areas will be adequately covered.

QUESTIONS

1. Describe the weaknesses and strengths of your menu:

   Weaknesses: _____

_____

   Strengths: _____

_____

   Your meal:

   Weaknesses: _____

_____

Strengths: _____

_____

2. What changes would you make the next time? _____

_____

_____

TABLE 24-1   Menu for One Day for Two Adults

Instructor_____	Name _____
Unit _____	Date of Meal_____

MENU FOR ONE DAY:[a]

DETAILED MENU OF MEAL TO BE PREPARED BY STUDENT:

[a]Star the meal that will be prepared by the student.

TABLE 24-2 Comparison of Menu to Basic Food Groups

	Basic Food Groups		Planned Menu		
Group	Recommended Serving/Day	Serving Size	Food	Serving Size/Person	Nutritional Adequacy
Meat meat, fish, poultry	2 or more	2-3 oz (60-90 g) cooked lean			
eggs peanut butter cooked beans or peas		2 2 Tbsp (30 ml) 1 c (250 ml)			
Milk cottage cheese ice cream cream cheese American cheese cheddar cheese	2-4 c (500 ml-1 l.)	1 c (250 ml) 1-1/2 c (375 ml) 2 c (500 ml) 2 c (500 ml) 1-1/2 slices 2 oz (60 g)			
Grains bread cooked cereal or product	4 or more	1 slice 1/2-3/4 c (125-180 ml)			
Fruit-Vegetable fruit vegetable	4 or more including 1 source of Vitamin C daily, and 1 source of Vitamin A 3-4x/ week	1 piece 1/2 c (125 ml)			
Others	none; amounts determined by caloric needs	—			

TABLE 24-3 Comparison of Nutritive Value of Menu to RDA

Food	Quantity	Weight (g)	Nutritive Value									
			Energy (Cal)	Protein (g)	Fat (g)	Carbo-hydrate (g)	Iron (mg)	Calcium (mg)	Vitamin A (I.U.)	Vitamin C (mg)	Thiamine (mg)
Total for day											
RDA for female[a]			2,100	46	—	—	18	800	4,000	45	1.1
RDA for male[a]			3,000	54	—	—	10	800	5,000	45	1.5
Less than 2/3 RDA					—	—					
Less than 1/3 RDA					—	—					
% calories											

[a] Age 19-22.

TABLE 24–4 Market and Equipment Order

Instructor _____   Name _____

Unit _____   Date of meal _____

                                                             Time of meal _____

Item	Specification	Quantity Needed	Market Unit Size	Market Unit Cost	Cost/Market Unit
Food					
Equipment			—	—	—

Total Cost of Meal _____

Cost/Person _____

TABLE 24–5   Itemization of Tasks for Meal Preparation

Task	Estimated Time (minutes)

TABLE 24–6   Itemization of Tasks for Meal Preparation in *Descending* Order of Time

Task	Estimated Time (minutes)

TABLE 24-7   Work Schedule

Starting Time	Person	Task

TABLE 24–8   Meal Service Plan Form

Instructor _____   Name _____

Unit _____   Date of Meal _____

Meal _____   Time of Meal _____

Type of Service _____

1. Diagram individual cover:

2. Diagram table arrangement:

Key:

1. _____   8. _____

2. _____   9. _____

3. _____   10. _____

4. _____   11. _____

5. _____   12. _____

6. _____   13. _____

7. _____   14. _____

TABLE 24–9   Table Appointment Order

Instructor _____   Name _____

       Unit _____   Date of meal _____

                                                        Type of meal _____

                    Meal _____

Item	Design or Color	Quantity	Purpose
Dinnerware			
Serving pieces			
Flatware			
Glassware			
Napkins, Cloths, and Mats			
Decorations			
Accessories			

TABLE 24-10   Meal Evaluation Form

Instructor _____   Name _____

     Unit _____   Date of meal _____

                                     Type of meal _____

                         Meal _____

1. Selection of menu   Maximum points
   a. Economical   _____ 5
   b. Palatable   _____ 25
      i. varied sizes and shapes   _____ 3
      ii. interesting textures   _____ 3
      iii. varied colors   _____ 3
      iv. compatible flavors   _____ 4
      v. contrasting temperatures
         and preparations   _____ 4
      vi. creativity   _____ 4
      vii. degree of doneness   _____ 4
   c. Satiety   _____ 5
   d. Practicality   _____ 5
   e. Nutritive value   _____ 10

2. Preparation of food
   a. Correct methods   _____ 5
   b. Correct seasoning   _____ 5
   c. Organization   _____ 5
   d. Efficient use of time   _____ 5

3. Service of food
   a. Attractive table appearance   _____ 5
   b. Correct table settings   _____ 5
   c. Appropriate type of meal service   _____ 5
   d. Efficient service   _____ 5

4. Atmosphere of meal
   a. Quiet, relaxed, and congenial   _____ 5

5. Cleanliness of unit   _____ 5

                                              Total _____ 100

Appendix
Food Evaluation

General Notes on Sensory Evaluation

The environment of the testing room should be comfortable, well-lighted, free of noise and distractions, and neutral in color. All plates and containers should be identical and made of clear glass. Plastic containers are acceptable if they do not impart a taste. The samples presented should be homogeneous in appearance, temperature, quantity, and freshness.

Experiment I

1. Select 3 of the following:*

   a. cabbage   d. cottage cheese   g. cooked broccoli
   b. cucumber   e. squash   h. cooked spinach
   c. peaches   f. vanilla pudding   i. cooked potato

2. Puree 1/2 c (125 ml) of each selected food in a blender.
3. Pour into a container and cover. All foods should be at room temperature for the experiment.
4. Prepare 4 blindfolds made from black, plastic garbage bags covered with cheesecloth.

Experiment II

1. Select 3 of the following:**

   a. apple   d. white turnip   g. yellow squash
   b. onion   e. parsnip   h. cucumber
   c. potato   f. cauliflower

2. Puree 1/2 c (125 ml) of each raw food in a blender.
3. Pour into a container and cover. All foods should be at room temperature for the experiment.
4. Have the students wear sunglasses or use a room lighted with red light.
5. Obtain 4 noseplugs if possible.

 * Do not season any cooked product.
** Peel and seed when appropriate.

Experiment III

1. Prepare the following mM solutions of sucrose with deionized water.

3 mM:1.03 g/l	24 mM:8.21 g/l
6 mM:2.05 g/l	36 mM:12.32 g/l
12 mM:4.11 g/l	48 mM:16.43 g/l

2. Use the following procedure:

   a. Weigh the appropriate grams of sucrose as indicated in step 1.
   b. Place in a 1-liter (1000 ml) volumetric flask.
   c. Fill to the mark with deionized water.
   d. Stir until sucrose is dissolved.
   e. Pour into storage bottle and label concentration. Do not store more than 1 week.

3. Samples and blanks (plain deionized water) must be brought to identical room temperatures prior to use.

Note: The quantity indicated here (1 liter) will make enough volume for approximately 30 students, with some allowance for waste. Approximately 30 ml of each concentration will be needed for each student tested.

Recipe Index